The CROSSLEY ID GUIDE

Britain & Ireland

Richard Crossley & Dominic Couzens

Crossley Books
Princeton University Press

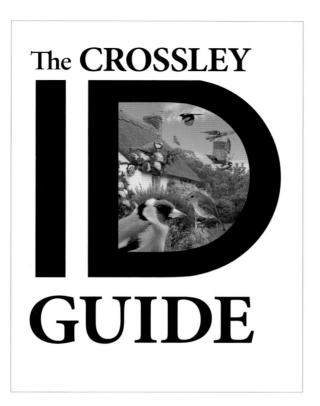

Published by Princeton University Press, 41 William Street, Princeton, New Jersey 08540
In the United Kingdom: Princeton University Press, 6 Oxford Street, Woodstock, Oxfordshire OX20 1TW
nathist.princeton.edu

Library of Congress Control Number: 2013938975

ISBN: 978-0-691-15194-6

British Library Cataloging-in-Publication Data is available

This book has been composed in Times New Roman
Printed on acid-free paper
Printed in Singapore
10 9 8 7 6 5 4 3 2 1

CONTENTS

To Debra, Sophie, and Sam

For always being there

Thank you

PREFACE

I started collecting eggs as a 7-year-old in Wykeham Forest, Yorks. My life changed forever when my school teacher, Mr Sutton, took a bunch of us birding to Burton Gravel Pits, near Lincoln when I was 10. It seems like yesterday! Technology has changed the world since then, but the fundamentals of bird ID have remained the same.

The Crossley ID Guide: Britain and Ireland is aimed at beginners and intermediate birders, yet can be enjoyed equally by anyone who simply likes to look at birds or enjoys the beauty of the British and Irish countryside.

The 'Crossley style' plates offer unique visual layouts which show birds as we really see them in the field. Most of the engaging and informative text is superbly written by highly respected nature author Dominic Couzens. The text reinforces the visual impact of the plates.

Today, with digital technology, we can create in-focus images from near to far that better represent what we really see in nature. This new approach to book design and photography can catch people off-guard, but it allows us to capture the true beauty of nature while sharing information at the same time. We can portray the different plumages and ages of birds on the same page as well as revealing the habitats in which they live and how they behave.

Identifying birds is all about the fundamentals: size, shape, behaviour, probability, and colour patterns. These are all linked—a bird's size, shape and colour are all in direct response to its habitat and will determine its behaviour. Since these are connected, it is important to have all of them in one image. This creates a complete and understandable connection that is logical to the mind—particularly important to the novice birder. A lifelike rendition of this image provides a better match.

Understanding these dynamics is the key to the design of *The Crossley ID Guides*. They intend to give the reader the tools to be a better birder rather than giving answers without understanding. In many ways *The Crossley ID Guides* are a halfway-house between traditional field guides and being in the field. Yes, you can have a pint or a glass of wine while you are birding!

For those who say we rarely see this many birds together in the wild, I agree. But having such a wide variety of birds on one page in contrasting sizes and distances allows the reader to know what the species looks like from any angle, whether from above, below, or the side. I always taught my kids from a very early age that 'practice makes perfect', and that same rule is applied in this book. Repetition and familiarity are the best tools for learning any subject.

I feel very fortunate. I never thought I would be lucky enough to work at what I love passionately, the sport of birding. Today I 'play' professionally at creating books. My goal is to help popularise the beauty of the outdoors, with a better understanding and appreciation of nature. It is important if we are going to take better care of tomorrow.

From wetting my feet as a coauthor of *The Shorebird Guide*, my fascination with the way the brain functions and with book design have led to the *The Crossley ID Guide* series. These include *Eastern Birds, Raptors,* and the imminent *Waterfowl* and *Western* guides.

I continue to see birding as a 'voyage of discovery'. I hope this book helps you on your own journey.

Richard Crossley

Swimming Waterbirds p. 32–81

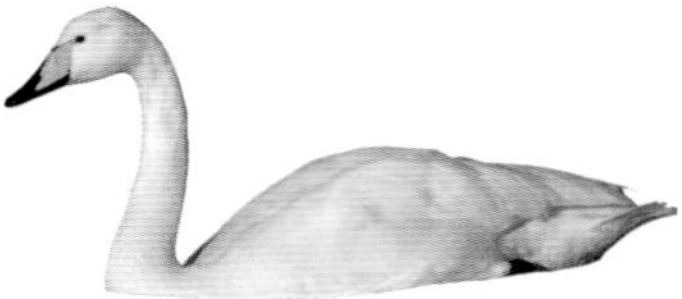
WHOSW p. 34

BEWSW p. 35

MUTSW p. 36

WHFGO p. 37

PIFGO p. 38

GREGO p. 39

BEAGO p. 40

CANGO p. 42

BARGO p. 43

BREGO p. 44

SHELD p. 45

EGYGO p. 46

MANDA p. 46

MALLA p. 47

GADWA p. 48

PINTA p. 49

SHOVE p. 50

WIGEO p. 51

AMEWI p. 52

GARGA p. 52

TEAL p. 53

POCHA p. 54

RECPO p. 55

FERDU p. 55

TUFDU p. 56

SCAUP p. 57

COMSC p. 58

SURSC p. 59

VELSC p. 59

EIDER p. 60

LOTDU p. 61

GOOSA p. 62

REBME p. 63

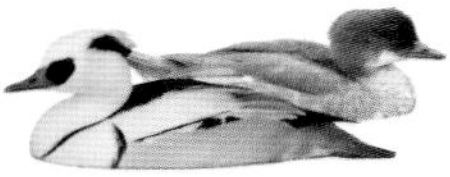

SMEW p. 64

GOLDE p. 65

RUDDU p. 66

SHAG p. 68

CORMO p. 69

BLTDI p. 70

RETDI p. 71

GRNDI p. 72

WHBDI p. 73

RENGR p. 73

GRCGR p. 74

LITGR p. 75

SLAGR p. 76

BLNGR p. 77

LITAU p. 77

GUILL p. 78

RAZOR p. 79

BLAGU p. 80

PUFFI p. 81

Flying Waterbirds p. 82–111

FULMA p. 84

CORSH p. 85

GRTSH p. 85

MANSH p. 86

BALSH p. 87

SOOSH p. 88

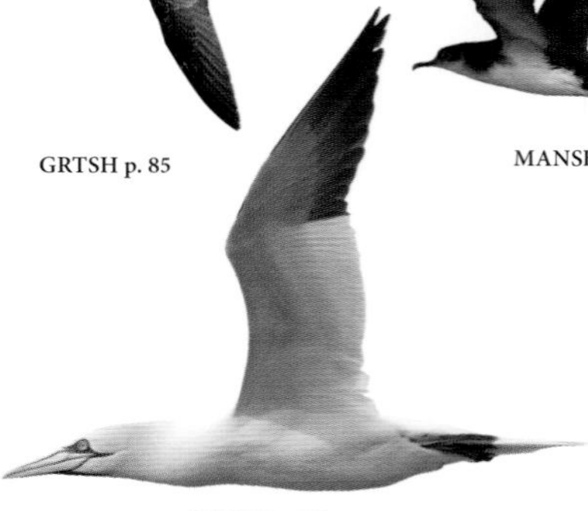
GANNE p. 89

STOPE p. 90

WILPE p. 90

LEAPE p. 91

WWBTE p. 91

BLATE p. 92

LITTE p. 93

COMTE p. 94

ARCTE p. 95

ROSTE p. 96

SANTE p. 97

GRESK p. 98

POMSK p. 99

ARCSK p. 100

LOTSK p. 101

SABGU p. 101

KITTI p. 102

MEDGU p. 103

COMGU p. 104

BLHGU p. 105

LITGU p. 106

RIBGU p. 106

HERGU p. 107

YELGU p. 108

CASGU p. 108

ICEGU p. 109

GLAGU p. 109

LBBGU p. 110

GBBGU p. 111

Walking Waterbirds p. 112–153

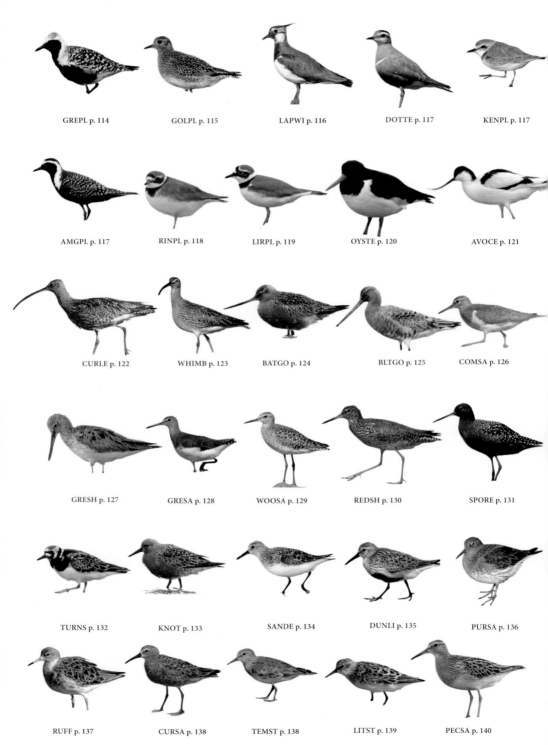

GREPL p. 114

GOLPL p. 115

LAPWI p. 116

DOTTE p. 117

KENPL p. 117

AMGPL p. 117

RINPL p. 118

LIRPL p. 119

OYSTE p. 120

AVOCE p. 121

CURLE p. 122

WHIMB p. 123

BATGO p. 124

BLTGO p. 125

COMSA p. 126

GRESH p. 127

GRESA p. 128

WOOSA p. 129

REDSH p. 130

SPORE p. 131

TURNS p. 132

KNOT p. 133

SANDE p. 134

DUNLI p. 135

PURSA p. 136

RUFF p. 137

CURSA p. 138

TEMST p. 138

LITST p. 139

PECSA p. 140

BUBSA p. 140

WHRSA p. 140

GREPH p. 141

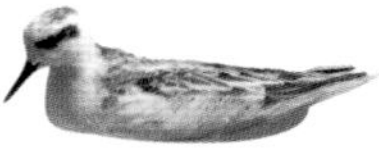
RENPH p. 141

WOODC p. 142

SNIPE p. 143

JACSN p. 144

STOCU p. 144

WHIST p. 145

CRANE p. 145

SPOON p. 145

BITTE p. 146

NIGHE p. 146

LITEG p. 147

PURHE p. 148

CATEG p. 148

GRWEG p. 148

GREHE p. 149

COOT p. 150

MOORH p. 151

WATRA p. 152

SPOCR p. 153

CORNC p. 153

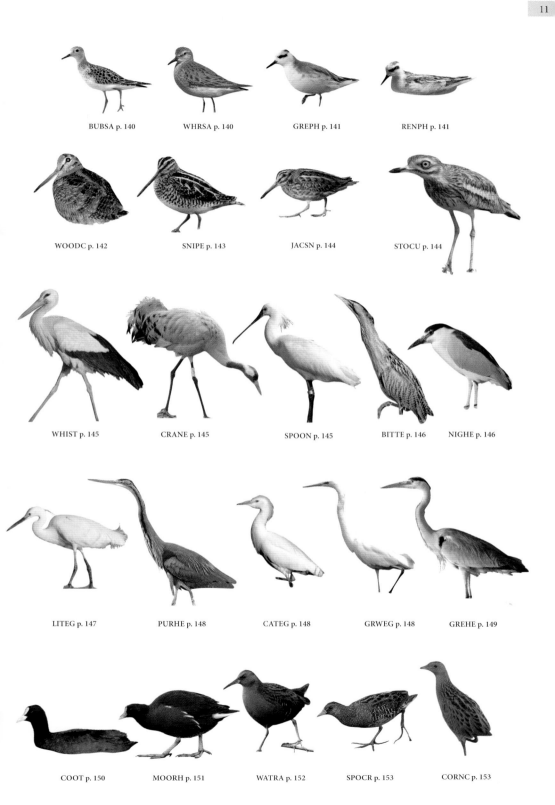

Upland Gamebirds p. 154–161

QUAIL p. 154 GOLPH p. 154 PHEAS p. 155 CAPER p. 156

BLAGR p. 157 REDGR p. 158 PTARM p. 159 GREPA p. 160 RELPA p. 161

Raptors p. 162–183

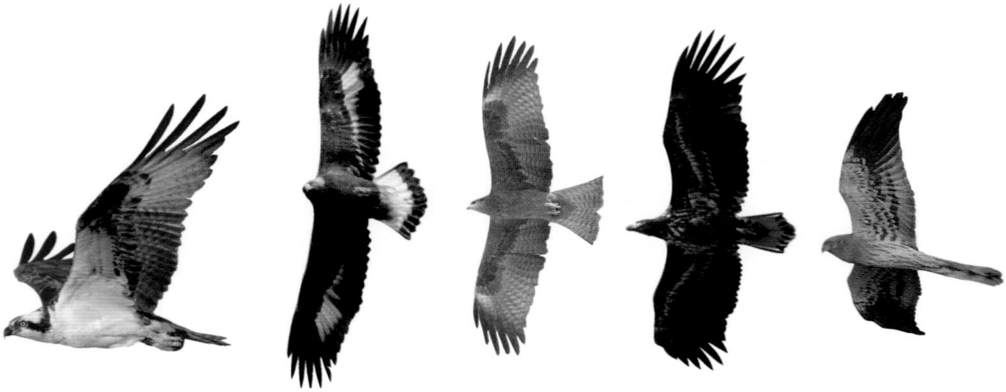

OSPRE p. 164 GOLEA p. 165 BLAKI p. 166 WHTEA p. 166 MONHA p. 166

REDKI p. 167 MARHA p. 168 HENHA p. 169 BUZZA p. 170

HONBU p. 171

ROLBU p. 171

SPARR p. 172

GOSHA p. 173

REFFA p. 173

KESTR p. 174

MERLI p. 175

HOBBY p. 176

PEREG p. 177

BAROW p. 178

TAWOW p. 179

SHEOW p. 180

LOEOW p. 181

LITOW p. 182

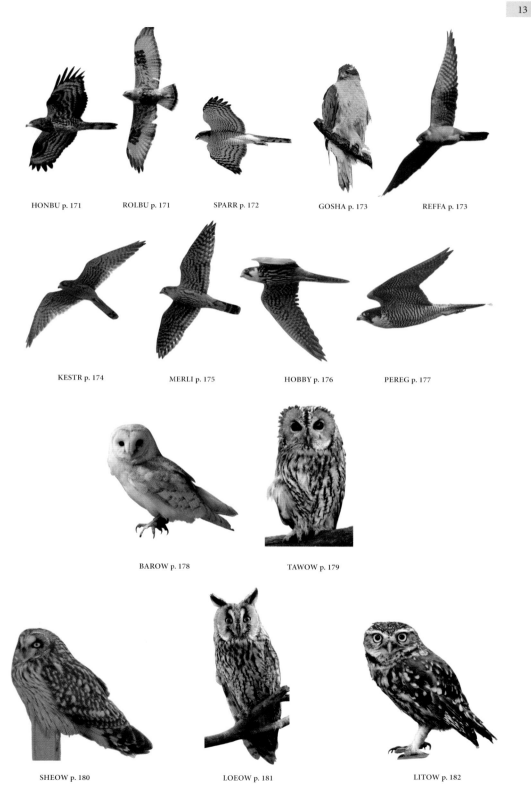

Miscellaneous Larger Landbirds p. 184–211

ROCDO p. 184–185

WOODP p. 186

STODO p. 187

COLDO p. 188

TURDO p. 189

RINPA p. 190

KINGF p. 191

BEEEA p. 192

HOOPO p. 192

GREWO p. 193

GRSWO p. 194

LESWO p. 195

WRYNE p. 195

JAY p. 196

MAGPI p. 197

RAVEN p. 198

ROOK p. 199

CARCR p. 200

HOOCR p. 201

JACKD p. 202

CHOUG p. 203

NIJAR p. 204

CUCKO p. 205

SWIFT p. 206

ALPSW p. 207

RERSW p. 207

SWALL p. 208

SANMA p. 209

HOUMA p. 210

Songbirds p. 212–295

GOLOR p. 214

REBSH p. 214

WOOSH p. 215

GRGSH p. 215

BLABI p. 216

RINOU p. 217

MISTH p. 218

SONTH p. 219

REDWI p. 220

FIELD p. 221

DIPPE p. 222

WAXWI p. 223

BEATI p. 224

LOTTI p. 225

GRETI p. 226

BLUTI p. 227

WILTI p. 228

MARTI p. 229

COATI p. 230

CRETI p. 231

NUTHA p. 232

TREEC p. 233

WREN p. 234

DUNNO p. 235

ROBIN p. 236

BLUTH p. 237

REBFL p. 237

SPOFL p. 238

PIEFL p. 239

BLARE p. 240

REDST p. 241

WHINC p. 242

STOCH p. 243

WHEAT p. 244

NIGAL p. 245

CETWA p. 246

DARWA p. 247

GARWA p. 248

BLACA p. 249

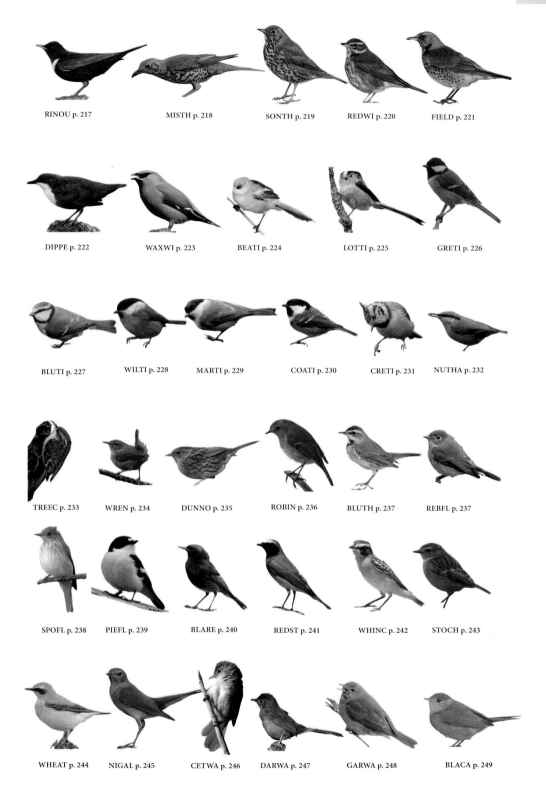

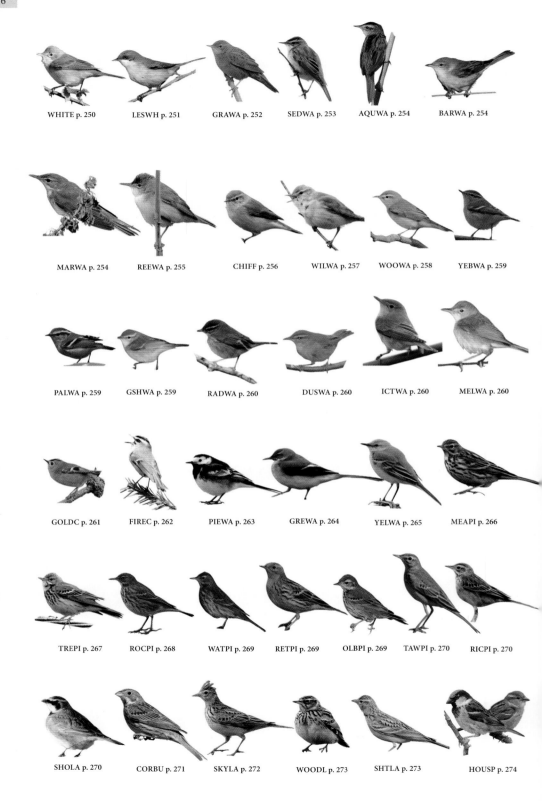

WHITE p. 250 LESWH p. 251 GRAWA p. 252 SEDWA p. 253 AQUWA p. 254 BARWA p. 254

MARWA p. 254 REEWA p. 255 CHIFF p. 256 WILWA p. 257 WOOWA p. 258 YEBWA p. 259

PALWA p. 259 GSHWA p. 259 RADWA p. 260 DUSWA p. 260 ICTWA p. 260 MELWA p. 260

GOLDC p. 261 FIREC p. 262 PIEWA p. 263 GREWA p. 264 YELWA p. 265 MEAPI p. 266

TREPI p. 267 ROCPI p. 268 WATPI p. 269 RETPI p. 269 OLBPI p. 269 TAWPI p. 270 RICPI p. 270

SHOLA p. 270 CORBU p. 271 SKYLA p. 272 WOODL p. 273 SHTLA p. 273 HOUSP p. 274

TRESP p. 274

BRAMB p. 276

CHAFF p. 277

LINNE p. 278

TWITE p. 279

COMRE p. 280

ARCRE p. 281

SERIN p. 281

SISKI p. 282

GREFI 283

GOLDF p. 284

BULLF p. 285

CROSS p. 286

SCOCR p. 287

PARCR p. 287

HAWFI p. 288

SCARO p. 288

REEBU p. 289

SNOBU p. 290

LAPBU p. 291

LITBU p. 291

RUSBU p. 291

YELHA p. 292

CIRBU p. 293

ORTBU p. 294

ROCST p. 294

STARL p. 295

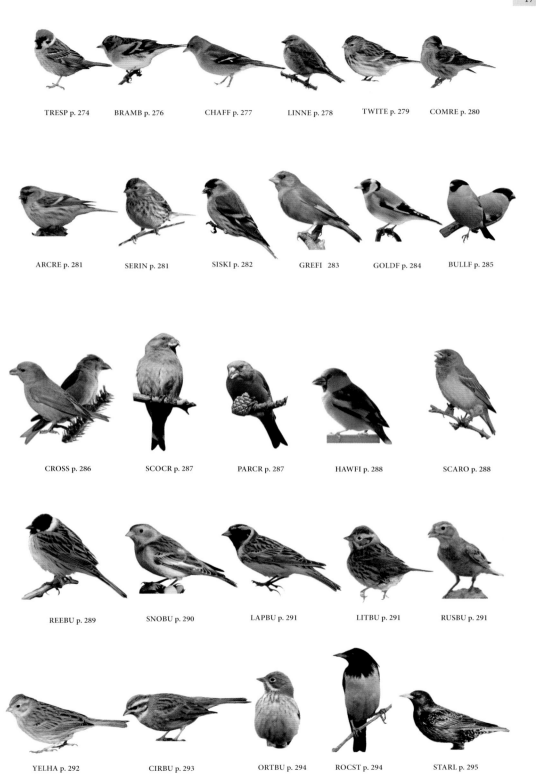

INTRODUCTION

Birding knowledge has evolved greatly over the last 40 years, but the basics of field identification have remained the same. Photography, however, has changed beyond all recognition. The digital age has revolutionised and popularised bird photography, and, in fact, the day when a pair of binoculars was essential for any new birder may be coming to an end. The camera could soon bring nonbirders into the great sport of birding. The idea of one person having the ability to take tens of thousands of images for books covering multiple continents would have been almost unthinkable until recent times. And as digital cameras continue to improve at a dizzying pace, more birders are becoming confident and proficient photographers, accelerating the trend of more photo-based guides. But, until now, these guides have essentially followed the same 'static' formula as artwork-illustrated books: concentrating on individual images isolated from the overall context of habitat—and from other birds. *The Crossley ID Guide* series changes this approach in a fundamental way.

HOW TO USE THIS BOOK

ORGANISATION

Traditional field guides largely use a taxonomic sequence, which, while aiming at scientific accuracy, doesn't always make sense in field birding. Taxonomy also changes, literally from day to day, making it hard to keep any guide current. This book splits the species into seven groups, based on habitat and physical similarities. It is no coincidence that a bird's appearance is largely influenced by its environment. It also means that taxonomic order is not broken as often as you might think. Similar-looking species are grouped together so they can be compared easily.

Unfortunately, the largest disadvantage of all bird guides is the impossibility of portraying size in a lifelike manner. The closest we can come is to note the bird's length, which is included here in each species account next to its name. The other is to show its size relative to other species. Because of the importance of this comparison, I have made it in two places in this guide.

Firstly, the inside front cover shows representative species from most families that cover the complete range of birds in this book. For the beginner, this is a good place to start, and it is where you can narrow your search for any bird you are trying to identify.

The pages immediately preceding this introduction feature all species covered in the book. As with the birds shown on the inside front cover, all of these have been carefully measured. This is the best place in the book to make direct size comparisons. These pages should also be used to study shape and, to a smaller degree, patterns of colour. In most cases, a species will be identifiable from these plates—but you will not learn much about the bird! Included under the species image is its name in shorthand with the page number. (These 5- and 2-letter codes are specific to the British Trust for Ornithology (BTO) and to ringers). It is on this page that you will find the species plate, the textual account, and the range map.

PLATES

The plates are intended to be the heart and soul of this book. Throughout, I have used images that I think most accurately represent the way each species looks in the field, or—put another way—as I would have painted them. They were chosen because they clearly portray each species' shape, plumage, and behaviour. One of the beauties of these plates is that you can control your canvas and include much more (lifelike) information than is possible with painted plates. These images were 'moulded', often after a considerable period of trial and error, to create an overall scene that is as lifelike as a printed image will allow. Each plate contains a massive amount of identification information within a relatively small area.

Here's the rationale for this approach:

1. Reality birding! One of the most important things to develop in becoming a good field birder is the ability to see the features that remain constant, regardless of distance. By creating depth in the plates, I show how a bird's appearance changes with distance.

2. Practice makes perfect! The book is designed to be interactive. Use the captioned birds in the foreground to try to work out the age and sex of birds in the background.

This won't be possible for some birds, but for most it will. At school and in other walks of life, it is not until you practise or get your hands dirty that you really learn. Most people are pleasantly surprised when they make a prolonged effort. If you can't do it here, it will be very difficult with moving birds. If you can, work out many of the answers yourself. You will be far better prepared for the real world.

3. A picture is worth 1000 words! And these plates contain many pictures, with a huge amount of information to process.

4. It's much easier for the human brain to absorb information from a single photographic image than from many separate images. We are more likely to create and retain a mental picture from one photo than from many. I still remember some images from the first bird book I got as a kid. The plates in this book are mostly in focus throughout their full depth, unlike other photographic bird guides. This is how most of us perceive the world.

5. All or most plumages are shown. Also included are birds in transition (moulting). Many books show birds in breeding and nonbreeding plumage. It typically takes weeks, sometimes months, and occasionally years, for a bird to moult the feathers that change its appearance from one plumage to the next. With a more complete picture, it is easier to visualise and understand the workings of moult and how it affects appearance, and it gives you a better chance of finding a comparable image of the bird you are trying to identify in the field.

6. Behaviour is a broad topic yet vital to many aspects of bird identification. Many examples of behaviour are included in the plates. All actions and movements shown, such as feeding behaviour or unusual poses, are typical for that species. Birds that occur commonly in flocks are usually depicted in this way.

7. Habitat plays a large role in identification. The plates capture a habitat or environment typical for that species. This is sometimes difficult because birds often live in a variety of habitats, and many species breed in very different habitats from those they occupy during the nonbreeding season. Hopefully you will recognise many of the famous locations.

8. Flight photos are provided for most species; many have multiple images. These were extremely challenging to take and almost certainly account for my hair loss over the past few years! You may ask, 'Why so many flight shots?' Well, we see birds in flight more than in any other pose. Birds in flight can be relatively easy to identify, but it does require specific focus on size and shape. A bird's structure on terra firma is mirrored in flight.

9. Species get proportional representation; that is, the commoner or more widespread species typically get full-page coverage. These species are treated more thoroughly. Half-page plates are typically used for scarce and more localised species. Species that get only a quarter page are rare migrants. This book covers all the regularly occurring species. It does not include the very rare species for which the British Birds Rarities Committee requests written submission (as of 2013).

The secret to becoming a better birder (and finding rarities) is knowing how to look at birds, and gaining an intimate knowledge of common species. When you know what something isn't (a common bird), it's usually fairly easy to work out what it is (a rare bird!).

HOW DO I LEARN FROM THIS?

It is hoped that many readers will like the appearance of these plates; others might at first find them overpowering, and perhaps even confusing. I could have made them simpler; however, I didn't want to compromise my effort to get people to understand the 'big picture' of bird identification. And, yes, I am asking readers to think of, and use, this book differently from other guides. There are many different types of guides, but they are different in appearance from *The Crossley ID Guide* and its goals. Although this book can be used for reference, both in the field and at home, the principal reason for its design is reader interactivity—much like a school workbook. It is my hope that, by enjoying the plates and text, you will get a more complete picture of a bird's appearance and, just as importantly, how it behaves and where it lives.

When looking at a plate for the first time, try to view it with an open mind. Simply ask yourself, 'What do I see?' rather than 'What am I supposed to see?' In particular, look at the smaller images in the background, because chances are, this is what you will see in real life. By zooming a bird's image in and out, you can absorb the things that remain constant—shape, patterns of colour, and so forth. If you create a good mental image of these patterns, it will serve well in the field.

As you look at the plates, try to get a feel for this bird, its lifestyle, where it lives, and what it does. In this sense, how you view it should be no different from the way people view each other. If you are not interested in getting so involved in honing your skills, see if you can find the image of every bird in the plate. Many are not so easy to locate. As in real life, the harder you look, the more you will see.

If you can remember details about the plate after you close the book, you almost certainly learned much more than you might think. Remember, the best field birders keep it simple, so if you can look at a plate and create a picture in your mind of the bird involved, you are beginning to think like an expert.

CAPTIONS, TEXT, AND MAPS

Captions, text, and maps are intended to complement the plates and fill in pieces of information that can't be shown visually.

Below each plate are the species' common (English) and scientific names. If in doubt, you can cross-reference the scientific name, but taxonomy today seems to be in a greater state of flux than ever before, so scientific names, like common names, may change.

Next to the scientific name is a 5-letter code. This is the BTO code - 'shorthand' used mainly by ringers in Britain and Ireland for recording data. I have used this in the text for two reasons. The first is a space issue. Birds' names are often long and take up a lot of space at the expense of text. The second reason is that ringing codes are an increasing part of many birders' lives for note taking and texting. Typically, single-name species use the first 5 letters (Ptarmigan is PTARM), double-name species the first 3 and 2, respectively (Common Sandpiper is COMSA), triple-name species, 2, 1, and 2 (Great Northern Diver is GRNDI). The second code is a 2-letter BTO code used primarily as a quick way to record species on maps or notes. On a number of the rarer species, there was inadequate space for the two letter code. These can be found on the BTO website www.bto.org

A species' average length is shown next to the ringing code. Length is measured from tail tip to bill tip on stretched birds. When there is a large difference in size between sexes, measurements for both are shown.

On most plates, each plumage, age, and sex is labelled once. A label placed between two or more images is applicable to all. Where all plumages are similar, for example Tawny Owl, there is no label. In these cases, the birds are considered impossible or very difficult to age or sex in the field under usual conditions.

On some plates you will see captions indicating that two plumages are the same, for example 1st-s ♂/ad ♀. In some cases, it is possible to age and sex the bird from the photograph, but the age and sex may not be indicated on the plate. This is going to be a bone of contention for some. The reason is that, in many cases, such birds in the field cannot be aged or sexed with certainty all the time.

Identifying birds is fun and rewarding. Trying to age and sex all the birds you see is just an extension of basic identification and can be equally enjoyable. As mentioned earlier in the introduction, try to use the larger captioned images to age and sex the smaller birds farther away. If you look closely and carefully, you will find it's often not so difficult. The clues always lie in the larger images. Using this simple approach, you will be training yourself to analyse and identify the birds you see in the field faster and in enhanced detail. In school, we learned by working out answers on our own. If we are given the answers, as all the other guides provide, it is very hard to improve. As my kids will tell you, one of my favourite sayings is 'Practice makes perfect'.

When you read the text, it should reinforce and enhance all you have learned from the plate. Abundance and status are very important factors to consider when identifying birds and so we have included numbers from the following sources. Population numbers for Britain are from the recent paper by A. J. Musgrove et al., *British Birds*, February 2013. There are no recently published numbers for Ireland, and we have used Gibbons et al. (1993). Habitat is also key. Knowing where a bird lives plays a significant role in successful bird identification.

The text then discusses behaviour. Like humans, birds tend to behave in certain ways. We can invariably identify loved ones by the way they move, by their particular mannerisms or quirks, and even by the places they tend to visit. But just as with humans, it sometimes takes time to learn these. Obviously, the more time you spend around people or birds, the better you get to know them. Try to read the text and get a sense of the bird—what it is likely to be doing and how it will do it. Cross-reference your mental image with the plate. Get to know the bird inside and out!

Within the 'ID' section all the important field marks of that species are mentioned, starting with reference to size and shape. From there, the text moves to other features that are constant in all plumages. Specific details of the characteristics that help in recognition of each plumage are then discussed. These field marks help you identify the bird to species and also age and sex it. These can be considered the same as captions pointing to specific field marks on plates in traditional field guides.

It is hoped you will notice many of these field marks if you look at a plate carefully! If you do, you will be sure to remember them in the field. If not, cross-reference the plates. Take your time and go one point at a time. For very similar species, the text will point out the features to focus on.

Try not to rush to read the text; read slowly and with reference to the plates.

HOW TO BE A BETTER BIRDER

LOOKING VERSUS SEEING

The biggest mistake most birders make is rushing to get to a name rather than learning about the species: how it behaves and what it looks like. We often look rather than see!

LEARNING TO LOOK: TAKING FIELD NOTES

Birding, as with most things in life, is about the basics. In this case it's learning to see. We can be told how to learn, but ultimately it's down to us to make it happen. The best field birders in the world, at some point in their lives, were made to look at birds closely, a crucial step in their (self)-training. I believe that all experts have taken detailed field notes, which is the best foundation for becoming a good or great field birder. Leading field trips, being a bird artist, or writing books also forces you to look at birds in this concentrated fashion. Only when you are put on the spot do you realize how little information you have really absorbed. This realisation compels you to look much more critically at every detail of a bird's plumage and behaviour. For those who take field notes, you already understand its value as a habitual exercise; you are able to fill in pieces of the identification puzzle more accurately. In this way, you have already become a better field birder.

Of course, in the end, this is an entirely personal choice for all birders; however, taking a photo to study on a computer also has advantages and is often now the tool of choice. Looking at the minutiae and beauty of birds on a computer screen is compelling. Although photos are poor for assessing size and behaviour, they are great for showing details that were not apparent in the field. A word of caution: beware of putting too much stock in the bird's apparent colour in a photo. Depending on model, settings, and lighting, a camera can create a wide array of colour tones in the same image. Add to this the wide-ranging colour rendition produced by computer monitors and photo-editing software, and it is not wise to put too much faith in assessing subtle shades of grey, brown, and green in digital photos. Features such as wing bars and ear coverts can often show more or less contrast than in real life; however, computers can be a fantastic learning tool—just be a little careful and try to look at a series of photos rather than just one or two.

When looking at a bird, try to look at a bird for what it is rather than what someone else tells you it is supposed to be. We are all influenced or biased by the world around us and the things we have read or heard. Remember, the bird in front of you is your immediate reality. Watch it and you will learn it. Believe your own eyes! You will understand the bird in a way that books and photos cannot teach you. And remember, a bird's size, shape, and behaviour usually do not vary too much from individual to individual, even though the plumage may. The same is true of humans. We change clothes seasonally, but underneath we remain the same.

The following may prove useful:

Take 1: My name is Richard, I am white, pink cheeked (though my cheeks get a lot rosier after exercise or booze). My complexion is paler in winter and darker after I spend time in the summer sun. My 'derriere' is white because it never sees the sun. I have brown hair and I'm not very tall.

Is this a good description and would you be able to recognise me based on it? The answer is obviously 'No'.

Take 2: My name is Richard. I am about 5 feet 9 inches tall. I weigh around 185 pounds—I could do to lose a couple, though I am fairly broad. I am in my 40s, Caucasian, with short brown hair. You can often find me birding or photographing birds.

Is this a better description? The answer is certainly 'Yes', simply because it gives more specific information about my size, shape, and other physical attributes, as well as habits. You might use a similar approach to provide a decent description of yourself.

Now—a tough question. Do you know what a Goldfinch looks like? If so, please get a piece of paper and write a full description (without recourse to a field guide). Or at least describe it in your head. Let's look at your description of the Goldfinch. Was your mental image based on size, shape, and behaviour as well as on colour? Maybe not. But if you start to recognise birds as you do people, you will be using the same set of skills used by the best field birders in the world.

I firmly believe field identification of birds can be broken down into these key areas (in my personal order of importance): size, shape, behaviour, probability, colour, and sound.

SIZE

Somewhat surprisingly, perhaps, it turns out that we're remarkably good at judging other people's heights, in fact to within 2 per cent accuracy on most occasions. The truth is that we spend most of our lives practising, so, not surprisingly, adults tend to be much better at judging height than children. We all judge relative size in birds to some degree but often put little emphasis on size in the field. Focus on size and try to make as accurate an assessment of this feature as you can. Compare the bird you're trying to identify with other nearby birds you have already identified. With practice, you can become accomplished at determining size, which is critical since it is the least variable characteristic in birds. Sometimes you will know you are very accurate with your assessment of size, but at other times it will be only a rough estimate. Naturally we can also get this wrong, particularly when views are brief or distant. The secret is to know your limits.

STRUCTURE AND SHAPE

Along with size, structure and shape are fundamental to the identification of nearly all birds. Shape is remarkably consistent in individual species. Colour and lighting have little or no effect on determination of a bird's shape and structure. Always try to describe a bird's shape in language that makes sense to you. We each interpret or understand words such as *fat, rounded, slim*, and *long* differently. As an author, I am compelled to use these terms when describing a bird, but you should create your own language and sense of scale to describe the same bird in terms that make sense to you.

BEHAVIOUR

Learning the 'personality' of a bird is hugely important. This takes longer to master than assessing a bird's size and shape. Knowing the behaviour of birds with which we are familiar is essential in the field. Behaviour encompasses many aspects of identification, just as it does in our interrelationships with humans. For instance, consider the type of habitat a species favours, how it moves, and whether it's a loner or gregarious. For example, a Sanderling is instantly recognisable when it relentlessly chases waves along the beach, a clinching identification feature regardless of size, shape, or colour.

PROBABILITY

We use probability in bird identification, sometimes more than we would credit. Does the bird usually or always occur in this location and in this habitat? When you go birding in an unfamiliar area, you always start with this basic question, consciously or subconsciously. On your local patch you are always more confident, since you have built up experience of species' occurrences and distributions. These are almost subconscious, reflex identifications built on years of careful field observation, and a just reward for learning to see.

COLOUR

We love the myriad colours of birds and stunning photographs that capture them in all their astonishing beauty. Often we can't help but feel overwhelmed by a blast of colour as we chance upon a stunning azure Kingfisher. The problem is that Grey Plover (a bird consistent in size, shape, and behaviour) changes its colours. In one season it is usually white, grey, and black, but it has to change its feathers (moult), and so it goes through a period when it shows a complex combination of feathers and therefore a changing pattern of colours. I won't dwell on the challenge of learning plumages of females, juveniles, 1-year-old males, and so forth in Grey Plover! Other important factors influence identification by colour, such as time of day, whether sunny or cloudy, position of the sun, amount of shade, feather wear and fading, aberrant (abnormal) plumage, and of course normal variation between individuals within the same species.

We are naturally attracted by colour. Despite this attraction, stick to identification basics: "Is the bird in front of me the correct size and shape for the species I believe it to be?" "Does the species I've identified even occur here?" Colour can be extremely variable, so it is important to focus less on the tone of the colour itself and more on the overall pattern it creates, that is, the relative colours of different parts of the body.

Ultimately, colour is undeniably important in bird identification, and for beginners, in particular, it will almost always be the first feature to attract the eye. But the secret is to learn how to use colour in combination with all the other identification factors described above.

VOCALISATIONS

Songs and calls are a large part of bird identification. Many birds are identified without even being seen. Even if you hear an unfamiliar sound, it helps you locate a bird you might not have known was there.

Having lived in England, Japan, and the United States, as well as travelling extensively, I have had to learn a lot of unfamiliar sounds. The best way I've found to learn songs is to try to describe them to myself. Try to write them down thinking about pitch (high or low, and whether going up or down), length of vocalization, and rhythm. A few birds have songs that are phonetically described. I found these useful. Listening to tapes helped the most, particularly in confirming identification after listening to a bird. There is no substitute for real-world repetition.

The variation in vocalization within species and even in individuals is large, as clearly shown in sonograms. Immature birds tend to be the most variable. Other factors, such as acoustics, weather, and which way the bird is facing, all have an impact. As when looking at birds, it is important to differentiate between 'certain' and 'probably' and know your limits.

TOPOGRAPHY

Birds are covered in feathers. These are split into batches or groups known as *tracts*. Knowing these tracts is a great help in bird identification. Colour patterns within these feather tracts are usually the same. The major exception is when birds are growing (moulting) new feathers.

I remember eavesdropping on a conversation in a pub on the Isles of Scilly when I was 16. Some of the top young English birders in the next booth were talking a language I didn't know. They were discussing primary projections, tertial fringes, greater covert bars, alulas. They were using these terms to identify, age, and sex birds. This 'tertial talk', as I now call it, sounded overwhelming and more like double Dutch, but it inspired me to start looking at birds more closely. As I began to learn the different groups of feathers, how they were used by a bird, and how their appearance changed, it had a big impact on my birding skills. The language of brilliant birders was not so difficult to learn.

One of the keys to learning topography is being able to see birds repeatedly and well. Bird feeders near your windows are perfect for this. I also find it useful to think of bird topography in human terms. Most of us know words like forehead, crown, legs, feet, breast, belly, and even scapulars. With a good grounding, it is easier to work out the missing parts such as tertials and coverts. Of course, birds change their shape, most notably when they open their wings. Understanding the mechanics of this, and how things fit back into place on the closed wing, is also a great help.

On the confusing side, you will find that tracts of feathers don't appear the same on different groups of birds. For example, scapulars will often cover much of the wing on shorebirds but relatively little on warblers. Learning these differences unfortunately comes down to repetition and experience; however, taking field notes certainly helps you become familiar with them. As a result, when you see an unfamiliar bird, you are able to take in far more information in a shorter time, focus faster on important identification features, and, quite simply, become a much better field birder. Knowing the name of a bird is not important, but knowing how to look at it is crucial. The top people in any field are the best because they can analyse things better and faster than others.

MOULT

Birds do essentially the same things on a cyclical basis, including moulting. They moult for a number of reasons. It is important that feathers be kept in good condition to keep the bird warm, dry, and mobile. Of course, some like to look good to attract a mate! Having an understanding of moult and how it affects a bird's appearance is a large help not only in identifying birds but also in ageing and sexing them.

Moult is complex, but we can try to simplify it. Fundamental to a clear understanding of this process is to know that birds moult all their feathers at least once a year, replacing them after they have finished breeding. Many also have a moult in spring; this is frequently only a partial moult of head and body feathers.

BIRD TOPOGRAPHY

Songbird

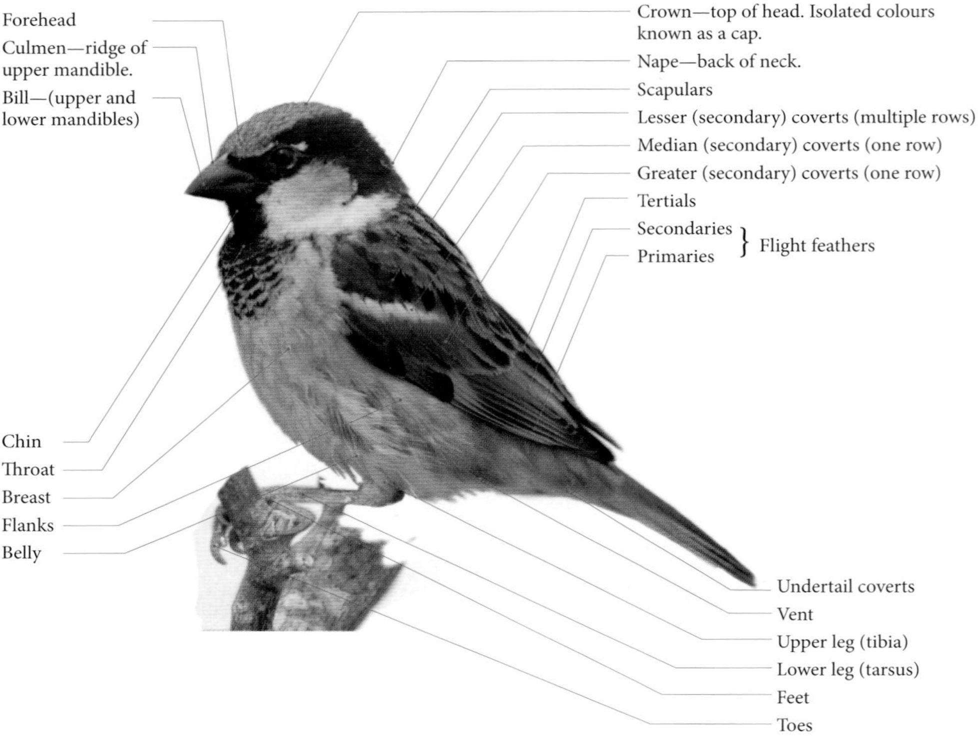
Forehead
Culmen—ridge of upper mandible.
Bill—(upper and lower mandibles)
Chin
Throat
Breast
Flanks
Belly
Crown—top of head. Isolated colours known as a cap.
Nape—back of neck.
Scapulars
Lesser (secondary) coverts (multiple rows)
Median (secondary) coverts (one row)
Greater (secondary) coverts (one row)
Tertials
Secondaries
Primaries
Flight feathers
Undertail coverts
Vent
Upper leg (tibia)
Lower leg (tarsus)
Feet
Toes

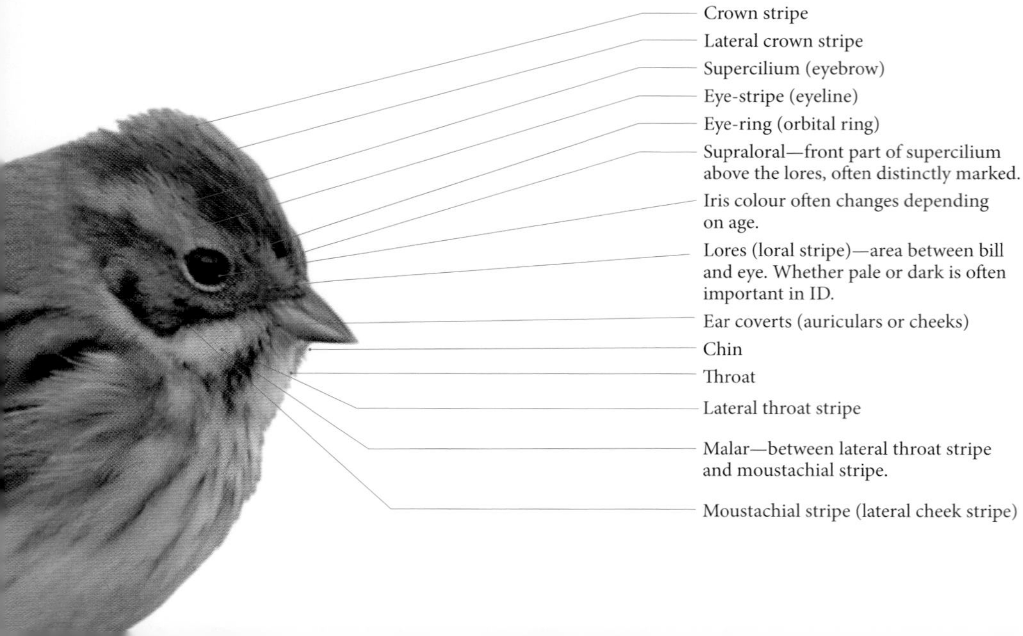
Crown stripe
Lateral crown stripe
Supercilium (eyebrow)
Eye-stripe (eyeline)
Eye-ring (orbital ring)
Supraloral—front part of supercilium above the lores, often distinctly marked.
Iris colour often changes depending on age.
Lores (loral stripe)—area between bill and eye. Whether pale or dark is often important in ID.
Ear coverts (auriculars or cheeks)
Chin
Throat
Lateral throat stripe
Malar—between lateral throat stripe and moustachial stripe.
Moustachial stripe (lateral cheek stripe)

Mantle—center of back.
Scapulars—shoulder feathers, typically large, that hang over inner wing.
Secondaries—inner wing flight feathers, usually 9 or 10 feathers. More on larger birds.
Tertials—the innermost 3 or 4 secondaries. They sit on top of the flight feathers, giving them protection.
Rump—lower back. Feathers often contrast with mantle.
Primaries—outerwing flight feathers, usually 9 or 10 feathers.
Uppertail coverts—cover base of tail. Often same colour as rump.
Wing point—position of wingtip relative to tail.
Tail feathers (retrices)
Primary projection—extension of primaries past tip of longest tertial, measured against tertials —here medium length, same length of tertials. Very important 'finger-print' in separating some species.

Raptor

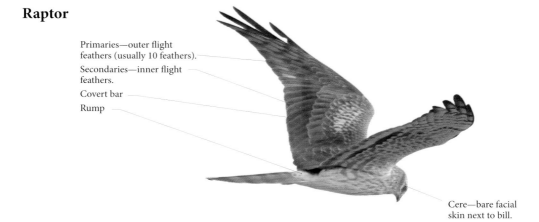

Primaries—outer flight feathers (usually 10 feathers).
Secondaries—inner flight feathers.
Covert bar
Rump
Cere—bare facial skin next to bill.

Carpal
Throat
Breast
Belly
Axillaries
Flanks
Leggings—feathers at base of legs.

Duck

Primaries—usually 10. Numbered from innermost (primary 1) to outermost (primary 10).
Secondaries—usually about 9 feathers plus 3 or 4 tertials. The number of feathers varies among species. Numbered from inner wing (seconadary 1) to outermost
Speculum—brightly coloured patch on secondaries.
Tail—colour often important in ID. Feather shape used in ageing.

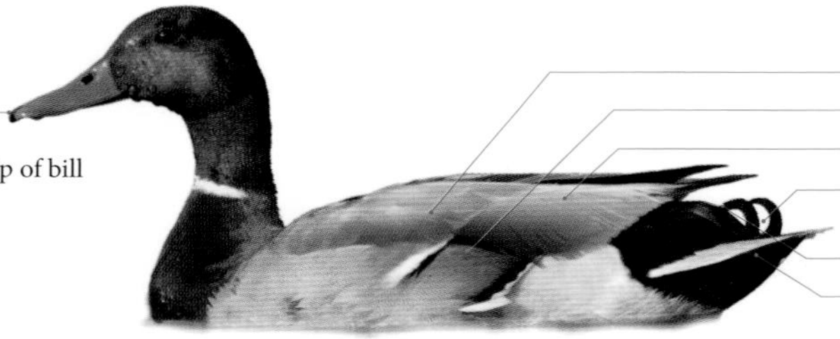
Nail—tip of bill
Scapulars
Speculum
Tertials
Tail—colour important in ID. Feather shape used in ageing.
Uppertail coverts
Undertail coverts

Gull

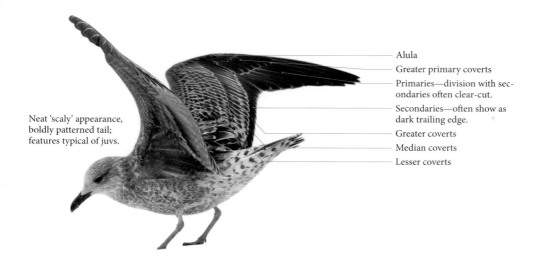

Neat 'scaly' appearance, boldly patterned tail; features typical of juvs.
Alula
Greater primary coverts
Primaries—division with secondaries often clear-cut.
Secondaries—often show as dark trailing edge.
Greater coverts
Median coverts
Lesser coverts

Gull

Uniform back—typical of adult or near adult gulls
Orbital ring—unfeathered skin surrounding eye.
Iris—colour often varies depending on age of bird. Usually darker in juvs.
Gape—fleshy edges at base of mouth. Often prominent in juvs.
Gonydeal spot—often red, shown by large gulls.
Gonydeal angle—usually stronger (more pronouced) in larger gulls.

Wader

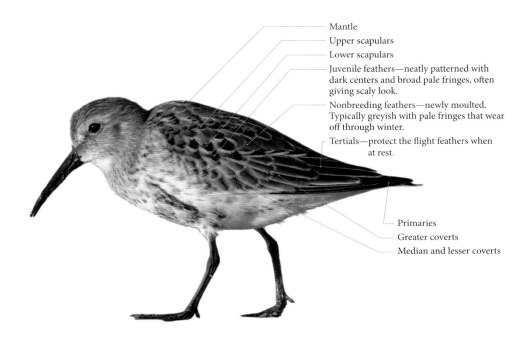

Mantle
Upper scapulars
Lower scapulars
Juvenile feathers—neatly patterned with dark centers and broad pale fringes, often giving scaly look.
Nonbreeding feathers—newly moulted. Typically greyish with pale fringes that wear off through winter.
Tertials—protect the flight feathers when at rest.
Primaries
Greater coverts
Median and lesser coverts

These spring moults are often a transition to brighter plumages to attract a mate or help the bird blend into its environment.

A feather starts as a follicle within a sheath (known as a *pin*)—just as our hairs do. As the follicle grows, it pushes out the old feather. Feathers grow anywhere from a couple of millimetres to a centimetre per day (larger birds' feathers grow faster, as you would expect). When they are fully grown, feathers are cut off from the circulatory system, so they can no longer grow. This also means the process no longer uses energy. Moulting takes up a lot of a bird's energy and for this reason has a large impact on its lifestyle and behaviour. The bird must keep a balance between the advantages of new feathers and the energy required to grow them. Large birds moult much more slowly than small ones, simply because of this large energy cost, and their moult can therefore be protracted.

Soft downy feathers are quickly replaced by the first strong feathers. These are known as *contour feathers*, and the first plumage they form is called *juvenile*. This is the only plumage in which all the feathers are the same age and have the same appearance and texture. Adults can also have a uniform appearance, but birds never moult all feathers simultaneously. These adult feathers therefore usually have subtly different colours and patterns of wear.

Small birds usually moult from a briefly worn juvenile plumage to an adult-like plumage. Some of these birds can be aged through the first year of life by looking at retained juvenile feathers, particularly some of the wing coverts and flight feathers. A number of large birds don't start to moult out of their juvenile plumage for more than a year. As a broad generalization, the larger the bird, the longer it takes to become an adult. For example, most small gulls take 2 years, medium-sized gulls 3, and large gulls 4 to reach adulthood.

In most birds, the difference in appearance between an often scaly or spotted brown juvenile and a boldly patterned adult is striking. Trying to understand what happens between these two appearances is very important. For the reason stated above, large birds tend to moult very slowly. In fact, they are in active moult the majority of the time. Their plumage usually comprises feathers of different generations. The newest feathers have adult-like characteristics compared with the oldest. This mishmash of feathers can appear confusing, but understanding what happens during development toward adulthood can help unravel many of the apparent mysteries of a bird's appearance. Also, understanding the sequence in which a bird moults feathers (most follow the same general patterns) is, in most cases, the best way to accurately age it.

In this book, unlike most other bird books, I have tried to put many of the transitional appearances in the plates. Birds never change their appearance overnight—it's a prolonged process. If you keep in mind that moult is an ongoing process, it will become easier to understand a bird's appearance.

The timing and patterns of moult vary. Many birds have to 'make the decision' to moult before, after, or during migration. There are no hard and fast rules; however, some patterns are clear. If you are a shorebird migrating from the Arctic to South Africa for the winter, you can't afford to be using energy for moult, and it would not make sense to have feathers missing from your wings; hence, long-distance migrants tend to moult either before or after migration, this being largely dependent on where food supplies are best. These birds always have long pointed wings—an adaptation to help them fly fast and far. Short-distance migrants, on the other hand, which don't have to fly as far, will often moult while migrating.

Feathers are moulted in different sequences depending on the species; however, it is almost always symmetrical across the wings and done such that a balance is maintained between them.

TERMINOLOGY

One area of confusion in bird books today is the different terminology used to describe them. This problem of terminology encompasses three features: age, plumage, and moult patterns. The reason for the confusion is due largely to lack of a clear and consistent terminology for describing each species' appearance.

The following is the most widely used terminology:

The Life-Year System

Traditionally this has been the most popular system. I have used it in this book. Fundamental in understanding how it works is knowing that a bird starts its life in the summer (assuming it hatched in the Northern Hemisphere). To calculate a person's age we need to know his or her birthday. Knowing a person's age provides a better understanding of behaviour and appearance; for birds it is the same. The following terminology relating to age is used in this book:

1st-yr: starts as a fledgling in the nest, usually late spring or summer, where its contour feathers grow out within a few weeks. This is *juvenile* plumage. Most birds moult a number of these juvenile feathers in autumn, and they are replaced by adult-like or older immature feathers, creating the *first-winter plumage* (*1st-w*). In spring, some species, for example Pied Flycatcher, or PIEFL, will moult in many new adult-like feathers, which are often bright, creating the first spring/summer plumage (*1st-s*). Often superficially like adults, they can be aged as first-summer by their dull and worn retained juvenile flight feathers and wing coverts. The term *first-year* (*1st-yr*) encompasses all three plumages—juvenile, first-winter, and first-summer—and is used in this book when there is insignificant difference in a bird's appearance through the first year. At the end of the summer, a small bird has gone through its complete annual moult. At this point it is an adult. On occasion, a bird will retain older immature feathers after the first year; in this case, it can be aged as a second-year bird. For others, mostly larger birds, the cycle is much longer, and they become second-year (*2nd-w, 2nd-s*), third-year, and so on until they reach adulthood.

Many adults have two different plumages or appearances in winter and summer (ducks are the major exception). The typically bolder plumage they moult into in spring, and also retain during summer, is called *breeding plumage* (*br;* also known as alternate plumage). The complete moult occurs in late summer/autumn and results in a typically drabber appearance called *nonbreeding* (*nonbr;* also known as basic plumage). A few species, such as Ptarmigan, have a third plumage called *supplemental*.

This terminology describes an appearance or plumage; however, these appearances can be variable. I do not think of these stages as plumages but as a period in time when a bird is a certain age. Knowing the date we are birding (or a photo was taken) is critical. If you are birding on August 2nd and you know the gull you are watching is approximately 1 year old, after a while you will learn the variation in appearance of birds of that age. Personally, I think of it as a 1-year-old gull just as I would a 1-year-old child.

The Calendar-Year System

As the name implies, the calendar-year system uses language based on calendar dates—January 1st being the first day of a new year. A Robin this year would be in its second calendar year on January 1st (but not in its second year of life). This is at odds with the way we age people, pets, and most things. This terminology is not widely used, but often enough to cause confusion with the life-year system. The calendar-year system has no advantages over others and has several obvious problems—it is best not used!

The Humphrey-Parkes System

The Humphrey-Parkes system is based solely on moult patterns. Because of the cyclical nature of annual moult and its relationship to physical appearance, use of this system has become more common, especially for ageing of gulls and raptors. It is particularly valuable when moult patterns are used as the way to age birds, rather than physical appearance. To a large degree, the systems are intertwined and arguably inseparable.

The first cycle includes all the different appearances or plumages of a bird until it starts to moult into its second basic plumage (2nd-winter). This includes juvenile, 1st-winter, and 1st-summer. Use of the term 'first cycle' is technically correct during this time period. By comparison, a juvenile bird, for example a Herring Gull as shown on page 107, that has moulted a few feathers is technically no longer a juvenile, though the majority of feathers are still juvenile. On one hand, the term *first-cycle* is correct but lacks detail about plumage; on the other hand, with the term *juvenile* you have a more detailed description of the bird's appearance and plumage, but it may not be correct. Take your pick!

In this book I use the term *juvenile*. You will see a number of images, such as Canada Goose, in which the bird has mostly juvenile feathers but has moulted a few feathers (see if you can tell which they are). These could have been labelled '1st-cycle' if I had chosen to write the book from that perspective, or '1st-winter'. Again, this is a judgment call. Where the bird has primarily juvenile feathers (>90%), I have usually called it a juvenile because it helps the viewer understand the appearance of the bird at this stage. Now you can look at all the birds labelled *juv* and see if they have moulted some of their juvenile feathers!

The major drawback of the Humphrey-Parkes

system is that it is at complete odds with other terminology. It is also an unfamiliar language for most people and hard to grasp. A bird is in its first cycle until it starts moulting into its second basic plumage when it is about 1 year old—usually first seen as newly growing flight feathers (primaries and secondaries). This transition is often impossible to see in the field. Two birds the same age can be in different cycles, and birds that are a year apart in age can still be in the same cycle. For example, yesterday (May 25th) I watched a second-cycle Herring Gull; how old was it and what did it look like? The answer: you don't know. It could have been a 1st-summer/1-year-old bird that has just started its second cycle or a 2nd-summer bird that has not started its third cycle.

Understanding these moult cycles and the different appearance of different generations of feathers is often critical in the correct ageing of some birds, however. At present, this terminology is poorly understood by most and often misused. It is best reserved for those with a solid understanding of moult.

Birds spend varying amounts of time moulting from one plumage to another and therefore will have feathers of both plumages at the same time. These transitional birds cause confusion; for this reason, I have treated transitional birds extensively in this book. Besides taking note of different colours and patterns, always remember: one feather may be new and another old, and different amounts of wear are often easy to see.

FACTORS AFFECTING APPEARANCE

If all this talk of changing plumages, moult, different feathers, and so on sounds confusing, it is—for everyone. But simply knowing about it and understanding that confusion exists is helpful.

Other things can change a bird's appearance that we must also consider. When a bird's feathers are old, particularly in the summer months, they have been subjected to many hardships. Sunlight bleaches feathers, making them paler. The wear and tear of time does the same thing. Not only are colours usually faded, sometimes considerably, but the feathers are also, quite simply, beat up and heavily worn. Certain groups, such as gulls, can look remarkably scruffy and dishevelled in the summer months. Juveniles have softer feathers than those of adults; these latter are more prone to wear and fading.

Some birds appear atypical or outside the norm. These are known as *aberrant*. Although uncommon, they are frequent enough to warrant consideration when things don't seem to add up. Some are particularly pale: leucistic; some completely white: albinistic; and, very rarely, all black: melanistic. Often an aberrant bird will still show the basic patterns of 'normal' colour, so always look for these. Size, shape, behaviour, probability, and vocalization generally stay the same, so, although these birds are initially puzzling, actual ID is usually fairly straightforward. The only changed feature is colour.

And of course there is the dreaded 'H-word'. The word hybrid comes up a lot today in the serious birding world. As we become more knowledgeable, with the technology to record sight and sound ever more accurately and the ability to dig deep with tools such as DNA analysis and blood sampling, the study and understanding of hybridization grows apace. In some groups, such as gulls and ducks, hybridization is fairly common. In others, such as shorebirds, it is very rare; however, the biological imperative to breed is strong. Even in shorebirds, the frequency of known hybridization is increasing and no doubt will continue to do so as time passes. The appearance of hybrids ranges across the spectrum, from total similarity to one parent, to displaying intermediate characters of both. The latter occurrence is the most common. If you find a bird that is puzzling because it seems to show features of two different species, you should consider the chance that it could be a hybrid.

Lighting also has a great effect on the appearance of birds. When the sun is high and bright, contrast is at its greatest: dark colours look blacker and pale colours look whiter. The lower the sun in the sky, the richer and more saturated the colours become. At sunrise and sunset, whites become creamy or have red tones and contrast is at its lowest. On overcast days ('flat light'), colours tend to have a more 'accurate' representation. Learning to understand the tricks of light is very important.

In this book, most plates are made up of images taken in flat light for a more accurate representation.

Size illusion can also occur. When one looks directly into the sun, birds can look slimmer than they really are. While much has been written about size illusion, however, I still believe the most important thing is to look longer and more carefully.

Sometimes birds get sick, or their normal way of life is interrupted, perhaps because of unexpected bad weather or shortage of food. As with humans, birds have to adapt as best they can. Sometimes they will have to change their normal way of life. For example, if a shorebird heading to the Arctic to breed becomes ill, or can't make the journey in time because there is not enough food to replenish fat reserves, it might alter its normal behaviour. If it can't breed, why go to the breeding grounds or moult into a bright breeding plumage, something that takes a lot of energy? If it is sick, it cannot afford to waste energy moulting, as this is not vital to its survival. It may then stay farther south than normal and not moult into what is effectively an unnecessarily bright plumage.

Some birds show outward signs of illness or abnormality. Birds can also have deformed unfeathered parts, most obvious in bill shapes; seeing birds with abnormally long bills is not rare. Cosmetic colour changes also occur as a result of rust staining, particularly common in groups such as ducks. A poor or atypical diet can also have an impact on colouring.

There are always factors that can change a bird's appearance; take them into account but don't be sidetracked; stick with the basics!

SWIMMING WATERBIRDS

GEESE

Few sights in birding are more inspiring than a huge flock of honking geese 'blasting off'. Because they are large birds and usually occur in flocks, often by the hundreds or even thousands, they can be easy to find and watch. They tend to be very vocal and are often heard before they are seen. Flocks spend most of their time grazing in fields but can also be found on larger bodies of water. Pairs mate for life and form family parties with the offspring through the winter. 'Watch posts' keep guard and quickly spook the flock at the first sign of danger.

Large flocks frequently act as 'carriers'. Other rarer species join the flock and start to move with them, ending up many miles away from their usual range. It's surprising how hard it is to pick the odd one out in large flocks—so keep looking! However, beware, as there are all sorts of oddball escaped captive birds to contend with. Working out which ones are genuinely wild vagrants is always a bone of contention.

DUCKS

Ducks are a fantastic group of birds. Only when you look at them really closely can you appreciate their intricate markings, iridescent colours, and true beauty. The contrast between gaudy males and, let's say, 'subtle' females (sexual dimorphism) is no more obvious in the bird world than among ducks. For ID purposes, working out the male can easily be based on patterns of colour alone. Ducks are frequently seen in pairs, so a great starting point for identifying a confusing brown duck is to check whether it's the partner of a bright bird close by; however, the basics of size and shape pertain to ducks just as they do to any other group of birds. They are often in mixed flocks, or other groups are nearby, for comparison of both size and shape. Making this comparison is particularly important because female-type plumages are commoner than bright ones simply because young and eclipse males share this appearance for much of summer, autumn, and, sometimes, early winter.

Eclipse is the term used to describe the dull female-like plumage into which males moult on their breeding grounds. This moult sometimes takes place near the nesting site, but breeding birds often migrate to a different location that can be hundreds of miles away. During this period the birds moult all their flight feathers at once and so are flightless for several weeks. The moulting site needs cover and plentiful food supplies, and it must allow them to dive to escape predators. One reason for this duller plumage is its value as camouflage while they are flightless. Summer is also a time with plentiful food supplies, so the disadvantage of being flightless is less serious than when moult occurs later in the year. Males usually moult back into their more easily recognisable bold colour patterns (often called 'bright' plumage) during the autumn. Females usually moult several weeks earlier than males and are often on the nest during this period.

In recent times there has been discussion whether 'eclipse' is actually a breeding or nonbreeding plumage. This naming scheme leads to confusion when dealing with ducks. I have described the plumage and use *eclipse* in the accounts to refer to birds moulting out of their bright plumage.

Sexing birds is often difficult during eclipse and sometimes possible only by focusing on the upper-wing pattern. Adult males retain their boldly patterned coverts, though these are usually not visible on sitting birds. Eye colour always stays the same; bill colour is often duller in adult males. Watch for distinctively marked bright adult male feathers moulting back in. As time passes, they appear as a variable mix of dull brown-grey feathers and bolder bright plumage feathers. Most adults have finished their moult by November or December.

Telling young males from eclipse males is often particularly perplexing and not well documented in guides, in part because it is genuinely difficult but also because there are still gaps in our knowledge.

Juveniles look superficially like adult females. Most have warmer brown tones. Juvenile feathers are softer and not so durable as those of adult wildfowl. Juvenile feathers also have a different shape from those of adults. Flank feathers and wing coverts are smaller and rounder, and usually have more solidly coloured centres (those of adults often have complex markings). The tail feathers of juveniles are narrower and more pointed than in adults; these become heavily worn through the autumn, a feature that can readily be seen with close views. Feathers often have an inverted V chipped out at the tip that becomes more obvious through the winter. Tertials, most noticeable in males because of their larger size, are very broad in adults and more rounded at the tip; juveniles' tertials are shorter, narrow, and pointed. The scapulars are also shorter, smaller, and more pointed in juveniles—again more noticeable in males.

First-winter (1st-w) males are birds that have a combination of juvenile feathers and newly moulted (bright) feathers. This combination, often a mix of brown and brighter feathers, is similar in adults. Working out age and sex is difficult, but with good views and practice, the above criteria will help you identify many birds. This is complex stuff in many cases, some of which is beyond even experts, so do not despair if it seems difficult. Remember, most adults have completed their moult by November or December (some earlier), so most birds not fully moulted into bright plumage after this date are likely 1st-w males. These birds often show signs of immaturity into spring.

Most immature birds winter in the southern portion of the species' range; adults tend to stay to the north. Many species of wildfowl breed in the Arctic and visit us only in the winter, most arriving from September onwards and departing by April.

Ducks are typically placed in two groups: dabbling, and diving. Dabbling ducks (genus *Anas*), as the name implies, dabble or tip up, to feed just under the water's surface. Diving ducks include sea ducks (scoters, Eider, Long-tailed, Scaup, and Goldeneye), sawbills (mergansers), and stiff-tails (Ruddy). The feet of diving ducks are set farther back on the body, which helps them swim under water. They sometimes stay under water for more than a minute and can dive to considerable depths in search of food such as molluscs and fish. They typically run across the water on take-off. Dabblers 'jump off' the water on take-off.

Hybridisation is relatively common in ducks. Just about any combination is possible. The parentage of many hybrids can often be worked out, as they usually show characters of both parents. It is often easy to work out the ID of one of the parents, but the second has to be left as 'possible' (a chance of) or 'probable' (likely to be). Sometimes it's just not clear whether a bird is pure or not.

Whooper Swan *Cygnus cygnus* **WHOSW/WS** L. 150cm

UK: s. 9-14 pairs
w. 15,000

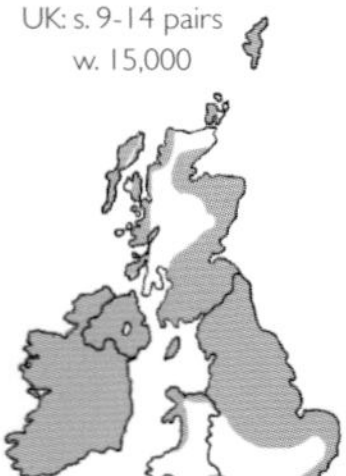

Locally common winter visitor, arriving Oct from Iceland, probably always in a single flight. Most often seen in small parties grazing in arable fields or swimming on flooded meadows, ponds, and sheltered bays. Often vocal—one of the sounds of winter, particularly heard when flocks commute to lakes or floods from their feeding grounds. Named after its whooping bugle given while flying or sitting, often uttering 3 notes in triplicate. **ID:** Same size as MUTSW but slimmer, with different bill shape and colour (triangular black and yellow). BEWSW v sim but smaller, more compact, shorter neck, blockier-headed with less angular shape. Subtly different bill pattern best thing to focus on with good views. Whooper usually sits tall with slim neck held proudly straight and erect, in contrast to MUTSW. Sleeping or feeding birds with submerged head and neck can be recognised from MUTSW by their shorter tail. Adult: all white. More yellow on bill than BEWSW, extending past nostril to sharp point. Juv: paler and less mottled brown than MUTSW, no black around eye. Bill yellow and pale pink.

Bewick's Swan *Cygnus columbianus* **BEWSW/BS** L 121cm

UK: w. 7,000

Very localised winter visitor Nov–Feb to flooded meadows, lakes, and salt marshes. Occurs regularly only in a few scattered areas, but sometimes wanders during harsh winter conditions. Frequently grazes in agricultural fields, routinely mixes with other swans. Mellow hooting yelp travels long distances; calls usually 2-syllable, not in 3s as WHOSW. Higher pitched, without bugling quality of WHOSW. Flock sizes vary from a few birds to dozens, usually in family packs. **ID:** Slightly smaller than WHOSW, with shorter and thicker neck; size difference not usually apparent without direct comparison. Profile different, with rounded crown, shorter bill, and relatively larger head. With head tucked in, shorter tail than MUTSW quite easy to pick out. Breast bulges less than WHOSW. Adult: black-and-yellow colouration on bill roughly half and half; yellow makes blunt angle to black (more pointed in WHOSW). Famously, each individual has unique bill pattern. Juv: dingy grey-white. Bill a shadow of adult pattern, yellow and pink, initially nearly all pink to base, becomes darker through winter. 2nd-yr: often retains a few grey juv feathers.

Mute Swan *Cygnus olor* **MUTSW/MS** L 152cm

UK: s. 6,400 pairs
w. 79,000

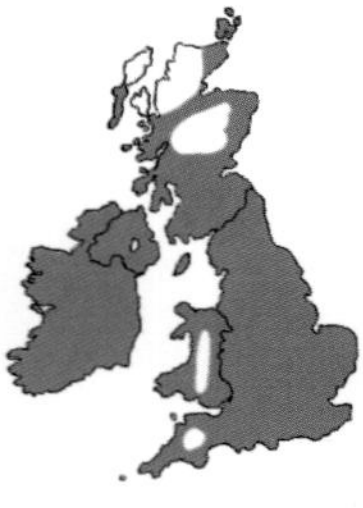

The familiar swan, ubiquitous on all kinds of waterbodies, including rivers, village ponds, and town parks, even on the sea in places. Elegant and beautiful, or big and nasty—take your pick, as both can apply. Territorial pairs take over patches, attacking other birds that dare to come nearby. Young and those without territory live in flocks year-round. Nest large and conspicuous. Young protected zealously; an adult, standing its ground, has hissed fear into many a human. Neck often held arched rather than straight as in other swans. Wings sometimes held high and arched, always when bird in an aggressive posture. Makes a running take-off with wings thrashing water. Wings make diagnostic whistled hum in flight (silent in other swans), which replaces flight call (hence 'mute'). Calls: a variety of hisses and snorts. **ID:** The largest swan with thick neck, square-headed look, and noticeably long tail. Bill pattern usually makes ID straightforward. Adult: white, often with yellowish neck. Striking orange bill with large black knob; ♂ larger than ♀. Juv/1st-w: variable, usually medium brown, mottled. Moults through autumn/winter into whiter plumage. Rare juv 'Polish' birds are all white. Bill initially dull, becomes pink through winter, black at base.

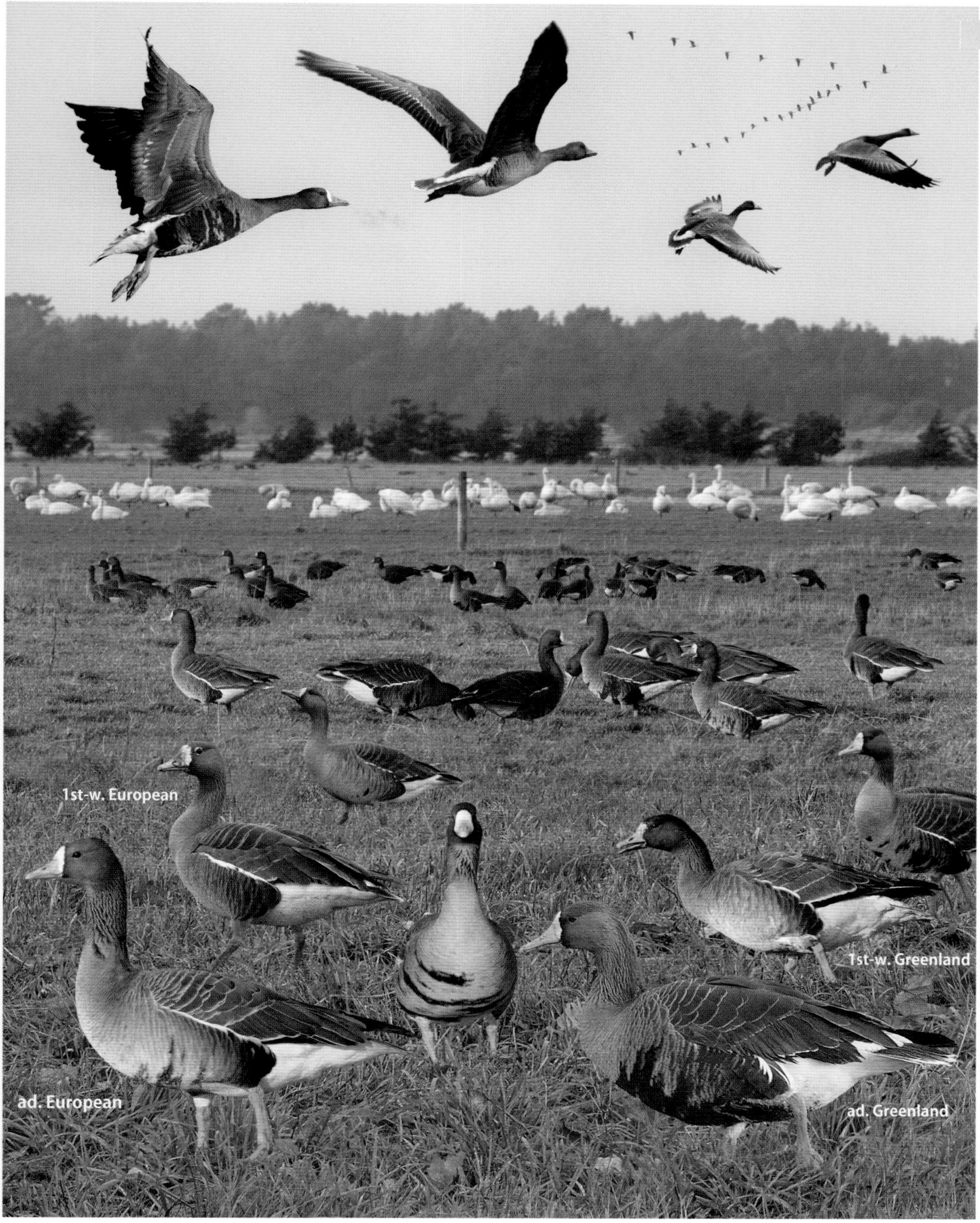

Greater White-fronted Goose *Anser albifrons* **WHFGO/WG** L 72cm

UK: w. 16,000

Uncommon and localised winter visitor to widely scattered locations. Two races winter at favoured locations: 'Russian' White-fronts in eastern and southern England, 'Greenland' White-fronts in Ireland and west Scotland. Russian birds often arrive late in winter, even Dec. Typically occur in small flocks, except at Slimbridge in Gloucestershire. Found in family parties within flock. Call disyllabic, with yelping, laughing quality. **ID:** Adult: given good view, easily identified by dark brown splodges on belly, and by conspicuous white forehead, hence white 'front' (French for forehead). Individuals of other species occasionally have white at bill base, but usually narrow and poorly defined. Otherwise medium-sized, stocky, grey-brown goose with orange legs; bill orange/pink lacking black tip. Juv: bill briefly dull yellow becoming pink, with uniform grey head and underparts. Birds develop black belly and white around base of bill and then forehead at variable rates from Sep through first winter. 'Greenland' birds are slightly larger and longer necked than 'Russian' birds, with longer, more distinctly orange bill, also have slightly bolder breast splodges. 'Russian' birds have pinker bill and slightly paler back.

Pink-footed Goose *Anser brachyrhynchus* **PIFGO/PG** L 68cm

UK: w. 360,000

As with most wild geese, a localised winter visitor. Tends to be found in large, noisy flocks (up to 40,000 birds) in favoured areas such as Norfolk, Scotland. These flocks commute between open-water roosts and farmland feeding areas at dusk and dawn, making wavy lines and V shapes against the sky, one of the sights and sounds of the British winter. Tends to fly quite high. Arrives from Iceland in Oct, leaves by Mar. Has distinctive *ang-ang-WINK-WINK* call (say it quickly) that condenses to a roar from huge flocks. Within flocks, family parties can be made out. **ID:** Rather a small, compact goose with dark-headed appearance, the dark making sharp contrast with pale breast. Has short neck and rounded head. Legs pink, but judging colour can be difficult. Bill distinctly small, dark, and triangular with some pink towards tip. Frosty-grey back and pale rump make good distinctions from BEAGO; flank darker than upperwing, reverse in BEAGO. In flight, dark underwing and extensive pale grey on upperwing; broad white tail tip. Juv: sim to ad, but flanks less obviously barred and neck less grooved.

Greylag Goose *Anser anser* **GREGO/GJ** L 82cm

UK: s. 46,000 pairs (3,200 'wild') w. 230,000 (85,000 'wild')

Common and widespread big, meaty goose–the ancestor of all domestic geese. Occurs widely, but populations have different origins. In most of England the resident Greylags are the descendants of farmyard geese, which is why you often find white individuals and others with odd markings. These now occur on large lakes, gravel pits, farmland, and marshes, often in numbers. Breeding birds of northern Scotland (including Outer Hebrides) are truly wild and nest on moorland, marshes and lakes. Wild birds from Iceland winter in Scotland, visiting Oct–Mar like other geese, feeding on agricultural land and roosting on lakes. Has familiar cackling, nasal, rather grating call lacking musical quality of other geese. **ID:** Huge triangular bill distinctive, as is two-toned underside of the wings. A big, pale, heavy-looking goose with thick neck. Ad: Head and neck not much darker than breast, so little contrast; eye easily visible. 'Grooves' along neck often obvious. In flight, upperwing, especially forewing, distinctively smoky-grey, with short brown mid-panels; rump pale grey. In flight neck 'pinched in' behind large head. Bill usually pink, legs also pink. Juv: lacks 'wet comb' grooves in neck; flanks lack bars, so look scaly.

Bean Goose *Anser fabalis* **BEAGO/BE** L 75cm ***730 winter***

Rare and localised winter visitor to sw Scotland (Carron Valley) and East Anglia (Yare Valley), feeding on pastureland and roosting on large lakes or floods. Small flocks occur fitfully elsewhere. Occurs in two confusing forms, 'Tundra' and 'Taiga', which are different in shape and size; perhaps two species. Most in the traditional sites are Taiga Bean Geese. Typically occur in smaller flocks than other geese. Calls are deep, with bassoon-like quality. **ID:** Wedge-shaped head and bill with flat crown. Dark goose with orange legs, and black-tipped bill with some orange colour. Back and rump darker than GREGO and PIFGO; white bars made by covert edges may be more obvious than in other grey geese. Dark head and neck contrast with paler breast, as PIFGO – BEAGO are most easily picked out in mixed flocks by their orange legs. Taiga form: Big, equal in size to GREGO, with long thin neck giving swanlike impression in flight. Long, narrow-based bill is mainly orange, with black tip and base. Tundra form: Smaller ('tundra under'), with shorter neck and bill. Shape similar to PIFGO, but bill longer, mainly black with orange subterminal band.

Exotic Waterfowl—commonly kept in wildfowl collections. Escapes can be found anywhere! Some tame, others less so! Look for bands on legs, clipped wings, or a missing hindclaw. In our region, the 5 species below also turn up as vagrants, typically in 'wild' flocks of wintering geese.

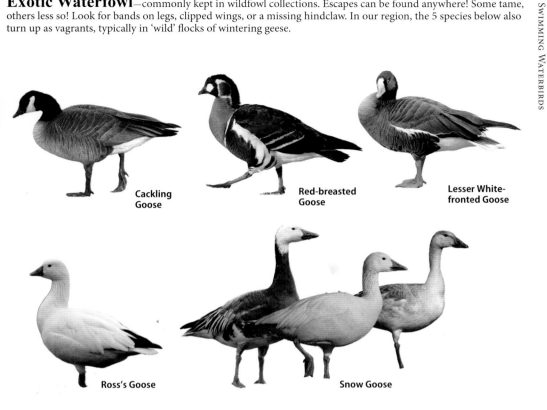

Cackling Goose

Red-breasted Goose

Lesser White-fronted Goose

Ross's Goose

Snow Goose

Exotic Waterfowl—the following geese are frequent escapes and vagrancy is unlikely or impossible.

Bar-headed Goose

Emperor Goose

Swan Goose

Canada Goose *Branta canadensis* **CANGO/CG** L 95cm

UK: s. 62,000 pairs
w. 190,000

Common, widespread, overbearing goose introduced from North America as long ago as 1665; acts as if it owns the place. Found abundantly in parks, ponds, farmland, and wetlands, even estuaries. Sociable and very noisy, makes its discordant, slurred, 2-syllable *ah-HONK!* at any opportunity: in flight, in disputes, in greeting. At times, calls sound moaning and resigned, at others, broken-voiced. Constantly bickers, with head-down shouting matches or splashing on water. Yellow-green goslings often gathered into crèches. Grazes on grass, also swims on the water, even up-ends. Groups frequently simply loaf on grass doing nothing at all. Has no fear of people. **ID:** Large goose with long neck, flies in imperious, almost swanlike manner, usually no more than just above rooftop height. Easily recognised by black neck and white face patch–a 'cut-itself-shaving bandage'. Crown and bill black, scaly brown pattern to plumage. Groups often contain individuals (usually juv) with poorly defined white patches, or with white faces. Juv has smaller and more rounded feathers on flanks and wing coverts. Neck often with brown mixed in. A very few vagrant individuals of smaller races/species such as Cackling Goose *(Branta hutchinsii)* occur each year in flocks of other goose species.

Barnacle Goose *Branta leucopsis* BARGO/BY L 64cm

UK: s. 1,000 birds (feral)
w. 94,000

Chiefly a localised winter visitor (Oct–Mar) to western Scotland and Ireland, where flocks feed on agricultural fields and roost on salt marshes. Birds wintering in the western isles (e.g., Islay) and Ireland are from the Greenland breeding population, while those in the Solway come from Svalbard. Less commonly, Russian birds appear as irregular visitors to eastern and southern England. In recent years, though, the goose has gained ground in the English hinterland as feral birds have established self-sustaining populations, occurring in lakes and in parks in similar way to CANGO. Very sociable, forming large flocks that make a sound like yapping dogs. Flocks form uneven lines, like those of BREGO, and typically fly higher than both BREGO and CANGO. **ID:** Much smaller and shorter necked than CANGO, with larger amount of white (often creamy) on face, including above eye. Some CANGO show similar face pattern (regular in juvs). Small black bill. Adult: black on neck reaches down to lower breast, and black bands on wings show against grey background. Juv very similar to ad but flank markings more evenly spread and upperpart markings less boldly contrasting.

Brent *Branta bernicla* **BREGO/BG** L 58cm

UK: w. 120,000

One of the most familiar of the wintering geese, mainly because it is found in estuaries in eastern and southern England, where birders concentrate; also widespread in Ireland. Unusual for its marine habitat, almost always seen in large flocks either swimming and up-ending in the water in search of eelgrass, or grazing in grassy areas and mudflats. Only occasionally seen inland. Birds arrive in Oct and may linger into Apr or even May, until tundra freezes. Birds in tight conversational flocks utter a pleasant, throaty, rolling gargle, which comes to a crescendo at take-off. Flocks in flight form wavy lines within the dense pack, rarely forming a V like other geese. **ID:** Only the size of a MALLA, small and compact with short, thick neck. An oily black goose with blazing white bottom. Adult: upperparts uniform, lacking distinct pale fringes. Juv/1st-w: broad white fringes to coverts, making 3 vertical lines. Initially dark necked, white necklace grows in through autumn. Three distinct races: 'Dark-bellied Brent' *(bernicola)* (south and east) with medium contrast between underparts and black neck. 'Pale-bellied Brent' *(krota)* (Northumberland, Ireland) with pale, almost creamy flanks and strongly contrasting black neck/paler breast. 'Black Brant' *(nigricans)* (from USA) rare; very smart, with large white necklace, very dark upperparts and underparts separated by blazing white flank.

Shelduck *Tadorna tadorna* **SHELD/SU** 62cm

UK: s. 15,000 pairs
w. 66,000

A common, widespread, and conspicuous duck of estuaries and sand dunes, also sparingly found inland on gravel pits and sandy places. Easily told by its large size and bold plumage. In contrast to other ducks, male and female very similar. Often seen on estuarine mud, head down, dabbling at its feet; also up-ends in shallow water. Highly strung, with frequent skirmishes breaking out in groups. Nests on ground in old rabbit hole, sometimes in tree. Attractive black-and-white young often in crèches. Strangely, almost entire population relocates from Jul to Oct (some later) to mudflats on north coast of Germany, leaving few behind, mostly juvs. Smaller moulting groups include Bridgwater Bay, Somerset. Quite noisy, the female making a series of belly laughs with a sarcastic ring, often accompanied by fast, breathy whistles of male. **ID:** Adult: looks black and white, but head and neck dark bottle-green. Has chestnut breast band. Longer necked than other ducks such as MALLA. Long pink legs. ♂: deep pink bill with large knob. ♀: bill lacks knob. Powdery white patch at bill base; narrower, messy breast band. Juv: beware—looks like different species. Washed-out plumage, dirty white belly, and anaemic scaly brownish above. Grey-brown head with obvious white eye-ring, white forehead and chin.

Egyptian Goose *Alopochen aegyptiacus* **EGYGO/EG** L 68cm ***s. 1,100 pairs w. 3,400***

Resident. Weirdly out-of-place African species first introduced in 1700s. Didn't become established in 'wild' until 1960s in East Anglia; has spread since to a few parts of England, increasing. Relative of SHELD, but occurs on or near freshwater lakes and reservoirs, nesting in tree holes or in banks, sometimes under bushes. Has peculiar wheezing call. **ID:** Pink legs look almost too long for heavy body. Adults: 'shades' around eyes, together with dark brown spot on breast, makes ID easy. Dirty neck and pinkish plumage, with darker back. Transformed in flight, with large, clean, white inner-wing patch above and below. Juv: lacks breast patch and marks around eye. Odd shape gives it away.

Mandarin *Aix galericulata* **MANDA/MN** L 45cm ***s. 2,300 pairs w. 7,000***

Exotic-looking duck introduced from ne Asia, the escaped population becoming established after 1900. Thrives in lakes or rivers with overhanging trees or bushes; nests in tree holes. Has habit of perching on branches or logs in water. Feeds in water on surface, also forages at night on land for acorns and the like. Often flies fast along track of water-course, below height of trees. Very agile in flight, fast wingbeats. Male makes excited, breathless whistle; female, a croaking quack. **ID:** ♂ colourful with orange 'sails' towards back. ♀: small, best identified by white eye-ring and whisker; neatly mottled underparts. Eclipse ♂: as ♀ but bill redder, less white on face, bigger crest. Juv: as ♀ but more uniform, less neatly mottled below.

Mallard *Anas platyrhynchos* **MALLA/MA** L 58cm

UK: s. 103,500 pairs
w. 710,000

The familiar and common duck, found in habitats ranging from urban parks, farm fields, waterbodies of whatever size, to the wildest places—sometimes even the sea. The one to learn well, as this species is the basis for learning all dabbling ducks! Often tame and approachable. Ancestral stock of many domestic ducks, and groups in parks often contain birds with odd plumage (all-white, mainly black, and the like) and different proportions ('yuk ducks'). Call: the stereotypical, nagging *quack quack* duck call given by females only, often in laughing sequence. Male's calls include a weak whistle and much quieter quack. Birds display right through autumn and winter with shakes of bill and tail, flaps of wings, apparent stretches, and the like. Hefty and powerful in flight, slight whistle to wings. **ID:** Fairly large, well proportioned, and muscular. Blue speculum (can appear purple) bordered by black and white. Ad ♂: striking green head with white collar; funky upturned black central uppertail coverts. Bill is bright yellow to yellow-olive with black nail. Eclipse ♂ (Jun–Sep): retains yellower bill. 1st-w ♂: identical to ad ♂. ♀: dullish grey-brown, paler on head and neck with dark crown and eye-stripe. White outer tail feathers. Variably yellow-orange bill with mottled dark centre. Juv: briefly held plumage similar to ad ♀ but warmer brown with darker centres to feathers.

Gadwall *Anas strepera* **GADWA/GA** L 51cm

UK: s. 690–1,730 pairs
w. 25,000

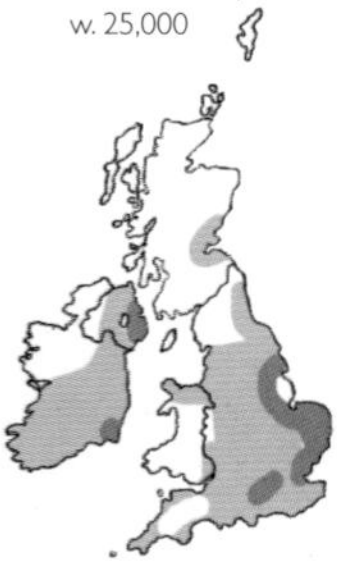

Fairly common duck of shallow wetlands, seen mostly in pairs but sometimes larger groups. Small breeding population on well-vegetated freshwater sites, but much more abundant in winter, often on lakes and reservoirs. Superficially nondescript, thus easy to overlook, particularly when mixed in with other more striking dabblers. Female gives a dull flatulent quack, similar to MALLA but harder toned. Male's calls a gentle burp and feeble whistle. **ID:** Slightly smaller than MALLA. Distinctive nipped-in neck and steep forehead often give a square-headed look. Head is larger in ♂ than ♀. Sits high in the water. Striking in flight: upperwing with white inner secondaries bordered by black, boldest in ♂, which also has chestnut coverts. White patch is often visible on sitting birds. Underparts also striking with distinct white underwing and central belly bordered by dark. Ad ♂: intricately patterned with striking black butt. Eclipse ♂ (Jun–Nov): sim to ♀ but retains bold wing pattern. Ad ♀: often confused with MALLA and other ♀ ducks; look at shape and cleanly demarcated orange-sided bill, pale head/neck contrasting with darker body. Strong eye-stripe. Bill often darker in summer. Juv: more neatly patterned and buffier than ad ♀. ♂ grows bold adult-type feathers through 1st winter.

Northern Pintail/PT *Anas acuta* **PINTA/PT** L 58cm

UK: s. 9–33 pairs
w. 29,000

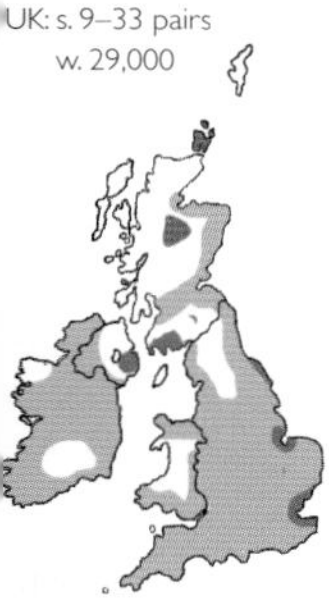

Fairly common in freshwater and coastal marshes and flooded river valleys; winter concentrations occur locally. Sometimes forms very large tight flocks. Small groups often fly in loose lines or Vs. Long neck adapted for reaching further down than other ducks, so frequently up-ends. Rather quiet. **ID:** Usually best to ID by structure alone: slim, long necked, long tailed, with erect posture, creating very distinctive elegant appearance—a really beautiful duck! This slim appearance is just as obvious in flight. Relatively plain upper wing. Ad ♂: striking with brown head and white neck stripe—overall impression is of a bird with a very 'thoughtful' and somewhat dapper look. Long tail with black butt distinctive at long range. ♀: plain and pale brown, particularly on face and neck; simple but elegant. Bill blue-grey, darkest in centre. Eclipse ♂ (Jul–Nov): appears as ♀. Retains bolder covert pattern, grey-and-black striped bill and has longer grey scapulars until it starts moulting new adult-type feathers in autumn. Juv: like ad ♀ with flanks more diffusely spotted and barred. In flight, ♂ is white bellied with grey flanks, ♀ browner with coarse flank markings. Speculum green (browner with narrower trailing edge in imm ♂) bordered by chestnut at front.

Northern Shoveler *Anas clypeata* SHOVE/SV L 48cm

UK: s. 310–1,020 pairs
w. 18,000

Fairly common in a variety of shallow wetlands, almost always fresh water. Breeds in marshland or wet grassland. Usually in small loose groups but can be in larger numbers in suitable habitat. Sometimes feeds in tight packs that move in circles, birds filtering food from the mud kicked up by neighbours. Bill often swished from side to side as it sieves out food; bill may appear 'glued' to water surface. Takes off with characteristic drumming wingbeats. **ID:** A rather small but heavily built duck that sits low in the water, and has a stonking spatulate bill. The bill, combined with short neck and broad head, adds to its distinctive front-heavy look and should be enough to ID most birds. ♂: unmistakable. Bright white accentuates green head and chestnut flanks. Depending on light, head can look purple or black. ♀: often looks pale due to broad fringes to feathers. Bill variably orange with bright edges. Eclipse (Jul–Nov) and imm ♂ (Jul–Mar): variable with multiple spots and arrows on breast/flanks with a range of chestnut, white, and green until after Dec. Ad ♂: retains pale iris year-round, darker in imm ♂; partial pale face crescent. In flight, ♂ has a striking blue, green, and white inner wing; duller and greyer in ♀, but still relatively bold.

Eurasian Wigeon *Anas penelope* **WIGEO/WN** L 48cm

UK: s. 300–500 pairs
w. 450,000

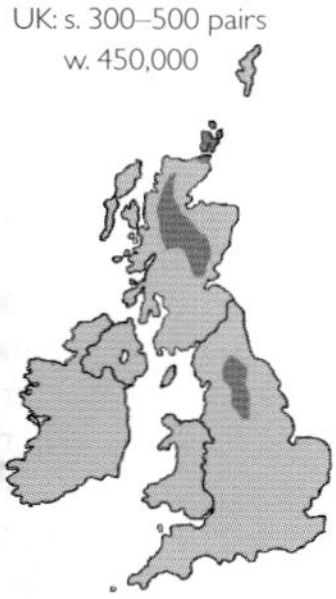

Numerous wintering duck found on estuaries, reservoirs, ponds, flooded meadows, and even the sea. Breeds uncommonly near shallow freshwater pools with nearby bushes or trees. In winter extremely sociable and often in large flocks. Male makes a very distinctive, exclamatory, excited whistle *wheeoo!* that goes up, then down in pitch; female makes a gruff growl. Often seen grazing out of water on grass, birds closely packed together; also feeds in shallow water by dipping head in. Often flies high in tight and frequently large flocks. Shy. **ID:** Medium-sized duck with large, rather rounded head. Bill blue-grey with black tip, rather short and strong. In flight has narrow wings and quite long, sharp tail. ♂ easily identified by straw-coloured forehead; rest of head tan–reddish brown. Breast pink, and closely barred grey body split by white midline. Tail black, contrasting with white flanks. Very prominent white forewing, which often identifies flocks flying past. ♀: darker than similar species, mottled red-brown. Flanks unmarked rufous, head often greyish, subtle dark shading around eyes, belly contrastingly white. Some greyer, others redder than average. Eclipse ♂: sim to ♀ but often stronger red colouration, white wings still visible. Juv: sim to ♀, often less white on belly. 1st-yr ♂s acquire grey-brown forewings.

American Wigeon *Anas americana* **AMEWI/AW** L 50cm ***w. 8***

Very rare, almost invariably found within larger flocks of WIGEO. **ID:** Similar to WIGEO, and ♀ can be tricky to distinguish. Has slightly larger head with more peaked forecrown, shares small bill, chunky body, long tail, and short legs. Ad ♂: has distinctive head pattern compared to WIGEO, with creamy yellow forehead and crown and eye enclosed in iridescent green streak that flows down to nape. Body is brownish pink, not grey. Shares WIGEO's white forewing patch. Ad ♀: white axillaries ('armpits') reliably distinguish from ♀ WIGEO. Most easily found by grey finely flecked head (contrasts with brownish red breast).

Garganey *Anas querquedula* **GARGA/GY** L 39cm

UK: s. 14-93 pairs

Scarce summer visitor (Mar–Oct) to freshwater marshes and meadows with much fringing vegetation in England. Easiest to find in the autumn, when migrants pass through the country with flocks of Teal. Always shy and retiring. Male makes extraordinary call like shaking a box of matches. **ID:** Slightly larger than TEAL, but always looks longer bodied and with high stern. Bill much longer, heavier, and grey in colour. Ad ♂: basically cereal brown but with grey side panel and brilliant white half-moon supercilium over eye. Eclipse (Jul–Nov), ♀, juv, and 1st-w: similar to ♀ TEAL but with stripy face and no white streak under tail; breast, belly, and flanks with single scales (double in TEAL) giving bolder two-toned appearance. Look for dark eye-stripe and crown, pale supercilium and white spot at base of bill, together with whitish throat. In flight, wings pale, speculum lacks TEAL's brilliant green.

Common Teal *Anas crecca* **TEAL/T.** L 36cm

UK: s. 1600–2800 pairs
w. 220,000

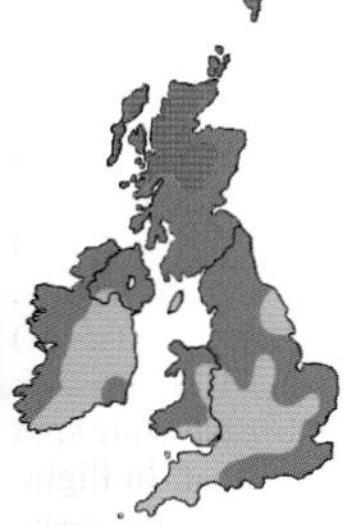

Common in winter on wetlands, meadows, and tidal mudflats. Scarce breeding bird of marshes and upland moors and bogs. Forms compact groups, easily flushed with fast, vertical take-off. Fly close together in sync, twisting with very fast wingbeats, like waders. Male often heard giving persistent bell-like or sonar-like blip. Female makes flat, hoarse *quack*. **ID:** Compact, sits high in the water. Large square head on a short neck with small bill—the rubber duck of ponds. In flight, plain-winged except for green-and-black speculum bordered by white and rufous. Ad ♂: rich chestnut head, with green mask edged with thin buff border. White horizontal flank line and black-bordered yellow butt stand out. Eclipse (Jul–Nov) and 1st-w ♂ (through winter): very similar, moult bright plumage at different times. ♀: distinct dark eyeline, often with cheek stripe on uniform brown speckled face. Buff line on tail side surprisingly obvious, even at long range. North American subsp. 'Green-winged' Teal rare. ♂ differs by lacking white horizontal breast line (but conspicuous vertical white streak down front of belly); also less distinct buff lines surrounding green head-streak.

Pochard *Aythya ferina* **POCHA/PO** L 46cm

UK: s. 350-630 pairs
w. 48,000

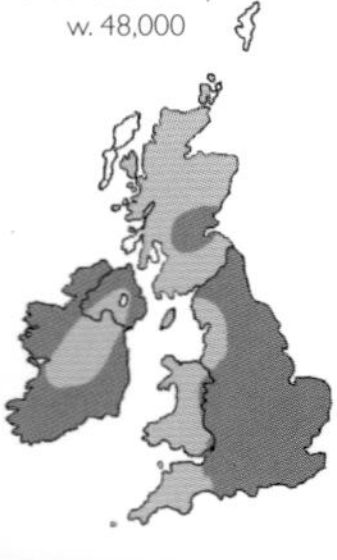

Sleepy diving duck common in winter on freshwater lakes, reservoirs, and gravel pits. Scarce breeding bird beside quiet lakes with plenty of emergent vegetation. Usually in waters at least 2m deep, where it is fanatically sociable, invariably in groups, often of hundreds. A quirk of behaviour is that, since it routinely feeds at night, it is often seen asleep. Mixes freely with TUFDU. Male makes very quiet sound like wheezing bellows, female loud purr. **ID:** Head shape distinctive, with smooth 'ski-jump' slope from peak on top of head down to concave culmen. Short-bodied, with long neck and bill. In flight shows featureless grey wings, lacking obvious bars. Ad ♂: tricoloured, with red wine-coloured head, black breast and rear, and grey middle. Ad ♀: undistinguished soft brown-grey duck, darker back and front. But note conspicuous pale eye-ring, streak behind eye, and powdery spot at base of bill. Body plumage grey, flecked darker. Eclipse: like faded br plumage, black replaced by dark grey. Juv: as ♀ but browner. 1st-w ♂ sim to ad with retained brown juv primaries.

Red-crested Pochard *Netta rufina* **RECPO/RQ** L 55cm ***s. 10–21 pairs, w. 320***

Rare exotic-looking duck of deep freshwater lakes with emergent vegetation. Truly wild birds are rare, but species popular in captivity and small feral populations have become established in the south. A diving duck that behaves more like a dabbler, sits high on water in regal style, mainly dabbles and up-ends. Flies strongly. **ID:** Big and long bodied, with long neck, high rounded crown, long bill. Ad ♂: tangerine-orange head, crown seems to glow; cheap-looking coral-red bill. Ad ♀: contrasting head, with conspicuous pale cheeks set against dark crown and nape (like ad ♀ COMSC); bill dark grey with pink tip. Eclipse ♂: as ad ♀, but red bill and eye. Some individuals paler plumaged.

Ferruginous Duck *Aythya nyroca* **FERDU/FD** L 40cm ***w. 10***

Rare visitor from southern Europe to well-vegetated freshwater lakes in the south. Shy and sneaky, often among vegetation or just out of water, and generally difficult to see. May be sluggish but dives a lot when feeding. Usually seen singly, but mixes with other species of diving ducks. Beware hybrids which can strongly resemble FERDU. **ID:** Small, short-bodied, rather uniformly rust-coloured diving duck with brilliant white, neatly defined undertail. Head shape with peak in middle of crown, strong downslope on forehead and nape; bill long and grey, with white band near tip. In flight shows big flash of long white wing bar, white belly. Ad ♂: strong chestnut colouration, white eye. Ad ♀: similar but less rusty, dark eye, flanks more scaly. Eclipse ♂ like ♀, white-eyed.

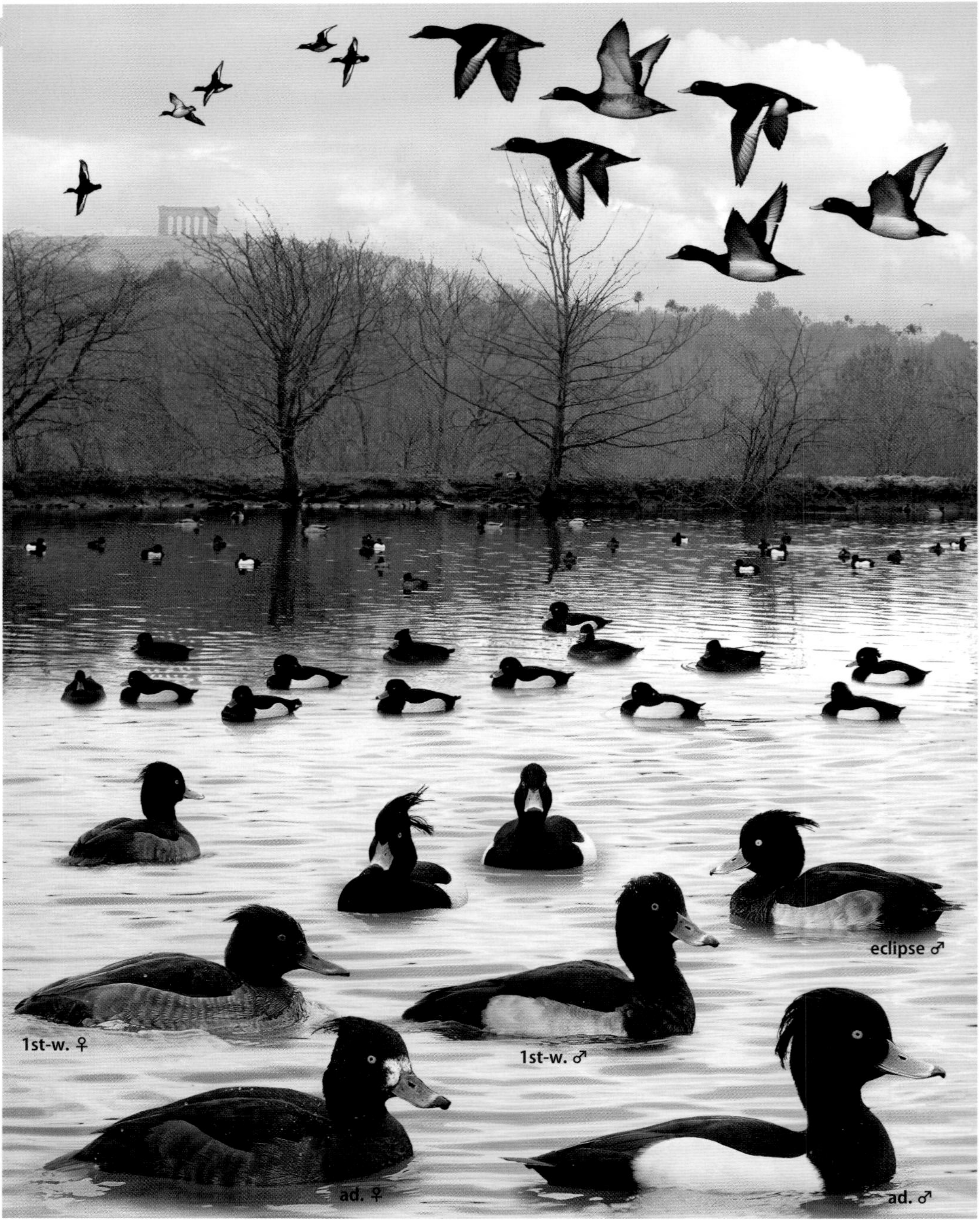

Tufted Duck *Aythya fuligula* **TUFDU/TU** L 44cm

UK: s. 16,000–19,000
w. 120,000

Common, lively duck, breeding by freshwater lakes, reservoirs, and slow-flowing rivers. Abundant on many freshwater wetlands in winter, including urban parks, where it sometimes competes with MALLA and gulls for bread. Dives for food (freshwater mussels, insect larvae, vegetation), submerges with forward leap. Forms large flocks; often sleeps in daytime. Subtle courtship in winter, when males utter quiet giggle, and both sexes stretch neck, as if peering over wall. **ID:** Small diving duck with some kind of crown adornment: large tuft in ♂, sometimes just a bump in imm. Head shape with high forehead, flat crown, and steep nape. Fast wingbeats in flight, obvious white wing bar. Ad ♂: neat purplish black, with sharply defined white side panels, large crest. Ad eclipse ♂ (Jun–Oct): smaller tatty crest, white side panels grubbily brownish. Ad ♀: brown version of ♂, with dark brown replacing black, and side panels pale brown with dark scales. Short crest. Juv: washed-out version of ♀, often with white at base of bill, brown eye. 1st-w ♂: like ♂ but side panels not perfect white, brown tinge to plumage.

Greater Scaup *Aythya marila* SCAUP/SP L 46cm

UK: w. 12,000

Uncommon marine duck, wintering in coastal bays and estuaries, and on the sea, so usually ecologically separate from similar TUFDU. Often over mussel beds or near sewage outfalls. Much rarer on large freshwater lakes, small numbers only. May form large, dense flocks out at sea. **ID:** Bulky diving duck with broad head and evenly domed rear crown, thick neck, and bulging cheeks. Lacks any kind of crest or tuft. Broad bill flared at tip with black restricted to nail (TUFDU has more of bill tip black). Broader-beamed than TUFDU; comparing size is a good ID starter. Ad ♂ br: frost-grey back instantly distinguishes from TUFDU; iridescent green head often appears black. ♀: large, well-defined white patch around base of bill. Body greyer and scalier than TUFDU, not solid brown on back. Worn birds (late winter/summer) often show a white cheek patch. Eclipse ♂ (Jul–Oct)/1st-w (Jul–Mar): female-like with solidly dark head; acquires grey back through winter. Juv: as ad ♀ but initially darker brown iris and more uniform brown. Less white on face. 1st-w ♂ grows adult-like paler flank and upperpart feathers through the winter.

Common Scoter *Melanitta nigra* **COMSC/CX** 49cm

Common and widespread sea duck, often seen in tightly packed flocks offshore, inky spots on the water. Flies frequently in irregular lines, the flocks often densest at the front, like the head of a tadpole. On water actively dives for molluscs, flocks often in sync. Typically dives with small leap, wings closed; has unique habit of wing-flapping while holding head down. Males repeat a fluty whistle with 'lost' tone. Some migrate inland and are sometimes seen on larger bodies of inland water. Rare breeding bird on moorland lochs, often nesting on small islands. **ID:** Smallest and chunkiest of the sooty-black–plumaged scoters with diagnostic bulky round head allied with distinctive bill shape and colour. Pointed tail is often obvious. In flight shows conspicuous pale primaries. Ad ♂: glossy black with yellow-orange knob on bill. 2nd-w ♂: may show browner throat and slightly reduced knob but most are as adult. ♀/1st-yr: conspicuous pale throat and face contrast sharply with dark cap and nape. This area becomes darker through winter in 1st-yr ♂, and bird develops yellow-orange knob on bill. 1st-yr has a pale belly that is easy to see in flight.

Surf Scoter *Melanitta perspicillata* SURSC/FS L 50cm *w. 13*

Rare sea duck from North America. **ID:** Slightly larger than COMSC but noticeably smaller than VELSC. Overall in flight compared to VELSC, weight is at the back of the undercarriage. Neck is long and slim, head pointed, wings longer, slimmer, angled back, and pointed. Lands with wings held pointing skyward (45° in VELSC). Ad ♂: incredible bill pattern suggests colours of a clown's costume. Striking white nape and forehead on black can be seen at long distance. Ad ♀: dark brown with a capped appearance. Usually 2 pale patches on face. Some ♀s have pale napes. 1st-yr: usually averages slightly paler; most easily aged by pale belly—easy to see in flight.

Velvet Scoter *Melanitta fusca* VELSC/VS 54cm *w. 2,500*

Uncommon winter sea duck mostly to eastern and northern coasts. Usually found in similar places to COMSC, but also in choppier waters close to rocks. Typically in small numbers. Groups tend to spread out. In contrast to COMSC, dives without forward leap, sinking with wings open; also keeps neck straight when wing-flapping. Often hauls out on rocks. **ID:** Bulkier than COMSC, with long body, thick muscle-bound neck ('on steroids'), and wedge-shaped bill. Usually can see some white on wings, even on swimming birds. In flight, vivid square white patch on inner wing. Legs red. Ad ♂: smart velvet-black plumage, with small white teardrop around white eye, plus large yellow patch on base of bill (not top as in COMSC). Ad ♀: dark brown, usually with pale powder patches between bill and eye, and on cheeks. Juv/1st-w: as ♀ but face patches often more obvious, pale belly. ♂ soon acquires dark head, yellowish bill through winter.

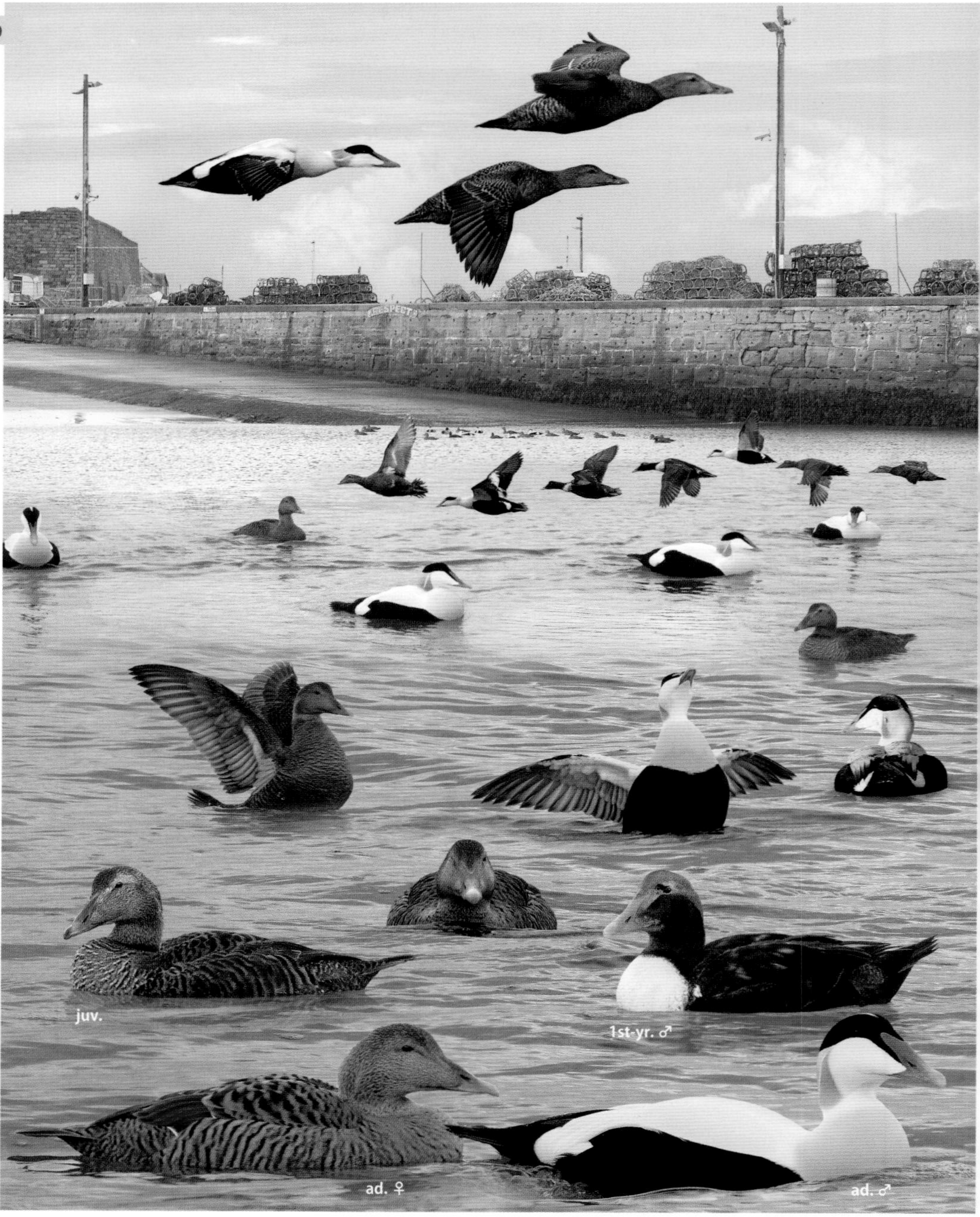

Common Eider *Somateria mollissima* **EIDER/E.** L 60cm

UK: s. 27,000 pairs
w. 63,000

Common marine duck of rocky coasts, estuaries, and low islands. Common offshore rather than far out to sea, and often hauls out on sandbars and rocks. Feeds actively at turning of tide, on mussels and other shellfish, which it crushes in its outsize, powerful bill. Dives with forward flip, wings open. Flies powerfully but needs running take-off. Extremely sociable, and often breeds in colonies; in past times (and still in Iceland) farmed for famously thick, insulating eider down. Young amalgamate into crèches. Male makes gorgeous, breathy, highly suggestive *ah-oo-oh!* (Frankie Howerd-like) while throwing head back, female growls. **ID:** Large and heavy, with unique profile created by long sloping bill and forehead ('Roman nose'). 'Lobes' from bill reach up towards eye. Ad ♂: bold plumage reverses usual waterbird pattern: white above, black below. Creamy breast, 'food-colouring green' patches on head. Ad ♀: plain brown at distance; looks featureless in flight with dark speculum. Plumage brown, barred darker. Juv: as ♀ but darker with denser barring, pale supercilium. 1st-yr ♂: increasingly 'pied' through winter with prominent white breast. Eclipse ♂ (Jul–Oct): dark head, belly, flanks, obvious white tertials and coverts, blotchy back. 2nd-yr ♂ usually retains a few imm feathers.

Long-tailed Duck *Clangula hyemalis* LOTDU/LN L 44cm

UK: w. 11,000

Charismatic Arctic sea duck, found off the coast in winter, commoner as one goes north. Capable of living far out to sea. Very rare inland. Usually in small scattered flocks. Groups often chase each other around in agile pursuit-flight, twisting from side to side. Makes a belly flop and big splash in water when landing. Very vocal, with beautiful yodelling call. Size, shape, behaviour, and colour all contribute to its very dainty but elegant appearance. **ID:** Complex moult with several colour patterns. Smallish with thick neck but small head and bill. General impression usually of a flock of very tastefully pale-coloured dainty ducks, with a lot of variation, some with long tails. Ad ♂: has long tail and subtle browns, greys, and whites that any decorator would be proud of. Much darker in breeding plumage. Ad ♀: similar to 1st-yr with warmer brown upperparts and breast: greyer in imm. 1st-yr ♂: variable with grey scapulars growing through winter and pink developing on the bill. In flight, forms tight groups; look for all-dark wings with fast wingbeats on pale birds. Often rocks from side to side, auk-like.

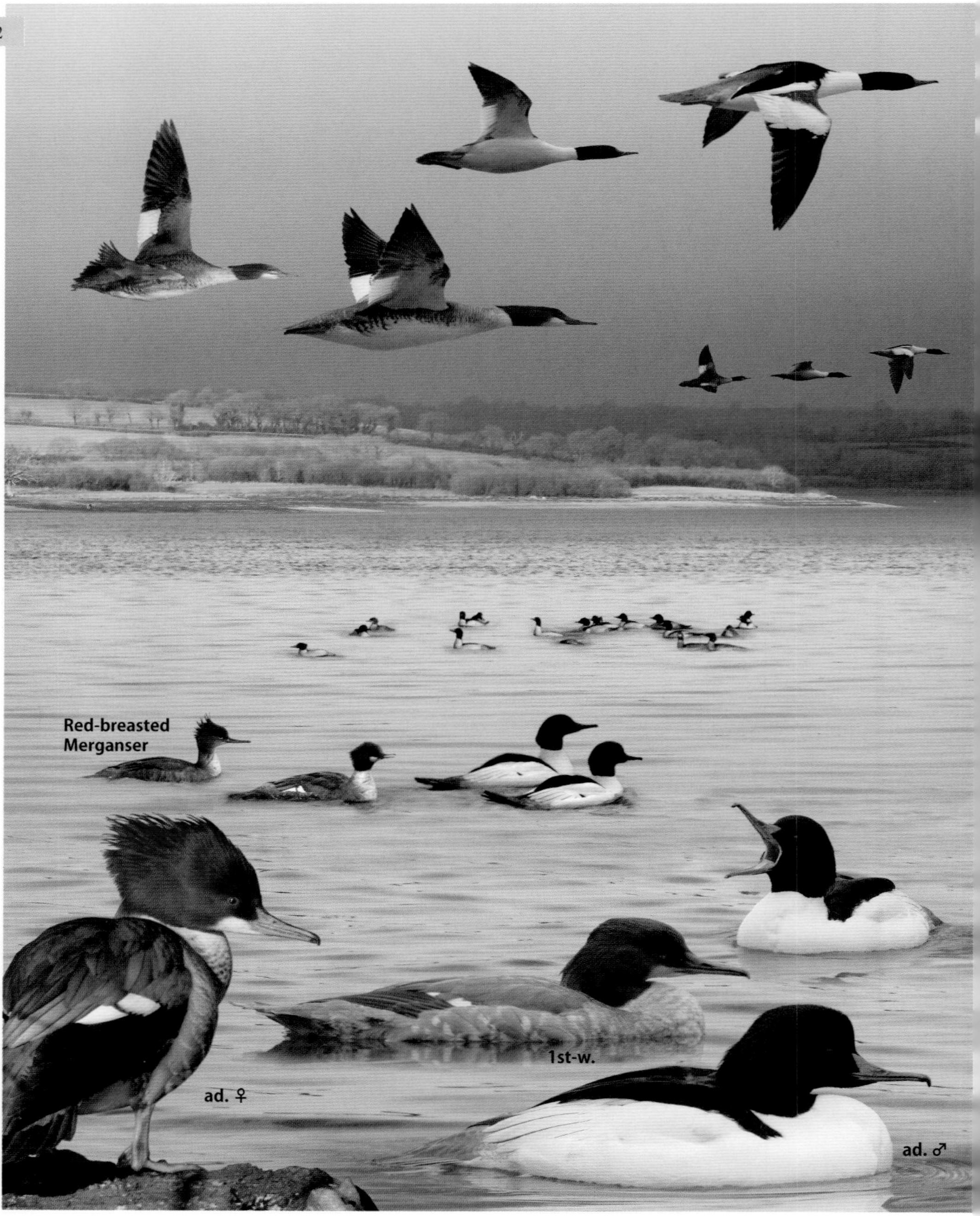

Goosander *Mergus merganser* GOOSA/GD L 62cm

UK: s. 3,500 pairs
w. 12,000

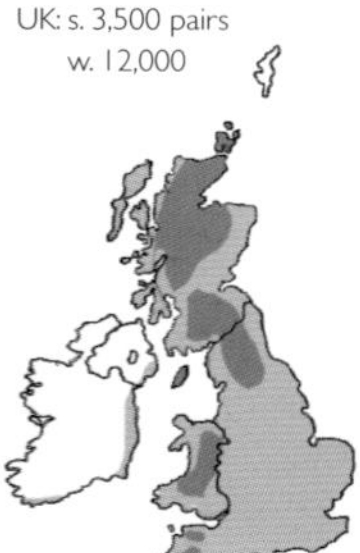

Impressive and very shy duck of rivers and large lakes, chasing fish underwater for a living. Breeds in upland areas near woods or forests, but winter habitat stretches to larger lakes and quiet rivers in the lowlands. Nests in tree holes. Rarely near salt water. Like other sawbills, has serrated bill for holding fish. **ID:** Largest merganser. Slim but muscular with large head and thick neck giving front-heavy look. Long red bill broadening onto large head. Typically sits low in the water, head held down and with long tail giving a stretched-out look. Crest usually 'flattened down'. Ad ♂ br: appears mostly white, yet has subtly 'clotted-cream'-coloured underparts. Dark back and green head that usually appears black at distance. Eclipse ♂: as ♀ but keeps white coverts. ♀ and 1st-yr: rich chestnut head with sharp border and well-defined white chin. Breast pale. 1st-w: usually paler loral area. REBME lacks clean-cut appearance and has darker neck, is smaller, has differently shaped head with spiked hairdo. 1st-yr ♂: does not develop greyer scapulars until spring. In flight has torpedo-like appearance with long neck and body; often flies in lines.

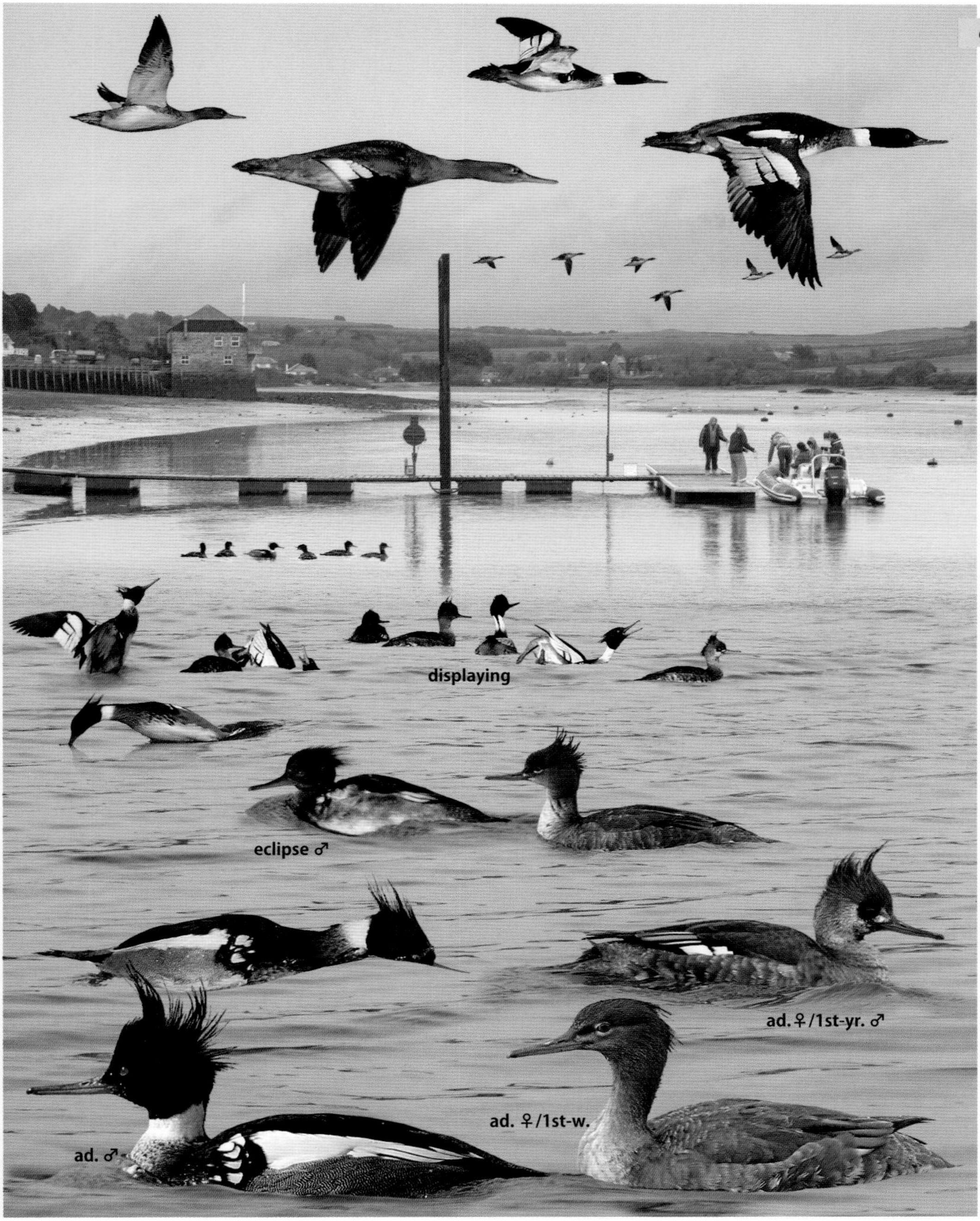

Red-breasted Merganser *Mergus serrator* REBME/RM L 55cm

UK: s. 2,400 pairs
w. 9,000

Fairly common breeding bird in the north and west; scarce in England. Found on the upper reaches of rivers, lakes, estuaries, and along coasts, breeding on the ground among boulders and roots. In winter widespread and common along most coasts. Usually in small groups. Often migrates later than other ducks in spring. Terrific display, in which males raise their bottoms and then ritually stretch their necks up towards the sky, can be seen through winter. Common on sea watches, when long, straight neck and long body noticeable (but beware grebes, which have weaker, more flickering flight). **ID:** Noticeably smaller and slighter than GOOSA. Punky crest, thin bill, steep forehead, smaller head, thin neck, and overall shape give distinctive profile. Complex body patterns never match 'cleanness' of GOOSA. Ad ♂: green, spiked head bordered by a white collar. A mosaic of black, grey, and white lacking the clean creamy white appearance of ♂ GOOSA. Eclipse ♂ (Jun–Oct): similar to ♀ with retained white coverts. ♀/1st-w: lacking clean-cut appearance of same-age GOOSA. Pale bordered black lores. 1st-w ♂ and older ad ♀ develop dark around eye and bright red iris. ♂ moults into adult-like plumage through summer.

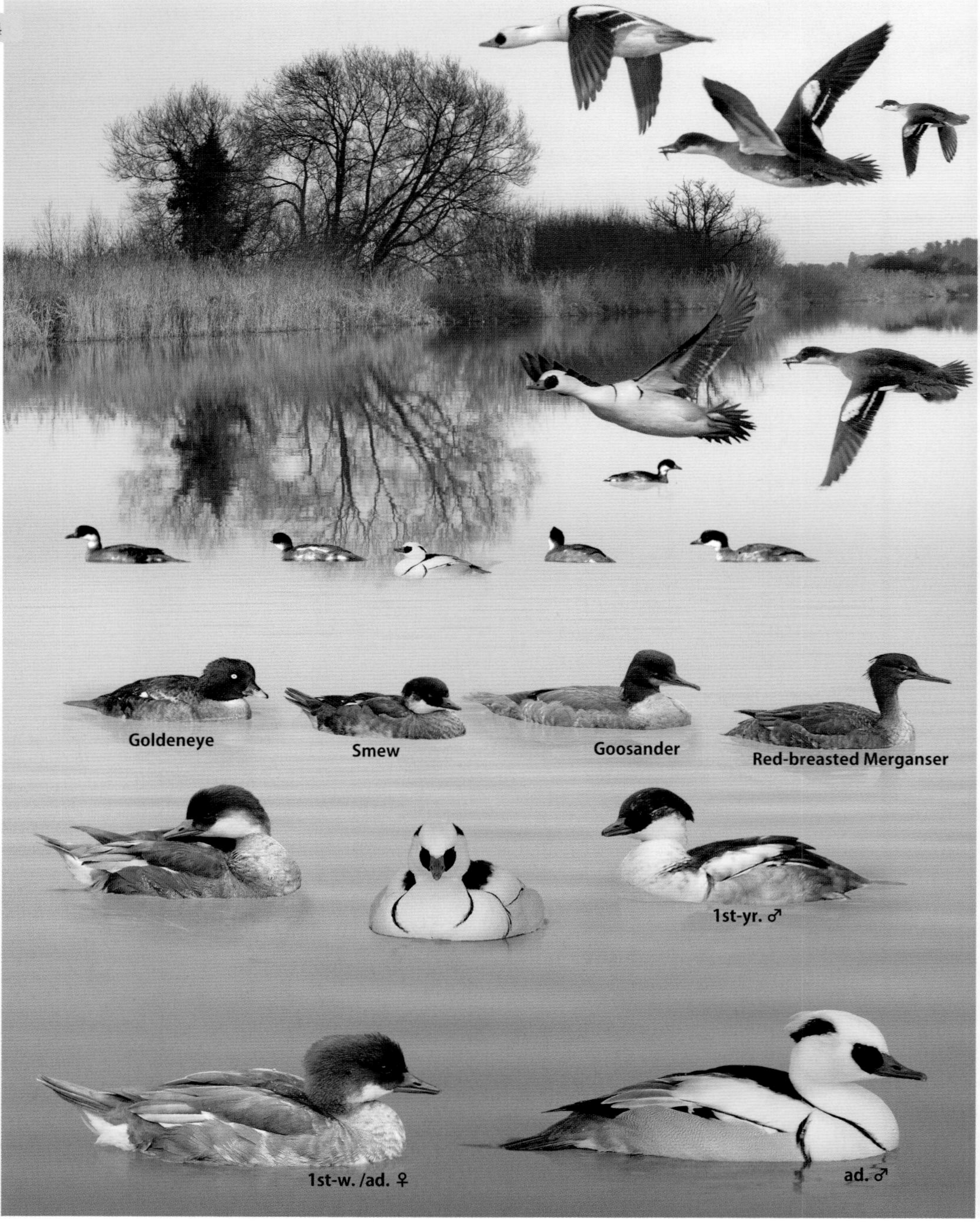

Smew *Mergellus albellus* **SMEW/SY** L 41cm

UK: w. 180

Regular winter visitor to deeper freshwater lakes and gravel pits in southern England Oct–Mar, uncommon to rare elsewhere. Indivs often don't arrive until Dec. Usually in small groups. May also be found on the sea. A very small, perky, shy diving duck, often difficult to pick out on lakes full of wildfowl. Often seen in company of GOLDE and has similar habit of diving with annoying frequency. In Britain, females and 1st-winters vastly outnumber distinctive 'white nun' males. Almost silent. In flight has fast wingbeats, note extended straight neck. Midwing white wing bars may recall TEAL, but has white ovals at base of wing. Rapid take-off with little or no running take-off. **ID:** Small and compact with fairly long bill and thin neck. Dives with forward jump. Ad ♂: white with black mask and various stripes. Doesn't stand out as much as you'd expect; white disappears on water. Ad ♀: white cheeks contrast with reddish head. Dark grey body, white line along middle. 1st-w ♂: by Jan, cap and scapulars may be dappled with white, lores blacker.

Common Goldeneye *Bucephala clangula* GOLDE/GN L 46cm

JK: s. 200
w. 27,000

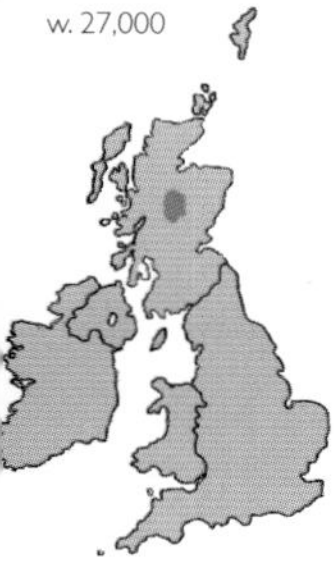

Scarce breeding bird in Scotland, along tree-lined rivers and lochs; a few in summer in England. Uses nest boxes and holes in trees. Widespread in winter, with some on deeper freshwater lakes, others on the coast. Male's wings in flight produce loud whirring whistle noise. Very wary and easily flushed. Puts head down before jumping up to dive. Animated displays in late winter: throws head back and also points bill skyward. **ID:** Medium-sized diving duck with an oversized head that juts out from the back of the neck. Large black triangular bill with variable amounts of yellow adds to distinctive head shape. Always alert and ready to dive, but still keeps a beady eye on you. Ad ♂: at a distance appears white bodied with dark back and upperparts. Oval cheek patch on green head diagnostic. White breast and head shape distinguish from TUFDU. Ad ♀: brown head contrasts with grey body. White midline along body (folded wing). Juv/1st-yr: as ad ♀ with darker iris. Eclipse and 1st-w ♂: similar but has extensive white in wing and develops a partial white face mark. Adult-like in summer.

Ruddy Duck *Oxyura jamaicensis* **RUDDU/RY** L 39cm ***w. 60***

Until recently a fairly common but localised resident, introduced from North America in 1950s. Currently subject to an eradication campaign to prevent interbreeding with threatened White-headed Duck *(O. leucocephala)* on Continent, so population low and widely scattered. Occurs on freshwater lakes with much fringing vegetation, in winter also on reservoirs. Often asleep in day; feeds at night. **ID:** Very small chunky and punky diving duck, usually easily identified by stiff, rod-like tail that points up at angle. Also very large bill sunk well into skull to make 'ski-jump nose'. Br ♂ rich chestnut, white cheek, blue bill. In winter, large white cheek patch and black cap retained, bill dark. ♀/young: dark mottled brown with horizontal white cheek stripe.

Domestic Wildfowl—often found on local ponds and are the first to approach when bread is being handed out. Tame and highly variable in appearance, they easily cause confusion.

Domestic Mallard

Muscovy Duck

xotic Waterfowl—commonly kept in wildfowl collections. Escapes can be found anywhere! Some tame, ıers less so! Look for bands on legs, clipped wings, or a missing hindclaw. In Britain and Ireland, a number of ecies of ducks occur regularly as vagrants. Others are far more contentious, but possible. Behaviour, arrival dates, ather patterns, and plumage conditions are just some things to check for when trying to assess their true status. ales are the boldly patterned of the pairs.

Blue-winged Teal

Cinnamon Teal

Wood Duck

Baikal Teal

Lesser Scaup

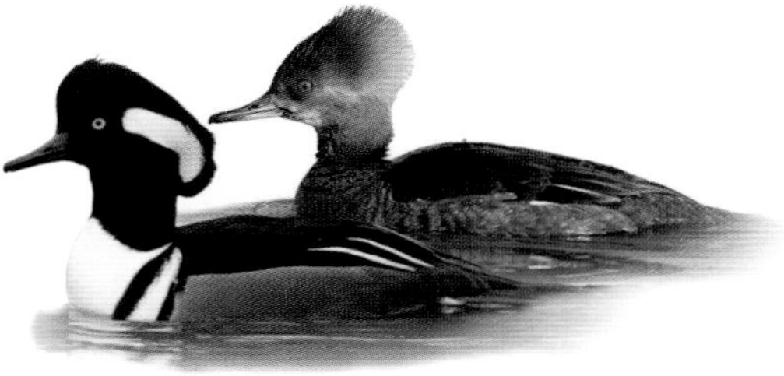
Hooded Merganser

Barrow's Goldeneye

King Eider

White-headed Duck

Marbled Duck

Falcated Duck

Shag *Phalacrocorax aristotelis* **SHAG/SA** L 72cm

UK: s. 27,000 pairs
w. 110,000

Smaller, thin-necked version of CORMO, mainly restricted to vicinity of rocky coasts where it occurs all year-round. Rare inland, almost invariably as juv singleton. Breeds in colonies on islands, sea caves, cliffs with broad ledges, often beneath overhangs. Usually flies low over sea, never soaring up to a great height as CORMO often does, rarely glides; often looks pot-bellied in flight. Shares habit of resting on rocks and jetties holding wings out, as if drying them. To dive, usually takes springy leap before entering water, which CORMO does much less often. **ID:** Usually noticeably smaller than CORMO. If not, concentrate on head shape: steep forehead, peak of crown above eye; bill looks thin enough to snap off easily. In flight, wingbeats quicker, slim neck usually held straight (no kink). Small yellow gape separate from eye. Ad br: diagnostic wispy crest, green sheen, no white in plumage. Nonbr: duller than br, small white patch on chin. Juv/1st-yr: Browner than adult, with pale pinkish bill and pale edges to coverts. Pale webs on feet.

Great Cormorant *Phalacrocorax carbo* CORMO/CA L 90cm

UK: s. 9,000 pairs
w. 41,000

Common widespread resident on coast; also inland, esp in winter, when on rivers, gravel pits, larger lakes, and other wetlands. Breeds chiefly on rocky coasts and islands, nesting on wide ledges, often high above sea; avoids caves. Also breeds uncommonly inland on trees. Large, black, goose-sized waterbird that spends much time in groups just sitting on rocks, jetties, islands, trees, and overhead wires, holding its wings out to dry in 'heraldic posture'. In water, swims low, with head pointing upwards at slight angle. Dives underwater for some time. Eats large fish, sometimes 'fighting' with them on surface. Strong flyer, may soar high; fairly quick, stiff wingbeats; frequent glides. Neck shows kink. **ID:** Thick necked and large bodied, with sloping back and fairly long tail. Thick bill is 'sunk deeply' into head, giving flat crown with peak at back of head, unlike SHAG. Eye set in skin contiguous with gape. Ad br: white thighs and bright white on chin, white flecks on crown and nape. Ad nonbr: all black except for large white patch on face and chin. Juv/1st-yr: brown, with variable white on underparts, often a lot. 2–3 yrs: progressively blacker.

Black-throated Diver *Gavia arctica* BLTDI/BV L 66cm

UK: s. 190-250 pairs
w. 560

Rare breeding bird in n and w Scotland, on large inland lakes (lochs) with islands. In winter widespread on the coast, but extremely localised and generally uncommon; rare on big lakes and reservoirs. In common with other divers, often 'rolls over' to preen, rears up in the water when wing-flapping and will often submerge head to check for prey before diving ('snorkelling'). As with other divers, wings entirely dark, in contrast to grebes and similar. In flight, note that neck is 50:50 light/dark. **ID:** Only slightly smaller than GRNDI, but not as bulky and doesn't bring CORMO to mind. Neck often looks snake-like. Holds bill horizontal. Ad br: very smart, with obvious black-and-white stripes down neck surrounding black throat. Ad nonbr: much smarter and more neatly contrasting than GRNDI, with conspicuous white patch on flank that appears as 'rising moon' above water-line. Clear line of demarcation between front and hind neck, with curve around ear coverts; eye not surrounded by white. Back usually slightly darker than neck (reverse in GRNDI), latter slate-grey. Juv/1st-w: paler and browner above than adult, at first with scaly pattern caused by pale feather tips.

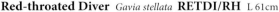

Red-throated Diver *Gavia stellata* **RETDI/RH** L 61cm

UK: s. 1,000-1,600 pairs
w. 17,000

By far the easiest diver to see. In winter, fairly common offshore and often seen in loose groups dispersed over the sea. In summer breeds on small pools within upland moorland and bogs in tundra-like habitat, and has habit of commuting between these pools and larger lakes, sea-lochs or bays. In winter, rare inland. Flies with faster and fuller wingbeats than other divers, and shows distinctive hunch-backed shape, with head sagging down. Flocks fly in undisciplined formations, often quite high over sea. Wings appear more angled back and feet protrude very little. **ID:** Smallest and slimmest diver, with small pointed head with thin bill characteristically tilted upwards, always obvious. Ad br: more uniform than other divers. Throat often appears black, not red, in unfavourable light. Ad nonbr: much whiter than other divers, esp on head and neck. Eye surrounded by white, head may look capped. Thin and straight-necked, without bulging breast of other divers; quite grebe-like. Close-to, white sprinkles on upperparts distinctive. Juv/1st-w: duskier on face and neck, with smaller speckles on back.

Great Northern Diver *Gavia immer* GRNDI/ND L 80cm

UK: w. 2,600

Uncommon but widespread winter visitor to coasts and some large inland lakes or reservoirs. Also regularly found in n Scotland and n Ireland in summer months, but not breeding. Impressive cormorant-like bird that holds dagger-shaped bill horizontal when swimming. Lacks CORMO's sloping rear end. Immerses for fish and often stays down for some time, emerging some distance from where it dived. Flies with relaxed wingbeats, goose-like pace, huge feet splayed behind. **ID:** Bulky, with thick neck, dagger-like bill and protruding forehead, often (not always) with apparent 'bump on head'. Ad br: smartly patterned with white 'blocks' on back; head and neck mainly deep bottle-green. Many wintering birds and spring migrants partially or completely moulted by early spring. Ad nonbr: brown above, pale below, with indistinct border between two on neck; whitish around eye, distinctive 'neck-nick', dark half-collar further down. Large pale bill with dark tip and culmen. Juv/1st-w: distinct pale fringes to upperparts, look scaly, become worn by spring. 1st-s: worn and faded juv plumage, pale fringes usually lost so looks like ad nonbr.

White-billed Diver *Gavia adamsii* WHBDI L 84cm *w. 13*

Very rare nonbreeding visitor from Arctic, to coasts, esp off n and w Scotland. Fairly common on Dogger Banks. **ID:** Slightly larger than similar GRNDI. Has more upright posture, with neck held back and appears slimmer; bill tilted up, giving regal appearance. Often shares 'bump on head' of GRNDI. Nonbr: very pale, particularly around eye and neck. Ad br: larger white chequers on upperparts and differently shaped white collar. Bill shape and colour always critical. Straight culmen with strong gonydeal angle, ivory coloured in nonbr, yellow in br. Culmen always pale; GRNDI always shows some dark (but beware GRNDI bill gleaming in sunlight). Pale bill may be visible at considerable distance.

Red-necked Grebe *Podiceps grisegena* RENGR/RX L 43cm *w. 57*

Scarce winter visitor to east and south coasts, and sometimes large inland freshwater lakes; rare in summer on richly vegetated wetlands, where it is shy and elusive. **ID:** Approaches GRCGR in size but resembles SLAGR and BLNGR in plumage, at least in winter. Thick necked with a stout, straight, yellow-based bill tilted slightly down. Capped appearance in all plumages. Eye dark. Ad br: adults have lovely head and neck pattern from Apr. Ad nonbr: dulled-down version of breeding, with greyer cheeks. Unlike GRCGR, no white above eye. Bill dull with limited yellow at base. 1st-w: very similar to nonbr. In flight, bold white secondaries and white leading edge to wing; thick neck.

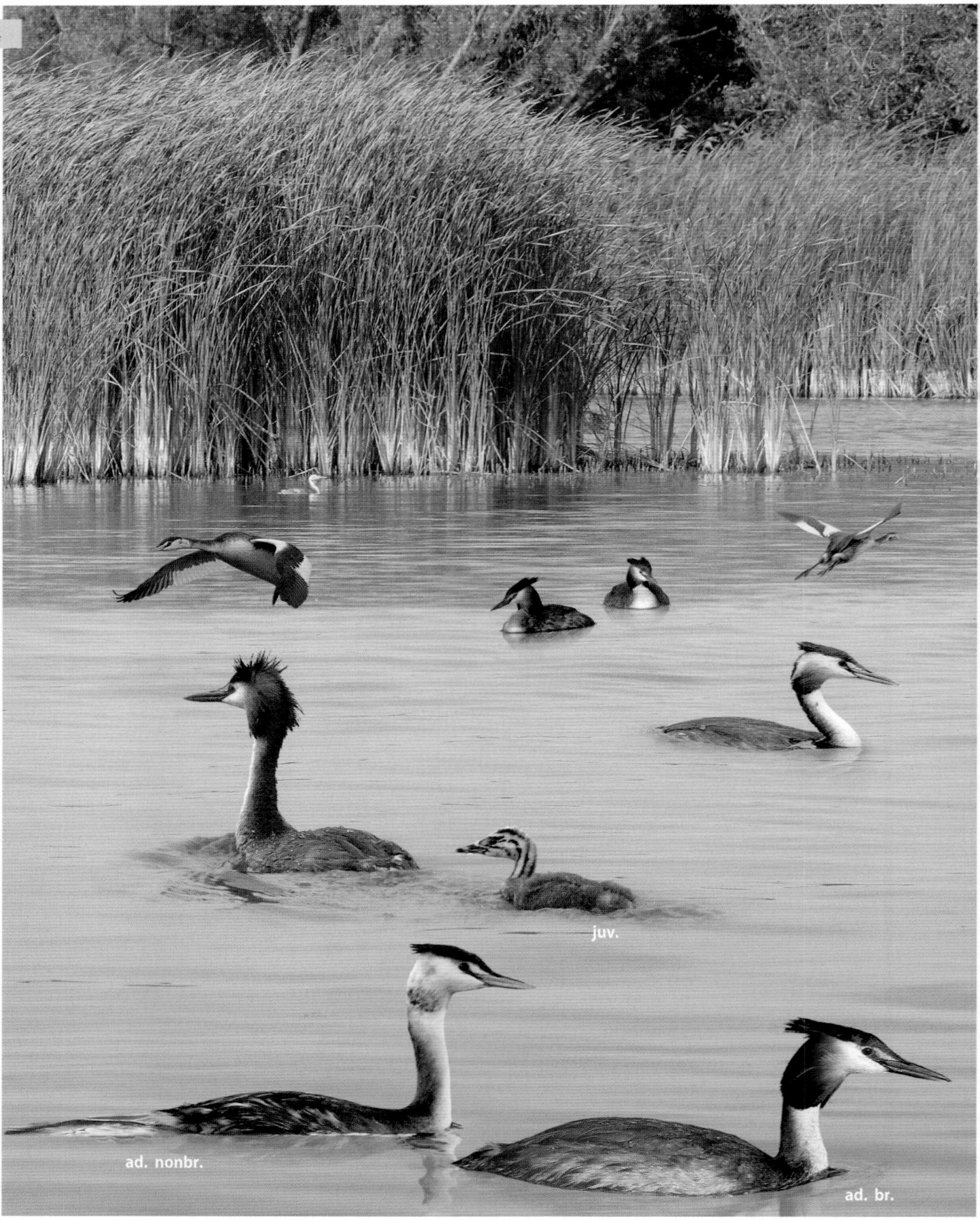

Great Crested Grebe *Podiceps cristatus* **GRCGR/GG** L 48cm

UK: s. 5,300 pairs
w. 23,000

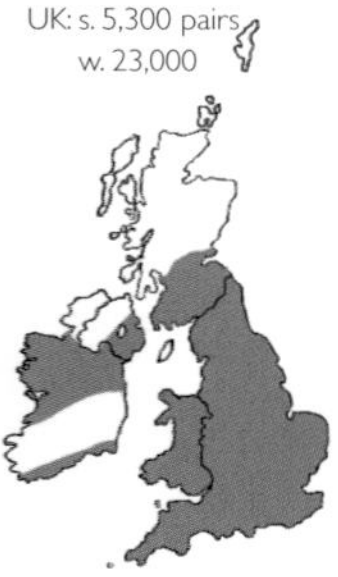

Common resident on lowland freshwater lakes and slow-flowing rivers, often in parks; also reservoirs and gravel pits. Frequently tame. In winter seen on sheltered coasts, often to people's surprise. By far the easiest grebe to see, known by nonbirders. 'Pyjama-striped' young rest on parent's back, plead for food with loud squeaking calls. Has famed courtship routine in spring and summer, when pairs face each other and mutually shake their heads, sometimes present weed to each other. Builds floating nest on water's edge. Pursues fish underwater. Dives with quick forward leap and often reappears some distance away from where it dived. Often sleeps with head and neck on back. 'Flickering' style of flight with rapid wingbeats, weak impression; shows a lot of white. Call is loud braying roar. **ID:** Largest and slimmest grebe. Ad br: unmistakable head pattern. Ad nonbr: much whiter than other grebes. Look for dagger-shaped pink bill, long thin whitish neck. The only grebe with white between crown and eye. Juv/1st-w: black stripes on head retained throughout winter, gradually lost.

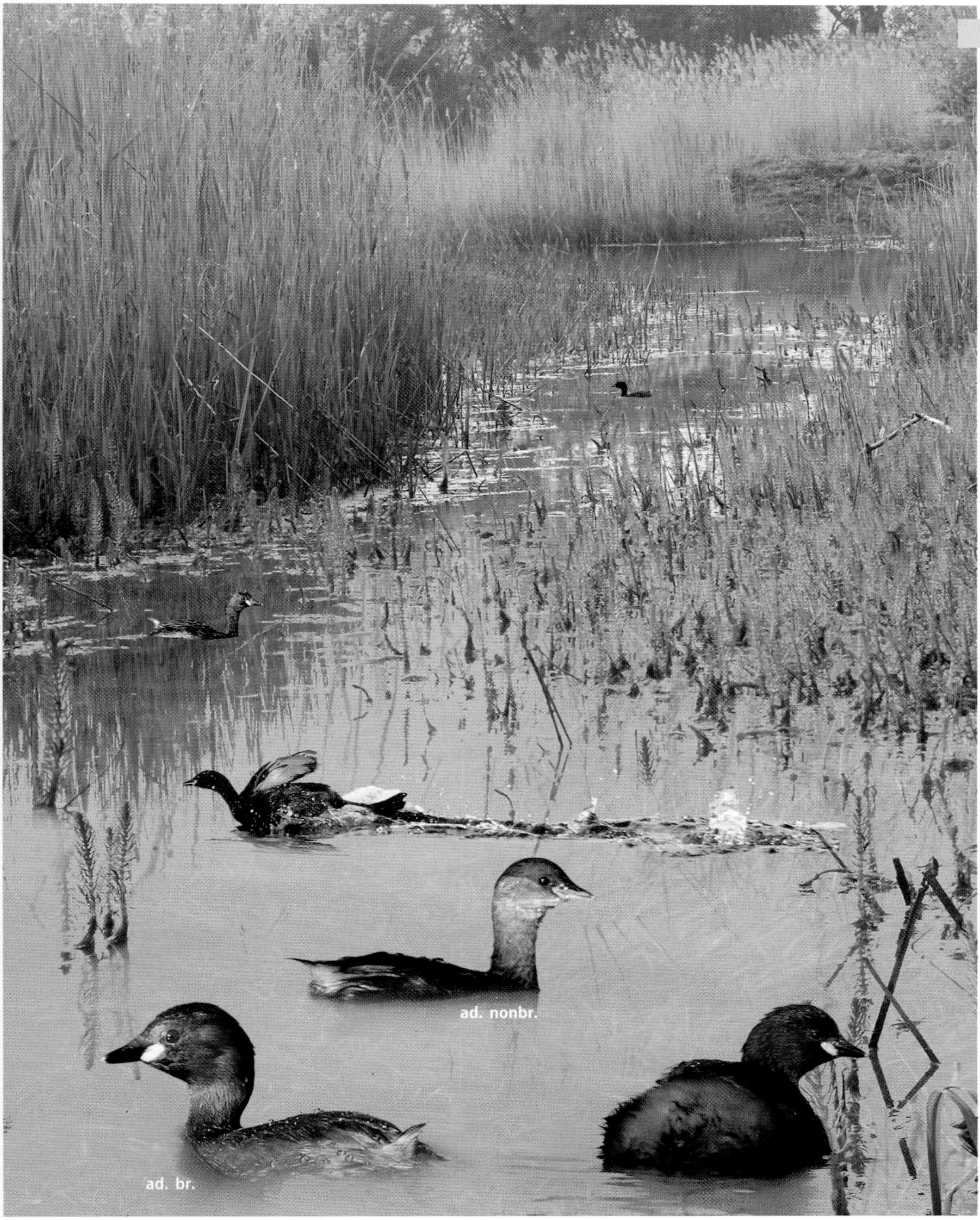

Little Grebe *Tachybaptus ruficollis* LITGR/LG L 26cm

UK: s. 3,900-7,800 pairs
w. 17,000

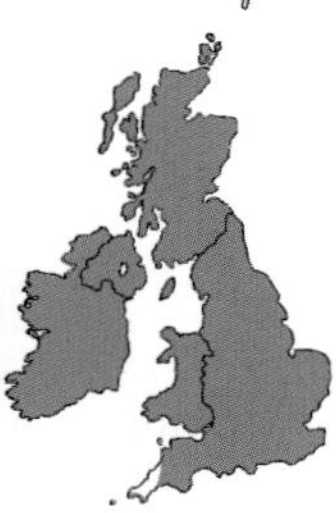

Widespread and fairly common on freshwater ponds, overgrown ditches, slow-flowing rivers, canals, and marshes. In winter, found on larger lakes and on some sheltered estuaries. With small size and fluffy tail, is like 'floating rabbit'. Often known by alternative name of 'Dabchick', which comes from 'dip chick', referring to habit of taking constant dips (dives) under water. Dives to feed on insects and larvae. Shy; able to surface with only its head and neck showing. May be spotted in open water, but soon retreats to side of river/pond and disappears among vegetation. Able to rush (skitter) over water surface to escape, rarely seen flying. Not sociable, usually 1 or 2, rarely in groups of more than 5. Very well-known call is like whinny of tiny horse, or slightly insane giggle. Pairs often duet. **ID:** Size, shape, and behaviour usually distinctive. Ad br: handsome, with rich chestnut on neck distinctive, and yellow-green base of bill diagnostic. In winter, much less contrasting than BLNGR or SLAGR, black and brown, not black and white. Also rounded head, yellowish bill, fluffier rear end, dark eye. Juv: may retain stripes on head into 1st-w.

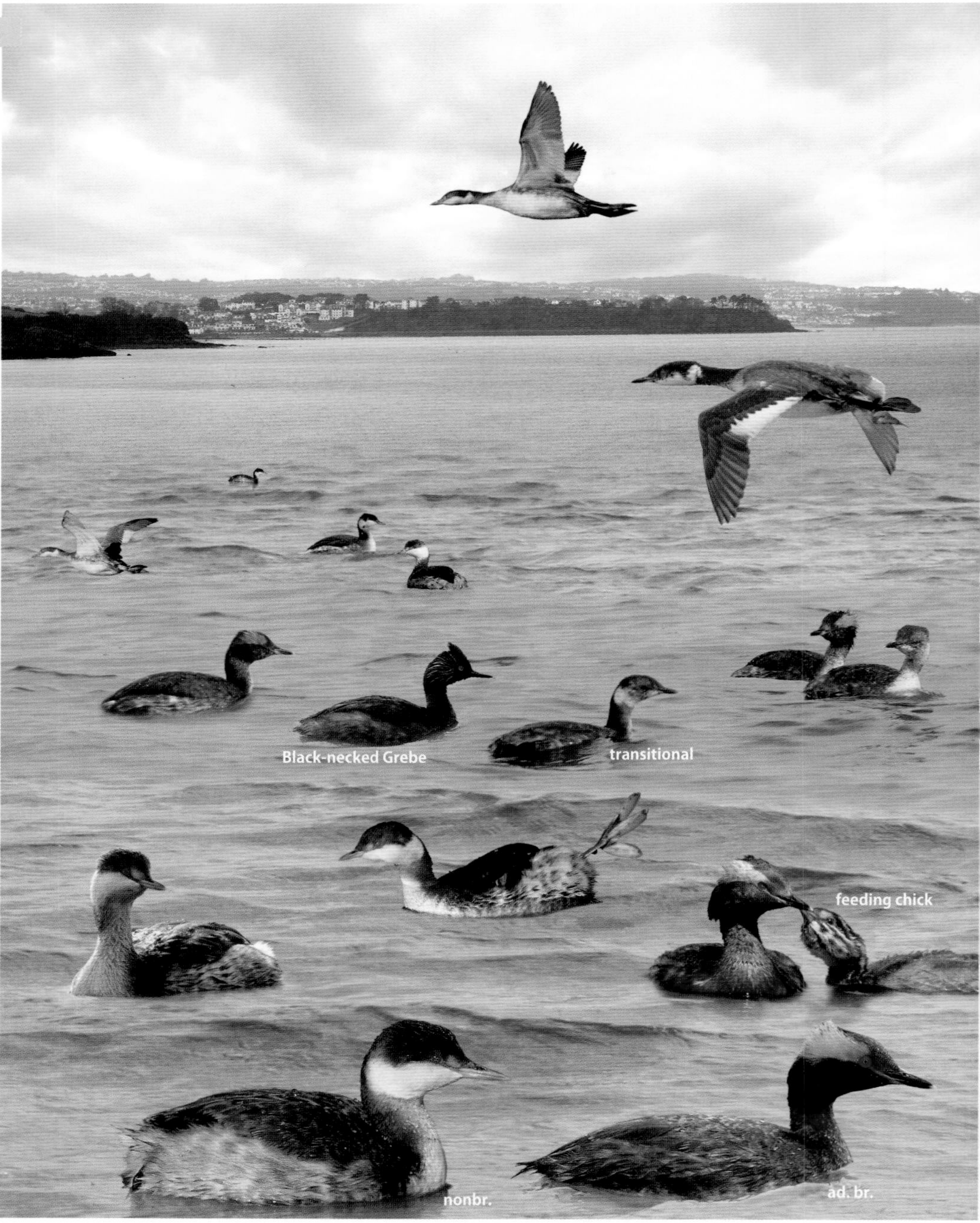

Slavonian Grebe *Podiceps auritus* **SLAGR/SZ** L 34cm

UK: s. 30 pairs
w. 1,100

Confined as a breeding bird to Scottish lochs; unlike BLNGR, doesn't need masses of floating vegetation. In the winter, much commoner and more widespread than BLNGR and often seen on sea watches; rare on larger inland lakes. Despite its size, quite a powerful fish-chasing grebe, usually diving with impressive forward leap. Much more able to cope with rough seas than BLNGR. Doesn't breed in colonies like BLNGR and doesn't take refuge among gulls or other birds to nest, as BLNGR does. **ID:** Fairly small, even proportions, not particularly fluffy at rear. Vertical posture with straight neck. Bill is straight, broad based, and helps to give head a pointed shape. Compared to BLNGR, crown looks flatter. Bill often pale tipped. Ad br: colours striking, but rufous can look black at a distance. Stunning red eye. 'Horns' reach back of head. Beware moulting birds in Feb to Apr, which can resemble BLNGR. Nonbr: appears black-capped ('northern' cloth cap) with clean horizontal divide through eye emphasised by stunning white cheeks—much dirtier in BLNGR. Small white spot on lores. Peculiar and distinctive shape in flight with head held higher than body. 1st-w. similar.

Black-necked Grebe *Podiceps nigricollis* **BLNGR/BN** L 31in ***s. 32–51 pairs, w. 130***

Scarce on richly vegetated freshwater lakes, sheltered coasts, and, esp on migration, reservoirs and gravel pits. Is unusually sociable for a grebe, breeding in small colonies and also occurring in small gatherings in winter. Frequent diver. Feeds on invertebrates and small fish. **ID:** A fluffy-looking grebe with habit of sitting very high on water, showing large exposed grey rear end. Strikingly fine bill is slightly upturned but often held pointing slightly downwards. It has a very steep forehead with a 'bump' on the top. Thin-necked compared to large head. Shape is always the most important factor in differentiating from similar SLAGR. Longer bodied than LITGR which shares fluffy rear end. Red eye (shared with SLAGR) obvious at close quarters. Ad br: bold yellow plumes on black neck and head (beware SLAGR often appears black-necked). Nonbr: lacks clean-cut appearance of SLAGR, shows darker neck and dark cheek patch well below eye; head pattern like 'riding hat'. Dark ear coverts surrounded by white which loops upwards at back. White on chin obvious.

Little Auk *Alle alle* **LITAU/LK** L 18cm

Scarce winter visitor from Arctic, regular in Shetland and Orkney but much rarer further south, mainly North Sea coasts. Occasionally 'wrecked' close to shore after northerly gales, otherwise keeps well out. Numbers in British waters vary year-on-year. Takes off without need to run over water like other auks. **ID:** Tiny, particularly on big ocean. Short, plump, and neckless with stubby bill. In flight, seen as chunky blur of wings with dark underside and thin white trailing edge. Nonbr: striking partial collar and white underparts, black lobe covering eye. Ad br: dark head and neck. PUFFI can look small, but not as tiny as LITAU, and PUFFI never has white neck sides.

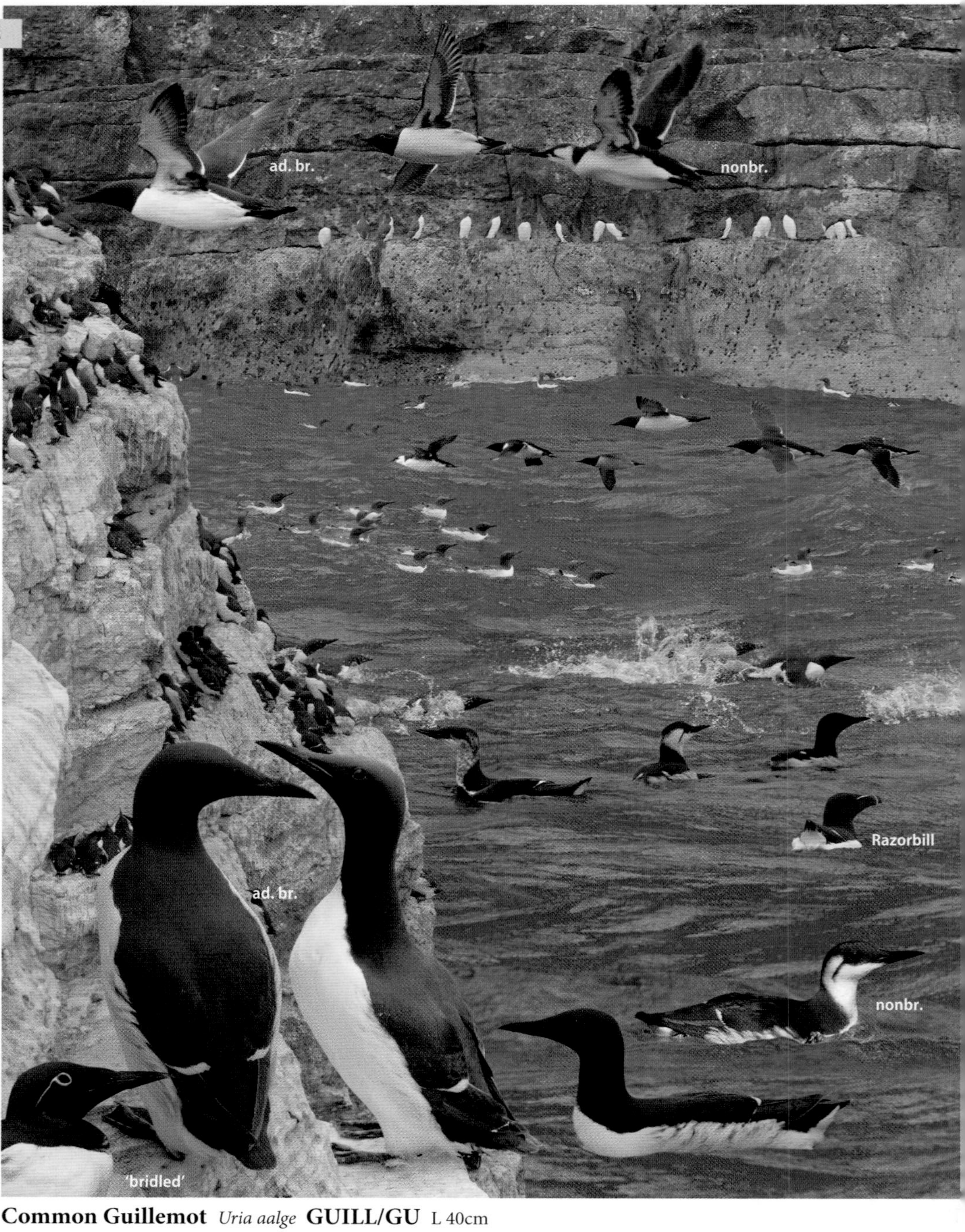

Common Guillemot *Uria aalge* GUILL/GU L 40cm

UK: s. 950,000 pairs

Widespread cliff-nesting seabird, also common offshore in winter. Has extreme lifestyle, nesting in densely packed colonies (densest in the world) with birds literally rubbing shoulders at times. These colonies are on cliffs, the eggs often laid on narrow, precarious ledges on sheer cliffs, entirely exposed to the elements. Birds at colonies make braying ululations that can be heard above roar of sea. Shape typical of auk, basically penguin-like, standing up erect, with feet set right back. Unlike penguin, flies with very fast, continuous wingbeats, usually low over water. Feet project well beyond tail. Near colonies, groups small and large parade past in flight, mill around together beneath cliffs on sea, often with other auks. In winter, common on sea watches, usually a little offshore. May go by in constant streams. **ID:** Distinguished by pointed bill and longer body than other auks. Ad br: except in far north, browner above than other auks, dark chocolate. White below with variable streaks on flanks. Some have white whisker behind eye ('bridled'). Nonbr: acquires white on side of head, usually with black streak down from eye. Br: plum. from Dec.; 1st-w. similar.

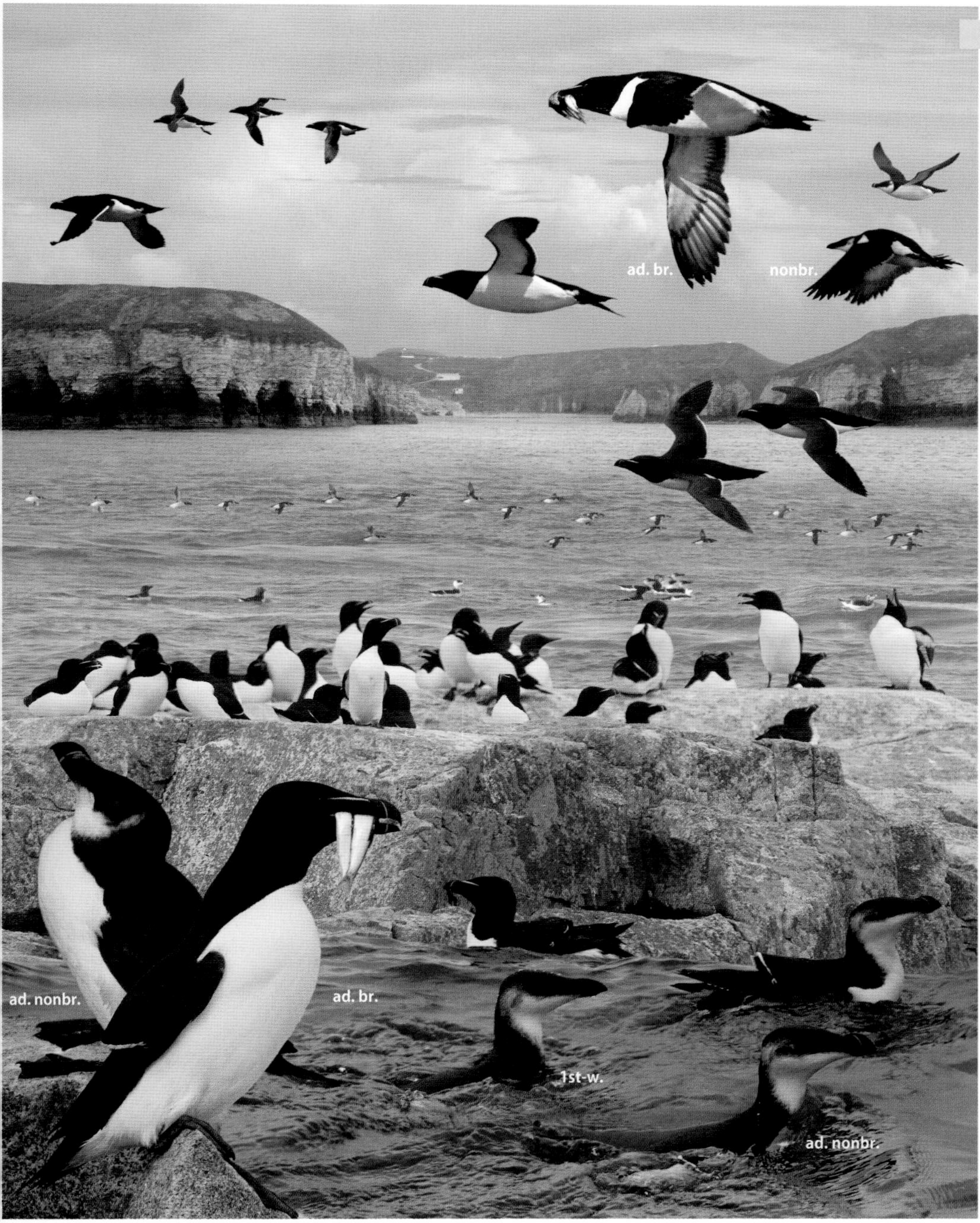

Razorbill *Alca torda* **RAZOR/RA** L 38cm

UK: s. 130,000 pairs

As widespread as GUILL and often shares same cliffs, but prefers much wider ledges and does not live in such cramped conditions. Not usually as numerous as GUILL in same locations. Lays single egg on ledge, incubated by both parents in shifts. Goes out to collect fish for chick, brings back several at once crosswise in its large, laterally flattened bill, rather than a single fish brought in lengthways, as GUILL. Overall slightly smaller and shorter-bodied than GUILL, with noticeably longer tail that points upwards distinctively in the water and covers feet in flight. At colonies, makes subtler, growling call rather like the creaking of a ship's timbers. Same habits as GUILL in winter, common offshore. **ID:** Bill is key field mark, deep and blunt, and black with obvious white vertical line near tip. Also has thicker neck than GUILL. Ad br: Smart, contrasting black above and gleaming clean white below. White line along top of bill to eye. Ad nonbr: look for blunt bill and much black on crown; doesn't have neat black streak on cheek. Clean white below, and also has unsullied white under wings. 1st-w: has smaller bill. It takes 4 years to reach full depth. Torpedo-like in flight.

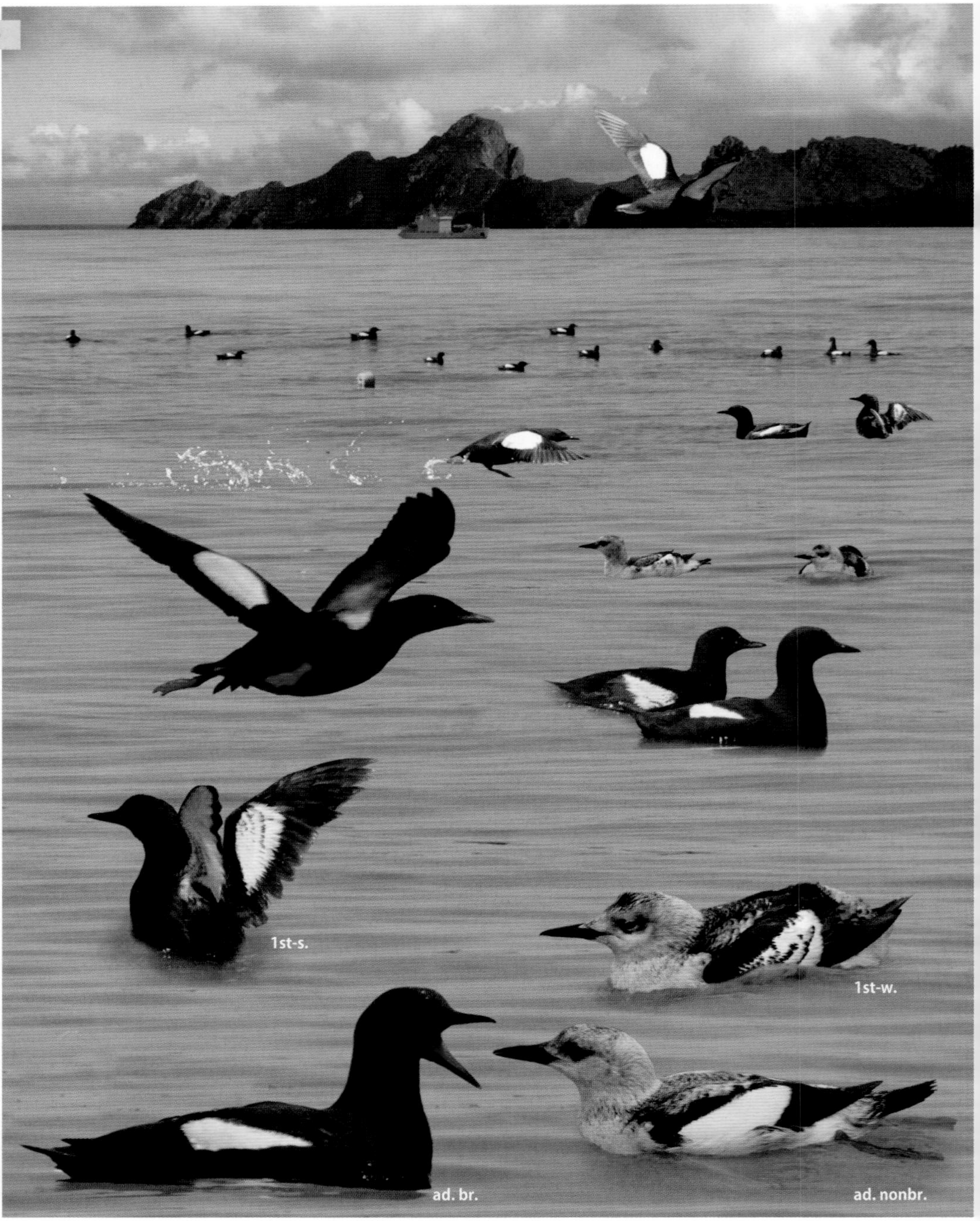

Black Guillemot *Cepphus grylle* **BLAGU/TY** L 31cm

UK: s. 19,000 pairs

Distinctive and unusual auk with remarkably different summer and winter plumages that look like different species. Locally common in Scotland and Ireland, on rocky shorelines with small islands with large boulders, under which it nests. Not in packed colonies like other auks, much more spread out, sometimes just in ones or twos. Feeds on seabed all year-round, so routinely found close to shore, often in sheltered bays. Lays 2 eggs, not 1 as with other auks. Unlike other auks, doesn't normally wander far from breeding areas in winter. Dives ('slips') under water powered by feet and wings. Makes very odd, 'electronic' peeping noises at colony. **ID:** Small, with dovelike head and fine bill. Bright red legs and mouth lining. Ad br: sooty black, with large white ovals on upperwing. Ad nonbr: dappled grey and black on body; wings still with white ovals and black wingtip. Looks whitish at distance and in flight. 1st-w: similar, but has dark spots on white ovals. Moults to 1st-s, which acquires dark body as adult, but with dark spots or bars on white ovals.

Puffin *Fratercula arctica* PUFFI/PU L 28cm

UK: s. 580,000 pairs

Popular and unmistakable seabird, occurring in summer widely on offshore islands, clifftops, and steep maritime grassy slopes. Makes burrow 1m long for nest, has single chick. Iconic sighting is of adult bringing fish to burrow, holding them crossways in enormous, triangular, colourful bill. Sometimes brings 10 or more fish at a time. Highly colonial, often with thousands of pairs. Low moaning is sometimes heard from burrows. In Aug, disappears far offshore, rarely seen until Mar, when returns to colonies. **ID:** Small muscular auk with sturdy bright orange legs, far better able to walk and run than congeners. Large triangular bill is laterally flattened. Fast flight on narrow black wings, dark underwing distinguishes from common auks, but shared with LITAU. Black collar and black patch on flanks. Ad sum: Bill bluish and orange, eye set amid triangle of skin, face whitish. Ad winter: bill smaller but still orange. Smoky grey face. 1st winter with much smaller bill. Summer bill becomes larger with more ridges up to age 4. In flight, look for darkish underwing, no white trailing edge to upperwing, and shape.

FLYING WATERBIRDS

SEABIRDS

Though birding logistics may sometimes be difficult when one tries to see these birds, this group in general is always intriguing. Britain and Ireland, surrounded by oceans, rocky promontories, and windy weather, has a long history as a great place to go for sea watching. Birds that typically live out at sea can sometimes be seen from land, but often only in the worst weather conditions. Onshore winds are typically vital—the stronger the better! Fog and rain also bring birds closer to land as does food availability. Knowing the most favourable weather conditions for your favourite sea-watching site is crucial. Usually a telescope is necessary for sea watching. In some cases, the easiest way to see seabirds closely is from a boat, particularly those species that travel far offshore in search of areas with plentiful food. Water temperature and food supply are connected and therefore play a significant part in distribution. The ocean is continually moving, and so too are the birds. In recent years boat trips for birders have been organised; these are highly recommended for a good look at pelagic birds. Boats that throw out food (chum) such as fish oil often get the best results.

Views of seabirds are often very brief and distant as birds disappear below the waves. Flight style is a key element in the ID of this group of birds. Size and colour patterns are also important, though often difficult to determine. Given the difficult viewing conditions, never be in a rush to put a name to a bird; many are best left unidentified. Never knowing what will turn up is one of the great fascinations of seabirding!

TERNS

Terns are a group of slim, angular-winged birds with long, forked tails. Because of their shape and buoyant flight style, they tend to look very graceful. Some species, such as Black Tern, only swoop and pick food off the surface; however, most terns hover and plunge-dive. Some do both. Most species are white with grey backs. They travel long distances and thus can turn up anywhere, particularly as they are quite easily impacted by wind and rain. Terns are colonial, often breeding on rocky islands or beaches, and always close to fishing grounds. They often compete for beaches with humans and are frequently protected behind roped-off areas. Get too close to nests and they will dive-bomb you. They mean business and do occasionally draw blood. They form mixed flocks, particularly on beaches where they gather to rest after fishing. Sorting through birds can be confusing initially, but with practice and understanding this challenge becomes great fun and always offers the chance of finding the 'goody'. ID is made trickier by the wide variety of plumages. It's easiest to break them down into three types: juvenile, nonbreeding/immature, and breeding.

Juvenile plumage is usually held for only several weeks in most species. These birds tend to be on or near their breeding grounds—a great clue! Juveniles can often be seen begging, since adults frequently continue to feed young after they leave the nest. Juveniles usually have scaly brown or black on upperparts, and their bills are usually dark and often paler at the base. During fall, many of the darker feathers are moulted or fade so they become similar to those of adult nonbreeders.

Adult nonbreeders and immatures generally have partial caps, develop dark on the bend of the wing (carpal bar), and have darker bills. Most terns don't become fully adult until they are about 3 years old. 1st-s birds are as nonbreeding birds, but have old, unmoulted feathers that are worn and faded, giving a scruffy look. 2nd-s birds usually as adult with white flecking on crown and darker bill, but variable and probably similar to some sick or failed breeding birds. An understanding of moult sequence is fundamental in correctly ageing these birds.

Breeding birds have solid black caps, brighter bills and legs, longer tail streamers, and clean grey upperparts. Breeding plumage is the most frequently viewed, because terns migrate south for the winter.

The extent of dark in the primaries is often used for identifying terns, but a large amount of variation exists, and the exact patterns are often difficult to determine in the field. To add to the confusion, breeding birds acquire a 'fluffy' filamentous bloom that makes the flight feathers pale. This wears off through the summer, and as the primaries become more worn they become noticeably darker, often causing confusion. Most plumages show secondary bars in flight, but these are variable and of little use in ageing birds.

Learning to ID terns is, as always, a question of getting back to basics. Learn the familiar species well, based on size, shape, and behaviour, and study the patterns of colour that remain consistent. Beware: if you get caught up in the minutiae of colour, you will become very confused!

SKUAS

Skuas are tundra breeders. Arctic and Great Skua breed in the far north, mostly on islands. They are pelagic the rest of the year, passing our shores on migration and occasionally in winter. They occasionally show up inland on migration.

Skuas have been at the centre of many a heated debate about their identification. The 'raptors of the sea', they harass other birds such as terns and gulls until those others drop or regurgitate their food. Powerful and agile flyers compared with similarly proportioned gulls, they are often seen distantly in poor weather conditions. Trying to discern their size and shape will provide the key to identification, but it is tricky for even the most experienced birders. Larger and heavier birds have a more powerful and direct flight than the more buoyant and less powerful smaller birds. Smallest and slimmest is Long-tailed Skua, largest and most bulky is Great Skua. Intermediate are Arctic (Kittiwake-sized) and Pomarine (Herring Gull-sized). Other important field marks are bill and central tail feather shape.

All skuas have dark upperparts with typically prominent white wing flashes. Underparts are highly variable plumage, ranging from all dark to mostly white underparts. Some are intermediate.

GULLS

Love them or hate them, gulls (genus *Larus*) are always fascinating and one of the great challenges in birding. As a 'larophile' in my student days, I found one of their major appeals to be that they could be found anywhere. They love densely populated urban areas, and are highly mobile (some will travel 30–40 miles to feed), so there is always the possibility of something new and possibly rare. Add to this their intrinsic ID challenges: multiple plumages, huge individual variation, and taxonomic uncertainties (several have recently been or will be split into new species), and you have the perfect recipe—depending on your personal birding likes and dislikes! My wife puts it more bluntly: 'I hate them. I have to stand out in the cold for hours, and they all look the same'. Maybe having our first date at Plymouth sewage outfall didn't help! We agree to disagree: perhaps you can relate? Although gulls frequently inhabit unattractive, often dirty places, I believe it's their overwhelming plumage variation that is key to many birders' unease with, and apparent lack of interest in, this group.

With practice, many species can be relatively easy, though a fair number are difficult to identify, and several are essentially impossible. This last category produces an assessment qualified by the more realistic terms 'probable' or 'possible'. To demystify gulls, you need to know a few things: firstly, different species take different lengths of time to develop adult plumages. As a generalization, small gulls take 2 years, medium-sized gulls 3 years, and large gulls 4 years. As a result, birds often take on appearances that can be very misleading in the field. However, all is not lost.

I usually break gulls into two groups: (1) younger immatures, and (2) adults or near adults (subadults). These groupings work for most species. They also have breeding plumage, but this is essentially the same as nonbreeding, the major difference being head pattern: hoods develop in some of the smaller species, and others become white and look cleaner for breeding.

The most confusing species are generally thought to be the large gulls because they show the widest variation. They can be overwhelming in the field at first. As you look at the plates, try to break the colour patterns into the two groups: younger immatures and older adult-type birds. Also go back to the basics of size and shape with a lot of emphasis on the bill. Herring Gull is the 'default' gull in most areas and the one species with which you must be familiar to significantly improve your field skills. For basic ID purposes, Herring Gull can be split into two groups: (1) those that are variably smudgy brown or grey with an overall grungy look (the first two years of their life), and (2) adults or near adults: cleaner-looking birds with a uniform grey back (adult feathers moulted in third summer [2nd-s]). Gulls often appear in large mixed flocks, so it is quite easy to compare birds. The darker 'backs' of older Lesser and Greater Black-backed Gulls should be obvious. Once you have worked them out, focus on darker immatures and then compare their size and shape to the nearby adults.

For the beginner, I would recommend trying to simplify things as much as possible, just as experts do. If you can get a good grasp of identification of the very common Herring and Black-headed Gulls, many problems in overall gull identification will disappear.

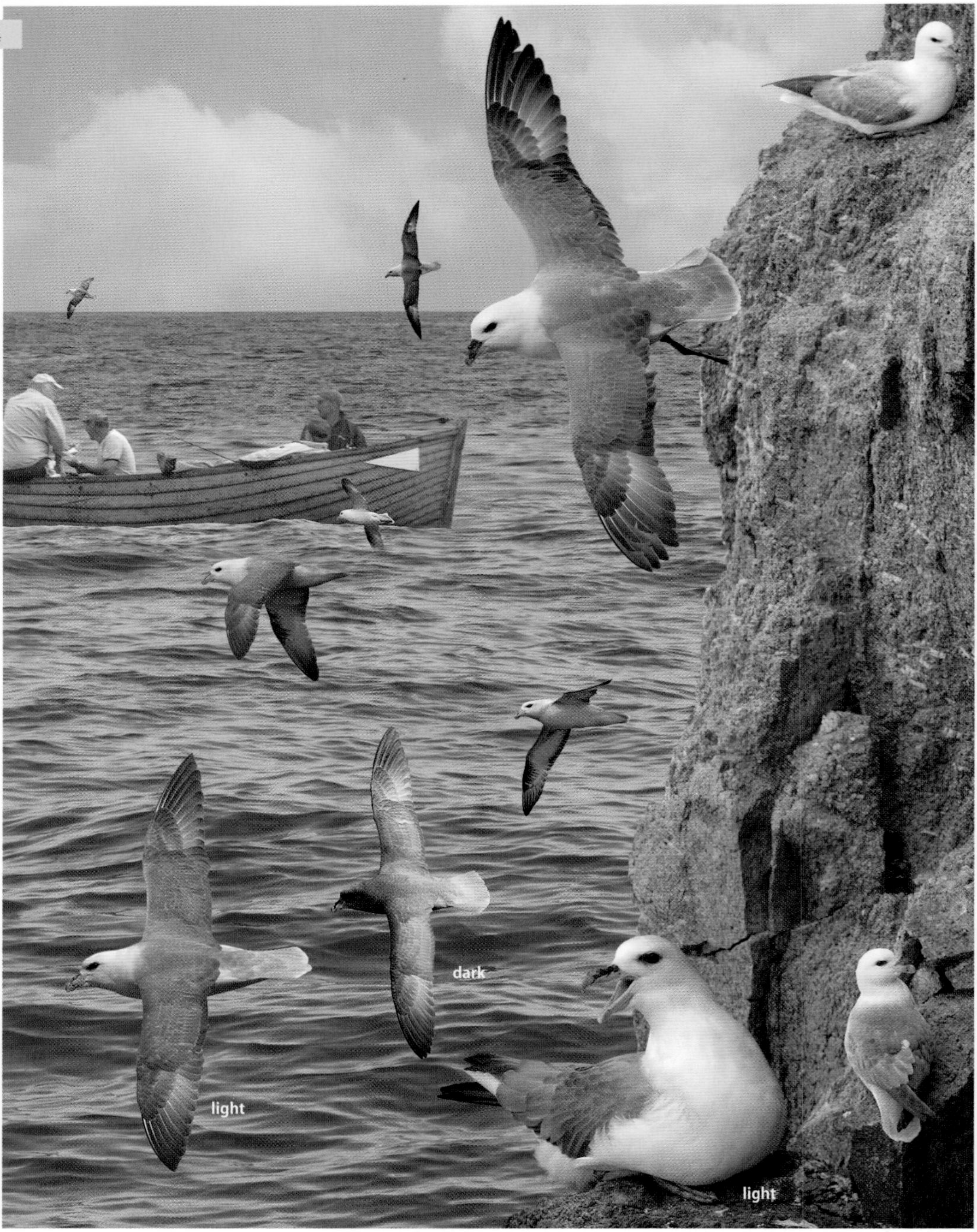

Northern Fulmar *Fulmarus glacialis* **FULMA/F.** L 48cm

UK: s. 500,000 pairs

Widespread breeding bird on cliff ledges all around coast. Birds can often be found near nest sites all year-round; may use burrows and sometimes building ledges. Very gull-like seabird, but flies with stiff wingbeats and wings held out straight. Powerful, yet agile, often gives good views as it flies along cliff-tops. Some winter far offshore, and immatures don't return to nest sites until 5 years old. Solitary, but found in numbers at food sources such as trawlers. Often follows fishing boats. Pairs make cackling at nest. **ID:** Heavyset muscular bird. Broad tail and neck with wings and body held straight. Shallow, stiff wingbeats followed by glides and high arcs in bad weather—beware of thinking it is a large Shearwater. Sits high in the water. It has to 'run' to take off. Stout yellowish bill with bulging nostril on top. Colours vary from light to dark, light birds much the commoner, dark ('Blue Fulmar') mainly in north. All have dark, inky smudge around eye (giving mean look), pale area at base of primaries, and grey tail.

Cory's Shearwater *Calonectris diomedea* **CORSH/CQ** L 46cm

Rare late summer and autumn visitor mainly to southwestern England and Ireland, seen off exposed headlands. Numbers vary from a few to thousands in exceptional years. When not breeding, usually found far offshore. **ID:** Largest shearwater; may recall immature gull, esp in its lazy flight. Heavy build with broad wings held hunched or bowed over and with emphasis on downbeat, giving pterodactyl-like feel. Elbow protrudes forward and outer wing angled back. Pale upperparts without strong head contrast shown by GRTSH. Underparts mostly clean white. Upperparts lack neater dark brown scaled look of GRTSH. Yellow bill. Be careful to rule out the much larger GANNE.

Great Shearwater *Puffinus gravis* **GRTSH/GQ** L 47cm

Rare late summer and autumn migrant, amazingly breeding in the South Atlantic off South America, yet seen from headlands off sw England, Ireland, and w Scotland. **ID:** Slimmer than CORSH, with very different flight: wings held straighter and with stiffer snappy wingbeats. Tends to arc more and higher than CORSH. Darker and more contrasting above with dark cap accentuated by white neck sides—striking at distance whether sitting or flying. This is always the easiest field mark to see. White uppertail coverts usually contrast more strongly with tail than in CORSH. Underparts usually appear white at distance; closer views show a smudgy belly and vent and intricately marked underwing. Slender bill always black.

Manx Shearwater *Puffinus puffinus* **MANSH/MX** L 34cm

UK: s. 300,000 pairs

By far the commonest shearwater; a summer visitor, most arriving in Mar and leaving in Sep, winters off South America. Breeds on western islands in burrows, but on migration may be seen on any coast. Parents take weekly rotations travelling thousands of miles to collect food and incubate the egg, entering their burrows under the safety of darkness. In the daytime they can often be seen in synchronised lines, and in evening often gathering close to shore near colonies. In flight, rapid shallow wingbeats are followed by long glides on slightly bowed wings as they rock from side to side, intermittently showing black then white. Wingbeats are stiff and wings are held rigidly out, giving neat cross shape ('ManX'). In rougher weather, they glide along the contours of the ocean before suddenly arcing high and steeply. Nocturnal calling at burrow is maniacal crooning. **ID:** Strongly two-toned black-and-white shearwater with dusky face and white wrapping around ear coverts. Worn late summer birds can look browner. White undertail coverts can be seen in flight and on sitting birds.

Balearic Shearwater *Puffinus mauretanicus* **BALSH/YQ** L 36cm

Mostly a rare but increasing late-summer (Jul onward) and autumn visitor, particularly to between Cornwall and Dorset, with a few seen well into the winter (MANSH usually absent in the winter). The only regular species in Britain currently globally Critically Endangered, with possibly as few as 9000 adults remaining in the world, breeding on the Balearic Islands of the western Mediterranean. **ID:** Easily overlooked among 'Manxies', Balearic is slightly larger and heavier but grungier-looking bird lacking the clean, contrasting, two-tone look. Typically looking browner, it also has darkish vent, lower belly and armpits, making it look 'dirty'. Balearic does not show white extending up the rear flank onto the edge of the rump as in MANSH, often noticeable at long distance. Typically looks plumper than Manx, the 'barrel-shaped Balearic'. Some individuals darker, so beware of SOOSH, which is larger, slimmer winged, and progresses with more relaxed, less rigid and stiff wingbeats that take it places in a hurry.

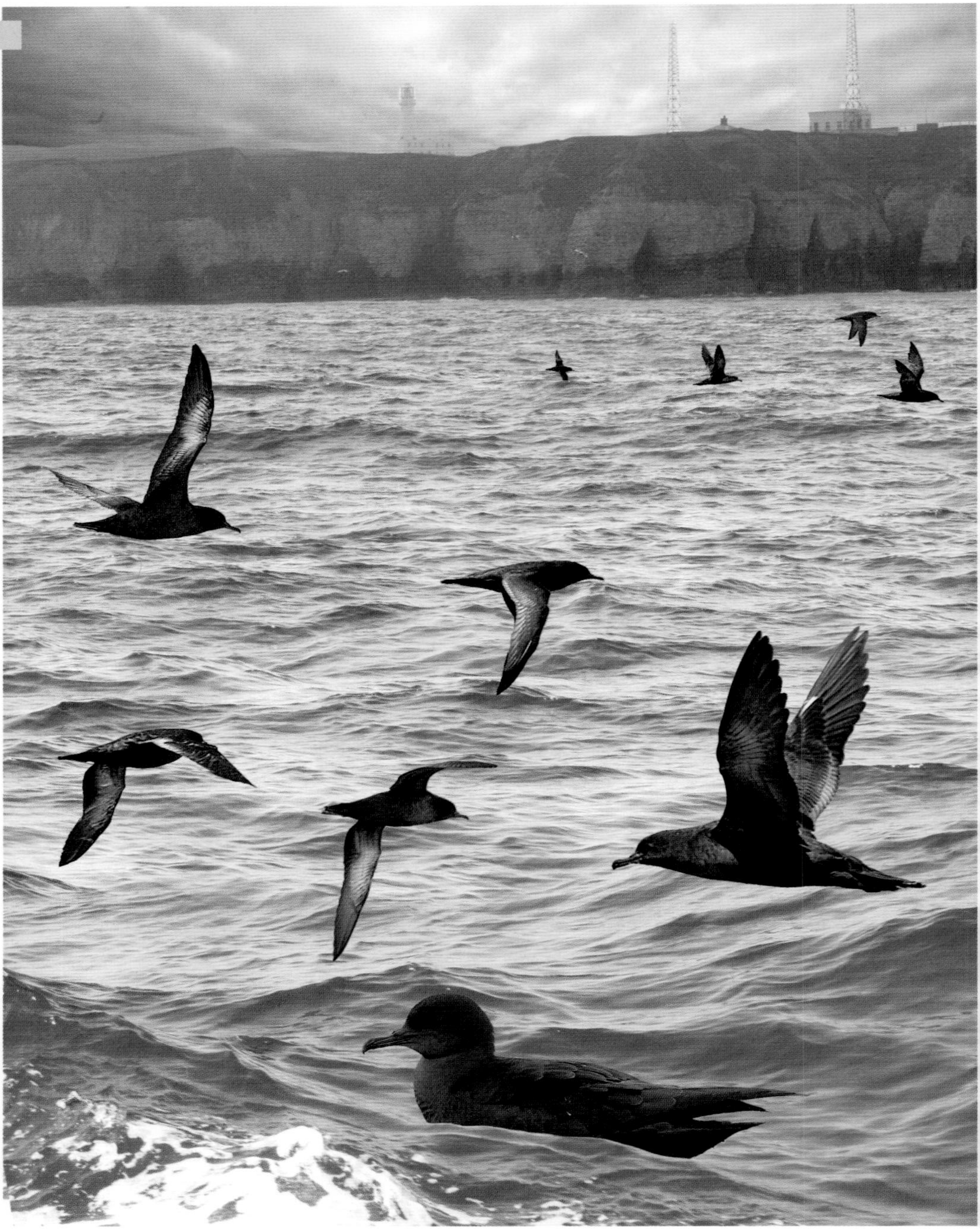

Sooty Shearwater *Puffinus griseus* **SOOSH/OT** L 46cm

Uncommon to rare offshore autumn visitor, mainly Aug–Oct. As with GRTSH, breeds in the Southern Hemisphere, but this species is easier to see in Britain and is much more widespread, regular for example on the East Coast. Sometimes seen from land, particularly in windy conditions. Numbers visiting vary considerably between years. **ID:** Fairly large—between GRTSH and MANSH in size. Fat bodied with a thick neck but slimmer head and slender black bill. The tail, like the head, gets narrower towards the tip. It is the wing shape that is most striking: narrow at the base, slim and pointed, giving distinctive profile. Arches high in windy weather, wings angled back and held stiff, but flaps and glides in calmer weather on bowed wings. Flight is direct, purposeful, and fast. At a distance, brown plumage usually appears black with (but not always) pale or silvery central panel in underwing (skuas can have similar colour pattern). The pale underwing is often visible at long range.

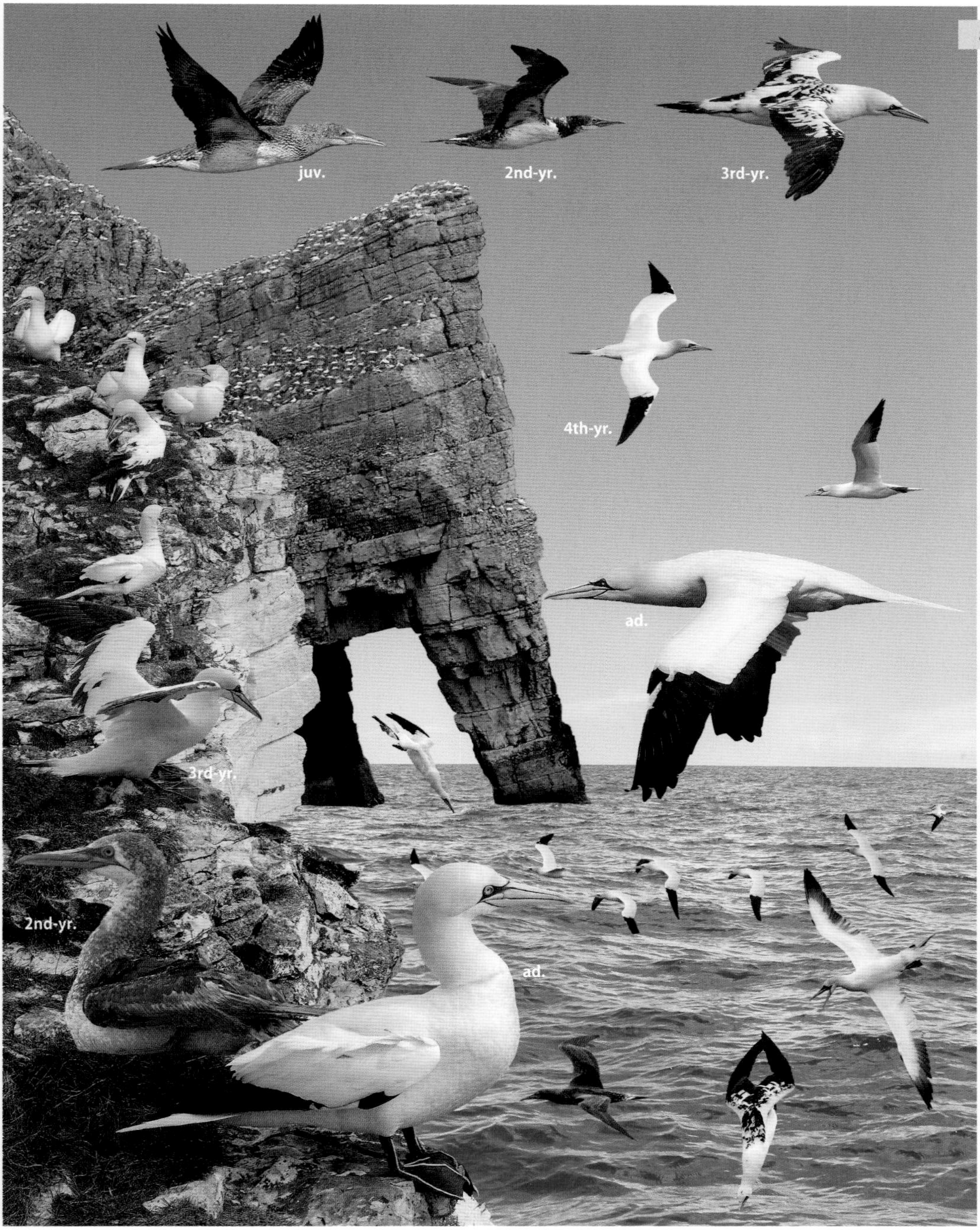

Northern Gannet *Morus bassanus* **GANNE/GX** L 94cm

UK: s. 220,000 pairs

Our largest seabird, common visitor to most coastal areas, near or offshore. Breeds locally in huge colonies on rocky cliffs and islands. In winter spreads right out over continental shelf waters, so is routinely seen from land and boat. Spectacular angled plunge-dives to catch fish. A powerful flyer with slow, stiff, shallow wingbeats followed by short glides. Typically travels in groups of 3–20 that create undulating, evenly spaced lines. Mostly seen in flight, it invariably confuses when seen sitting on water. Sick birds occasionally sit on beach. Large flocks quickly gather where shoals of migrating fish suddenly appear, creating impressive feeding frenzies. **ID:** Very large with long slim pointed wings, tail, and head—but all evenly proportioned. Size and shape distinctive. Large, pointed bill gives a snouted look, and tail also fairly long, so looks tapered front and back. Adult (4+ years): strikingly white with black wingtips and gold-toned head. Juv: all dark with pale spots and streaks. Starts to moult out of juv plumage and acquire progressively more white adult-type feathers over next 2–3 years.

Storm Petrel *Hydrobates pelagicus* **STOPE /TM** L 16cm ***s. 26,000***

A difficult bird to see, appears about the size of House Martin, and truly oceanic. Breeds in burrows on offshore islands May–Aug and comes to land only at night. Otherwise spends time out of sight of land, unless blown towards coast by summer or autumn gales. Best way to see it is to take pelagic trip in summer or autumn. Usually seen pattering low over waves; may disappear in troughs. Has quite swallow-like or bat-like flight, jinking and turning. **ID:** Smaller and slimmer than WILPE with narrower white rump. A very dark bird lacking obvious pale carpal bar. White line on underwing is essential to clinch ID. Fast, light, butterfly-like flight different from much larger LEAPE.

Wilson's Petrel *Oceanites oceanicus* **WILPE** L 16cm

Very rare late summer and autumn visitor offshore, mainly to south-western approaches: Scilly, Cornwall, sw Ireland. Seen every year on pelagic trips, almost never from land. **ID:** Similar to STOPE in its compact silhouette, but with broader wings that have shorter 'arm'. Note pale band on upperwing (as LEAPE, unlike STOPE) and plain underwing (ditto). Tail quite broad. Fluttery swallow-like flight followed by distinctive flat-winged long glides, often back and forth across water. As STOPE, flight path often quite straight. Legs and feet (yellow webs) extend beyond tail, sometimes easy to see. Wing profile usually straight trailing edge and evenly curved leading edge.

Leach's Petrel *Oceanodroma leucorhoa* **LEAPE/TL** L 20cm ***s. 48,000***

Seldom-seen British breeding bird on isolated offshore islands in nw Scotland. Uses gaps between boulders and holes in walls and buildings for nest, visiting only at night. Otherwise pelagic. Seen from land in autumn gales, particularly in north-westerlies, some reaching inland lakes. **ID:** Largest storm petrel, with slim proportions and long, strongly angled wings. Strong pale carpal bar reaches leading edge of wing, contrasts strongly with outer wing. Broad white in rump forms a shallow V. Tail forked, but can be difficult to see. Bounding Nightjar-like flight with deep, jerky wingbeats with strong downstroke. Rocks from side to side and zigzags, changes direction suddenly.

White-winged Black Tern *Chlidonias leucopterus* **WWBTE/WJ** L 22cm

Rare migrant, most frequent in autumn, late Jul–Sep. May be found in freshwater marshes, over lakes, and on coast. Most likely in south and east. Very rare in spring. **ID:** Similar to BLATE but slightly chunkier with shorter thicker bill—a Little Gull in a tern's body. White tail and rump in all plumages. Ad br: stunning! Noticeably two-toned above and below: black coverts contrasting underneath; above and at rest whitish tail and white upperwing coverts contrast with dark body. Red legs. Juv/1st-w: paler upperparts than BLATE with whitish rump, gleaming white underparts lacking breast patch. Darker saddle in late summer. Isolated cheek spot, whiter forehead. Pale central wing panel.

Black Tern *Chlidonias niger* **BLATE/BJ** L 23cm

Once bred, but now a regular spring and autumn passage migrant to coasts, freshwater marshes, reservoirs and gravel pits. Commonest offshore where often in flocks. Frequently mixes with other tern species. Much commoner in autumn (mid-Jul–mid-Oct), numbers varying between years, sometimes in hundreds at traditional sites such as Hornsea Mere, Yorkshire. A 'marsh' tern that rarely plunge-dives but gracefully swoops down to pick food off the surface, or insects in mid-air. Its flight is buoyant and bouncy, jinking and tilting from side to side. Often perches on jetties, buoys, and the like. **ID:** Small, compact, with short square or slightly forked tail (other terns have sharply forked tails) and broad-based wings. Grey upperparts in all plumages noticeably darker than other regularly occurring terns. Ad br: striking black head and body with contrasting white vent. By late summer, moulting birds are blotchy black and white below. Nonbr: black cap and lobe down to behind eye. Pale underparts with dark patch on breast sides. Juv: similar to nonbr but has dark saddle on back with pale-fringed feathers. Colour varies from grey to brown.

Little Tern *Sterna albifrons* LITTE/AF L 23cm

JK: s. 1,900 pairs

Localised and uncommon summer visitor (Apr–Aug) to a few shingle or sandy coastal beaches next to sheltered feeding grounds. A dinky miniature tern, much smaller than relatives. Flies with slightly mechanical, stiff wingbeats, wings strongly angled back; looks a complete lightweight, sometimes gives impression of giant butterfly. An inveterate hoverer, usually just a few metres above very shallow water, close to shore, often several quick dives in sequence. Excited, squeaky, nasal call extends to chittering sequence. **ID:** Strikingly small compared to other terns; half as big as COMTE. Big headed and thick necked with narrow-based long wings and short tail. Legs orange-yellow. Ad br: obvious triangular white forehead and long yellow bill and black tip (bill colour the reverse of SANTE). Distinct black wedge created by black outer 3 primaries. Nonbr and 1st-s (retain old outer primaries): different head pattern, with streaks extending onto crown. Darker bill, and dark carpal bar on upperwing. Juv: bill dark, mantle and scapulars scaled with dark chequer markings, like SANTE. Dark covers contrast with grey mid-wing panel and panel secondaries in flight.

Common Tern *Sterna hirundo* **COMTE/CN** L 33cm

UK: s. 12,000 pairs

Common summer visitor (Apr–Sep) to coasts, marshes, rivers, large lakes, and gravel pits. The only tern that breeds inland in most of area. Nests in colonies, usually on beaches and islands, but also on 'tern rafts' provided on water bodies. As with other terns, is more angular than a gull, with sharp wingtips, long sharp bill, and long forked tail. Has elegant flight with deep wingbeats. Noisy, with sharp, irritable 'kip' notes and drawn-out, grating squeals. **ID:** A medium-sized tern that looks light grey at a distance, esp out to sea. In flight, wings look centrally placed on body. When standing, tail does not project beyond wingtips. Ad br: long red bill with black tip, large head with flat crown; red legs. Wings show dark 'wedge' where dark outer primaries meet paler inner primaries, most obvious from below. Also shows fairly broad dark border to outer wingtip. Nonbr: as adult with white on forecrown, large carpal bar (can appear small), dark bill, duller legs, and darker secondary bar. Juv: upperparts dark with subterminal marks, and initially warm brown (soon fades). Strong carpal bar and dark secondary bar.

Arctic Tern *Sterna paradisaea* **ARCTE/AE** L 34cm

UK: s. 53,000 pairs

Common northern tern, breeds mainly in Scotland and Ireland. Essentially coastal but some colonies are inland, for example, along rivers. Regular migrant elsewhere, often passing through south during narrow window in May (may be seen on reservoirs) and then Aug–Oct. **ID:** Very similar to COMTE. ID based largely on size and shape—ARCTE slightly smaller, 'neckless', with more rounded head and very short legs. This gives front-loaded feel in flight. Overall, flight lighter and bouncier, with slightly quicker wingbeats. When standing, tail projects beyond wingtips. Calls similar, but includes harsher rattling sounds. Ad br: from COMTE by shorter all-red bill, fractionally darker underparts with more contrasting white cheeks, longer tail projection, and narrower black trailing edge to upper- and underwing in flight. All primaries translucent, so no 'wedge' (see COMTE). Nonbr/1st-s: best differentiated by shape, paler appearance. Juv: white secondaries striking in flight (compare to dark bar in COMTE), usually shows less obvious carpal bar. May have more black on head. Overall, looks distinctly whiter than COMTE at this stage.

Roseate Tern *Sterna dougallii* **ROSTE/RS** L 36cm

UK: s. 89 pairs

Very rare summer visitor to a few offshore islands, May–Aug, most numerous in Ireland. Colonies on rocky islands and sandy beaches, often with tall vegetation. Mixes with other tern species. More widespread on migration, but still rare; inland records almost nonexistent. Feeds over shallow water, hovers less than other terns, and tends to dive in at a shallow angle—suddenly breaking off from level flight. Often detected by its distinctive *chivick* call. **ID:** The palest tern in the flock with strikingly fast, shallow, but stiff wingbeats that can be seen at distance. Long tail, exaggerated by short, slender wings; tail streamers project well beyond wings at rest. Narrow dark wedge to outerwing. Broad white inner web to primaries. Strikingly fine black bill, often red at base, particularly later in summer. Ad br: pale upperparts, white underparts often with pink flush. Legs orange-red. Nonbr: speckled crown, white forehead. Juv: unique bold black, chequered subterminal markings to upperparts (lacking brown of COMTE). Darker headed than other juv terns.

Sandwich Tern *Thalasseus sandvicensis* SANTE/TE L 38cm

UK: s. 12,000 pairs

Usually the first tern to arrive in the spring, often in Mar, and may depart as late as Nov; a few even overwinter on southern coasts. A numerous, assertive coastal tern, breeding in colonies on islands and shingle beaches. Noisy, drawing attention to itself by grating *kareek* call, easily recognised. Shows rather laboured, full wingbeats, patrols over the water, head down. Hovers and dives from higher than other terns, with dramatic splash. **ID:** A very pale two-toned tern, only ROSTE is whiter. Distinctive by combination of long and narrow yellow-tipped black bill ('tipped in mustard in sandwich'), shaggy crest, fairly large size, and shape. Very slim, particularly in flight, with long angled wings. Black legs, and dark primary wedge. Ad br: crested black cap. Nonbr: reduced cap by midsummer. Black eye bold on white face. 1st-yr: as nonbr with dark-centred tertials. Juv: black subterminal markings to upperparts (like ROSTE). Bill usually with yellow or orange, quickly becomes black. Yellow tip by spring.

Great Skua *Stercorarius skua* **GRESK/NX** L 56cm

Breeding bird of the Northern Isles, also found widely around most coasts on passage and in winter; main winter habitat is pelagic (far out to sea). Heavy-bodied troublemaker on breeding areas, where chases and intimidates birds (often tail-gating, grabbing wings or tail) up to size of GANNE to force them to drop food brought in for young. Some individuals also predators on STOPE or PUFFI, others eat fish out to sea. Often dive-bombs human and other animal nuisances when eggs or young in nest, may draw blood. Makes irritable *guk guk* calls in a huff. **ID:** Looks like bulky, barrel-shaped immature gull with conspicuous white wing-flashes. Wings broad-based but pointed, and flight is steady, without looseness of gull. Tail short, blunt. Gives impression of menace. Adult: all brown plumage with straw-coloured streaks, head with mask. Juv/imm: darker than ad, rich brown, lacks streaks on body, most of head darker (looks hooded). Shows much less variable plumage than other skuas.

Pomarine Skua *Stercorarius pomarinus* **POMSK/PK** L 48cm

Scarce passage migrant Apr–May, then again Aug–Nov, usually about 300 a year centred around East Coast, Western Isles, and English Channel. 'Poms' often migrate in packs. Chases mainly gulls, less tenacious than ARCSK, but sometimes kills birds; main food lemmings in Arctic. **ID:** Large and powerful, a bruiser. Plumage like ARCSK, but bulk and flight recall GRESK. Long wings and long tail, with flat undercarriage and bulging sternum. Powerful, steady flight with shallow wingbeats, less gliding than ARCSK. Wings broad-based and long. Long thick bill. Large white wing-flashes. Second pale flash formed by pale bases to greater coverts on underwing absent in smaller skuas. Colour phases vary from light (90%) to dark (10%). Adult: long central tail 'spoons'. Dark malar region gives 'mean' look. Broad breast band. Nonbr: central tail feathers shorter and blunt tipped. Barred rump and underparts. Juv/1st-yr: barred underwing and strongly barred underside. Head often with grey wash, lacks warm tones of ARCSK juv, and peppered, not streaked. Note long and thick bill with obvious contrast of black tip and grey base.

Arctic Skua *Stercorarius parasiticus* **ARCSK/AC** L 44cm

UK: s. 2,100 pairs

Much the commonest skua in Britain and the easiest to see, passing most coasts on migration Apr–May and Jul–Oct. Breeds only in north of Scotland on coastal moorland and islands. Rare inland, but flies high and may be overlooked. Endlessly harasses and intimidates gulls and terns, catching dropped or regurgitated food, including during migration. **ID:** Smaller than HERGU and slim. Raptor-like seabird: wings often seem pointed and swept back. Fast direct flight with snappy wingbeats. Pointed central tail feathers in all plumages. Long slim bill. Ad light br: dark cap; lacks really 'mean' look of POMSK. Pale area at base of bill. Paler upperparts than POMSK, browner than LOTSK. Pointed tail, shorter than LOTSK. Dark birds brown, often looking black at distance, palest around neck. Ad nonbr: similar to imm but underwing solid brown. Usually has flank and vent barring. 2nd-yr: as ad nonbr with some retained juv feathers, notably on underwing coverts. Juv/1st-yr: variable colours from ginger to dark brown. All with narrow pale fringes to feathers, including primary tips. Head and nape streaked, and often noticeably warm brown.

Long-tailed Skua *Stercorarius longicaudus* **LOTSK/OG** L 50cm

Rare passage migrant, most regular in Western Isles and Ireland; May then Jul–Oct. Numbers vary. Often suddenly stops with wings raised and drops to water, swims. Inoffensively eats insects, unlike other skuas, and rarely chases birds. **ID:** Usually small and buoyant with tern-like flight; other skuas larger, heavier. Long tail, narrow-based wings with flattish undercarriage, deepest at sternum. Pigeon-like head shape with small bill. Typically only outer 2 primary shafts white. Ad br: white breasted, neat cap, and paler grey-brown back. Long central tail feathers. Juv: variable. Colder tones than other skuas. Blunt central tail feathers.

Sabine's Gull *Xema sabini* **SABGU/AB** L 30cm

Rare Arctic gull (100–200 seen per year), usually driven inshore by autumn storms; migrates far out to sea. A beautiful, diminutive gull with tern-like qualities and striking upperwing comprising triangle patterns. **ID:** Very large wings, small head, and forked tail. Often mistaken for larger juv KITTI, which has narrower M pattern across back. Ad br: black-bordered grey hood kept into autumn. Pale-tipped black bill. Ad nonbr: dark nape on pale head. 2nd-s: as nonbr with heavily worn flight feathers. Juv: dark neck and browner overall. Colour can be difficult to judge at distance. Black tail band.

Kittiwake *Rissa tridactyla* **KITTI/KI** L 39cm

UK: s. 380,000 pairs

Best known for forming large, dense, spectacular colonies on rocky cliff faces, the nests often placed on ludicrously small prominences far above the thundering waves. Widespread breeder, pelagic in winter, sometimes within sight of land, particularly in bad weather. Plunge-dives into water for fish. Named after its caterwauling *kitti-WAAke* calls, a dominant sound of seacliffs. **ID:** An attractive, dainty, clean, and well-proportioned gull. Medium-grey upperparts. Short black legs, yellow bill, and dark eye. Buoyant but powerful flyer with long, slim body and wings. Wings usually held straight and stiff. Sometimes elbow is pushed forward, creating W along leading edge of wing, making wings look slimmer. Stiff shallow wingbeats. Easy to overlook as COMGU, but slimmer, slightly darker, with distinctive squared-off black wingtip and different flight style. Ad br: white head. Nonbr: grey spot to rear of ear coverts. 2nd-yr: as adult but some have more extensive black in wing. Juv/1st-yr: bold W pattern on upperparts. Some have dark ear spot and collar, others all white as adult. Black tail band. Black bill becomes yellow in spring/summer.

Mediterranean Gull *Larus melanocephalus* **MEDGU/MU** L 37cm

UK: s. 600-630 pairs
w. 1,800

Uncommon but increasing gull found principally on the South Coast and East Anglia; badly named as it originates from Black Sea. Breeds on salt marshes and lagoons, but often feeds in fields inland from coast, on invertebrates, including flying insects; coastal in winter. Easiest to find among gatherings of BLHGU, but also associates with COMGU inland. **ID:** Medium sized, with relatively thick blob-tipped bill and long legs. Adults similar to BLHGU but larger, and wings broad-based and rather short, giving distinctive shallow, stiff wingbeats. Upperparts very pale. Makes distinctive, nasal, exclamatory *yeah* call. Adults easily identified by clean white wingtips, almost egret-like. Ad br: smart true-black hood, with white eye-crescents; bright red bill and legs. Ad nonbr: distinctive dark mask or 'bruise' behind eye. 2nd-w: as ad but confusingly, has uneven black marks behind wingtip. Juv: odd; dark back with white scales, plain head, whitish breast, black bill and legs; 1st-w sim to 1st-w COMGU, but less brown on wings, white underwing and underparts, dark mask.

Common Gull *Larus canus* COMGU/CM L 41cm

UK: s. 49,000 pairs
w. 710,000

Often claimed to be misnamed, but hardly rare. Often abundant in Scotland and Ireland. Easily overlooked as it is lightly built, but has plumage rather similar to its big brother HERGU. Colonial nester on islands in lakes and on moorland. In winter, often inland on playing fields, esp, agricultural fields; eats worms and the like. Regularly foot-paddles in puddles. Makes remarkable ear-splitting high-pitched squeal, unlike ringing tones of other gulls. **ID:** Bulkier and healthier looking than BLHGU, lacking any red on bill or legs. Adult: plumage sim to HERGU, but has much darker, cold-winter's-day grey on upperparts; also more rounded head, petite bill, and dark eye, giving peaceful expression. Slightly larger mirrors on wing, often show as conspicuous white blobs on end of wing. Ad br: white head, yellow bill, greenish legs. Nonbr: head and breast strongly flecked with peppery dots, bill green with black subterminal band. 2nd-w: as ad but more black on wings. Juv: brown scaly upperparts, brown mottled underparts. 1st-w: as ad nonbr but grey mantle contrasts neatly with well-defined brown coverts; black tail band, pink legs, pink bill with black tip.

Black-headed Gull *Chroicocephalus ridibundus* **BLHGU/BH** L 36cm

UK: s. 140,000 pairs
w. 2,200,000

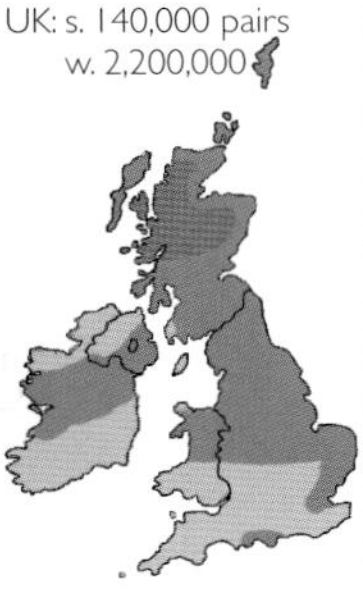

Superabundant small gull, seemingly everywhere in winter, from park lakes and playing fields to all kinds of marshes, seaside, rivers, reservoirs, gravel pits, and so on. Breeds on salt and freshwater marshes, lakes, and moorland. The gull seen competing with ducks for bread, following the plough, pulling worms from fields. As noisy as it is ubiquitous, making irritable *kek* and rolling *kreer*, lacks loud cackling of other gulls. Often in very large flocks. **ID:** 2-yr gull. Small and skinny with sharp wingtips, red/orange bill and legs. All stages show striking white isosceles triangle on upper forewing. Ad br: brown (not black!) hood, white nape, and white eyelids. Bill often bright red, legs dark red. Ad nonbr: hood disappears to leave dark ear spot and slight smudge around eye. 1st-w: orange-and-black bill, orange legs, more dark on primaries, brown carpal bar. 1st-s: as adult, but head not usually pure brown. Moults to adult winter. Juv: Odd plumage with dark tan or brown blotches on head and mantle, brown-spotted wings, often doesn't look like a gull at first.

Little Gull *Hydrocoloeus minutus* **LITGU/LU** L 26cm

Scarce passage migrant and winter visitor, seen both on the sea (winter) and also on inland freshwater marshes, reservoirs, and gravel pits. World's smallest gull (two-thirds size of BLHGU), has tern-like manner of foraging, wavering over water and dipping down to pick up edible fragments; faster wingbeats than other gulls. **ID:** Very small and compact, with slender black bill. Ads have diagnostic black underwings, white tips; wings rounded. Ad br: sooty black head. Ad nonbr: black ear spot, black crown. 2nd-w: as ad but black specks near wingtip. Juv/1st-w: black W across upperwing, dark secondary bar.

Ring-billed Gull *Larus delawarensis* **RIBGU/IN** L 45cm ***w. 22***

Very rare nonbreeding visitor from US, 50–70 records a year. Singles among gull flocks on coast, individuals often return to winter sites. Walks around a lot on long legs. **ID:** Closely related to COMGU, but larger and more thick-set, with much broader bill. Adult: pale eyes, yellow legs, paler back than COMGU (= HERGU), bill yellow with bold black subterminal band, smaller wing-mirrors than COMGU, smaller white tertial crescent. 1st-w: as COMGU but smaller pale fringes to dark tertials, brown flecks on mantle, grey band on greater wing coverts.

Herring Gull *Larus argentatus* **HERGU/HG** L 60cm

UK: s. 140,000 pairs
w. 740,000

Big, bad-tempered gull, the abundant loud-mouthed character in seaside towns and, increasingly, in some urban centres. Belts out a clanging 'long call'; also makes fast paced *ga-ga-ga-ga* in alarm. Often found at landfills in winter, sometimes in huge numbers, roosting on reservoirs, but essentially coastal. Nests on cliffs, beaches, dunes, buildings, and the like. **ID:** 4-yr gull. To birders the common, large, pink-legged 'default' gull. Big, with heavy body and blunt rear end. Large bill, with flat crown producing angry expression; angular headed. Ad br: paler grey mantle than similar species. Deep yellow bill with orange spot. Ad nonbr: copiously streaked/mottled head and neck. Bill paler. 3rd-yr: as adult with some dark in coverts, tail, and bill. Juv/1st-yr: blotchy brown all over, not as white on head as similar species. Dusky mask around eye, oak-leaf patterned tertials and greater wing coverts. Dark bill. 2nd-w: blotchy brown, but develops clean grey on mantle. Scandinavian populations (subsp. *argentatus*) slightly larger, with fractionally darker grey mantle and more white on wingtips.

Yellow-legged Gull *Larus michahellis* **YELGU/YG** L 63cm ***w. 1,100***

Scarce European visitor, particularly late summer to south coast on coastal marshes, reservoirs, tips. **ID:** 4-yr gull. Ads often look immaculate. Slightly larger than HERGU, but has long wings and pointed rear like LBBGU. Compared with HERGU, older birds show slightly darker mantle, yellow legs, extensive black square-ended wingtips, orange-red orbital ring, larger bill, pale head (only a few streaks around eye in winter). 1st-yr: unlike HERGU, notably white headed, dark tertials with narrow white fringes; very similar to large-billed LBBGU.

Caspian Gull *Larus cachinnans* **CASGU/YC** L 60cm ***w. 90***

Rare visitor from Eastern Europe to coasts and reservoirs, currently about 20 records per year. **ID:** Most easily recognised by unusual shape, with long, narrow, parallel-sided bill, weirdly small head on long neck, long legs, and more attenuated rear end than others. Eye dark, even in adults, and beady, looking too small for head. In ads the back is slightly paler than in YELGU and the legs have a greenish cast. Imm stages show white head with smudge around eye, dark tertials. Best to look for body shape.

Iceland Gull *Larus glaucoides* **ICEGU/IG** L 56cm ***w. 240***

Scarce winter visitor (Nov–Mar), commonest in northern Scottish harbours and isles. **ID:** 4-yr gull. Like snow-blasted version of HERGU, with white wingtips; in winter head and neck slush coloured, legs raw pink. Smaller than HERGU and GLAGU, with short, delicate bill and rounded, dovelike head with 'kind' expression. Elegant, not lumbering in flight, with long, pointed wings that give attenuated rear end at rest. Immature stages plain coffee coloured, with pale wingtips. 1st-w has blackish bill at first with little pink at base, but soon more like GLAGU.

Glaucous Gull *Larus hyperboreus* **GLAGU/GZ** L 65cm ***w. 170***

Hardy northern species, scarce winter visitor (Nov–Mar), esp to Scotland. Usually coastal, but sometimes turns up at inland reservoirs or rubbish tips in depths of winter. **ID:** 4-yr gull. Bigger and bulkier than ICEGU and HERGU, and compared to ICEGU, the other large gull with white wingtips, has longer parallel-sided bill and flatter head, giving fierce expression. Front-heavy, with shorter wing-point and primary projection. Immature stages have coffee-coloured plumage; check bill for neat black tip. Plumage whitens with age.

Lesser Black-backed Gull *Larus fuscus* **LBBGU/LB** L 58cm

UK: s. 110,000 pairs
w. 130,000

Numerous and familiar gull, breeding on moorland, dunes, grassy cliff slopes, and islands, often in large colonies. In winter, darker-backed birds from Scandinavia augment population, some breeders migrate south away from country. Small groups often seen migrating overland, esp Mar–Apr. Smarter, gentler version of HERGU, making a distinctive, more nasal call. Less common around tips, and more likely to catch fish at sea than HERGU. **ID:** 4-yr gull. Very elegant for a larger gull, with long, pointed wings and slender body evident at rest and in flight. Slightly smaller than most HERGU, and much smaller than hulking GBBGU. Has narrower bill and more rounded head. Ad/3rd-yr: dark grey mantle (between HERGU and GBBGU, but see below), yellow legs, extensive black on wingtips, usually 1 mirror. Head heavily streaked in nonbr plumage. 1st-yr: dark upperparts with dark area around eye. Often easy to spot in flight—uniform upperwing pattern, with completely dark outer half, dark underwing, contrasting with white 'rump' and dark tail band. Bill black with some pale after a year. Legs pink until 3rd year

Great Black-backed Gull *Larus marinus* GBBGU/GB L 71cm

UK: s. 17,000 pairs
w. 77,000

Very common on n Atlantic coast, less numerous S; often seen lounging on beaches. Scarcer inland. Survives frozen N by adopting versatile diet (using huge bill). Scavenges but also kills live prey, including birds such as AMCO. **ID:** 4-yr gull. A real tank. Our largest gull, and bulky with a killer-like thick bill. Darkest-backed common gull with short wings. Dark colours add to mean appearance, but overall impression is clean and bold. Younger birds' contrasting plumage is neat and fairly distinctive. If in doubt, look at that bill. Ad br: dark gray and white. Bright yellow bill with red spot. Pink legs. Ad nonbr: a few dusky marks on head but still essentially white-headed. Some have black bill spot next to red. 3rd-yr: variable number of imm feathers in wing, variable black on bill and, generally, some black in tail. Juv to 2nd-s: superficially similar with boldly checkered upperparts and well-defined markings on underparts. Pale-headed. Strongly patterned tail. Juv: mantle and scapulars show fairly uniform dark centers and broad pale fringes. New feathers, moulted through first winter, have more complicated internal markings. Bill typically mostly dark until 2nd-s, when also starts to get dark adult-like mantle.

WALKING WATERBIRDS

An incredibly diverse and interesting group of birds, waders (or shorebirds) are popular for two reasons: they are fairly common in suitable habitat, usually wet areas but also certain types of fields, tidal flats, and beaches; and a number of different species are often seen together, giving repeated opportunities for comparison.

The majority of species breed on inaccessible northern tundra and moors, so they are seen most frequently during migration or on their wintering grounds much farther south. Turnover at these spots can be high, so repeated visits will invariably yield new birds. Looking out onto a marsh at hundreds of birds can seem confusing initially, even overwhelming; however, with decent views (a telescope always helps) and prolonged careful observation, people are often surprised by how much can be learned; what may first appear as a lot of 'little brown jobs' can end up as 10 different species in an intriguing mix of plumages. Size and shape, as with all birds, are crucial in getting to grips with identification.

It can be difficult to get close to birds on a mudflat or marsh area, and judging size is not always easy. Remember, a bird's size is hard to measure precisely in the field, and the real value of size is for comparison between individuals. Careful observation of relative differences in size is very important. After size, look at shape. Important factors are bill length and shape, and leg length. Behaviour and feeding styles are also great clues for successful ID.

In some cases, birds have longer legs for wading in deeper water, and thus they need longer bills with which to feed. On the other hand, birds such as plovers are found on mud, sand, or short grass. They can run to their prey and pick it up in a deliberate fashion with their short bills (run-and-pick style). Colour is useful, but many birds tend to be shades of grey and brown, creating real ID challenges. More pertinent are the patterns of colour—the areas of light and dark and the contrast between them. Learning to think in black and white can be helpful here.

Probability can also play a major role. Often we identify a distant flock to species largely on the basis of the abundance of birds. For example, a thousand small waders crawling over a tidal flat on the Wirral will almost certainly be Dunlin. Familiarity with the area and a full appreciation of probability of occurrence is a huge help!

In many cases, it is important to age or know the specific plumage of the bird before we can identify it. As a broad generalization, juveniles look very tidy, often with lots of buff colouring and neatly patterned upperparts (many described as 'scaly'), and breasts with a buff wash or neatly patterned streaking. Adults often show a combination of breeding and nonbreeding feathers, lacking the neat pattern of juveniles. Adult waders typically moult twice a year: once in spring to create breeding plumage and once in fall to create nonbreeding plumage. Most juveniles also moult into nonbreeding plumage during fall and superficially look like adults but can usually be aged by retained juvenile wing coverts, which they keep through the winter. Some species moult into an adult-like plumage in spring, others typically appear as nonbreeding birds with a number of breeding-type feathers mixed in; however, it's variable, with some in complete nonbreeding and others in full breeding plumage. Many immatures stay on the wintering grounds; some move north while others reach the breeding grounds. They moult into nonbreeding plumage during the summer, typically earlier than adults.

A number of shorebirds travel amazing distances from the high Arctic to South Africa, often flying for days without stopping. Recent research has shown that they essentially shut down organs to conserve energy. The importance of being able to feed effectively during or before migration cannot be underestimated. Waders need to double their body weight within a week or two at these stopovers.

Birds that travel long distances all have one feature in common: very long wings, a feature that can be seen on sitting birds and is an important feature in ID for certain wader species, for example, Red Knot and Pectoral Sandpiper. These wing feathers are never moulted on migration (a hole in any wing is never a good thing!). Birds that winter locally or do not have to travel so far generally have shorter wings, giving them more agility, and they often moult while on migration. This is useful to know.

Waders are often seen in flight, frequently in mixed flocks. A raptor flying over often flushes everything. This can be frustrating but also provides a different set of ID playing cards. This is when waders are most vocal, and many have distinctive calls. Tail patterns and wing bars are good features to look for. Sometimes large flocks will divide and sort by species. The one out on its own is often the 'goodie' that was missed on the ground.

Herons and egrets are a common sight, particularly in coastal marshes. They are usually conspicuous because of their large size and tendency to feed in accessible, open areas. Their beauty always draws admirers. In the past, demand for their ornate plumes resulted in large declines in populations.

Heron and egret are loose terms, with some overlap. Egrets tend to be white and slimmer. They spear fish and small insects, but will catch other prey such as frogs and crabs. Prey is usually eaten whole, and it is not uncommon to see birds with swollen 'cobra-like' necks as they struggle to swallow their catch.

Moult timing in herons tends to be variable, as do the resulting plumages. Ageing these birds is often difficult. For a few weeks, at the peak of breeding season, when birds are courting ('high breeding'), bare parts, particularly legs and lores, change to brighter colours, usually reds and pinks. Herons tend to prefer warmer climates; hence there is a more southerly bias to their distribution. Global warming has resulted in a northerly range expansion of most species. Little Egret, with only a few records annually as recently as the 1980s, has shown the most pronounced increase. Nowadays, Little Egrets are fairly common, particularly in the south, and some roosts may have more than 100 birds.

Rails live in marshes. They are primarily nocturnal but often seen in the daytime. Adverse weather, particularly flooding but also freezes, will make them easier to find. They are often vocal but usually stay frustratingly well hidden, occasionally coming to edges, where they remain very wary. The term 'thin as a rail' comes from their slim profile, a body shape that allows them to fit between reed stems. They frequently run for cover and fly as a last resort. They sometimes swim to cross gaps and even go under water to escape predators. Rail chicks start walking the marshes with Mum when only a few days old—they are small and black. They lose the black feathers as they grow to full size in the following weeks. By September or October, most juveniles have moulted into adult-like plumage.

Grey Plover *Pluvialis squatarola* GREPL/GV L 28cm

UK: w. 43,000

Common winter visitor to estuaries and sandy beaches. May gather in large numbers at roost sites, but at low tide bad tempered, and individuals space themselves out, some maintaining territories. As with other plovers, has distinctive run-stop-pick feeding style, easy distinction from KNOT or REDSH. **ID:** Easily the largest and heaviest of the plover group, with muscular neck and large body. A big head and large bill give it a distinctive 'not-to-be-messed-with' appearance. Bill size rules out all other plovers, allows it to deal with tough shellfish. In flight, diagnostic black armpits, white rump, and far-carrying atmospheric 3-note *plu-wee-oo* call tend to be a giveaway. Ad ♂ br: boldly spangled upperparts with grey crown diagnostic at distance. White vent contrasts strongly with black underparts. Ad ♀ br: subdued browner and less striking version of ♂. On migration, many pass through in a mottled combination of br and nonbr plumage. Nonbr/1st-s: pale underparts, but upperparts still studded with white spangles; brown wash on breast sides. Juv: as nonbr but with more boldly fringed upperparts and distinct streaking on underparts.

European Golden Plover *Pluvialis apricaria* **GOLPL/GP** L 28cm

UK: s. 38,400–59,400 pairs
w. 420,000

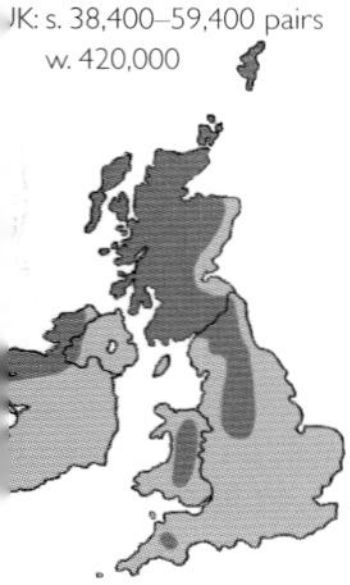

Fairly common breeding bird, mainly in northern bogs, moorland, and upland pasture. In winter, continental birds swell the population, and occur on farmland, fields, grassland, and, sometimes, estuaries. Often seen on inland fields with LAPWI, but when flushed, flocks separate, the GOLPL into tight units that form ovals or Vs high in the air, often wheeling around many times before finally landing. Feeds in stop-start manner typical of plovers. Gorgeous high-pitched display call has tragic ring, uttered from high aloft; at same time white underwings glint. Call high-pitched, crystal-clear, single short whistle.

ID: Smaller than GREPL, with much thinner bill. Plump wader with sharply pointed wings, white axillaries; fast wingbeats. As name implies, plumage always has golden wash, upperparts spangled. Ad br: beautiful gold-studded upperparts contrast with inky-black underparts from throat down to belly, including cheeks, bordered by white. In ♀, black not as bold, more diffuse around edges, little on head. Ad nonbr: black lost, giving dense streaking on breast, contrasts with whiter belly. Juv similar, neater pattern on upperparts. 1st-s may have little black on underparts.

Northern Lapwing *Vanellus vanellus* **LAPWI/L.** L 30cm

UK: s. 140,000 pairs
w. 650,000

Much declined but still widespread breeding bird on arable farmland, meadows, and wetlands; common in winter in similar habitats, sometimes estuaries. Prone to making evacuation movements during frost and snow. Feeds in large black-and-white flocks, forages by standing still, then elegantly running, almost on tiptoe, to snatch item from ground or to stand still again. Eats earthworms and other soil invertebrates. Rounded wings give unmistakable shape, flies with shallow, floppy wingbeats, at distance looks like ash blowing in wind. Loud, unmistakable whining call *pee-wit!* develops into whooping, madcap display song in barely controlled flight, which includes thud ding wingbeats and sound like peeling sellotape **ID:** Unique wispy crest, iridescent green/purpl upperparts, fudge-coloured undertail coverts wings contrasting black and white from be low. Ad ♂ br: tall wispy crest as long as head solid black throat, broad outer wings. Ad ♀ br shorter crest and 'messy' white-mottled throa and breast. Nonbr: throat white, black ban across chest, buff on face and nape; subtle scal pattern on back (buff fringes). Juv: as nonb but very short, stumpy crest and more obvi ous pale fringes to coverts, scapulars, tertials

Dotterel *Charadrius morinellus* **DOTTE/DO** L 21cm ***s. 630***

Rare summer visitor (late Apr–Aug) to high plateaux in Scotland, where breeds on flat rocky areas. Traditional migration stop-off points on open fields and hilltops further south. Hard to find but often tame; almost silent. Practises curious 'role-reversal', with more colourful female initiating displays, male incubating eggs and tending young. **ID:** Small compact plover with prominent supercilia; green legs; always shows white band across breast, good feature in nonbr. Ad br: white supercilium, rich chestnut breast, black belly; ♂ duller. Nonbr: pleasing brown-grey, with narrow buff fringes to wing feathers, band across breast. Juv/1st-w: dark wings with broad buff fringes giving strong scaly pattern.

Kentish Plover *Charadrius alexandrinus* **KENPL** L 16cm

Rare visitor to beaches and shallow saline pools, usually in spring. Frequently makes long runs, legs disappear in blur. **ID:** Distinguished from RINPL and LIRPL by distinctive shape, incomplete breast band, leg color. In flight, shows strong white wing bars, as RINPL. Ad ♂ br: black eye-stripe, rich reddish brown hind crown. Ad ♀ br/nonbr: pale bleached brown, with white forehead, white collar. Juv: paler.

American Golden Plover *Pluvialis dominica* **AMGPL** L 24cm

Rare vagrant sometimes found with flocks of stockier GOLPL. **ID:** Likely to be picked out by its dark underwings, contrasting with glinting white of accompanying GOLPLs, or in nonbr by its generally darker, greyish upperparts with lack of bright golden wash. May look like GREPL among Goldens, esp with prominent pale supercilium. In breeding birds, plumage much darker above and blacker below than GOLPL.

Common Ringed Plover *Charadrius hiaticula* RINPL/RP L 19cm

UK: s. 5,400 pairs
w. 36,000

Fairly common breeding wader of shingle and other types of beaches, plus islands and, in places, inland gravel workings and pits. Common in winter and in migration in similar habitats, and also occurs in large numbers at estuaries and mudflats. Bold head pattern is disruptive camouflage, to break up shape of bird. In breeding season, often suffers from disturbance on beaches, has famous 'broken wing' distraction display. Call is gentle, liquid *too-ip*, call elaborated into rolling song. **ID:** Much the commonest 'ringed' plover, and the only one likely ever to be seen in numbers of 10+ (up to 100s at estuarine roost). Stop-start feeding action distinguishes from other small waders. Has white wing bar and stumpy bill, often with orange base; orange legs. Ad br: bold black head-markings, broad complete black collar; orange bill with black tip (in ♀ slightly less boldly marked). Nonbr: similar but black turns dark-brown, bill pattern less clear. Obvious white supercilium. Breast band thickest at breast sides, pinched in at front. Juv: as nonbr, but pale fringes to upperpart feathers give subtle scaly appearance.

Little Ringed Plover *Charadrius dubius* LIRPL/LP L 14cm

UK: s. 1,200 pairs

Delicate but perky summer visitor to gravel pits, workings, and the margins of freshwater lakes and rivers. A very early arrival, often appearing in mid-Mar. Very different from RINPL in sticking to fresh water—not seen on estuaries or salt water; and never gathers in large flocks—half a dozen is a lot. More horizontal in posture than RINPL and has smaller head and attenuated rear end. Main display call is tern-like *cree-a, cree-a*, usually uttered at night. **ID:** 'Feminine' version of RINPL: more elegant and trim. Easily distinguished in flight by lack of white wing bar. Also thinner, black bill and duller legs. Lower rear edge of black ear coverts pointed (rounded in RINPL). Ad br: easily distinguished from RINPL by bright yellow eye-ring; also thinner black breast band, white band behind black band on crown. Juv: less obvious eye-ring than br, scaly on back head markings indistinct. From RINPL by lack of whitish supercilium. Ad nonbr: rarely seen, washed-out version of ad br.

Eurasian Oystercatcher *Haematopus ostralegus* **OYSTE/OC** L 42cm

UK: s. 110,000 pairs
w. 340,000

Familiar wader of estuaries and shorelines; also breeds inland by lakes and rivers, and sometimes in fields. Astonishingly noisy: volume settings are loud and very loud. Birds in pairs and flocks often perform piping display, bills pointed down and open, facing each other, and this can be deafening. In flocks birds feed well apart, but large numbers can gather at roost, closely packed. Main call is exclamatory *ke-BEEK*! Probes in mud for worms and shellfish and often hammers heavy bill to open them.

ID: Unmistakable bulky black-and-white wader with long, straight, bright orange bill, red eye-ring and plastic pink legs. In flight shows striking white wing bar. Ad br: black head and chest contrasting with white breast and belly; upperparts black. Nonbr: acquires white chin-strap across throat. Juv/1st-w: duller black with brown tint. Bill with 'dirty' tip (beware: sometimes similar on adults that have probed in mud) and legs pale pink-brown. Develops chin-strap and may retain it into 1st summer. Bill still with dark tip.

Avocet *Recurvirostra avosetta* **AVOCE/AV** L 44cm

UK: s. 1,500 pairs
w. 7,500

Scarce and localised lanky wader, mainly confined to saline lagoons and sheltered muddy estuaries. Instantly recognisable by unique, strongly uptilted 'designer' bill with fine, fragile tip. Feeds in elegant fashion, stooping down to sweep bill through shallows or very soft mud, moving head mechanically from side to side in 'watching tennis rally' fashion; touch receptors detect shrimps and other particles in solution. Is a proper wader, often paddling up to thighs and out of its depth, where it swims easily. Flies strongly with regular beats, legs trailing far behind, often in neatly disciplined flocks. Sociable, nesting in small colonies and forming winter gatherings, but quarrelsome, aggressive both to its own kind and to other birds. Noisy when breeding, uttering a loud, somewhat breathy *kluut*. **ID:** Unmistakable with decent view. White with neat black lines, unusual blue legs. Ad ♀ has shorter and more sharply uptilted bill than ♂. Juv: black markings tinged brown, with smudged brown coverts. Some brown-tinged feathers retained into 1st summer.

Eurasian Curlew *Numenius arquata* **CURLE/CU** L 55cm

UK: s. 68,000 pairs
w. 150,000

Familiar in spring and summer from upland moors and bogs, where its rich, ecstatic bubbling song, delivered in a flight-display, provides a rarefied soundscape. Also common on estuaries and coasts, esp in winter, where loud, liquid onomatopoeic *cour-li* call is equally atmospheric. A giant that dwarfs all other waders feeding or roosting on an estuary—it looks as though it could swallow a Dunlin whole. The exaggerated long, curved bill is used for probing into soft mud, down crab burrows, and under seaweed; also catches insects and worms in grass. Flies with slow wingbeats similar in pace to a large gull, flies in disciplined lines, usually low down; sometimes glides before landing. **ID:** Unmistakable tall, straw-coloured wader, but see WHIMB. Length and curvature of bill vary: ad ♀ has longest, most strongly curved bill, juv ♂ has shortest (sim to WHIMB). Barred tail and white slit up back. Has plain head compared with WHIMB. Wings show contrast between dark outer wings and pale inner wing. Sexes alike, but juv has more even streaks down breast.

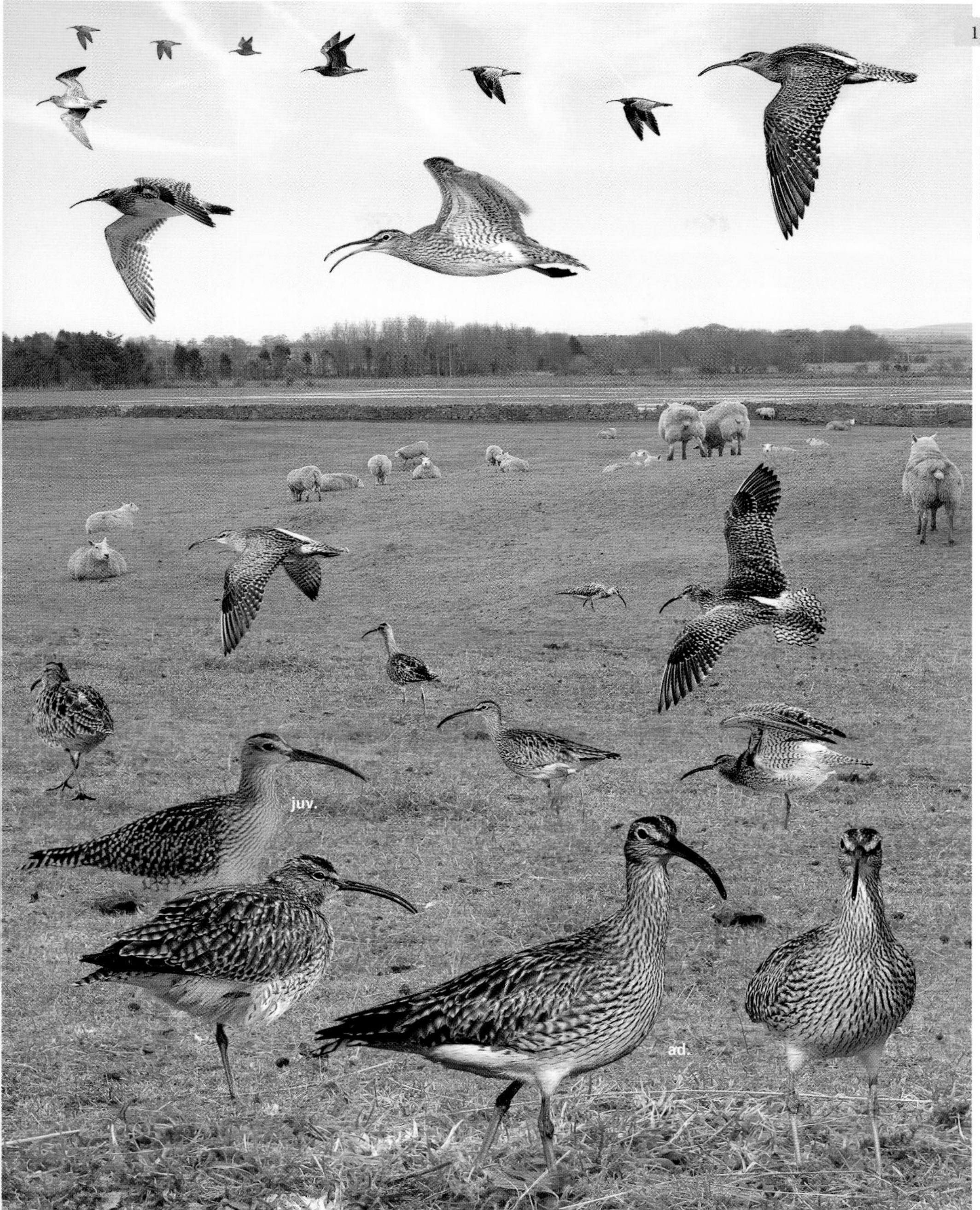

Whimbrel *Numenius phaeopus* **WHIMB/WM** L 41cm

UK: s. 400-500 pairs
w. 30

Rare summer visitor to northern bogs and dry heather. Widespread and numerous passage migrant Apr–May and Jul–Sep, occurring on beaches, rocky coasts, and grassland, as well as inland by reservoirs and gravel pits. Not usually among roll-call of winter estuarine waders. Often detected by fast-paced approx 7-note tittering call *pupupu...* on level pitch. Makes song-flight on breeding grounds like CURLE, but shorter, less wavering. **ID:** Very similar in plumage to CURLE, but decidedly smaller and with a different bill shape: bill tends to look straight with kinked tip, rather than evenly curved. Also shows more stripy head, with dark eye-stripe, pale supercilium, and dark crown-sides, with narrow pale stripe along top of crown. In flight, has noticeably faster, more purposeful wingbeats than CURLE. Wings are more evenly dark than CURLE's, but white slit up back is similar. Background colour is slightly darker than that of CURLE and, combined with smaller size and stripy head, can make it surprisingly easy to identify. Juv: fresher and subtly bolder upperparts than otherwise similar adult.

Bar-tailed Godwit *Limosa lapponica* **BATGO/BA** L 38cm

UK: w. 41,000

Numerous but fairly local winter visitor to selected larger estuaries; more widespread passage migrant. Well known for gathering in large numbers, feeding on mudflats and roosting in large groups, often well immersed up to belly. Often 'stitches', immersing bill in mud several times in quick succession, touch-feeding. Rare inland, sometimes touches down at reservoir banks or similar during migration in May. **ID:** Different shape than BLTGO, with shorter legs, esp above tibiotarsal joint ('knee'), and frankly, legs look too short for bird itself, conferring slightly awkward gait. Neck much shorter. Bill usually looks more uptilted than BLTGO's; in flight, shows plain wing with no white bars, instead long white slit up back and whitish tail with many bars. At all times, shows rather streaky, CURLE-like upperparts. Ad ♂ br shows typical brick red of godwit, more intense than in BLTGO and covers whole underparts to vent; ad ♀ red-wine stained on underparts; ad nonbr lacks red, just grey-brown, with long white supercilium and pink bill with black tip. Looks like straight-billed CURLE at distance. Juv similar, buffier.

Black-tailed Godwit *Limosa limosa* BLTGO/BW L 42cm

UK: s. 61–66 pairs
w. 44,000

The very small British breeding population (*limosa*) is found in flooded meadows and northern bogs, but most familiar in winter when Icelandic birds (*islandica*) are found on southern muddy estuaries, marshes, and wet pasture. If a godwit is seen on or near fresh water or inland, it is virtually always this species. Very much a paddler, wading in deep water to feed, immersing its head and bill completely to probe bottom sediment. Sociable but, like BATGO, not noisy, making the odd whining *wicka*. **ID:** Much lankier than BATGO, with longer legs (esp above 'knee') and longer neck. Easy to recognise in flight by its silhouette of long bill and long legs, by broad white wing bar, and by 50:50 black/white tail. Ad ♂ br: brick red on underparts only reaches to belly, not vent, amidst slightly messy barring; ad ♀ less brick red. Nonbr: no red, just plain grey-brown on head, neck, and upperparts, lacking streaks; white supercilium only in front of eye. Juv: reddish head and neck, grey with brown spots on wings/mantle. Race *islandica* generally shows more intense reddish colour.

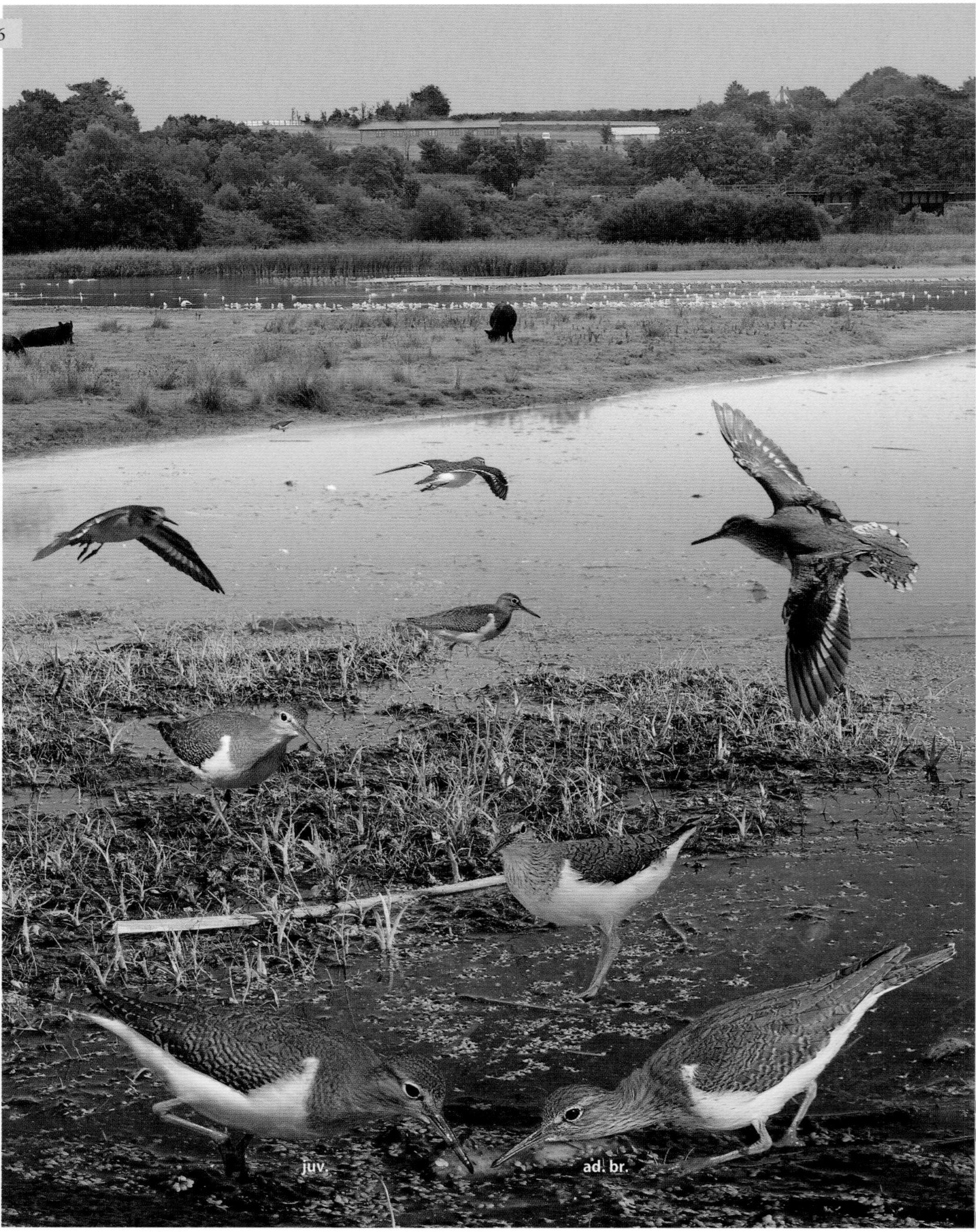

Common Sandpiper *Actitis hypoleucos* **COMSA/CS** L 60in

UK: s. 15,000 pairs
w. 73

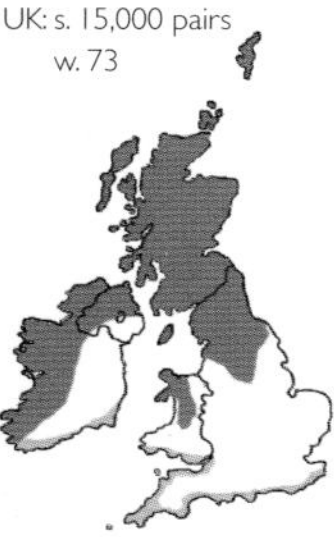

Highly distinctive summer visiting wader that breeds by fast-flowing streams and lakes in the uplands. Widespread on migration on lake shores, gravel pits, muddy lagoons, and the like, and small numbers winter on the shoreline of sheltered estuaries. Walks on its short legs in crouched fashion, continually bobbing its rear end up and down, which on its own is often enough to identify it. Also has most unusual flickering flight, low and very close to the water surface, using curious irregular, stiff wingbeats, wings bowed. Notes are piccolo-like and pure: call is 3–4 notes, falling in pitch, while song is a cyclical repetition of similar notes. **ID:** Shares fairly long, straight bill with *Tringa* waders, but legs shorter and tail sticks well beyond wings at rest. Olive-brown above in all plumages and neat white below, with slit or 'comma' reaching up breast sides around wing (not in GRESA or WOOSA); sharp contrast between breast and belly. Wings with central white wing bar. Sexes alike. Ad br: dark bars above. Ad nonbr: similar to juv but more uniform above. Juv: scaly above, dark bars on wings.

Greenshank *Tringa nebularia* GRESH/GK L 32cm

UK: s. 700–1,500 pairs
w. 610

Best known as a passage migrant on freshwater lakes, gravel pits, scrapes, marshes, and meadows, but also a rare breeding bird on Scottish bogs and moors. Small numbers winter. Quite nervous and easily flushed, and often first detected by its *pu-pu-pu* whistling flight/alarm call, in which the notes are even in pitch and tempo. Wades to feed; often hunts for fish, which might involve running fast in the shallows, quickly changing direction. Not very sociable, and often seen alone. **ID:** Tall, slim wader with greenish legs, long neck, long bill quite thick at the base and slightly uptilted. Bill is typically blue-grey with black tip. In flight, plain wings, white rump extends to make slit up back; tail white with a few incomplete bars. Always strong contrast between dark wings and white belly and flanks. Ad br: streaks all over head and neck, upperparts with some dark, some pale feathers; ad nonbr: head rather white, streaks on crown and hindneck only; upperparts pale grey. Juv: darker brown mantle/coverts/tertials with obvious white fringes; many streaks head and neck.

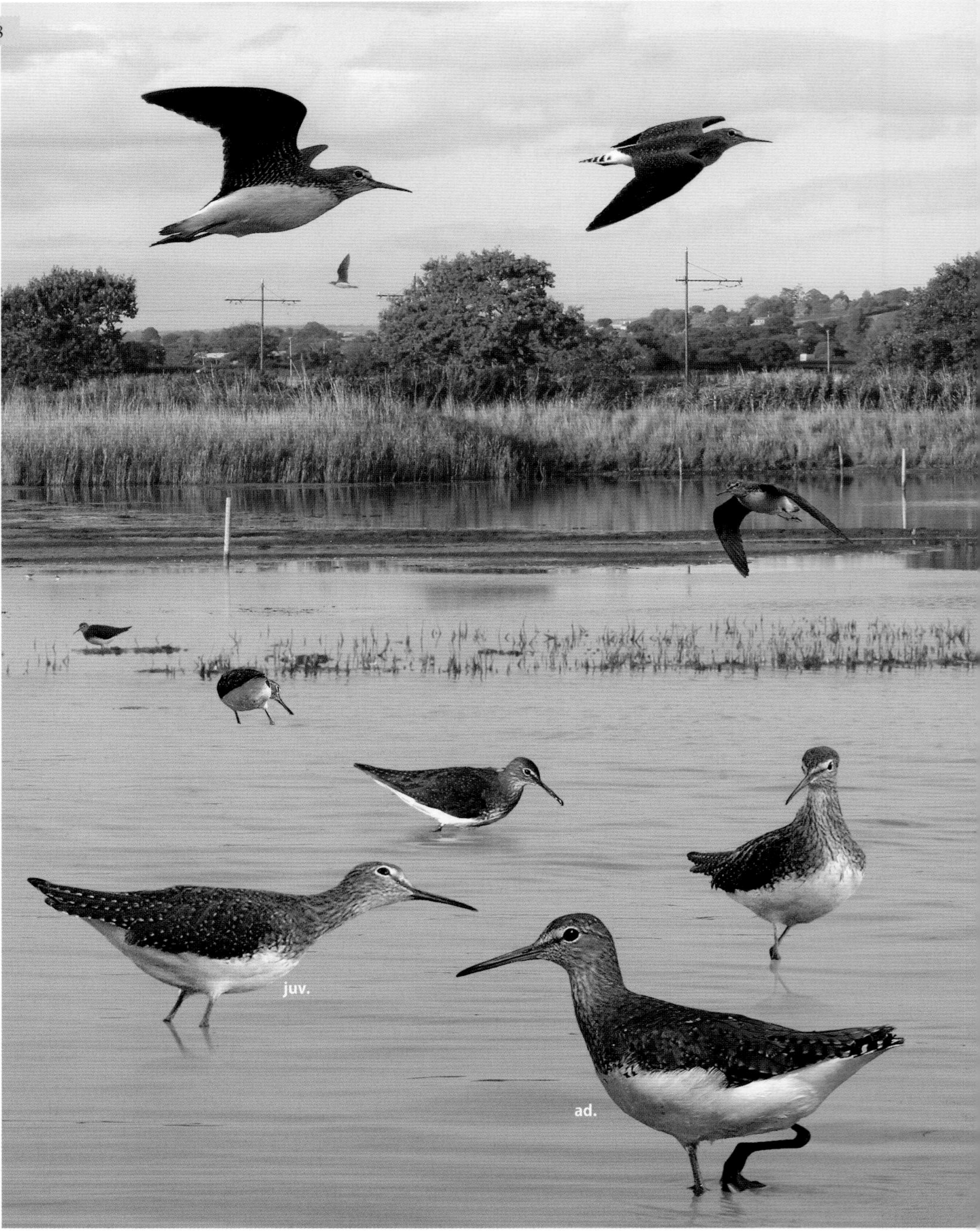

Green Sandpiper *Tringa ochropus* GRESA/GE L 22cm

UK: s. 1–3 pairs
w. 910

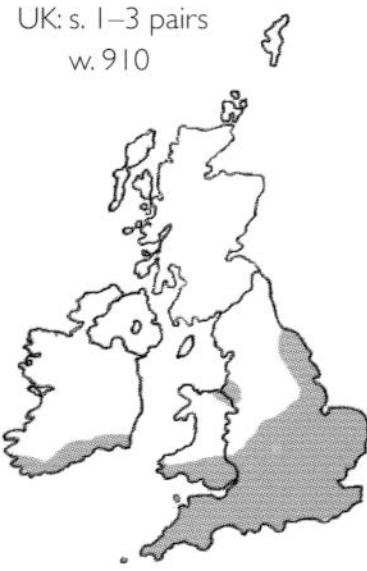

Fairly common passage migrant and winter visitor to freshwater ditches, rivers, marshes, and lake shores, where it often skulks and is seen only when flushed. Flies away in panicky style, flashing its HOUMA-like white rump as it twists and turns into the distance. Has very pleasant *do-weet, wee tweet!* alarm/flight call, the last note rising in pitch. Not very sociable, groups of half dozen at most. **ID:** Small, very contrasting wader with invariably very dark upperparts and pure white underparts, the line between them being rather horizontal, from the vent along to the strong demarcation between heavily streaked chest and white belly. Wings dark above, without bars, rump white and tail white with a few thick black bars. Upperparts dark with small white spots, with a white eye-ring and strong white supercilium in front of eye only. The legs are dark green and the bill is dark, straight, and slightly longer than the head. Juv: differs from ads by richer buff spotting on upperparts.

Wood Sandpiper *Tringa glareola* **WOOSA/OD** L 20cm

UK: s. 11–27 pairs

Uncommon passage migrant and very rare breeding bird. A few pairs in Scotland use lightly wooded bogs and clearings, while migrants turn up in a variety of freshwater locations, including marshes and lake edges. Birds pass through Apr–May and then in higher numbers Aug–Sep, juveniles earliest. Not as paranoid as GRESA, doesn't flush with same drama, makes gentler *chiff-chiff* call. **ID:** Similar to GRESA, but taller, longer necked and more elegant, with much paler, yellow legs. Also shows longer white supercilium reaching behind eye, light streaks on the breast making a diffuse, not sharp demarcation from whiter belly, and more obvious pale spots on upperparts. In flight, shares white rump with GRESA, but tail has narrower bars. In shape, looks like mini-REDSH, but with different-coloured legs, dark bill, longer supercilium, and lacks white wing bar. Ad br: distinctive, with prominent and copious white spots on dark upperparts, less clear on nonbr; juv warmer brown above with smaller, buff-coloured spots.

Common Redshank *Tringa totanus* REDSH/RK L 28cm

UK: s. 25,000 pairs
w. 130,000

Breeds on salt marshes, one of the few species present there in midsummer. Also found in moors, meadows, freshwater marshes, and bogs, while in winter it gathers on estuaries, often in large numbers. Extremely nervous and noisy; being near nesting pairs gives you a headache. Often perches on posts, bobbing head, or flies around you; may briefly raise wings above its head when standing. Song is pleasing, fluty, repeated *tu-oodle*, call is variation on *tew*, often *tew-hu-hu*, with first note longest. Feeding flocks often spread out on estuary, but roost, often in large numbers, in tight packs with other waders. **ID:** Unique wing pattern with broad white trailing edge, plus orange-red legs, easily identify it. Middling in everything: medium sized, mid-brown, with medium-length legs and medium-length bill. Bill as long as head, dead straight and with orange base and darker tip. Ad br: grey-brown, paler below, quite copious untidy streaking, esp on underparts. Ad nonbr: much plainer, with hardly any streaks, except on flanks. Juv: more orangey legs than ads, upperparts with strong buff speckling, more neatly streaked below.

Spotted Redshank *Tringa erythropus* SPORE/DR L 30cm

UK: w. 98

Uncommon passage migrant, with about 540 individuals appearing each year, a few in Apr and May and then many more Jun–Sep; rare winter visitor. Primarily in freshwater habitats, where relishes getting its feet wet, frequently immersed up to its belly and routinely swimming, when it will upend in the water like a duck—a distinctive behaviour. Also works creeks in estuaries. Makes distinctive call *chewit*, quite unlike REDSH. Fast flight. **ID:** Taller than similar REDSH, with much longer bill that has slight but noticeable droop at the tip. In contrast to REDSH, red on bill confined to lower mandible. Lacks any white on upperwing, just a white oval on back. Ad ♂ br: uniquely 'barbecued' wader, sooty black except for small white spots on upperparts; black legs. Ad ♀ br: faded sooty with white flecking. Ad nonbr: sim to REDSH but much whiter, with soft grey back and whitish below; no hint of brown. White supercilium very prominent in front of eye. Juv: very dusky, with heavy barring on underparts and whitish spots on upperparts. Distinctive. Bill and supercilium as ad nonbr.

Ruddy Turnstone *Arenaria interpres* **TURNS/TT** L 23cm

UK: w. 51,000

Common and widespread winter visitor to rocky and shingly coasts, beaches, groynes, jetties, and piers. A bird with real character: the 'sausage dog' of waders. Walks quickly on shoreline, seeming to sniff around like a terrier, head close to ground, looking for anything edible. Uses bill to turn over rocks and debris at wrack line to find hidden goodies. Also digs holes in beach, sand thrown everywhere. Typically in small groups, in which individuals recognise each other. Makes rippling call like lots of snooker balls struck together or beer crates being moved. **ID:** Pocket battleship: small with very short legs, thick-set long body, short chisel-shaped bill. In flight, has 'borrowed every bar and stripe going'. Plumage boldest in br ♂ and dullest in nonbr; in latter, plumage has the same basic pattern with complex bib and head pattern. Ad ♂ br: superbly marked tortoiseshell. Ad ♀ br: subdued messier version. Ad nonbr: most uniform plumage, generally duller brown. Sexes similar. Juv: uniform upperparts with well-defined white or buff fringes.

Knot *Calidris canutus* **KNOT/KN** L 24cm

UK: w. 330,000

Localised winter visitor and passage migrant to coastal areas, mainly larger muddy estuaries and beaches (breeds in High Arctic; some come from Canada). Scarce inland. Thousands may gather at roost and perform impressive aerial manoeuvres. When feeding, moves slowly, usually picking food off surface; lacks feverish air of smaller, similarly plumaged DUNLI. Also ploughs: placing bill in mud and furrowing forward. Call a nasal *whet whet*. **ID:** Unique shape. Built to travel long distances. Large body (fuel tank) with long pointed wings. Green legs look too short for it. A horizontal bird, often leans forward. Stout, fairly short straight bill. Sexes similar. In flight, tail and rump very plain pale grey; strong white bar. Ad br: rich rufous underparts; upperparts coarsely spangled. Ad nonbr: decidedly nondescript. Pale grey upperparts, breast streaking/barring extending onto flanks, black wingtips. The pale supercilium stands out at a distance. Juv: as nonbr but with dark subterminal lines and white fringes to upperpart feathers, so looks scaly. Fresh juvs can show pleasing buff wash on breast.

Sanderling *Calidris alba* **SANDE/SS** L 20cm

UK: w. 17,000

Fairly common winter visitor and passage migrant. In contrast to some other waders, eschews muddy estuaries for sandy beaches. Always on the run. It's the 'army' on the beach that chases waves into the sea, only to be chased back out, then returns for more. Its short legs move as fast as they can, a blur; feet lack hind toe, adaptation for running. Roosts in tight flocks higher on the beach. Feisty, squabbling with others. The boldest white wing bar in flight, with clean white underwing. Often calls, a liquid *qweet*. **ID:** Chunkier than similar DUNLI, with short black legs, thick neck, and rounded head. All-black straight bill. Sexes similar. Ad br: breast, head, and upperparts range from dull brown to bright chestnut to dark or pale grey and black. Colours fade through summer, often becoming pale orange and worn combinations of white through black. Moults late summer. Nonbr: striking white underparts, very pale grey upperparts. Dark bend of wing often striking. Large black eye stands out. Juv: pristine spangled upperparts, often buff washed when fresh but wear to white.

Dunlin *Calidris alpina* **DUNLI/DN** L 18cm

UK: s. 8,600-10,600 pairs
w. 360,000

Abundant wader, the yardstick by which other small shorebirds are compared. Often found in huge numbers at estuaries, sprinkled in tight flocks over mudflats, and forming impressive roosting aggregations. Regular migrant inland, and breeds in moderate numbers in moorland, bogs, and machair grassland. Feeding birds pick food from surface and make shallow probes; flocks may look feverish and busy. Quiet but distinctive call is buzzing *jeesp*. **ID:** Short black legs, fat neckless body with noticeably long and slightly downcurved black bill. Often looks hunchbacked. Ad br: striking rufous upperparts, pale head and belly 'dipped in black ink' (amount of black varies). Ad nonbr: uniform grey upperparts and breast with indistinct supercilium. Juv: rufous and buff-fringed upperparts with diffuse streaking on underparts (unusual in juv shorebirds). Arctic breeding race (migrant) *alpina* often has longest, most curved bill and most black on belly; British breeding birds of race *schinzii* intermediate; uncommon Greenland race *arctica* shortest bill, not much black, least colourful upperparts.

Purple Sandpiper *Calidris maritima* **PURSA/PS** L 21cm

UK: w. 13,000

Localised winter visitor to rocky shores, jetties, harbours, and piers, often with TURNS. Its habits, shape, and dark, swarthy overall appearance distinctive. Usually in small flocks, clambering over rocks in search of mussels; sometimes eats fish. Jumps from rock to rock, dodging waves, but is perfectly capable of swimming; not on muddy estuaries. Call insignificant *tit* or *twit*. **ID:** Always plump and dark; blends into rocks and seaweed. Boldly patterned in flight, with black stripe splitting white rump, narrow but noticeable white wing bar. Ad br: Rather plain and dark, but some feathers on upperparts have rufous fringes; mottled below. Ad nonbr: smoky grey upperparts and diffusely streaked underparts; purple iridescence often hard to see. Head plain and unstreaked, unusual for a winter wader. Typically orange legs and bill base create strong contrast. Often has white spot on lores. 1st-w: as nonbr with white-edged coverts and tertials. Many moult into breeding plumage on wintering grounds.

Ruff *Philomachus pugnax* RUFF/RU L 25cm

UK: s. 0–11 pairs
w. 820

Singular wader with significant size difference between sexes, related to breeding strategy, in which larger males (size approaches REDSH), with lavish and colourful plumes on head and neck, display together in small groups ('leks') on meadows to attract the cryptically coloured, smaller females ('reeves'), which mate and carry out breeding duties alone. Rare breeder, scarce on freshwater meadows and floodlands in winter, but fairly common passage migrant (Apr–May, Jul–Sep) to freshwater or brackish pools. Almost silent, even when displaying.

ID: Looks disproportionately large bodied with long legs but small, pigeon-like head. Stands tall. ♀ 20% smaller than ♂ and smaller bodied, a little larger than DUNLI. All have yellow or orange legs. In flight, has bold white V on rump. Bill slightly downcurved; often a white patch at base of bill. Ad br ♂: has stunning mixture of white, black, and tan. Neck feathers ('ruff') moulted by Jun, otherwise still boldly marked. ♀ has mottled breast. Ad nonbr: similar to breeding ♀ but duller. Often has pale feathering at base of bill. Juv: buff, paler on belly. Upperparts scaly with bold buff fringes.

Curlew Sandpiper *Calidris ferruginea* **CURSA/CV** L 18cm ***670 migrants***

Scarce migrant, mostly in autumn. Typically among other waders (e.g., DUNLI) on coastal pools and reservoirs. Call more jangling than DUNLI, with hint of Crested Tit's trill! **ID:** Sim to DUNLI but taller, longer necked, and with longer, more downcurved bill; in flight, shows white rump. Ad br: rare sight, a deep, rich chestnut, with white bill base; summer adults retain traces on underparts. Ad nonbr: plain grey and white, with white supercilium. Juv shows equally prominent supercilium, with peach wash to chest, relatively unmarked underparts; scaly upperparts.

Temminck's Stint *Calidris temminckii* **TEMST/TK** L 14cm ***1–4 pairs, 11 migrants***

Rare, low-profile wader, hard to find. Usually on fresh water, in marshes, ditches, and pools, often skulking out of sight in vegetation. Seen in May, then again in autumn. **ID:** In all plumages like a miniature COMSA, with white belly contrasting with dark chest and upperparts. Check for small size, fat body with short neck, short bill, green legs. Has distinctive horizontal posture and crouching gait; feeds slowly. Flies off fast and far. At rest, tail projects beyond wingtips (reverse of LITST). Ad br: plain, with tinge of olive green on upperparts. Juv: scaly above.

Little Stint *Calidris minuta* **LITST/LX** L 13cm ***460 migrants, w. 14***

Uncommon passage migrant, most familiar in autumn from birding hotspots on the coast, usually mixed up with DUNLI and other passage waders on pools and lagoons. Peak time is Aug–Sep. Less often on lakes and marshes inland; rare in spring. Tiny wader with quick movements. Often tame, not flushing very far, in contrast, for example, to TEMST. Picks from muddy margins, doesn't probe. Call: simple, high-pitched *tit*. **ID:** Noticeably smaller than DUNLI, but shorter, straighter, finer-tipped bill. Long legged, pot-bellied, and small headed. Ad br: breeding plumage more orange than red, strongest on ear coverts and palest around chin and throat. Spots mixed in orange on throat. Rufous upperparts include tertials and coverts. Ad nonbr: like tiny DUNLI, a little paler, with fewer streaks on breast sides. Juv: most British birds in this plumage. Early on, easily recognised by 2 prominent whitish V stripes on mantle; otherwise upperparts neatly scalloped with rich colours and white fringes; in contrast to sim age DUNLI, largely white breast and belly; pale head with split supercilium and white forehead.

Pectoral Sandpiper *Calidris melanotos* **PECSA/PP** L 21cm

Rare, but the most regular transatlantic stray wader. About 80 a year turn up at sewage farms, reservoirs, and freshwater margins, esp Aug–Sep. Walks around steadily picking at surface, head rocking slightly as it moves. **ID:** Named for ever-present pectoral band, exhibiting strong contrast between streaked chest and white belly. Legs pale yellowish green. Subtle dark eye-stripe, pale base to bill. Like a small RUFF or larger DUNLI. Chest is almost disproportionately large and bulging, yet overall bird is attenuated with long wings. All plumage patterns similar, but juv has white tramlines on back.

Buff-breasted Sandpiper *Calidris subruficollis* **BUBSA** L 19cm

Rare transatlantic fall migrant on the short turf of airfields or golf courses, away from usual wader habitat. Quite often in small parties. Moves with jerky strut. **ID:** Gentle appearance, large eye on bland face. Square head, short, thin bill, slim neck, and attenuated rear end. All plumages buff, recall taller and bulkier juv RUFF. Broad pale fringes to dark upperparts.

White-rumped Sandpiper *Calidris melanotos* **WHRSA** L 21cm

Rare on pools, lagoons, and reservoirs, usually in autumn. Very distinctive call, an unusual, short, high but nasal *tzeek*. **ID:** Quite fidgety, so diagnostic white rump will be seen eventually. Otherwise looks like small DUNLI, but has tapered rear end, long wings projecting beyond tail, shorter but equally decurved bill. Strong white supercilium, and all ages well streaked on breast.

Grey Phalarope *Phalaropus fulicarius* **GREPH/PL** L 21cm ***200 migrants***

Rare autumn visitor blown in from ocean by westerly gales, Sep–Jan. Breeds in Arctic and winters in Atlantic; pelagic. Not like a wader, instead seen swimming like a tiny white, very buoyant duck. Severe weather may bring some inland, for example, to reservoirs. **ID:** Larger than RENPH. Focus on noticeably thicker bill with pale area at base; also broader white wing bar. Ad nonbr: upperparts uniform pale grey, with narrow pale fringes. Often more extensive white on crown and paler grey nape than RENPH. Br ads unmistakable, ♀ smarter. Juv/1st-w: may retain buff on head and neck, and on fringes of tertials and coverts.

Red-necked Phalarope *Phalaropus lobatus* **RENPH/NK** L 18cm 20–30 pairs

Very rare breeder on Western and Northern Isles of Scotland, in freshwater pools. Rare migrant, commutes between northern Europe and Arabian Sea, may stop over in Jul–Aug. Swims with cork-like buoyancy, often spins to stir up food in shallow water. Moves quickly, jabs needle-like bill at insects and plankton. **ID:** Small square head and thin neck add to petite feel of this species. Thinner, longer bill than GREPH. Ad ♀ br: a beauty, marked with white eyelash as if to emphasize striking head. Ad ♂: a washed-out version of ♀. Ad nonbr/juv: broader white fringes to upperparts than GREPH, looks scalier; stripes on mantle.

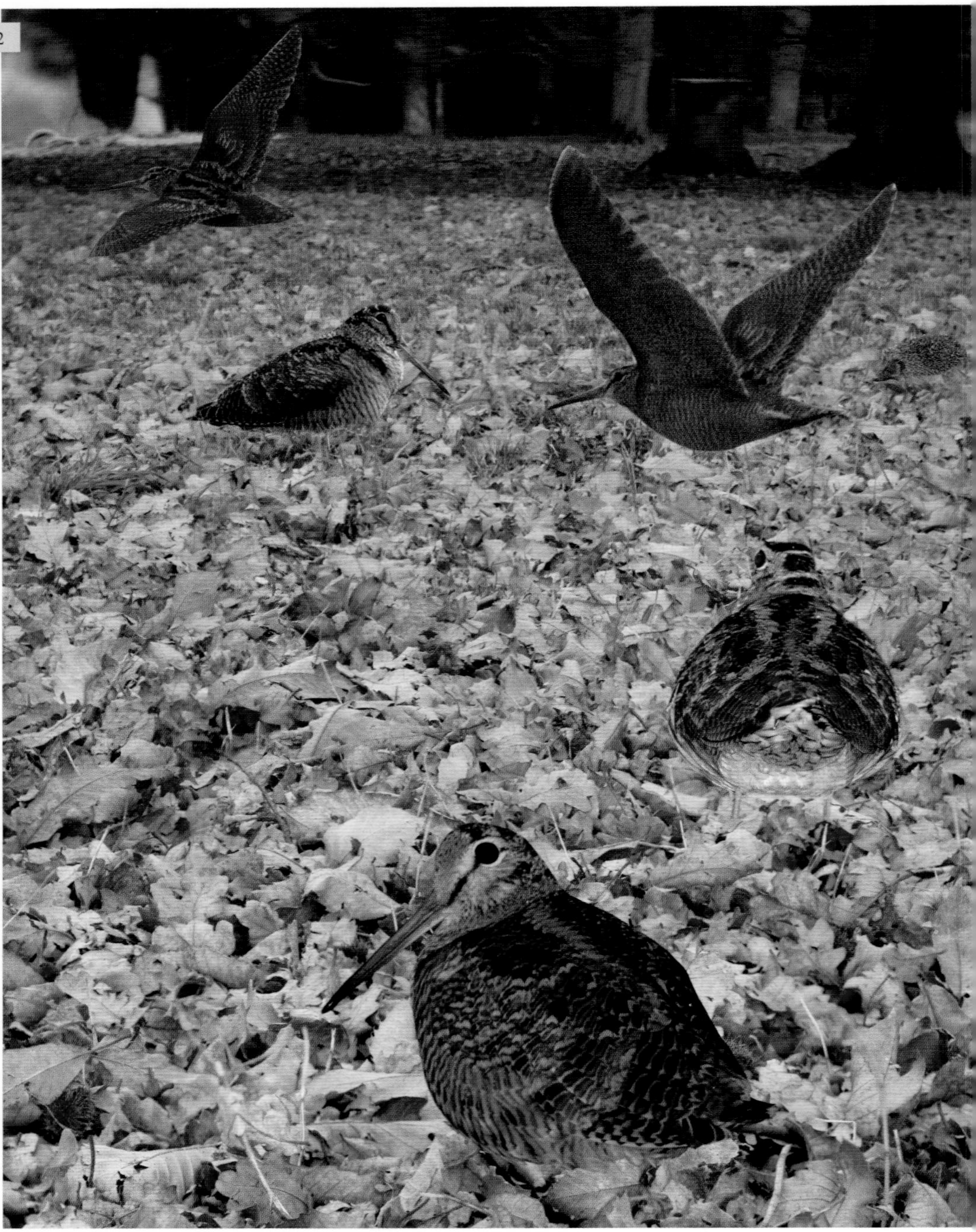

Woodcock *Scolopax rusticola* **WOODC/WK** L 34cm

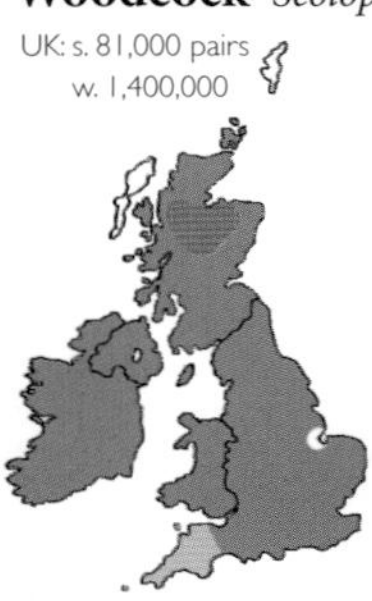

Oddly for a wader, breeds in damp woodland and also takes refuge in copses and deep scrub on passage and in winter. In deep frost and snow may be forced to take refuge in unusual areas like fields and gardens where the ground is soft enough to probe. Most typically seen on spring and summer evenings (or at dawn) performing courtship flight ('roding') in very wide circles, just above treetops. Flies with flickering wingbeats, and makes periodic explosive squeak preceded by low, froglike croaks ('frog squashed'), latter not always audible. Even in twilight, curious shape is distinctive, plump with rounded wings and long bill held downwards. Other encounters may be flushing medium-sized brown bird from woodland floor, which bolts off with loud wing noise but no call, and may keep low and veer between tree trunks. **ID:** Like giant SNIPE, but more richly and warmly coloured for perfect camouflage among litter of woodland floor. Large eye on pale head (enables bird to have nearly 360° vision) and pale transverse stripes across dark crown. All plumages similar.

Common Snipe *Gallinago gallinago* SNIPE/SN L 26cm

UK: s. 80,000 pairs
w. 1,100,000

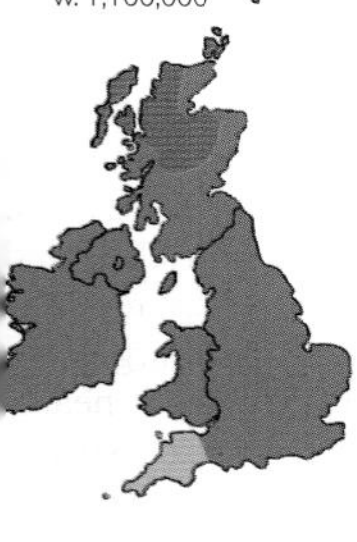

Widespread and common breeder, migrant, and winter visitor. Found in wet bogs, fields, and marshes, including salt marshes. Usually not seen until flushed, but heavy snow or frost may force it into open. Explodes from underfoot with rasping *scaarp*, like a loud kiss of the back of the hand. Flies off in panicky zigzag pattern. Usually drops back into cover at some distance, runs off, and disappears. Feeds methodically, probing long bill into soft mud, often several probes from same standing position. Sits on posts and other perches on breeding grounds. Dramatic and familiar display on breeding grounds: flies high into sky making 'drumming' sound (a little like sheep *baa*), circling territory, often in half-light. May be seen crouched among tussocks; cryptic plumage makes it difficult to see. **ID:** Has longest bill-to-body ratio of any British bird; bill entirely straight. Legs rather short. Cryptic plumages all similar. Heavily barred flanks and underwing contrast with white belly—striking in flight. Pale crown centre, stripy head.

Jack Snipe *Lymnocryptes minimus* JACSN/JS L 18cm *w. 110,000*

Widespread but incredibly skulking winter visitor to marshes, ditches, wet fields and overgrown pools, Sep–Mar. Hardly ever seen owing to its epic ability to freeze when threatened, only flushing when almost stepped on. Often lands nearby, only to disappear. Exhibits odd habit of rocking up and down while feeding (larger SNIPE does this, but not to same extent). **ID:** Smaller than SNIPE with very obviously shorter bill, clear even in flight. Distinctive head pattern: dark crown, split supercilium, and dark border to pale cheek. 2 obvious golden stripes flowing down either side of back. Lacks flank barring.

Stone Curlew *Burhinus oedicnemus* STOCU/TN L 42cm *s. 350 pairs*

Unusual semi-nocturnal localised summer visitor (Mar–Nov) on Salsibury Plain and the Brecklands. Often catatonic in daytime. Chases after large invertebrates with quick plover-like runs. Often flicks tail down when running. Strange wailing raptor-like screams at twilight and through the night. **ID:** Extraordinary bug-eyed appearance. Cryptic plumage blends into its sandy and chalky environment. Conspicuous in flight, with bold black-and-white patterns, visible in poor light, gives stiff beats of bowed wings. Juv has subtly less obvious white supercilium and covert bar than ad.

White Stork *Ciconia ciconia* **WHIST/OR** L 108cm
Rare visitor on marshes and fields, mostly Apr-May. Flies with neck outstretched, slow wingbeats and regularly soars. Birds on Continent make famous stick nests, on buildings or telegraph poles. Stalks over shallow water to catch frogs and fish. **ID:** Unmistakable. Juv has dark-tipped bill.

Common Crane *Grus grus* **CRANE/AN** L 108cm
Rare migrant in marshes and farm fields. Tiny population in Norfolk Broads. Flies with neck outstretched and slow, controlled wingbeats. Bugeling call heard miles away. Sociable. **ID:** Enormous. Bushy 'tail' like an ostrich. Adult: black-and-white neck and red patch on crown. Juv: dull brownish head.

Spoonbill *Platalea leucorodia* **SPOON/NB** L 85cm ***s. 2 pairs, w. 20***
Rare wading bird found near shallow water. Wades while sweeping its oddly shaped bill from side to side to find invertebrates. The few breeders nest in trees close to marshes. Wintering birds are often on estuaries. Often seen asleep, since it routinely feeds at night. Flies with distinctive stiff wingbeats, holding neck extended, with long bill and long legs obvious. **ID:** Unmistakable, but beware egrets. Long, spoon-shaped black bill with yellow tip. Ad br with bushy crest and egg-yolk flush on breast, lost in nonbr. Juv with black wingtips, paler bill. Imms have reduced black in wing tips.

Eurasian Bittern *Botaurus stellaris* **BITTE/BI** L 75cm ***s. 80 pairs, w. 600***

Rare breeding bird of large reed beds and marshes; in winter may be found in smaller reed beds and beside rivers. Secretive, easiest to see when it makes brief flights over reeds, esp early and late in day. Also shows itself in icy conditions. Can be hard to see even when close, owing to amazing cryptic plumage, augmented by slow movements and occasion al habit of swaying with reeds. Makes remarkable far-car rying 'booming' song, like blowing over open beer bottle **ID:** At first glance like brown heron. Slightly quicker wing beats than heron, thicker neck, quite owl-like rounded wings

Black-crowned Night Heron *Nycticorax nycticorax* **NIGHE/NT** L 62cm

Rare migrant, also with a couple of populations of captive origin living freely, in Edinburgh and Norfolk. Mostly nocturnal; birds fly from waterside roost trees (e.g., willows) to marshy feeding grounds at twilight. Call a loud *wock*. When feeding, crouches, occasionally walking a few paces hoping for better luck. Typically eats fish. Compac shape, striking in flight, emphasized by rounded wings **ID:** Stocky with short neck and big head. Adult: black crow and mantle, grey wings, red eyes. Juv: completely different streaked brown with pale spots. 2nd-s like faded version of ad

Little Egret *Egretta garzetta* **LITEG/ET** L 60cm

UK: s. 660–740 pairs
w. 4,500

Flourishing recent colonist, now resident on coast and inland in southern England and Ireland, first nested 1996. Breeds in colonies, often on treetops with GREHE. Feeds on fish and invertebrates, sometimes standing still in GREHE fashion, but also runs after fish in the shallows with impressive turn of speed, using wings as balance. Unhurried, well-balanced flight, though much quicker beats than GREHE. Often seen in small groups; often stands hunched. Call is irritable growling. **ID:** Easily recognised, elegant small heron with black legs and incongruous yellow toes; dark bill long and fine, neck long and narrow. White plumage invariably immaculate. Ad br: long white plumes on nape, shorter on breast and back, brief orange blush to lores. Lost in nonbr. Juv: greenish legs.

Purple Heron *Ardea purpurea* **PURHE/UR** L 84cm

Rare visitor to marshes and large reed beds, Apr–May and again Jul–Sep; has bred. **ID:** Slimmer than similar GREHE, with clearly thinner neck and longer, thinner bill. Always looks darker. In flight, 'keel' made from retracted neck a little more obvious, and feet splay more. Ad: like dark GREHE, with stripy neck; darker underwing in flight. Juv: reddish brown with dark-spotted wings and back.

Cattle Egret *Bubulcus ibis* **CATEG** L 50cm

Rare but increasing visitor, at any time. Has useful habit of feeding alongside livestock, including cattle, horses, and sheep, often far from water. Takes insects disturbed by their feet. Sometimes in small groups. Nests in marshes. **ID:** Sim to LITEG but antithesis in shape: short bill, thicker neck, compact shape, 'double chin'. Bill yellow, not dark, and lacks yellow feet. Ad br: colourful, with orange-ochre patches, lost in nonbr. Juv: dull legs.

Great White Egret *Ardea alba* **GRWEG/HW** L 50cm ***w. 35***

Recently bred, but still very rare. Usually in larger marshes. Seen singly. Flies with slow, steady wingbeats. **ID:** Basically looks just like white GREHE, of sim size, thus much larger than LITEG. Long legs give odd, front-heavy silhouette. Longer bill and thinner neck than GREHE. Ad br: impressive back plumes ('aigrettes'), dark bill. Ad nonbr/juv: all-yellow bill, dark legs and feet.

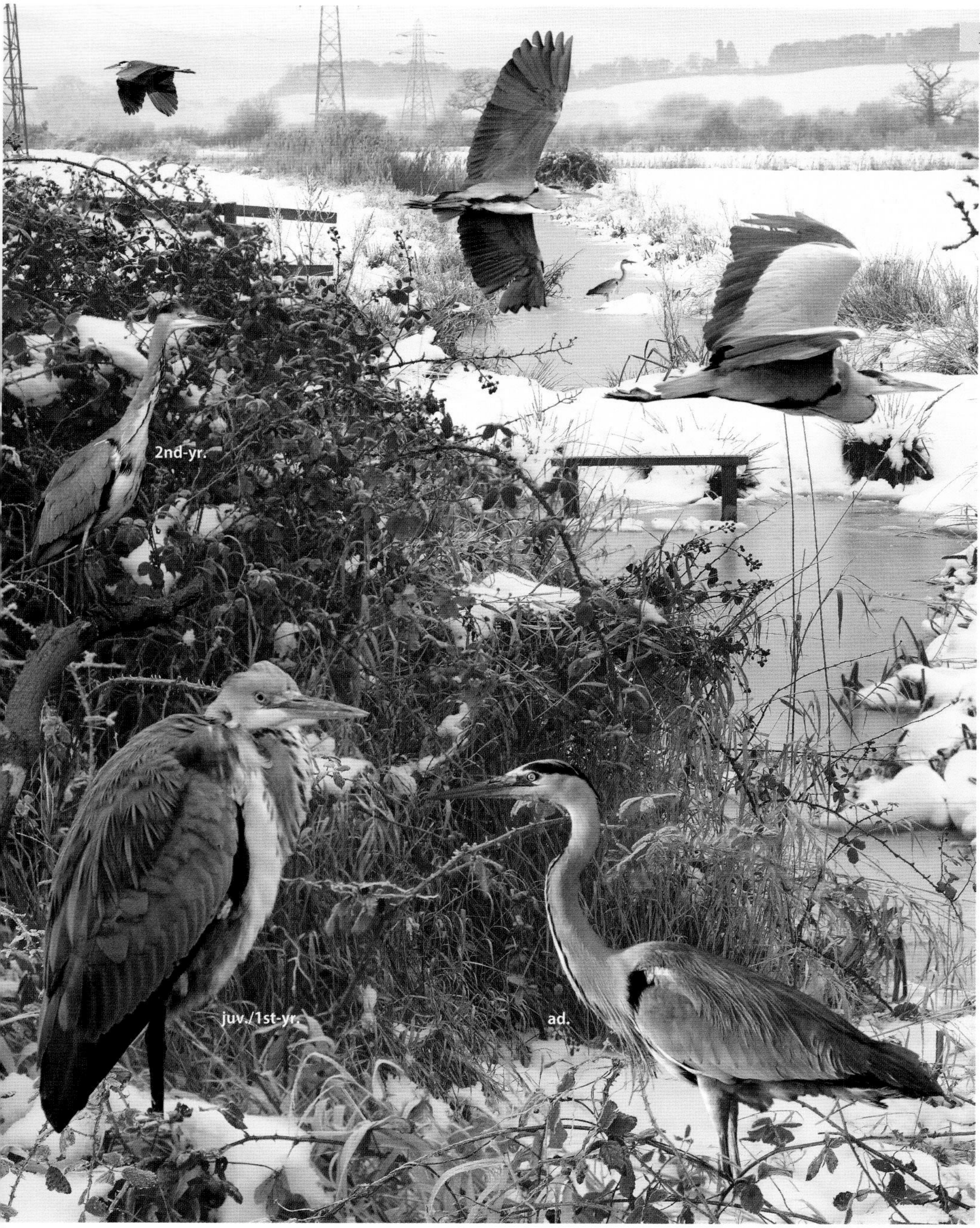

Grey Heron *Ardea cinerea* GREHE/H. L 94cm

UK: s. 13,000 pairs
w. 63,000

Our common heron, found beside lakes and in marshes, estuaries, damp fields, parks, and even gardens. Has famously patient feeding style, standing beside water or paddling up to its belly, waiting to ambush fish within reach, then grabbing (not spearing) with lightning strike. Just as often, stands cheerlessly with neck retracted, loafing and appearing fed up. Feeds alone, but will share roosting sites, grudgingly. Flies with very slow, deliberate wingbeats; holds neck retracted; may elicit mobbing from other birds. Regularly flies high, soars. Call a loud, irritated yell *krank*! Breeds in colonies on top of tall trees, making huge stick nests. Odd grunts and other sounds emanate from colony. **ID:** Big sturdy heron with heavy bill. Ad: white head and neck with black stripe behind eye and forming neck plume. Yellow bill flushes briefly pink in early spring. Juv: dark grey crown, grey neck. In 2nd year acquires black stripe, but neck still grey.

Coot *Fulica atra* COOT/CO L 37cm

UK: s. 31,000 pairs
w. 190,000

Very common resident on freshwater lakes, reservoirs, gravel pits, and marshes, familiar from town parks and village ponds. Often found with ducks, and shares habit of swimming on open water, but has sharp-tipped whitish bill and blue feet with lobes, not webs. Dives below surface with little leap for waterweed, also may up-end. Will graze on grass. Although sociable, famously irascible, often seen with head held down, showing white frontal shield to real or imagined foe, wings raised in 'bottom-up' posture. Where Coots gather, they bicker, with splashing confrontations sometimes ending in pattering retreat over water surface. Noisy, making furious *kit* call and clamorous *kowk*, with variations. Builds easily spotted nest of waterweeds. **ID:** Ad: sooty black with white bill and frontal shield. Juv: very different, paler grey with white throat and breast. Downy chick black with much red/orange around neck.

Moorhen *Gallinula chloropus* **MOORH/MH** L 34cm

UK: s. 270,000 pairs
w. 330,000

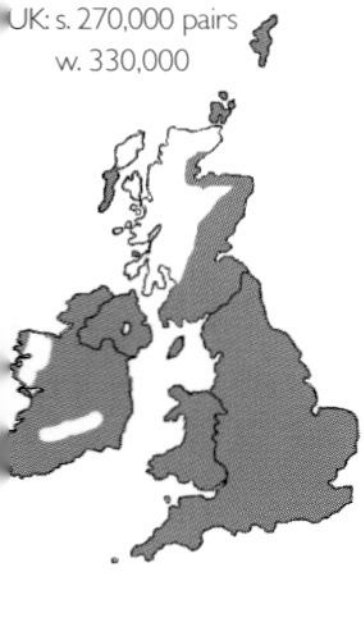

Abundant waterside bird, a little more secretive than COOT and more inclined to hide itself within thick vegetation. Capable of climbing around in reed beds and even up into lower branches of trees. Equally often swims on open water, making heavy weather of its stroke, with nod of head like cyclist labouring uphill. Rarely dives like COOT. Has continual habit of flicking tail upwards, revealing brilliant white undertail coverts. Flies low, and with effort, often runs with wings flapping into cover to avoid danger. Tetchy like COOT, birds puff up and fan their undertails in warning and aggression; rivals will fight face to face on water, kick-boxing each other. Main call an explosive *ker-ruck*, as if suddenly startled. **ID:** Sim to COOT but longer tailed, with green legs, feet not lobed; red garters. White undertail split by black stripe; white 'dotted line' along flanks. Ad: red frontal shield with yellow tip. Juv: browner than COOT, less white on front, bill dark—retained into 1st winter. Downy chick like giant black bumble bee, pleads pitifully with pathetic wings flapping.

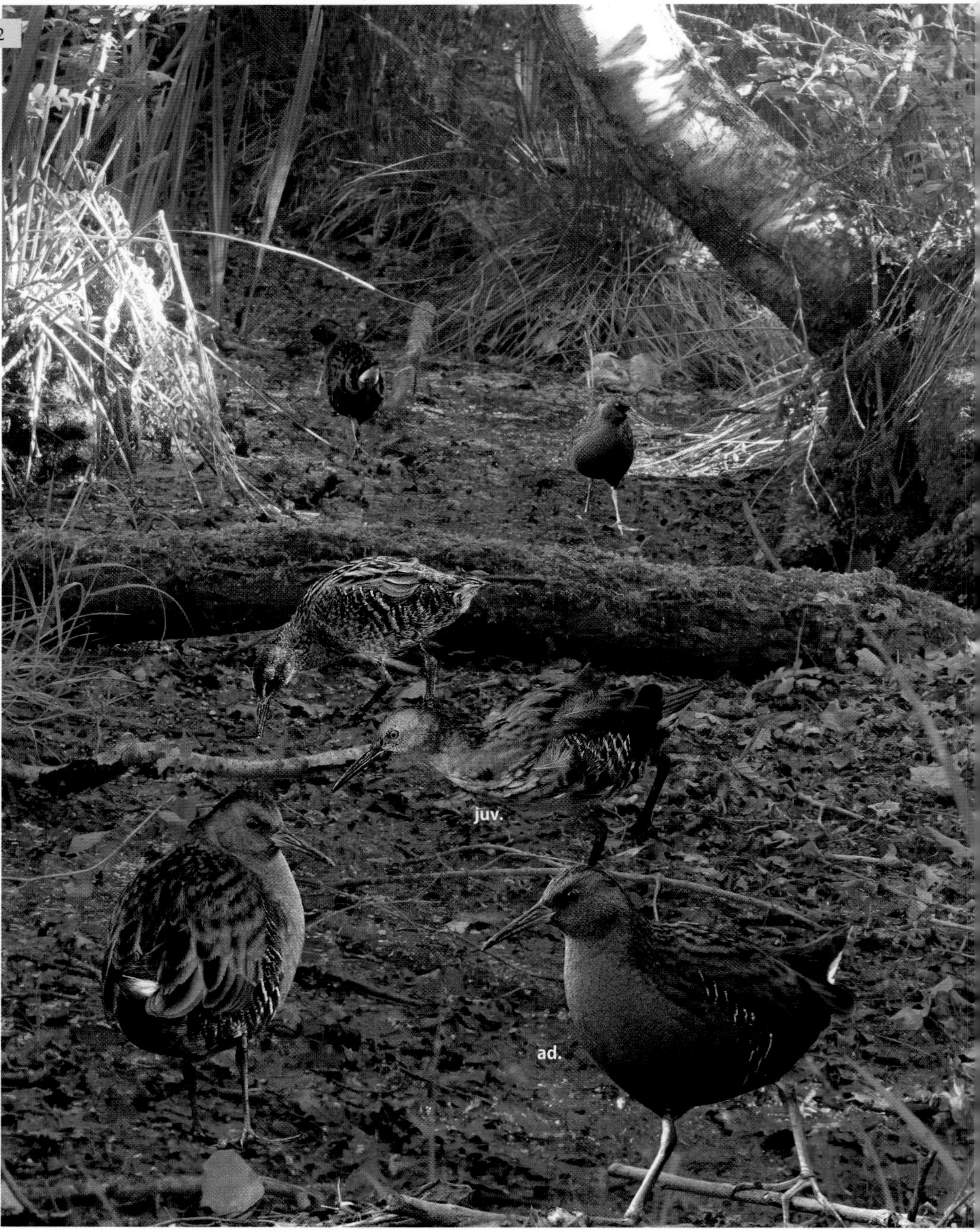

Water Rail *Rallus aquaticus* **WATRA/WA** L 26cm

UK: s. 1,100 pairs

Famously elusive marshland resident, a prize for birders who detect it scampering on mud at the base of reed beds, or running along the edge of streams and rivers. 'Thin as a rail', it is able to squeeze between thick forests of stems in marshland vegetation. Most active at dawn and dusk, and shy; most often seen from hides. In very cold weather may show itself more. Feeds by picking and probing in mud, shallow water, vegetation. Doesn't dive but readily swims. Noisy, best-known call like a sudden outbreak of squealing from a pig, dying away disconsolately. Also makes brief *kit* notes, gentler than COOT calls. **ID:** Smaller and slimmer than MOORH, with diagnostic long bill. Rich brown, mottled black on upperparts, with black-and-white barred flanks; creamy undertail. Ad with red bill, smart blue-grey breast and most of head; red eyes. Juv with whitish throat and supercilium, dark patch by eye, lacks blue-grey on breast and has pale bill.

Spotted Crake *Porzana porzana* **SPOCR/AK** L 23cm ***s. 80 pairs***

Rare summer visitor and passage migrant, to larger freshwater marshes. Very hard to see, probably easiest Aug–Sep when juveniles pass through. As with WATRA, best chance is to see one on mud at base of reed stems, close to water. In spring, makes loud 'whiplash' song, heard late at night. **ID:** Much smaller than WATRA, may look like a juv of that species! Always note short, thick bill with orange-red base, plus eponymous white spots on underparts, also green legs. Adult: grey supercilium and neck sides. Juv lacks grey.

Corn Crake *Crex crex* **CORNC/CE** L 28cm ***s. 1,200 pairs***

Rare summer visitor (late Apr–Sep), not to marshes but to lush meadows and hay fields, particularly in Hebrides and Ireland. Exceptionally skulking and difficult to see. Makes remarkable loud song, repeated *crex, crex*, sounds like running a comb over an almost empty matchbox. Song usually begins after midnight and is highly evocative. Very rarely seen on migration. Sometimes flushed from thick cover, flies in floppy style, legs dangling at first. **ID:** WATRA sized, but with short, blunt bill and warmer brown colouration. Looks like streaky brown bird with long legs. Rich chestnut wings obvious in flight. All plumages similar.

Quail *Coturnix coturnix* **QUAIL/Q** L 17cm ***s. 540 pairs***

Rare and mysterious summer visitor arriving in unpredictable numbers each year, initially from late Apr, sometimes with second surge in Jul. Usually found in wide open fields of cereal and on chalk grassland. Hardly ever seen, only when flushed unexpectedly (often by dog), when flies low with whirring wings, not far. Presence usually indicated only by male's far-carrying, ventriloquial *wet-me-lips* song, uttered several times in succession before a pause. Song usually heard at twilight or in darkness, sometimes stimulated by rain. **ID:** If flushed, is STARL sized, compact bird with narrow pointed wings and pointed tail. Ad ♂ has black throat and head stripes, browner in ♀.

Golden Pheasant *Chrysolophus pictus* **GOLPH/GF** L 67-88cm ***s. 50–100 pairs***

Forest pheasant introduced from China to a few widely scattered plantations, for example in Norfolk and sw Scotland. Very secretive and notable for preference for dark, shady woods of conifers and even rhododendrons. May be seen at edge of rides or on roadside early and late. Male call: *ker-check!* **ID:** Much smaller than PHEAS, with proportionally longer tail. Ad ♂ unmistakable. Ad ♀ darker than PHEAS, with denser barring.

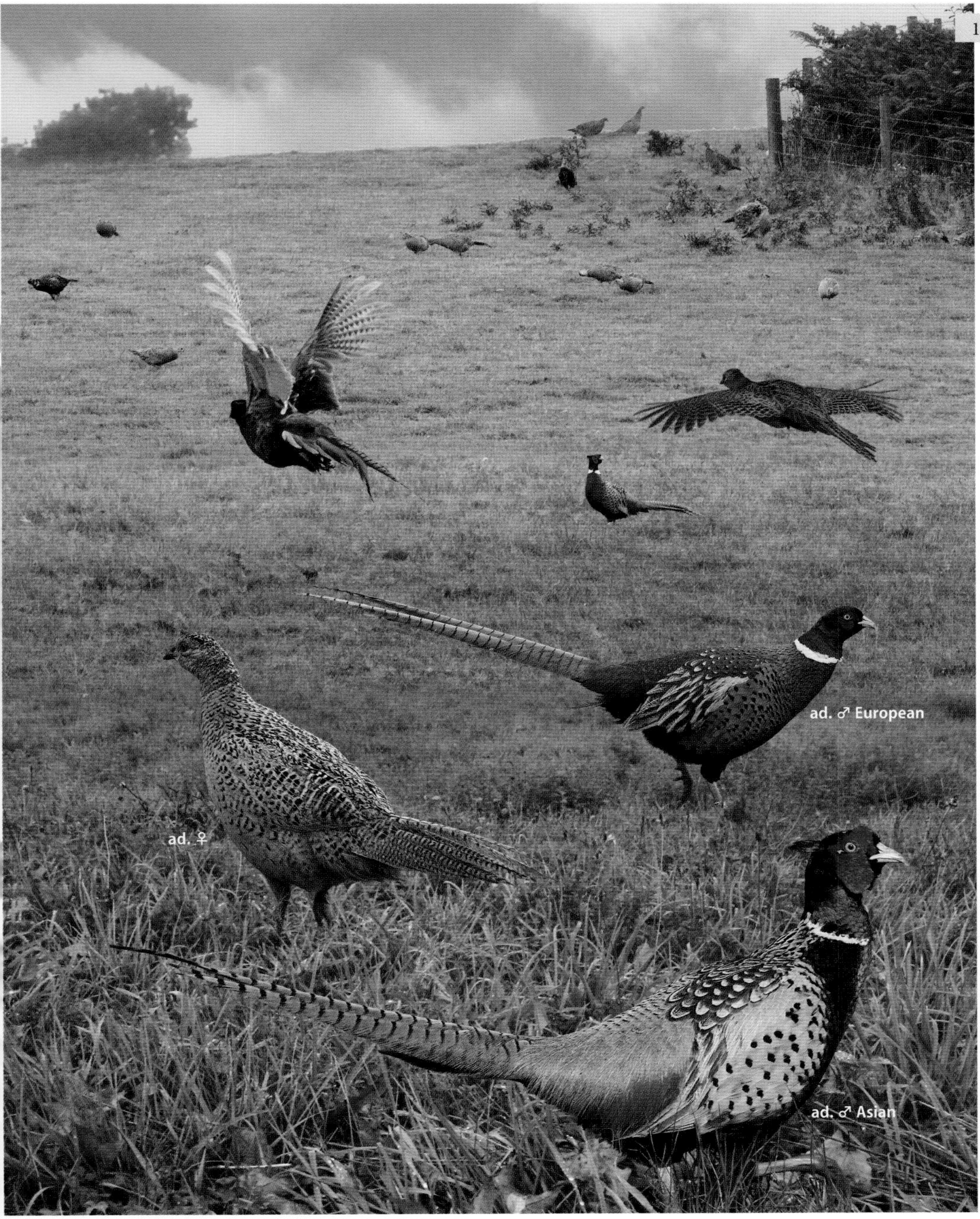

Pheasant *Phasianus colchicus* **PHEAS/PH** L 63–89cm

UK: s. 2,300,000 pairs

Here for 1000 years, but still looks exotic for British landscape. Thrives where open ground (esp farmland) abuts copses and woods, where nests are placed; also in marshes. Local populations fluctuate because of releases from breeding programmes, mostly catering to hunters. Struts around slowly and deliberately, often stopping to put head up in air to check surroundings. Seems completely unable to adapt to traffic, and runs panicking when quick flight would solve problem; often run over. Frequently in loose-knit groups and often roosts in trees. In flight, bursts from the ground, wings making constant noise. Once away, makes intermittent short glides, doesn't go far. Male's call is a very loud, far-carrying *kock-ok*, uttered with wing-flaps in display. **ID:** Very large with distinctive long tail in all plumages, shorter in ♀. Ad ♂: unmistakable copper-toned stunner with bold red face. Variable: some all dark, some with white ring around neck, the cross-breed lottery. Ad ♀: variable, from pale to dark brown. Fairly uniform and nondescript with spotted flanks. In flight, long pointed tail usually stands out. Juv: short tailed, partridge sized, streaked.

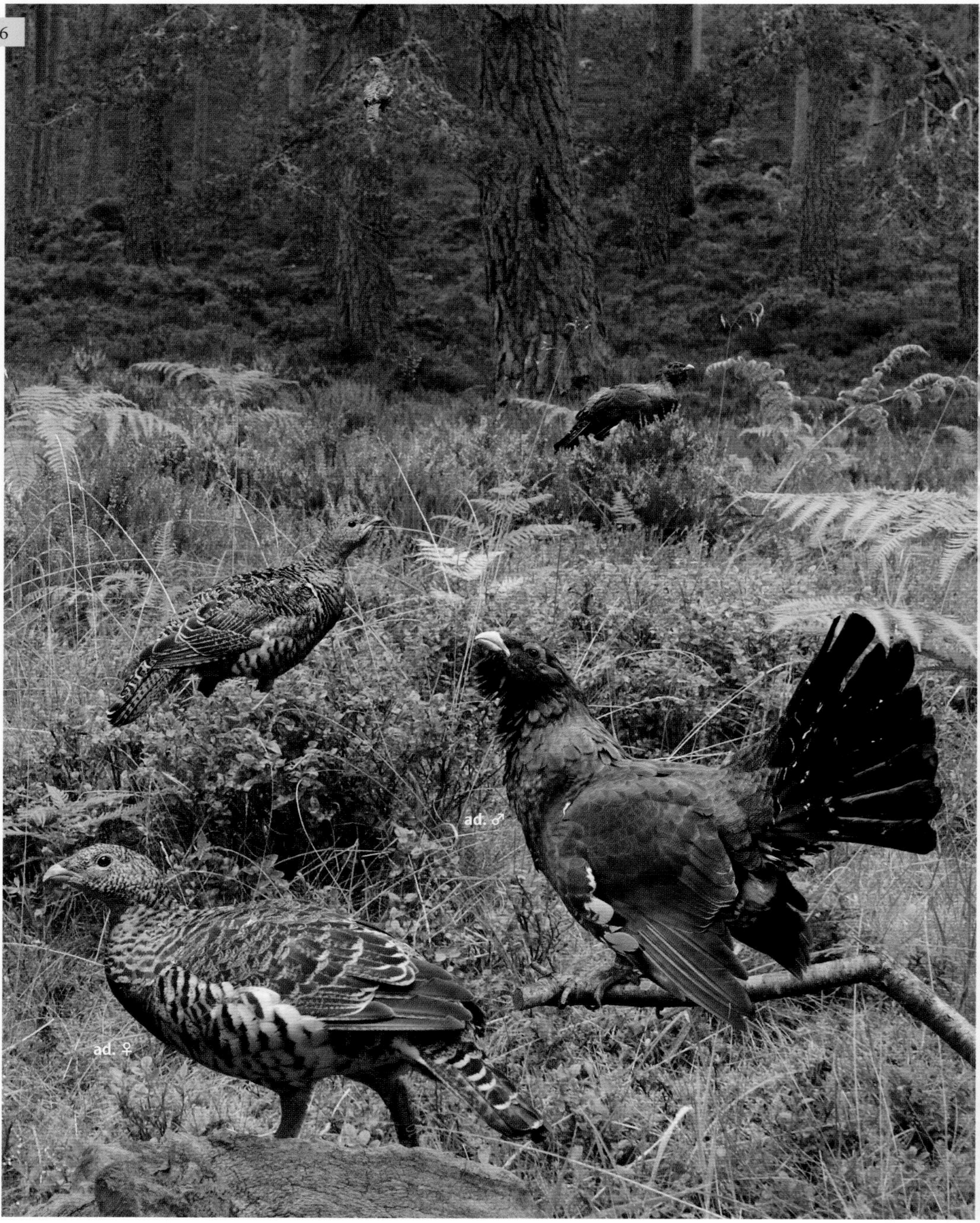

Capercaillie *Tetrao urogallus* **CAPER/CP** L 62-86cm

UK: w. 800–1,900

Rare grouse of woodland, confined to remnants of native Caledonian pine forest, and a few other forests maintaining mature trees and ample clearings. One of the hardest British birds to see, despite enormous size of male, almost approaching a turkey. Often feeds quietly and inconspicuously in pine tree tops in winter, eats needles. Also forages on ground among lush ground layer of berry-bearing plants. In very early mornings may come to side of road for grit. In early spring, males display at lek, where they make soft but outlandish belching noises, plus extraordinary song with double-clicks accelerating to cork-popping climax. Female mates at lek and performs other breeding duties alone. Flies away dramatically with explosive wingbeats. **ID:** Big, heavy, thick-billed. Ad ♂: huge, yellow bill, white flanks, plain wings; white-speckled black tail can be fanned in display. ♀ like large, bulky PHEAS, with shorter, broader tail. Richly barred and speckled, superb camouflage. Sim to ♀ BLAGR but much bigger, with heavier bill and notably warm orange-brown patch on breast, and loose barring on whitish flanks.

Black Grouse *Tetrao tetrix* BLAGR/BK L 48cm

UK: s. 5,100 pairs

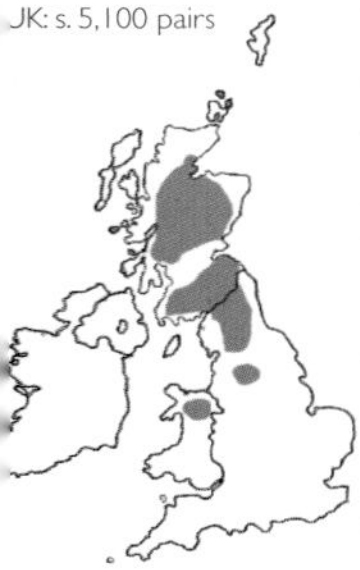

Upland grouse with need for both open ground and woodland, found on the edges of moors and bogs, for example, and near farms. Most famous for its gatherings of displaying males, known as leks, which form morning and, to a lesser extent, in the evening both in spring and autumn. At leks the black-and-white males display in sight of rivals in small territories, and females call in to assess them. After mating, female carries out all breeding duties. Lekking males make remarkable intense crooning noises, interspersed with explosive hisses, like firing geysers. Easier to see than CAPER, sometimes perching in treetops and feeding in branches, but can be elusive. **ID:** Much smaller than CAPER, size of PHEAS, with small head and bill. Ad ♂ iridescent bottle-blue, with red comb over eye, white undertail, and white wing bar. Long tail diagnostically lyre-shaped. ♀ bigger than REDGR but smaller than CAPER, with close-set barring and long tail; white wing bars diagnostic; underwings with more white than ♀ REDGR. Eclipse ♂ sim, but black tail (late summer).

Red Grouse *Lagopus lagopus* **REDGR/RG** L 40cm

UK: s. 230,000 pairs

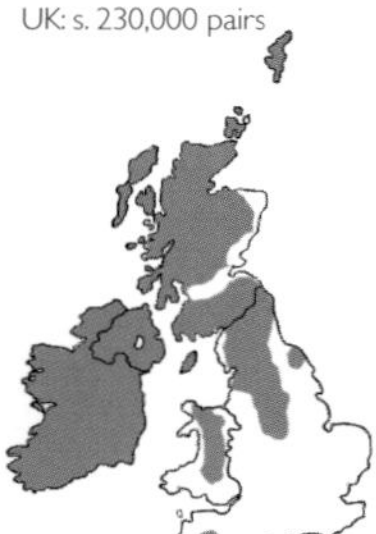

Fairly common resident on treeless moorland and bogs, habitats dominated by its staple diet of heather. Important gamebird, moors often maintained just for this species, and shooting famously allowed from Aug 12 ('Glorious Twelfth'). Often found in groups, larger in the winter, and is often located by its very distinctive guttural call *go-back*—a fantastic sound! In spring, displays by lifting into the air, stalling and gliding to ground with tail spread, calling all the while. Easiest grouse to see, often flushed by hill walkers, and then will fly some distance with bursts of wingbeats, intermittently wings still and arched down. Also often seen with just head breaking horizon or peering between heather stalks, checking on intruder. **ID:** Coloured to blend in with heather moors, sexes more similar than other grouse. Plumage rather plain, lacking wing bars or pale patches, but feet feathered white. Ad ♂ has broad red comb, darker wings and tail, ♀ slightly duller, more heavily barred and smaller red comb. Small patch of white on underwing.

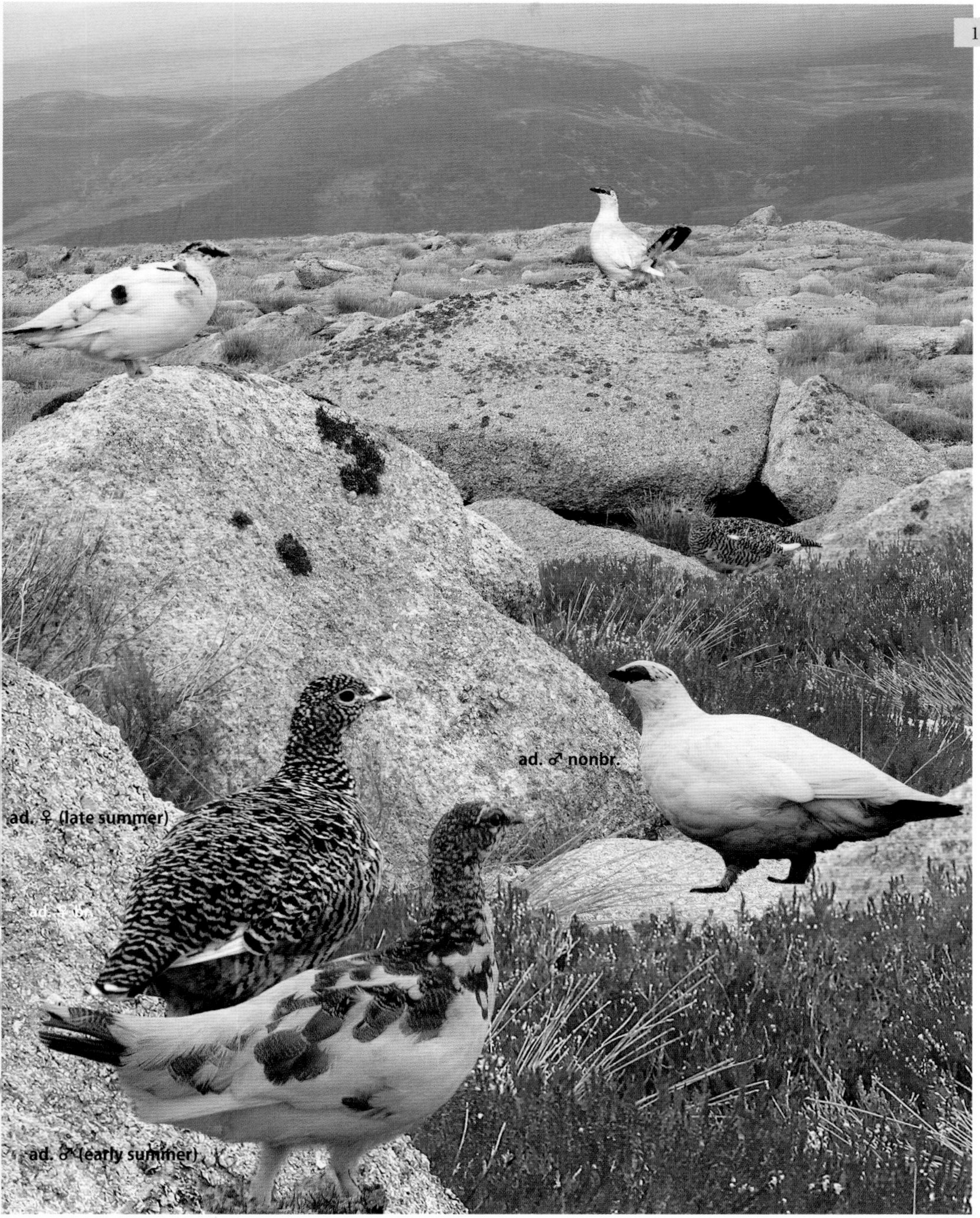

Ptarmigan *Lagopus mutus* **PTARM/PM** L 35cm

UK: s. 2,000–15,000 pairs

Even hardier than REDGR, found on highest mountaintops above 1000 m in Scottish Highlands, usually in barren landscapes with not much vegetation and plenty of rocks. Can be quite tame, and is less likely to flush theatrically than REDGR, preferring to run. Found in small parties in winter, usually roosts in snow. Has similar flight display to REDGR, but very different call, a series of clicks that sound a bit like retching. **ID:** Slightly smaller than REDGR with narrower-based bill. Famously changes plumage according to prevailing state of habitat, with white blotches on plumage in spring and autumn when snow patchy, and all white in midst of winter. Nonbr: all white with black tail corners, ♂ has black lores with red comb above. ♀ is all white with pale lores and reduced red above eye. In br, plumage always greyer or yellower than similar REDGR. Ad ♀ br: yellow-brown tones. Ad ♂ br: barred grey lacking warm tones of ♀, black eye-stripe. Barring on the underparts become more extensive through the summer.

Grey Partridge *Perdix perdix* **GREPA/P.** L 30cm

UK: s. 43,000 pairs

Generally uncommon gamebird of agricultural fields and pasture, benefiting from hedgerows and wide field margins. Also found on some upland pastures, and overall inhabits moister locations than RELPA. Ground addicted and most reluctant to flush, preferring to run away. For much of year, lives in small groups ('coveys'), usually family units, which stick together when alarmed. Very hardy, coveys often hide under windbreaks in winter, but roost on the ground. Male in spring makes call sounding like turning a key in a rusty lock; other calls similarly hoarse and high pitched. Frequently bathes in dust. Has largest average clutch of any British bird, 15 eggs. **ID:** Often stands erect as if on guard. Compact, with orange corners to very short tail. All plumages have grey neck and broad rufous flank bars. Ad ♂: striking dark belly patch with orange face. Ad ♀: lacks belly patch and has paler face divided by grey ear coverts. Juv: plumage held for 2–3 months, face and underparts dull and lightly streaked; no belly patch.

Red-legged Partridge *Alectoris rufa* RELPA/RL L 33cm

JK: s. 82,000

Introduced species that does well on dry, light soils and wide open fields; numbers are maintained by release of captive-bred birds by estate owners. Broader habitat spectrum than GREPA, sometimes in scrub and heath, and unlike its relative, will often perch on fence posts and even roofs of barns or houses. Coveys have less cohesion and are more likely to separate when flushed. Runs more readily, while GREPA often squats and relies on camouflage. Some birds released on estates are hybrids or are actually Chukar, a species from se Europe. Call is extraordinary series of clucks repeated rhythmically and often at accelerating pace, may sound remarkably like puffing of steam train. Often heard best at night. **ID:** Same size, and at distance surprisingly difficult to tell from GREPA. Given decent view, white throat, black necklaces, and darker, closer-set bars soon become obvious; legs red. In flight, looks greyer and plainer on back. Juv: odd creamy brown, with fewer flank bars.

RAPTORS

Raptors are one of the most popular groups of birds in the world. Many species are large and powerful and spend a lot of time in flight, covering large distances largely in search of food. Sightings of raptors are often brief, and more prolonged views are often of distant soaring 'specks'. Add to this poor light conditions, and identifying many birds with certainty is impossible. When trying to identify raptors, it is most important to try to work out a bird's size and shape. Judging size can be difficult and gets harder with distance. Comparing with other nearby species is helpful. Larger species have slower wingbeats; thus with even the most distant birds you can get a sense of size. Be careful about trying to be too precise with judging size, and remember that size can vary widely within a species. Female raptors are typically larger than males.

Judging shape is critical and key to identifying most species. Sometimes the shape will change depending on whether it is soaring, diving, or flapping, as well as the angle of observation. It does not usually take long to get an accurate sense of the bird's appearance if you watch carefully. Working out which group of birds it belongs to is always the first step. A falcon such as Kestrel has pointed wings, and an accipiter such as Sparrowhawk has rounded wings. Shape also determines flight style. In large raptors, juveniles are usually slightly slimmer winged than adults.

It takes several years, and multiple plumages, for larger raptors to reach adulthood. Most buzzards moult into adult-like plumage after a year, though many retain a few juvenile feathers, so they can be aged with careful observation. Accipiters take 1–2 years (2–3 plumages), eagles 4–5 years (5 plumages), and falcons 1 or 2 years, to reach adulthood. Most raptors keep juvenile plumage for a year. Understanding this moult sequence is key to ageing and ID.

To simplify, these birds can be broken into five groups: eagles and Osprey, buteos, accipiters, falcons, and miscellaneous species.

Eagles and Osprey. Eagles and Osprey are hunters.

Buteos/Buzzards. This group comprises medium to large raptors with broad and typically long wings but shortish broad tails. They spend a considerable amount of time soaring.

Accipiters. Smaller than buteos. They have rounded wings and proportionately longer tails. They also soar. Short rounded wings are designed for agility rather than speed, so manoeuvring in woodland and other tight spaces is not a problem.

Falcons. Small to medium-sized. The slimmest raptors, falcons have narrower and more pointed wings, and are designed to travel at high speeds for hunting. Peregrine Falcon has been clocked at more than 200 mph.

Miscellaneous species. A number of other raptors such as kites don't fit neatly into any of the above groups.

Exploitation has always had a major impact on raptor populations, with the sale of birds or eggs a profitable business in some areas. The Wild Birds Protection Act 1954 and Wildlife and Countryside Act 1981 in the United Kingdom have made it impossible to legally collect or even keep wild birds' eggs unless they were procured before 1954. Increased surveillance and harsher penalties, including prison sentences (the Countryside and Rights of Way Act 2000), have helped to reduce the number of collectors but they still remain a significant problem. Other species such as Kestrel have declined in certain areas partly because of loss of suitable habitat and changes in agricultural practices. Migrant raptors, such as Hobby, still face exploitation by trappers and hunters in the Mediterranean.

In recent times, hawk watches for some of our scarce species such as Honey Buzzard, Goshawk, and Osprey have been established and are very popular. The reintroduction programme for Red Kite, which had dwindled to a few pairs, has been remarkably successful, to the point where they are now fairly common in many areas of Britain, including the heavily populated south-east.

OWLS

Owls are a mesmerising and often mysterious group of birds, particularly as they are mostly nocturnal. Their habits and cryptic plumage make it easy to walk straight past them. A collection of regurgitated pellets, whitewash (feces) on or under trees, or a group of agitated songbirds—usually led by tits and 'crests—can often give away their presence. Even if you know where they are, they can be tricky to see. After a second and third look into foliage, you often see them miraculously appear. Patience and perseverance is the name of the game. Some species frequently roost communally out of breeding season and have favourite locations. Common sense should prevail, as they are sensitive and easily flushed.

Some owls have 'ears'—actually just tufts of feathers that help camouflage them—and facial discs that help direct sound into the hidden ear openings. Although owls have good eyesight, their incredibly sensitive hearing can determine both direction and distance, allowing some species to catch food even when they can't see it. They hunt from perches as well as on the wing. Serrated edges to the outer primaries allow air to pass through, helping the owl to fly silently. At night, the best way to locate owls is by listening. They give a variety of hoots, whistles, barks, and other weird noises. Another way to find them is to make high-pitched mouse-like squeaks, which they will often come to investigate. Bad weather, particularly wind, makes it difficult for owls to hunt. If you want to see one, you will have the most joy if you look on the first calm evening after a storm.

Osprey *Pandion haliaetus* **OSPRE/OP** L 55cm

UK: s. 200–250 pairs

Charismatic and popular summer visitor Mar–Sep to large water bodies with plenty of fish; rare but widespread passage migrant, to Oct. Frequently seen hunting, diving, or carrying fish torpedo-style from lakes, rivers, or the sea. Famous for spectacular plunge-dives, led by huge feet and talons. Frequently cuts out before hitting the water or comes out empty-handed. Patrols waterways, often in circuits, hovering intermittently. Sits on prominent perch to rip prey apart, but also on the ground in marshes. Head-on, profile is flat winged, or a shallow W. Feeble cal when flying or sitting, a high-pitched *choop* **ID:** White head with a dark eyeline. Slim wit wings typically angled back but straighte when soaring. White body and underwin contrast with dark carpal and barred fligh feathers and tail; a unique combination. Be ware, though, of confusing with gull. Ad ♀ averages darker breast band. Juv: superficial ly as adult but with pale-fringed upperpart and buff on breast and underwing coverts

Golden Eagle *Aquila chrysaetos* **GOLEA/EA** L 80cm

UK: s. 440 pairs

Rare resident in wilder areas of Scotland, plus a few in Cumbria, mainly in mountainous regions, but also along the coast and on islands. A very big, impressive raptor that typically catches birds such as PTARM and mammals such as Mountain Hare, sometimes snaring them when one member of a pair flushes the prey and the other ambushes it. May also stoop down rapidly on prey, and will also scavenge. Formidable flyer that can maintain control even in harsh winter gales. **ID:** Very big, with 2m wingspan. Very long, narrow-based, pinched-in wings with obvious 'fingers'; much longer tail than BUZZA, and more protruding head. Feathered legs visible when perched. In common with BUZZA, soars with wings held up in a V shape, unlike other big raptors. Flight notably controlled, with steady glides and slow wingbeats. Ad (5th yr onward) all dark with narrow grey bands in tail; golden nape. All imm with striking white patches in tail base and wings, most obvious on 1st-yr and become progressively less extensive.

Black Kite *Milvus migrans* **BLAKI/KB** L 58cm
Rare visitor, with fewer than 10 records/year, peaking May. **ID:** BUZZA-sized, with long tail with very shallow fork, not always visible. Broad-tipped, parallel-edged wings that are flexed backwards as REDKI in level flight; soars with wings slightly bowed, unlike harriers. Loose flight style sim to REDKI. Plumage darker than REDKI, without reddish tones. Upperwing with pale band across coverts. Juv more mottled, with dark eye mask.

White-tailed Eagle *Haliaeetus albicilla* **WHTEA** L 80cm
Small reintroduced Scottish population; rare winter visitor further south. Huge, with massively broad wings, protruding head, and enormous bill, plus oddly short, wedge-shaped tail. Often on ground. Feeds on fish and seabirds. **ID:** Ad pale brown head and large yellow bill; white tail. Juv: darker head and bill, brown tail with white feather centres, pale armpits, wings more 'pinched in'. Older imms remain mottled below, white tail not complete until 5th yr.

Montagu's Harrier *Circus pygargus* **MONHA/MO** L 44cm ***s. 12–16 pairs***
Rare summer visitor, May–Sep, breeding in agricultural fields. **ID:** Slimmest and lightest of harriers, with light body and sharp wingtips, buoyant flight like a tern, quarters over grassland and dry areas. Ad ♂: dark secondary bar on upperwing, underwing coverts mottled orange-brown, lacks clean breast band. Ad ♀ underwing ginger coloured, more strongly barred than HENHA, dark face mask. Juv: strong rufous underparts.

Red Kite *Milvus milvus* **REDKI/KT** L 61cm

UK: s. 1,600 pairs

Exciting raptor now thriving in many areas after reintroduction schemes, allied to a native population in Wales; a number of feeding stations exist. Requires small woods and copses next to open country, often in hills. Mainly a scavenger, drawn to tips and road kills, but can catch such food as birds. Flight highly manoeuvrable, often twists its tail slightly to adjust; can dive and swoop. **ID:** Larger than many expect, with diagnostic long, deeply forked tail and long fingered wings. Flies with characteristic loose style with deep wingbeats; in level flight, wings are pressed forward at carpals, and slightly bowed. Pale 'window' inside dark wingtips; tail warm reddish brown, superb when catches sunlight; pale diagonal band on upperwing. Head often pale, greyish white. Juv with paler vent and pale tips to greater wing coverts, producing pale line above and below.

Marsh Harrier *Circus aeruginosus* **MARHA/MR** L 52cm

UK: s. 320–380 pairs

Rare summer visitor (Mar–Sep) primarily to large freshwater marshes with extensive reed beds. Small numbers overwinter. Usually seen quartering, flying low and slow in an effort to spot prey on ground or to flush it out; feeds on birds, esp young, along with a few small mammals. In summer, performs marvellous food passes, the male calling as it brings in food and the female rising from the reed-bed nest to catch dropped offering, often turning upside down. Male makes LAPWI-like whine; alarm *quek-quek*. **ID:** An obvious harrier with its long, narrow wings, usually held up in a V, and very long tail. Bigger and broader winged than other harriers. Ad ♂ tricoloured above, black (wingtips), brown (coverts and back), and grey (secondaries and tail); wings from below lack dark trailing edge; streaked brown on belly. Ad ♀ larger than ♂, mainly dark brown with variable creamy markings on shoulders; crown and throat cream, with dark eye mask. Variable pale breast band. Juv sim, but darker brown including underwing, no breast band or shoulder marks, throat and crown rich buff.

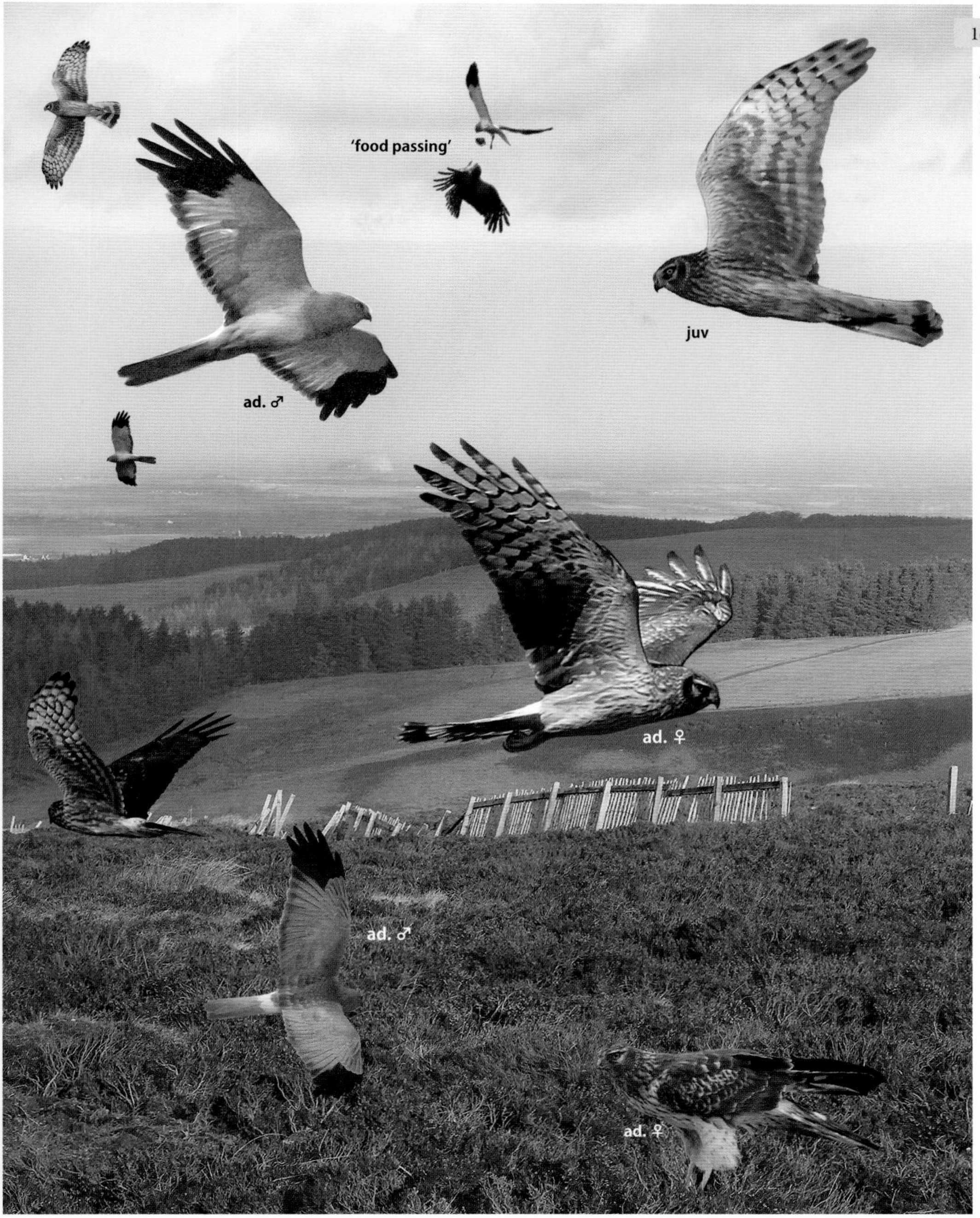

Hen Harrier *Circus cyaneus* **HENHA/HH** L 47cm

UK: s. 630 pairs

Uncommon raptor of open areas, often chilly and windswept. A winter visitor to the south, to salt marshes and other wetlands, grassland, heaths, and farmland. Rare breeding bird on upland moorland. Typical low, slow-quartering flight of harriers, with wings held in a dihedral. Long, narrow wings and tail immediately obvious. It rocks from side to side, then dives down to grab or chase birds and mammals. Performs food-passes as MARHA, and the male spectacular rollercoaster 'sky-dances' high in air, barely in control. **ID:** Quite large, although slimmer than MARHA. Typical long-tailed harrier shape. White rump. Owl-like facial disc, slim build, and long legs obvious when perched. Adult ♂: 'grey ghost', grey upperparts and chest; white underparts contrast sharply with chest, black wingtips. 2nd-yr ♂: variable, often sim to ad with more brown in plumage. Ad ♀ 'Ringtail': large white rump, barred tail, streaked breast on buff background, pale neck ring. Juv: v sim to ad ♀ but with finer streaking on rufous underbody and has rufous upperwing coverts (buffier in adults).

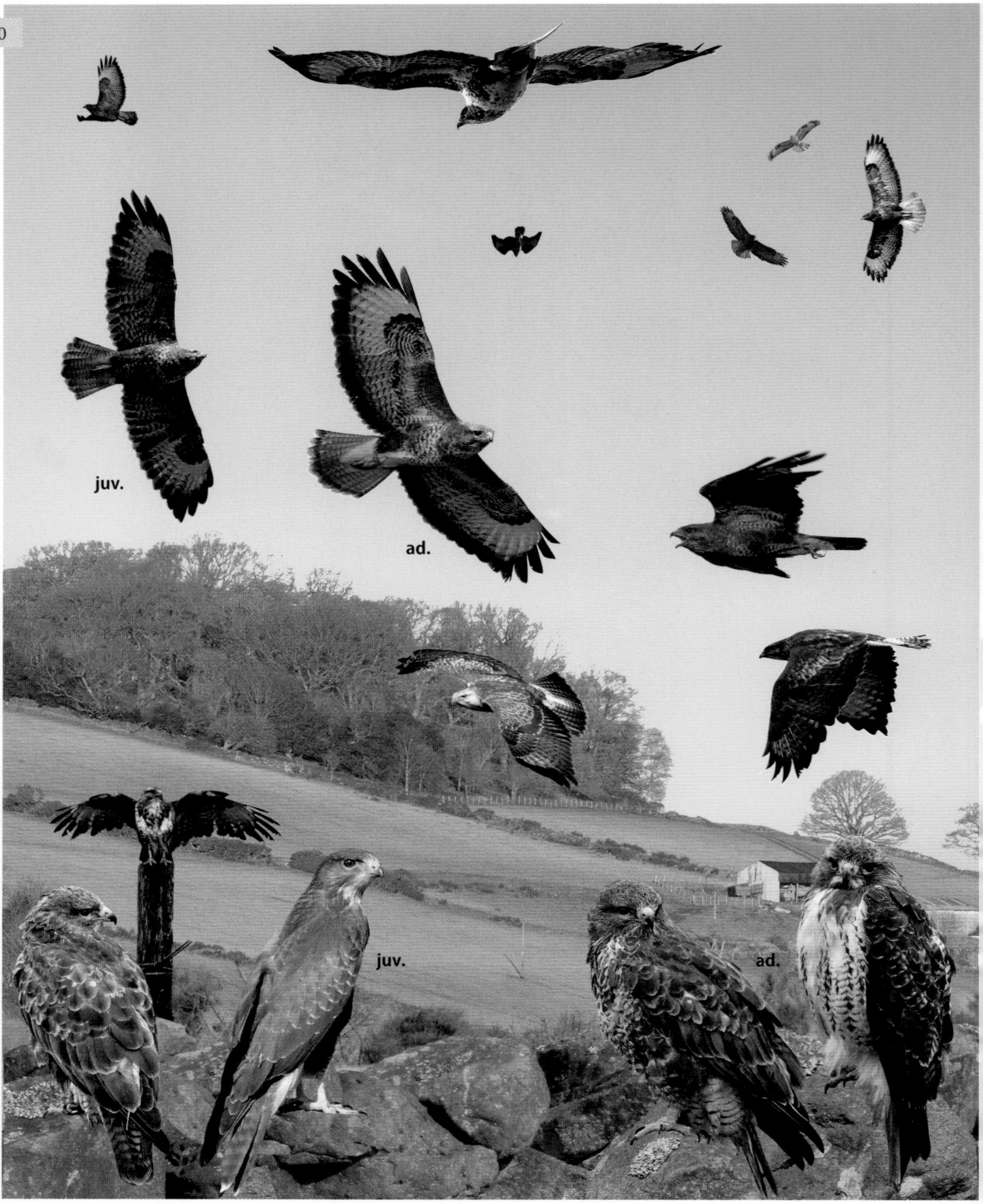

Common Buzzard *Buteo buteo* **BUZZA/BZ** L 54cm

UK: s. 57,000–79,000 pairs

By far the commonest large raptor in Britain, once found mainly in hilly areas of the west and north, now almost everywhere. Thrives where it has small woods for nesting and open country for hunting. Very adaptable, from being able to catch mammals (e.g., young rabbits, rats) with a dive from above, right through to wandering over fields searching for worms. Is able to hover and hang still in the wind, and to hunt from a low perch, pouncing on rodents; also scavenges. The most territorial raptor, often heard uttering loud, wild-sounding mewing. Often several can be seen circling in the air at once. Has display in which dives with wings closed and uses momentum to swoop up again. **ID:** Broad-winged raptor with very small head and short tail (shorter than wings front-to-back). Soars with wings held up in shallow V; in level flight, flexes wings forward at carpals, wingbeats quick and stiff. Extremely variable plumage, from dark to creamy white, a challenge. Many have pale band across chest. Pale inner primaries/secondaries below. Ads with clear black band on end of tail, and broad black trailing edge to wing, narrower in juv. Juv: often streaked/mottled below. Upperparts uniform with pale fringes.

Honey Buzzard *Pernis apivorus* **HONBU/HZ** L 56cm ***s. 33–69 pairs***

Rare, secretive summer visitor (May–Sep) to larger forests, feeding on bee and wasp grubs, some vertebrates. Doesn't show itself like BUZZA, feeds quietly on forest floor or sits in canopy. Doesn't hover, is largely silent. In flight display, briefly flicks wings high above back. **ID:** Sim to BUZZA but in flight, head protrudes more, tail is longer, and longer wings are broad in middle, slightly pinched in at body. Soars on flat, not raised wings, wingbeats slow, regal. Tail with broad terminal band and 2 inner bands, dark stripes on underwing. Plumage incredibly variable. Ad: yellow eye, ♂ greyish head, ♀ more mottled below with extra wing band. Juv browner with narrower trailing edge to wing.

Rough-legged Buzzard *Buteo lagopus* **ROLBU/RF** L 55cm ***w. 32***

Rare winter visitor, numbers vary. **ID:** Larger than BUZZA, with more pointed wings and longer tail with conspicuous white base above and below. Underwing whiter and more contrasting than BUZZA, with more obvious dark carpal patches. Belly usually contrastingly dark. Hovers much more than BUZZA; in level flight, wingbeats slower, not as stiff. ♀ and juv: brown bellied, paler head; pattern reversed in ♂. Ads have broader solid trailing edge to underwing.

Sparrowhawk *Accipter nisus* SPARR/SH L 30–38cm

UK: s. 35,000 pairs

Common and widespread in woods, open country, and gardens, where a predator of small birds at feeders. Catches by ambush; sits quietly concealed, then makes unseen, accelerating, low approach (e.g., from behind hedge) until final surprise strike. Eats only birds. Often seen soaring, flies upwards or forward with short series of flaps followed by glides. Presence often first detected by songbirds scattering or pigeons circling. Nests in woods. **ID:** Small raptor with pencil-thin legs, KESTR sized, but doesn't hover and doesn't sit much in open. Shares long tail of falcons, but has relatively short, broad wings with blunt tips. Tail is narrow based, square ended with sharp corners. Plain greyish above, except for dark bands on tail; densely but neatly barred below. May have white patch on nape. ♂ small, with orangey cheeks and underparts, ♀much larger (one-third bigger), with whitish underparts, narrow pale supercilium and rufous on cheeks. Juv: sim to ad ♀, browner, with scaly upperparts and heavier barring on underparts.

Goshawk *Accipter gentilis* **GOSHA/GI** L 50–60cm ***s. 280–430 pairs***

Rare but widespread forest raptor, often associated with large coniferous stands, but also uses deciduous woods and may hunt over open country. Eats mammals as well as birds, hunts as SPARR, not at bird feeders. **ID:** Larger than sim SPARR, ♀ as big as BUZZA, but ♂ less obvious bulk. Quite different shape, with longer and broader arm (inner wings) and more pointed wingtip; long tail round tipped and tends to look much more hip-heavy; head protrudes more. Dark face mask and white supercilium. ♂ grey above, whitish below with fine barring, ♀ browner above. Juv buff below, with drop-shaped streaks, not bars down breast. Brownish above. 2nd-yr: mostly adult-like, with some retained juvenile feathers.

Red-footed Falcon *Falco vespertinus* **REFFA/FV** L 30cm

Rare passage migrant, mainly Apr–Jun, roughly 10 sightings a year. Insectivorous falcon like cross between HOBBY (catches insects in agile flight) and KESTR (hovers with loose-looking wingbeats, perches on wires and often on ground). **ID:** Silhouette like HOBBY with longer tail. Red legs. ♂ all-over sooty grey but for reddish thighs; upperwing silvery. ♀ totally different, rusty reddish brown underparts and crown, white face, small black mask, upperwing grey with black bars. Juv: as ♀ but black streaked below on buff.

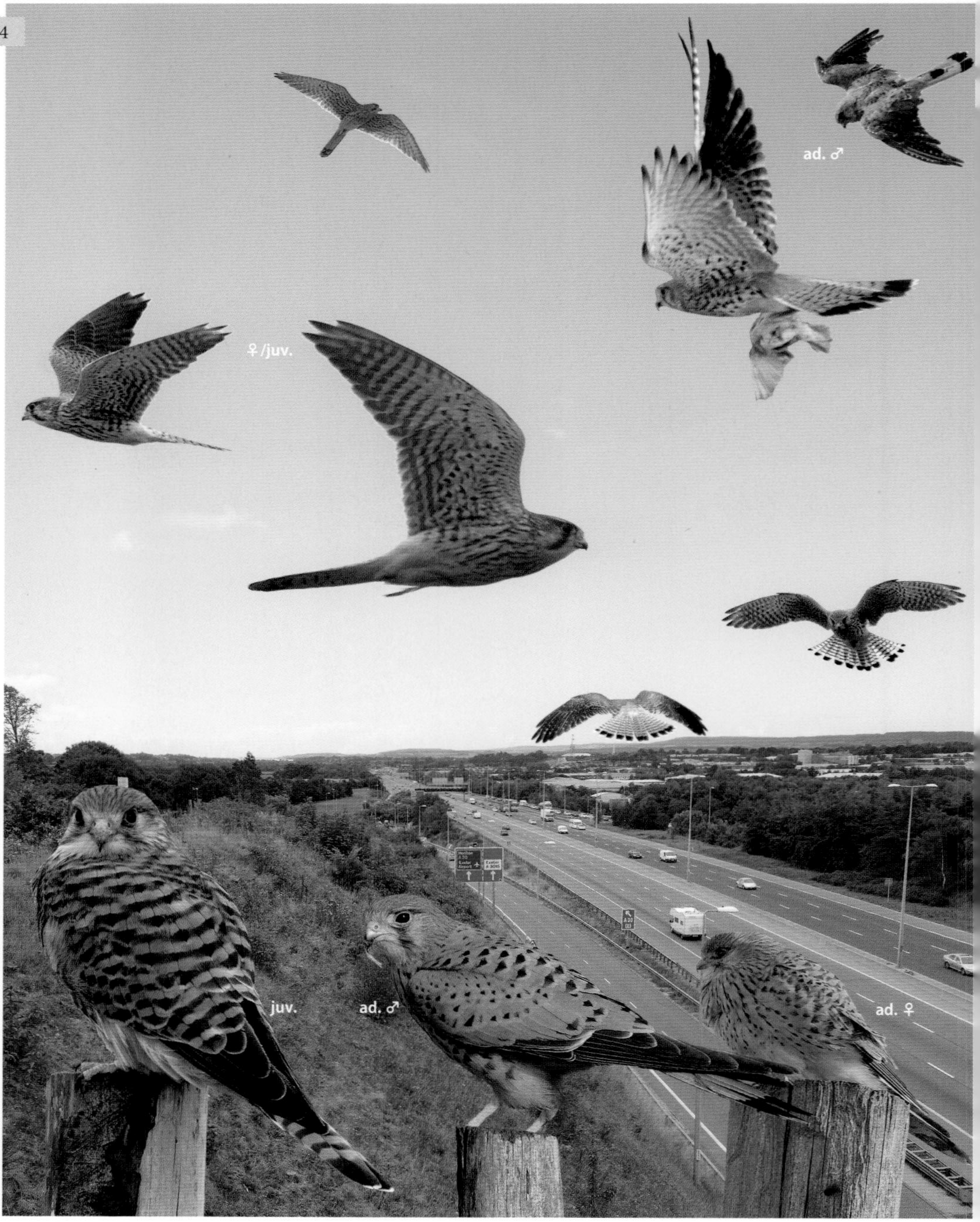

Common Kestrel *Falco tinnunculus* **KESTR/K.** L 34cm

UK: s. 46,000 pairs

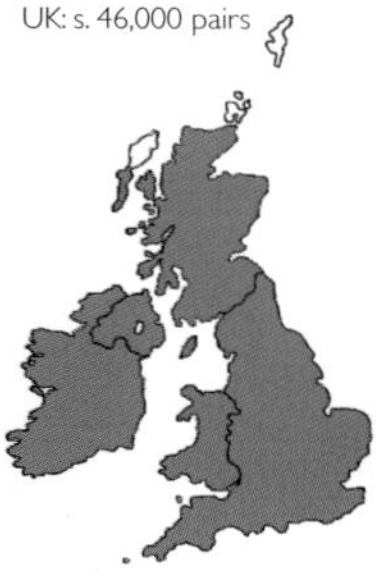

Common and widespread raptor that draws attention to itself by its persistent hovering. Holds body at angle and head perfectly still while flying on the spot with steady, winnowing wingbeats. Often adjusts position while hovering, and eventually drops down lower before final, talons-first plunge into mammalian prey, such as voles or mice. Can hunt in moonlight and often at dusk. Often seen perched on wires, bushes, and poles. Inhabits open country, sometimes reaching into cities and regular along roads. Hoarse *kek-kek-kek* call. Male shows off shimmering pale underparts in display-flight. **ID:** Longer tail than most falcons, and has noticeably less powerful flight, with full but weak wingbeats. Outer wing dark brown, contrasting with chestnut inner wing; moustachial stripe small but clear; underparts buff with lines of spots. Ad ♂: rich chestnut upperparts, grey head, tail clean grey with broad black subterminal band. Ad ♀: brown head and tail, the latter with several bars, as well as dark subterminal band; overall more heavily streaked/spotted. Juv: v sim to ♀. Underparts more streaked than spotted. Imm ♂ has dark bars on grey tail.

Merlin *Falco columbarius* **MERLI/ML** L 30cm

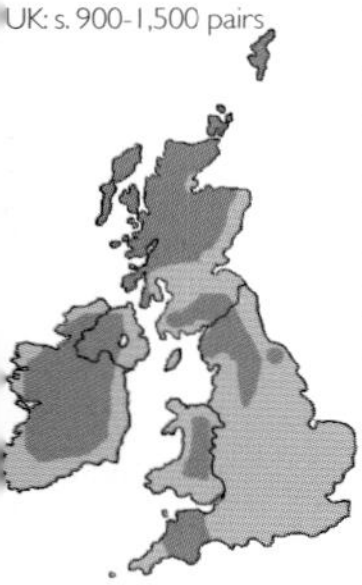

Uncommon breeder on upland moors and plantations; in winter moves to lowlands, including the coast and can be seen anywhere on migration. By far our smallest raptor, males barely larger than a thrush; female like small KESTR. A feisty dasher; despite size, causes panic among flocks of birds when it appears unexpectedly. Sits on low but prominent posts and snags (but not overhead wires like KESTR), then sets off like a 'bat out of hell', chasing its prey with fast but stiff wingbeats. At times, follows every twist and turn of fleeing bird (e.g., SKYLA), as if it were a guided missile. **ID:** Similar to a very small PEREG, sharing broad-based wings, but with a narrower tail. It always looks more compact than KESTR. Rather dark plumaged, with weak moustachial stripe. Ad ♂: blue backed with dark shaft streaks; orange underparts. Tail grey with white tip and broad black subterminal band. ♀/juv quite different, with dark brown upperparts and buff underparts with heavy streaks that become almost arrow-shapes on flanks. Tail brown with several whitish 'rings'.

Hobby *Falco subbuteo* **HOBBY/HY** L 34cm

UK: s. 2,800 pairs

Agile aerobatic summer visitor (Apr–Oct) that plies summer skies for insects and birds. Breeds mainly in vicinity of heathland and farmland, but ranges widely over open country and, esp, wetlands (bogs, reservoirs), sometimes in concentrations that nest in isolated tree. Famed for ability to catch fast aerial birds (e.g., SWIFT, SWALL) in flight, but also hunts pipits and larks. From late spring onward, hunts dragonflies and beetles, seizing in low passes over bogs and lakes, then delivering from feet to bill in mid-air. Call loud, slurred, ringing *kyew, kyew*. **ID:** KESTR-sized raptor. Look for giant, slow-moving SWIFT—v sim shape, with long, swept-back, very sharply pointed wings and comparatively short tail. Narrow-based tail and wings (see PEREG). Ad distinctive, with black mask, white face and collar, reddish brown thighs, and broad black streaks flowing down white breast. Upperparts greyish. Juv: buff face and underparts; upperparts scaly. Lacks reddish thighs, buff instead.

Peregrine *Falco peregrinus* **PEREG/PE** L 44cm

UK: s. 1,500 pairs

Supreme aerial predator that traditionally nests on remote cliff faces but now found in many cities, using buildings and large bridges. Widespread but uncommon; in winter, wanders and can be found almost anywhere. Hunts birds in incredible stoops, skydiving from great height; when hits, may break neck of pigeon and wipe it out with puff of feathers. Also approaches from low down, may make several dives at one victim. Often terrorises concentrations of birds on estuaries, lakes, and so on and at roosts (e.g., STARL). Stiff, shallow flaps with wings held flat and straight. Call is loud complaining ringing, almost quacking in tone. **ID:** Fairly large, with anchor shape. Broad-based, sharp-tipped wings and short tail enhance compact, muscular look and distinguish from other predators. Dark upperparts, broad moustache, and barred/streaked underparts. Adult: broad black moustache bordered by white cheek. Slate upperparts. Underparts white, sometimes buff-washed, with variable black barring. Juv: brown upperparts and streaked underparts with pale crown.

Barn Owl *Tyto alba* **BAROW/BO** L 34cm

UK: s. 3,000–5,000 pairs

Exciting 'ghost' of the night-time countryside, found mainly in unimproved grassland and pasture, overgrown field corners, marshy areas and dykes, esp wherever rodents are plentiful. Roosts and nests in old buildings, barns, trees, and nest boxes. Coming out to hunt at dusk, courses open areas low to ground or sits on perch watching or listening for dinner, often seen in car headlights. Tends to look at you when disturbed, with striking white heart-shaped face, before silently disappearing into the night. Caught in a flashlight, this is the 'white' owl. Call: given by adults and young at nest site or in flight, a shrieking hush-like *sssshhhhh*—like scolding naughty kids. It can be heard at long range. Begging young will call almost constantly. **ID:** Medium sized with tan-and-grey upperparts. Unmistakable heart-shaped facial discs and small black eyes. Long legs often dangle when hunting. Underparts usually white in ♂ and with orange/buff in ♀, the latter with more spots on plumage. In silhouette, wings appear slightly longer and more pointed than in 'eared' owls, but flight style similar.

Tawny Owl *Strix aluco* **TAWOW/TO** L 38cm

UK: s. 50,000 pairs

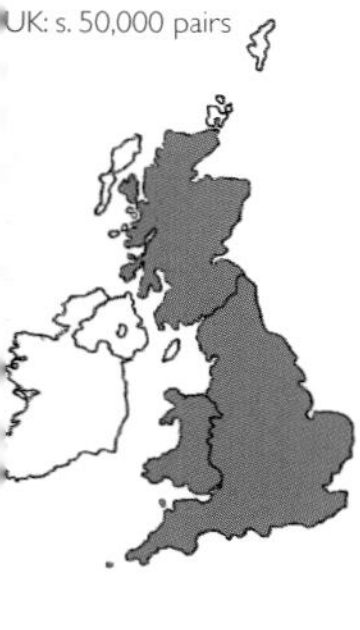

Our best-known owl, quite common in woodland, even in gardens and towns, but often difficult to see. Truly nocturnal and hides during day, although sometimes angry *chink* calls of BLABI and others may alert observer to bird mobbed at roost. Famous for its gorgeous haunting hoots, given by male: initial sonorous hoot followed by gap, then a sequence of quavering hoots, the whole sounding soulful and mysterious. Both sexes give loud *ke-wick!* contact call, and fledglings give squeaky wheeze. Hunting method is to perch high (e.g., on lamp-post) and drop onto prey (e.g., mice, rats); often hunts by roads and streets. Flight rather straight, with quick, stiff wingbeats, nothing like wavering of other medium-sized owls. Roosts in hollow tree, among creepers and the like. **ID:** Large, big-headed owl with short, rounded wings. Black eyes on broad facial discs. Marvellous, richly patterned plumage, mixture of brown streaks and speckles, white spots and blotches. Fledging fluffy grey-white, like child's toy.

Short-eared Owl *Asio flammeus* **SHEOW/SE** L 38cm

UK: s. 620–2,180 pairs

Open country owl, in marshes, grassland, bogs, and moors. Uncommon, but in some winters large numbers come south from Scandinavia, after boom vole years. Roosts and nests on the ground. Much easier to see than LOEOW, will hunt in the daytime, though far more likely to be seen at twilight. Gracefully courses over open areas, flying low, but often changes direction quickly or stops suddenly, dropping on an unsuspecting rodent. Sometimes seen sitting on ground or low posts adopting distinctive horizontal posture. Often uses communal roosts in winter at favoured locations. Male gives fast-paced deep hoot, and may wing-clap in display; also calls *chee-op!* **ID:** A medium-sized brown owl, with long wings. Streaks on underparts confined to chest and breast, peter out to pale belly. Marbled upperparts. Short, barely visible ear tufts, yellow eyes, dark eye surround gives sinister look. In flight, has blacker wingtips than LOEOW above and below, plus broader tail bars, narrow white trailing edge to wing.

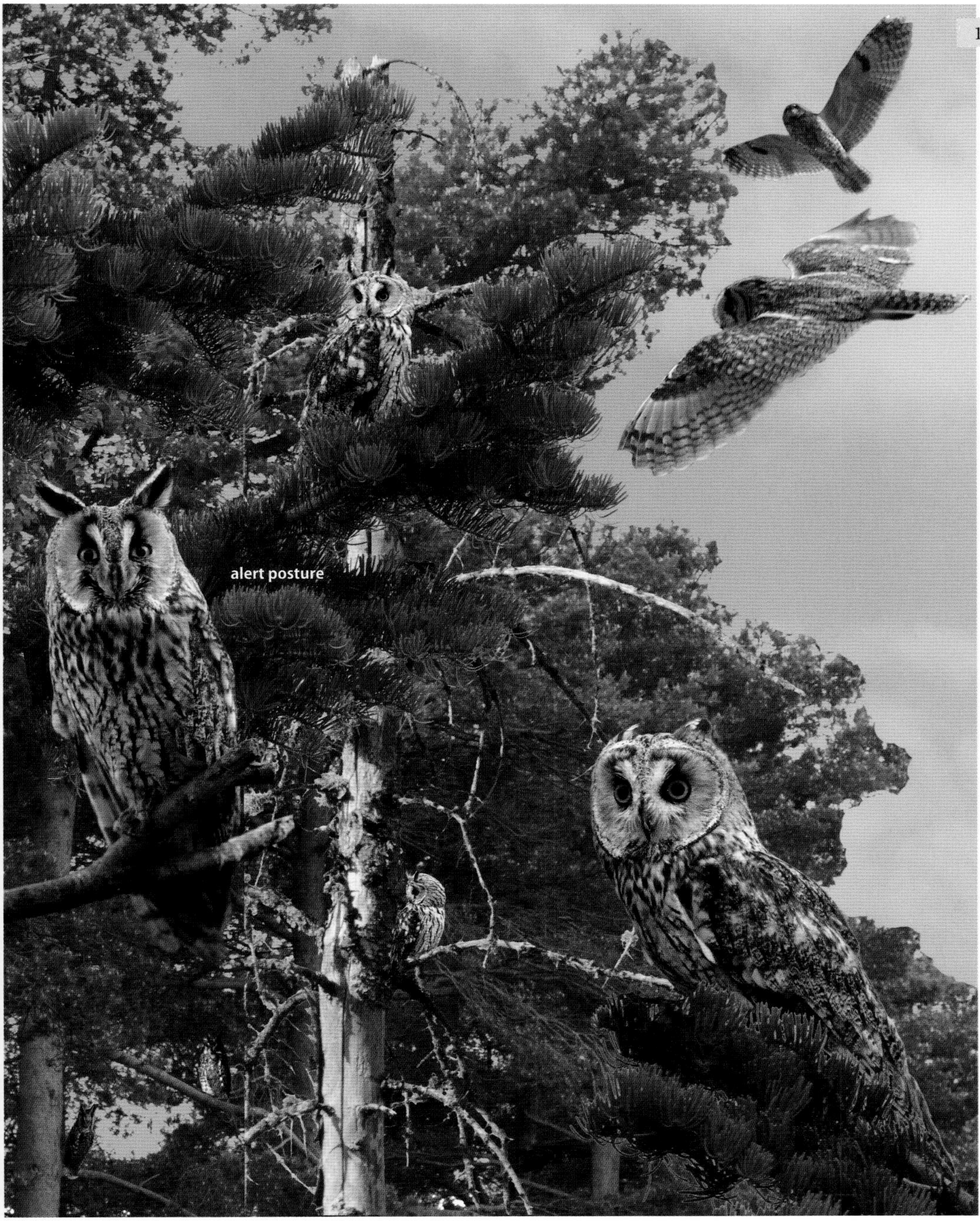

Long-eared Owl *Asio otus* **LOEOW/LE** L 36cm

UK: s. 1,800–6,000 pairs

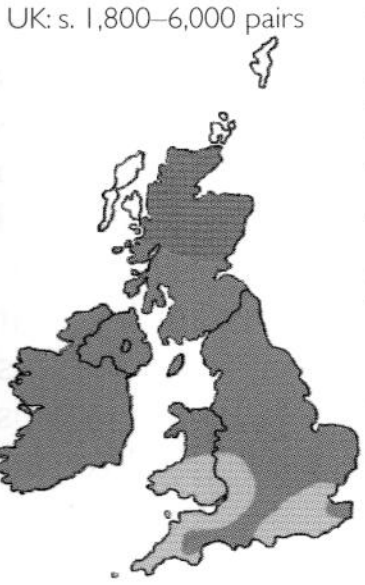

Uncommon deep inside forest, both coniferous and deciduous. Widespread but local, except in Ireland, where replaces TAWOW. Melts into the trees—you know it is there, watching you try to find it. Nocturnal, coming out to feed over open country when pitch-black, rarely before. Away from breeding grounds, roosts are usually communal, sometimes with several birds in one tree. Sits upright and slim (camouflage posture). Easily flushed; wings are heard hitting branches as it flies to another tree. Many sounds include deep hoot at slow pace, plus nasal alarm call (like restrained sneeze) and loud plaintive call of fledglings, like squeaky gate. **ID:** Smaller than TAWOW, and longer bodied. Very different wavering flight with relaxed, deep beats. Like SHEOW, but longer ear tufts, red eyes, and orange face with black lines through eye. Breast barred as well as streaked and much darker—easiest difference to see in flight (daytime). Other differences in flight are more rounded wings, shorter tail, and finely barred outer primaries that lack contrast and dark tip of SHEOW; narrow bars on tail.

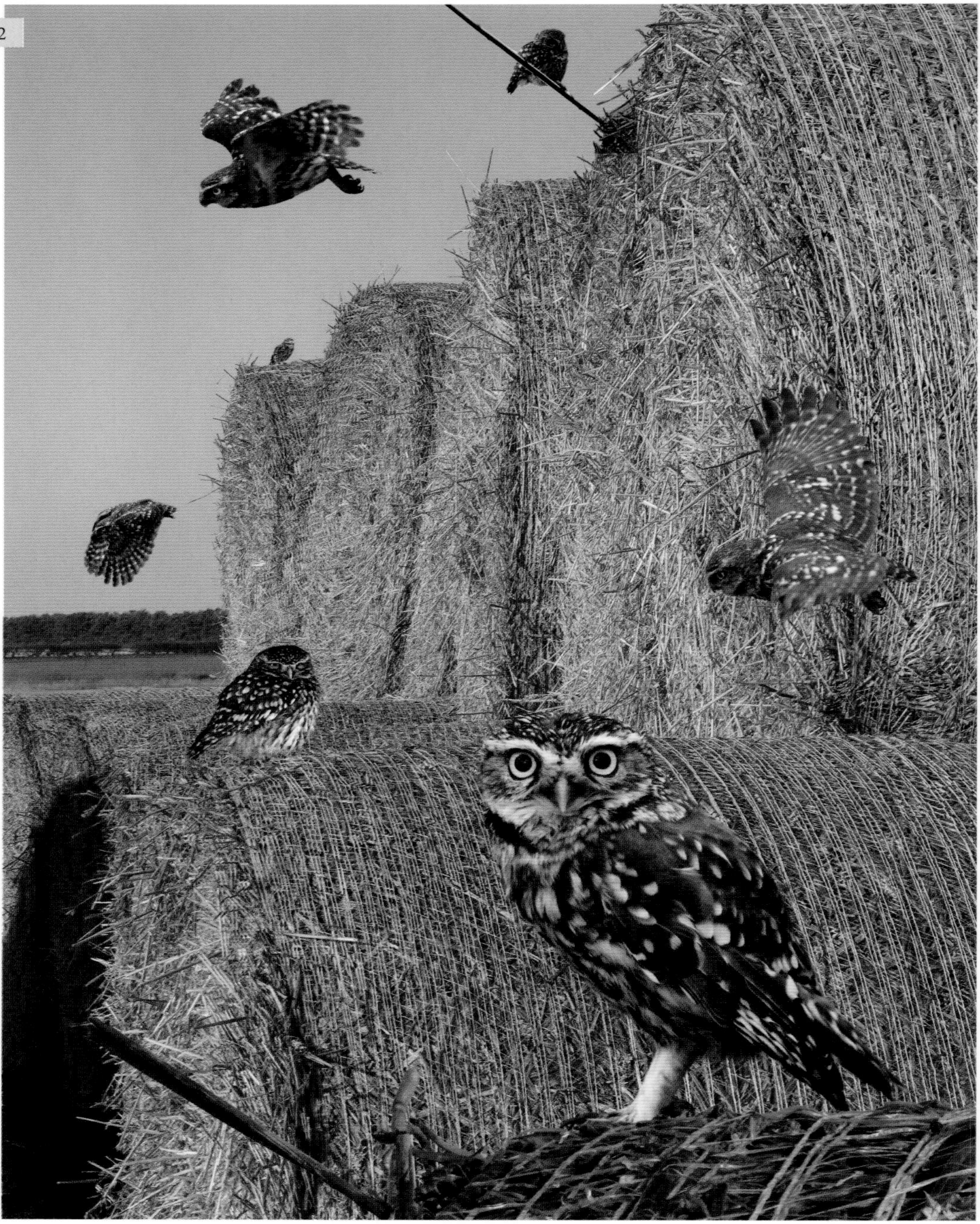

Little Owl *Athene noctua* **LITOW/LO** L 22cm

UK: s. 3,300-7,700 pairs

Probably the easiest owl to see, since it is often active in daytime and at dusk and dawn. Prefers areas where open ground (for hunting) is next to old trees (e.g., willows) with plenty of cavities for hiding and nesting; often this includes farmland, and pollarded willows by watercourses. Feeds on insects in the summer, also worms, birds, and small mammals. Introduced from Holland in 19th century. Often perches on telegraph poles, haystacks, roofs, fence posts, from which it may drop down onto prey; also perches in trees, staying still, low, close to trunk, out of wind. Bobs up and down on perch, looks angrily at observer. Flies low with heavy undulating flight, rather like MISTH. Call an explosive *kiew*, a loud mewing; male has hoot on single note, quite high pitched for an owl, with slight upward inflection at end. **ID:** Very small for an owl (like plump thrush) with upright posture. Look for fierce yellow eyes and white eyebrows (white patches on nape look like false face). Otherwise white-spotted mid-brown. Juv lacks spots on crown.

MISCELLANEOUS LARGER AND AERIAL LANDBIRDS

Pigeons and doves usually build shallow stick nests. They call frequently and are often more easily heard than seen. Many species' calls are soft and rhythmic. Their wings often make noise on take-off. Juveniles lack neck-side patches.

Woodpeckers are a popular group of birds. Their toes are long and strong for clinging to tree trunks. Their bills act as chisels and they have long tongues for grabbing grubs and insects. They excavate holes for nesting—a new one each year. In spring, they repeatedly tap trees at great speed (drumming). The speed, length, sound volume, and intonation make each drum identifiable to species, the same way songs do. Woodpeckers have a strikingly undulating flight pattern shared by few other species—a key ID feature. Surprisingly, Wryneck is part of the woodpecker family.

Crows are not everybody's favourite birds. They are essentially black, very similar, and often described as 'evil looking'. They are intelligent. Research has shown that crows can count and do addition and subtraction. Some pose tough ID challenges, compounded by their monotone colour. White wing patches are quite common, particularly in immature birds. These birds are can be aged through the first year by their dull brown retained flight feathers and wing coverts.

Swifts, martins, and swallows are summer visitors most often seen zooming around, hawking insects. As harbingers of spring in the north, their graceful flights and swoops can mesmerise. They often form mixed flocks, particularly out of breeding season. These can be large to the point where they seem like clouds of gnats in the distance. Nesting on and in buildings, bridges, other man-made structures and sand banks, many use dried mud to build their homes. All have proportionally long pointed wings. ID can be tricky, but with practice, you will find that most species have

Feral Pigeon *Columba livia* **ROCDO/DV** L 33cm

Rock Dove *Columba livia* **ROCDO/DV** L 33cm

UK: s. 550,000 pairs

Common and familiar just about anywhere from city centres to arable areas, particularly where grain is plentiful. Familiar urban birds descended from cliff-nesting wild stock, now confined to cliffs and islands off Scotland and Ireland. Domesticated worldwide—aptly named Feral Pigeon. Nests and roosts on buildings, ledges, and bridges, in loose colonies. Shamelessly displays on ground, male chasing female, also bowing head and making familiar crooning *look at the MOON!* Noisy wing-flapping when flushed. Flight display is glide with wings held up in V. Famously fast in flight; flocks differ from other pigeons in having varied colour combinations; often circle round. **ID:** Wild stock are grey, darkest on head with iridescent green neck patch, 2 black wing bars and white rump. Eyes red. Centuries of domestication have resulted in many colour variations ranging from all white to nearly all black. Most have dark-bordered pale underwing and white rump, distinguishing from flying WOODP and STODO. Juv: duller, lacks iridescence, and has dull orbital ring.

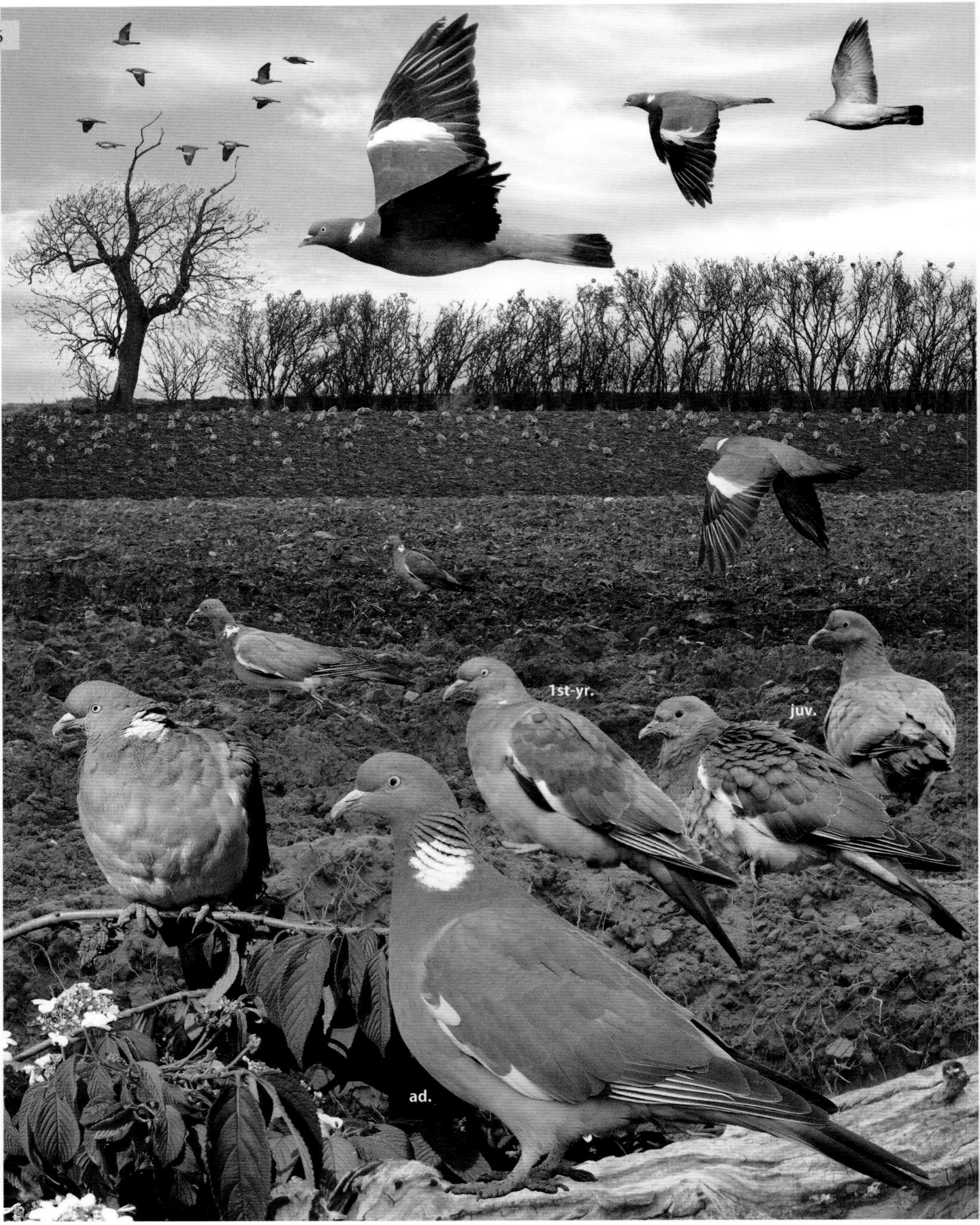

Woodpigeon *Columba palumbus* **WOODP/WP** L 41cm

UK: s. 5,400,000 pairs

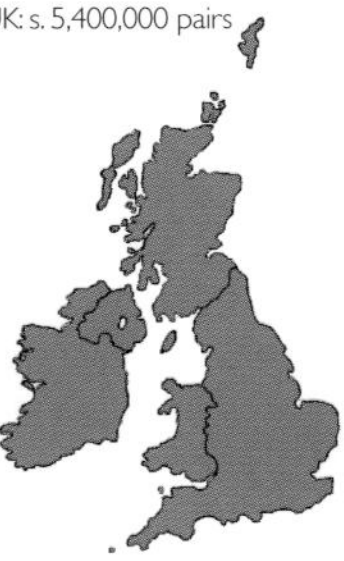

Ubiquitous pot-bellied pigeon, scourge of arable farmers and gardeners who prefer smaller visitors. Theoretically a woodland bird, making an appallingly flimsy stick nest in shrubs and low branches of trees, but also occurs in cities and gardens, farmland and hedgerows. Evocative song is sequence of crooning notes *take TWOOO COOS taffy*, heavy emphasis on second and third syllables; uttered from high perch such as tree branch or rooftop. Flight display in straight line: bird rises with wing-flaps, stalls as if shot, glides down. When landing, raises tail and slowly drops it. Often sits on tops of trees and overhead wires. Sociable when feeding, flocks can be in 100s or even 1000s, latter esp in late autumn. **ID:** Large pigeon with heavy body and long tail. Conspicuous white neck patch is unique, as is white wing-crescent in flight. Yellow eye staring (resembles stick-on eye of toy). In contrast to ROCDO and STODO, primaries white-edged. Sexes alike. Juv: lacks white neck ring and has dark eye and bill, but wing pattern as ad.

Stock Dove *Columba oenas* **STODO/SD** L 33cm

JK: s. 260,000 pairs

Britain's 'other' pigeon, easily overlooked but still fairly common in parkland, farmland with scattered old trees, and also rocky places, including cliffs. Requires a hole for nesting, in tree, rock crevice, or even the ground. Less 'in your face' than other pigeons: song is very quiet, three-note *oo-OO-e* repeated a few times in a cycle, a soft sound from treetops very easily missed in bird chorus. Display is equally understated, just a circuit or figure-of-eight around the treetops with wings in shallow V. Frequently mixes with other pigeons in flocks, but will form modestly sized single-species flocks. **ID:** Compact pigeon with short tail and blunt-looking wings. Close up, note the dark eye; storm-cloud grey wings, head, and upper back; 2 small black bands on wing; and pale bill. Has iridescent green neck patch and rich pink breast. In flight, wings are grey centred above with black edges, lacking silvery white underwing of ROCDO. Smaller and more compact than WOODP, with faster wingbeats. Sexes alike. Juv: lacks neck patch, but shows wing pattern (including bars on wing created by spots) of ad.

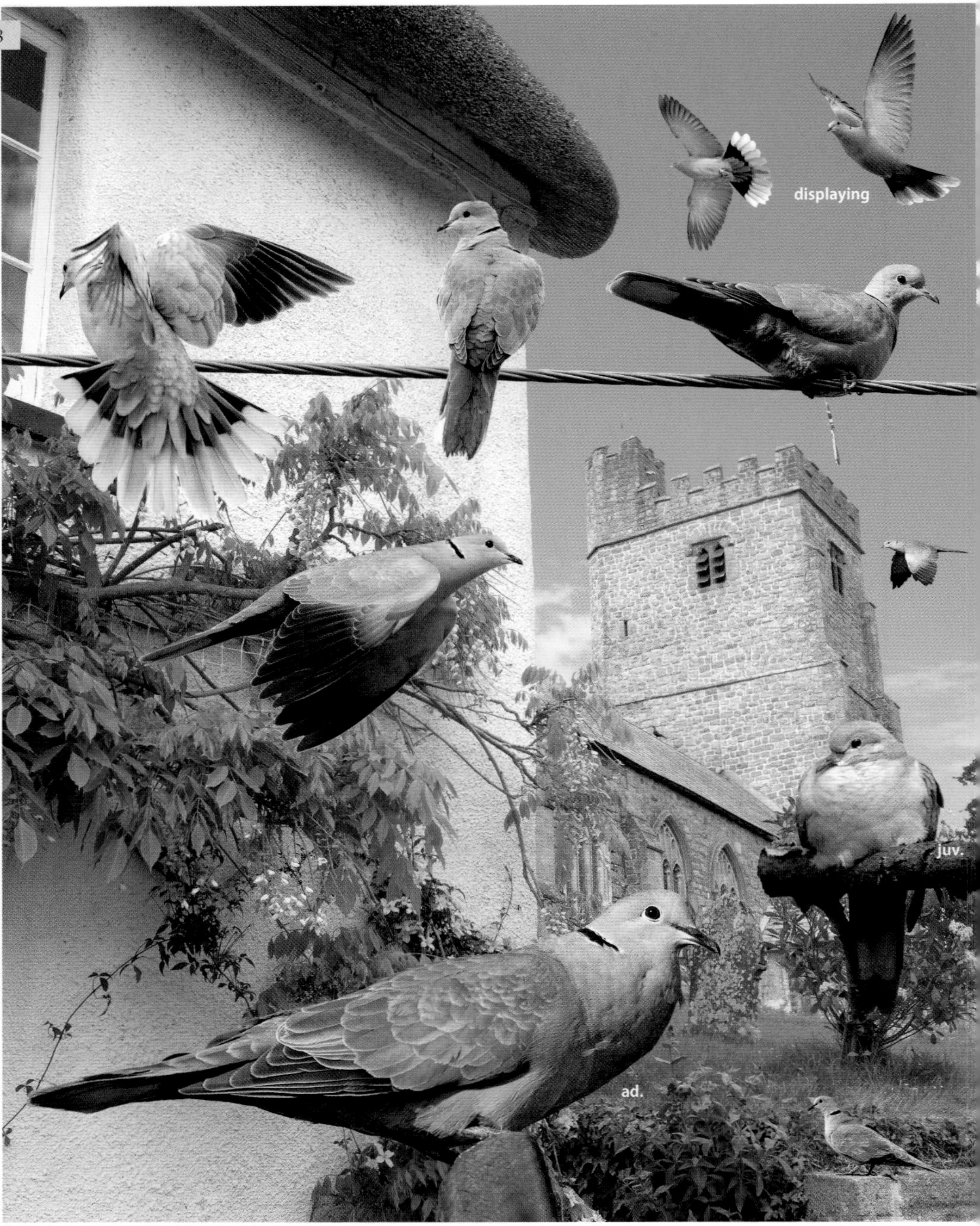

Collared Dove *Streptopelia decaocto* **COLDO/CD** L 32cm

UK: s. 990,000 pairs

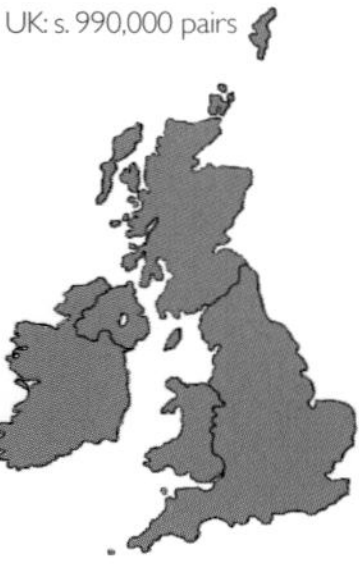

Common dove of suburbia, farms, and villages, not usually in urban centres, woodland, or 'wilder' places. A common sight on aerials and rooftops, from which it launches into display flight, climbing upwards at a steep angle and then gliding back down in a rough spiral with wings and tail splayed. Also perches on wires. Stick nest in shrub, often low conifer. Makes monotonous 3-note cooing in rhythm of football chant *U-NIIII-ted*; also calls after alighting, a curious mewing with tone of party trumpet. Moderately sociable; forms flocks but usually maximum of 15–20. Feeds on the ground with pigeon strut, often unpopular at bird tables. **ID:** Anaemic soft grey-brown plumage lacks contrasts of other pigeons, but does have white-edged black neck ring making half-collar, and darker wingtips. In flight from below, tail is black at base with broad white tip, underwings pale (see TURDO). Has slim, long-tailed shape, flies with characteristic half-beats or flickering. Juv: lacks necklace of ad and is slightly duller, with slightly scaly upperparts.

Turtle Dove *Streptopelia turtur* **TURDO/TD** L 27cm

UK: s. 14,000

Fast-declining summer visitor (Apr–Sep) to woodland edge and agricultural land with copious hedgerows. May also occur in rural gardens and villages. Has eastern bias in range and abundance and requires certain weed seeds to be available. Shares COLDO's habit of using raised perches, including wires, but will also perch unobtrusively at side of tree canopy, more hidden. Song is soft, soporific purring, hard to pinpoint; no alighting call. Has similar display to COLDO, but leaves from top of bush or tree rather than wire. **ID:** Gorgeous, delicate, slim dove with bright chestnut tortoiseshell pattern on wings, zebra-crossing black-and-white patch on neck, and rich pink on breast. Head has greyish tinge and there is swollen red around eyes. Rich patterning on plumage easily distinguishes perched bird, but in flight told from COLDO by black underwings contrasting with white belly. Black undertail with white tip. Flies with rapid, flickering wingbeats at quick pace, often tilting from side to side. Sexes alike. Juv: lacks neck ring, but wings have ghost of distinctive ad pattern.

Ring-necked Parakeet *Psittacula krameri* RINPA/RI L 40cm

UK: s. 8,600 pairs

Incongruous garden bird in Greater London and a few other suburban outposts, still increasing after being introduced in the 1960s. Probably survives mainly on garden handouts but increasingly found wild in parks and even commercial orchards and plantations. Potentially a pest. Nests in holes in trees, often very early in the year. Exceptionally noisy, uttering piercing staccato call and multiple variants. Birds live by day in small parties, but gather in a few large roosts at night. Often flies high. **ID:** Slim bodied, with long, sharp-tipped wings and very long, tapered tail. Quick wingbeats give fast, agile flight. Unlikely confused with anything else. Bright shining grass-green, with bluish hue on nape and tail. Typical parrot bill is bright red in adults; eye pale. Ad ♂ has black throat and black ring around neck, bordered behind on nape by narrow pink band (hence alt. name of Rose-ringed Parakeet); ♀ has just suggestion of ring. Juv: dark bill, yellower plumage.

Kingfisher *Alcedo atthis* **KINGF/KF** L 16cm

UK: s. 3,800-6,400 pairs

Fairly common inhabitant of slow-flowing rivers, streams, and lakes, nesting in mud banks by excavating a tunnel. In winter broadens its habitat to include lakes without banks, garden ponds, reservoirs, and, as a last resort, seashores. Smaller than many people expect, and easily missed owing to habit of flying very fast and low over water. Call, not well known, is excellent detector, a shrill, piercing whistle (similar to short blast on dog whistle). Will perch quietly just above water on tree branch, reed, post, or even wall, nodding head frequently to judge distance, then diving in with splash. Sometimes hovers if perches not available. Very territorial, so disputes are frequent, easily confused with courtship chases. Batters captured fish on perch to subdue, then swallows headfirst. **ID:** Deep orange underparts and brilliant iridescence unmistakable. Sparrow sized, with huge head and long, pointed bill; small coral-red legs. Ad ♂: all-dark bill; ad ♀: orange at base of lower mandible. Juv: upperparts duller with greenish cast, legs dark.

Bee-eater *Merops apiaster* **BEEEA/MZ** L 28cm

Rare but annual visitor in small numbers, esp in fine late spring weather; has bred. Often migrates high, giving birders a chance to detect the very distinctive, far-carrying, liquid *quilp, quilp* call as bird flies over. Also has habit of perching on wires, from which may make foraging flight to snap up flying insects. Has distinctive flight, alternating quick-fire flaps with long, often circling glides. **ID:** Unmistakable plumage: note yellow throat. Pointed wings and long tail with pin tip; underwings with black trailing edge. Juv: duller; shorter tail.

Hoopoe *Upupa epops* **HOOPO/HP** L 27cm

Rare, exotic visitor that has bred in Britain. About 100 turn up each year, singly, usually overshooting their northward migration in fine weather, and being seen near the coast. Feeds on closely cropped grass remarkably furtively, and easily overlooked; often first seen only when takes off on springy, moth-like flight (similar to JAY) on broad black-and-white wings. Has floating hoo-poo-poo song with quick pace. **ID:** Completely unmistakable, but beware—smaller than you expect (large thrush sized). Long, downcurved bill used for probing. Crest is raised in alarm. Flies low.

Green Woodpecker *Picus viridis* GREWO/G. L 32cm

UK: s. 52,000 pairs

Common ground-feeding woodpecker of woodland edge, parkland, heaths, and large gardens. Subsists on ants and hence is typically seen working on swards of short or long grass, probing bill into ant nests in soil, insects lapped up by tongue. Easily overlooked as it feeds quietly, but then suddenly flushes from ground, uttering loud, panicky call and flying low and with deep undulations to nearest tree, flashing yellow rump. Then lands on trunk and peers quizzically from behind, half-hidden. Song is loud, ringing laugh dropping slightly in pitch. Doesn't drum. **ID:** Size of large pigeon, but has typical woodpecker shape, with large head and chisel-shaped bill, stiff tail. Ad: rich yellowish green above, paler below, with brilliant crimson crown and nape, and black mask surrounding white eye. Ad ♂: crimson-centred moustache; ad ♀: black moustache. Juv: very distinct, with heavy dark spotting on pale underparts and head, and pale spotting on green upperparts. Crimson crown obvious flecked with white; juv ♂ has crimson moustache and juv ♀ has black moustache.

Great Spotted Woodpecker *Dendrocopos major* GRSWO/GS L 23cm

37,000–44,000 pairs

Common woodpecker of all kinds of woodland, and regular in parks and gardens. Usually seen on trees, and frequently perches near top of tree when just landed; black-and-white plumage allows it to melt away in latticework of winter twigs and branches. From Jan to May makes familiar 'drumming' sound, equivalent of song, when bill struck on sonorous wood to make short drum-roll that seems to fade quickly. This isn't sound made when excavating nest hole. Also makes loud *kick* alarm/contact call. Often visits bird tables, may hang upside down, which it also does among leaves in summer, gleaning insects. Flies with heavily undulating flight, a few flaps followed by interval of closed wings. Aggressive; birds often chase around the tree trunks. **ID:** Size of starling or small thrush. Black and white with blood-red undertail. Two large splodges of white on shoulders; breast dirty white, but not barred. Ad ♂: square red spot on nape; ad ♀: lacks red; black nape continuation from crown. Juv: confusingly has all-red top of crown, pink-stained undertail.

Lesser Spotted Woodpecker *Dendrocopos minor* **LESWO/LS** L 14cm ***s. 1,500***

Scarce, declining woodpecker confined to deciduous woodland in England and Wales; also visits hedgerows; however, typically lives furtive life in treetops and is famously tricky to see. Best chance is to hear male's loud, excited, peeping display call (a little like modern-day alarm clock), a volley on a single note. Drumming is longer than GRSWO's and doesn't fade, somewhat like blast of electric drill. **ID:** Always looks much smaller than GRSWO and is more delicate, with smaller bill; moves faster in branches, tends to creep among slender twigs. Has white 'ladder steps' up black back, and has streaks on breast; no red on vent. Ad ♂: bright red crown; ad ♀: black crown with pale forehead. Juv: sim to ♀, more streaked below.

Wryneck *Jynx torquilla* **WRYNE/WY** L 16cm

Rare migrant, usually to coastal scrub and open woodland, commonest in autumn (Aug–Sep); once bred. A weird ant-eating bird with cryptic mixture of browns and greys; long tongue as woodpeckers. Twists neck around if threatened. Feeds on ground in close-cropped soil, or in shade of vegetation, progressing with jerky hops; also laps insects from branches and posts. Sits across perches rather than clinging vertically like woodpecker. Flight with shallow undulations, often low. **ID:** Barred below, greyish with black bands above. Short, pointed bill.

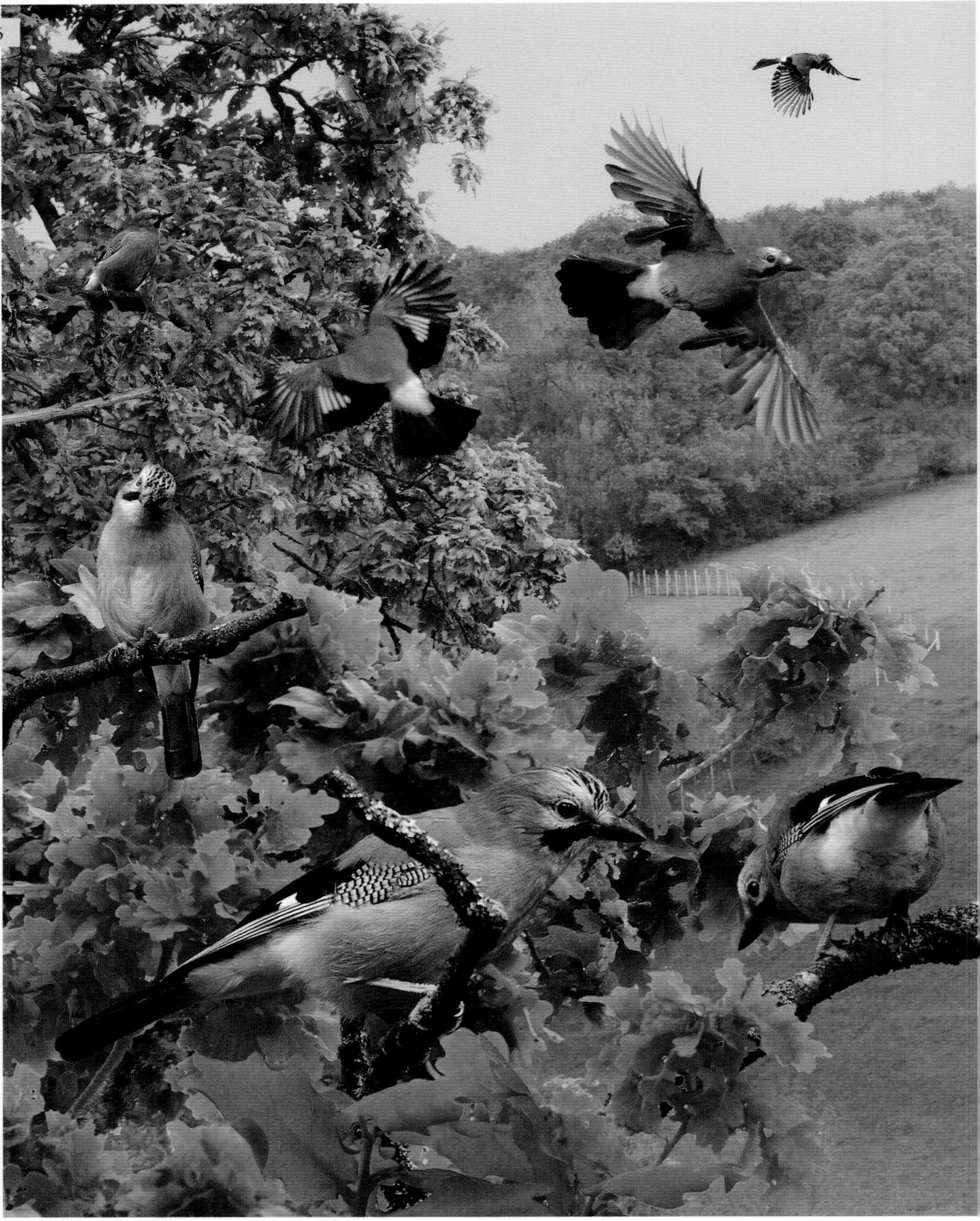

Jay *Garrulus glandarius* **JAY/J.** L 34cm

UK: s. 170,000 pairs

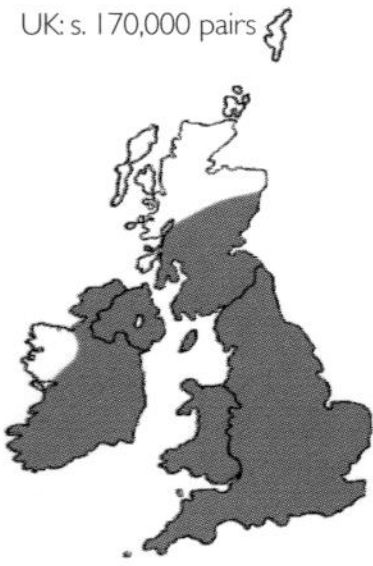

Common but secretive woodland bird, occurring both in deciduous and coniferous stands. Sneaks into gardens, parks, and the like—wherever there are mature trees. In most places favours oak trees, and in autumn (late Sep–Nov) collects acorns for winter food store, and then can be seen readily, commuting between territory and oak wood. When disturbed, very noisy, uttering harsh, screeching, discordant calls (source of name *jay*); can be deafening if, for example, roosting owl is found. May also make soft, sweet medleys. Unobtrusive in breeding season, often eats eggs and nestlings. Lives year-round in pairs, but small gatherings may be seen in autumn. Makes confident 2-footed hops on ground. **ID:** Plumage has unmistakable 4-colour combination, crowned by kingfisher-blue and black barred wing panel. Dark pink body plumage also unusual, with bold black moustache and black tail; crown streaked. In flight, white rump is most obvious feature. Sexes alike, juv hardly differs. Flight style itself distinctive, with somewhat floppy, unsteady style, despite full wingbeats.

Magpie *Pica pica* **MAGPI/MG** L 46cm

UK: s. 600,000 pairs

Very common resident in a variety of habitats, including suburbia, woodland edge, hedgerows, farmland, and moorland. Much increased over last 40 years, and not always popular owing to habit of raiding birds' nests in full view of distressed householders. Has greatly benefited from increase in easily available road kill, and suburban trees often ideal for distinctive domed nest, built of thorny sticks at the tops of hedges. Lives in pairs, or joins small nonbreeding flocks. Roosts of 10s of birds form, and similar-sized, excited gatherings occur in territorial disputes. Often perches on top of shrub or tree, and flirts tail. Feeds mainly on ground, where walks, skips, and runs. Doesn't horde bright objects at all, despite reputation. Alarm call loud chattering, friendlier than JAY's screech, has mischievous ring; contact call slightly strained *chee-ik.* **ID:** Unmistakable owing to black-and-white colouration allied to long, graduated tail. Feathers on tail and outer wing bear oily looking green/purple iridescence. Flies busily on straight course on weak-looking wings, tail something of a hindrance behind. Sexes alike; juv flight feathers less glossy, has shorter tail.

Raven *Corvus corax* RAVEN/RN L 64cm

UK: s. 7,400 pairs

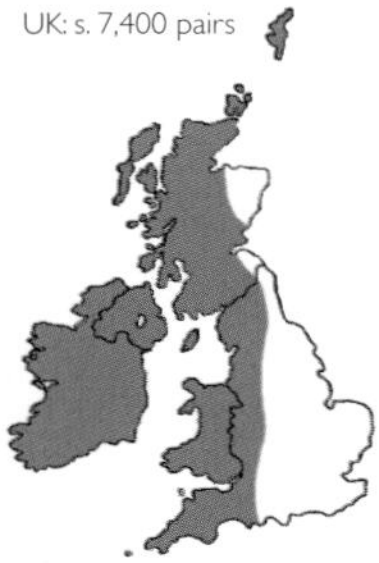

Fairly common resident, esp in the west and north, where it tends to occur in 'wilder' habitats, including mountains, moorland, upland forest edge, cliffs, and sheep country. Now spreading eastward and may occur in lowlands, esp in vicinity of rubbish tips. Often in ones and twos, rarely in larger groups. Patrols its large territory by wing, its deep, croaking *bronk* call often the only sound in harsh environments. Gatherings occur around carrion. Often nests or perches on prominent radio towers, power lines, cliffs, or trees. Seems to love flying and often performs aerial displays—rolling dives with wings tucked in before swooping up again. Also frequently turns upside down when flying. **ID:** Huge – as big as a BUZZA. Easily confused with CARCR, but has much bigger bill and longer wings and tail, the tail clearly wedge shaped and the wings swept back and more pointed, giving distinctive cross shape. Flies with slower, deeper wingbeats. Often soars with feathers spread, becoming much more crow-like. Long, shaggy throat feathers. Juv/1st-w: uniformly dull black with brown cast and pale gape.

Rook *Corvus frugilegus* **ROOK/RO** L 46cm

UK: s. 1,100,000 pairs

Widespread and very common in agricultural areas where there are copses of tall trees; also moorland, towns, and villages. Requires tall trees for breeding, builds stick nests in canopy. Colonies ('rookeries') are obvious in winter landscape, and birds begin to attend them in earnest from Jan onward. Extremely sociable at all times; feed in large flocks on fields, where birds dig into the earth for invertebrates, and at noisy roosts. Call is a flat, tuneless *caw*, without menace of CARCR (Rook caw is like crow that's had anger counselling); also broken-voiced high-pitched sounds from colony. Has rolling gait on ground. **ID:** Black with slight purplish gloss. Most distinctive for dirty white base to bill, easy to see, reaches to eye. Also has steeper crown than CARCR, strong angle to bill, which is more pointed. Looser feathers around legs give 'baggy shorts' effect. In flight, tail more wedge shaped than CARCR, and wings are beaten at slightly quicker pace and more loosely. Sexes alike. Juv: lacks white bill base until Feb, so v sim to CARCR, but bill more pointed.

Carrion Crow *Corvus corone* CARCR/C. L 46cm

UK: s. 1,000,000 pairs

Abundant, adaptable, domineering all-black 'wide boy' among birds, found in woods, farmland, villages, towns, cities, rubbish tips—indeed almost anywhere. Omnivorous, taking everything from living animals to berries and acorns. Intelligent: drops shellfish on beaches to break them, dunks bread in ponds, remembers locations of short-term caches. Builds stick nest high in tall tree, the pairs having no company, unlike colonial ROOK ('only one crow's nest on a ship'); however, non-breeding flocks do occur and large numbers may roost together. Makes a variety of caws, including loud, irritable bursts of 3 notes that welcome the morning. Feeds on ground, can walk or move with sinister, 2-footed hops; wears permanently threatening mien. **ID:** All black with subtle bluish sheen. Bill is dark grey (see ROOK); curved culmen gives stout tip; crown is rather flat, lacking ROOK's peaked forehead. In flight, progresses with slow yet quite shallow wingbeats. In flight has squarer tail than ROOK or RAVEN and slightly broader, less pointed wings than either. More inclined to soar and less inclined to frolic in the air than ROOK. Sexes alike, juv slightly browner.

Hooded Crow *Corvus cornix* **HOOCR/HC** L 46cm

UK: s. 260,000 pairs

This is the hardy crow of the west and north coast of Scotland, of Ireland, and the Isle of Man; rare elsewhere but may wander down east coast, even to England. Formerly considered a subspecies of CARCR. Seen on sheep pasture, on mountain slopes, moors, by roadsides, on the seashore, on cliffs, in towns, and even on the edge of woodland. Nest is usually in a tree, but also cliff ledge. A little more sociable than CARCR. Call is usual caw, but often more rolling in nature than that of CARCR. **ID:** Size and shape as CARCR. Distinctive and handsome, with black head and chest, black tail and black wings, all contrasting with ash-grey body. Often hybridise in zone of overlap with CARCR, producing mixtures that can look like either parent or between. Look for darker belly and vent, black mixed in scapulars, and overall darker tones than pure HOOCR.

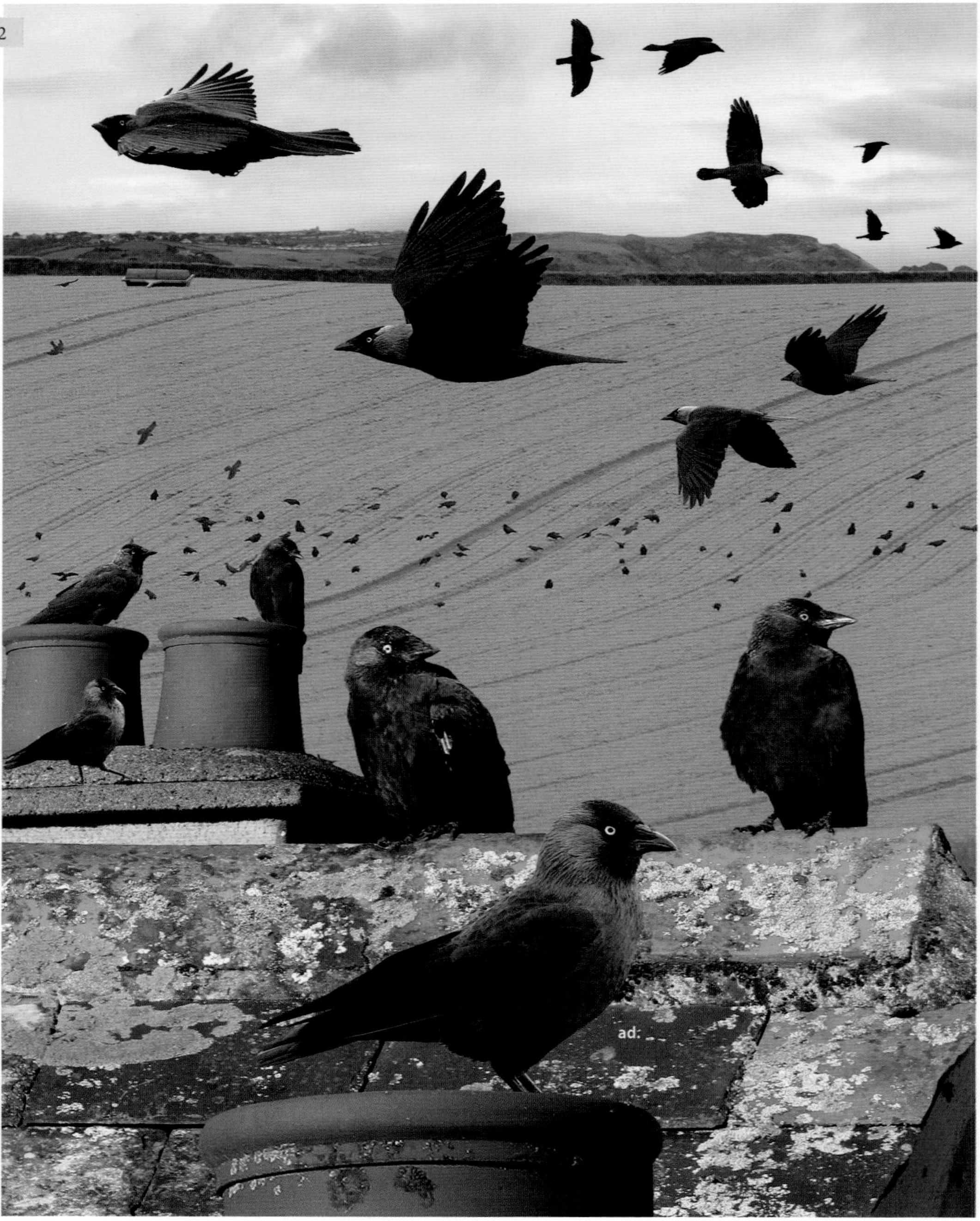

Jackdaw *Corvus monedula* **JACKD/JD** L 33cm

UK: s. 1,400,000 pairs

Familiar small black crow, occurring in farmland, cliffs, rocky places, villages, towns, parkland, and on the edge of woodland. Named for its sharp, exclamatory call *chack*, uttered in flight and in many social situations. Breeds in loose colonies using holes in trees, rocky cavities, and chimneys for the nest site. In towns, neighbouring houses may each have a pair or two. Pairs for life and members of pair inseparable, seen flying alongside each other in dense wheeling flocks. May form very large roosts, which bed down late after much commotion, and sometimes members perform impressive aerial manoeuvres of soaring and chasing. Feeds on ground, often among grass. Has jaunty walk, lacks menace of CARCR. Often perches on back of sheep, or even deer, either as lookout or taking insect pests. **ID:** Smallest black crow, with distinctive short bill noticeable in flight. 'Grey shawl' on back of head, contrasting with black forecrown and staring white eye. Sexes alike. Faster wingbeats than other crows, pigeon paced, and wings are rather narrow. Sexes alike. Juv: has darker eye, plumage browner.

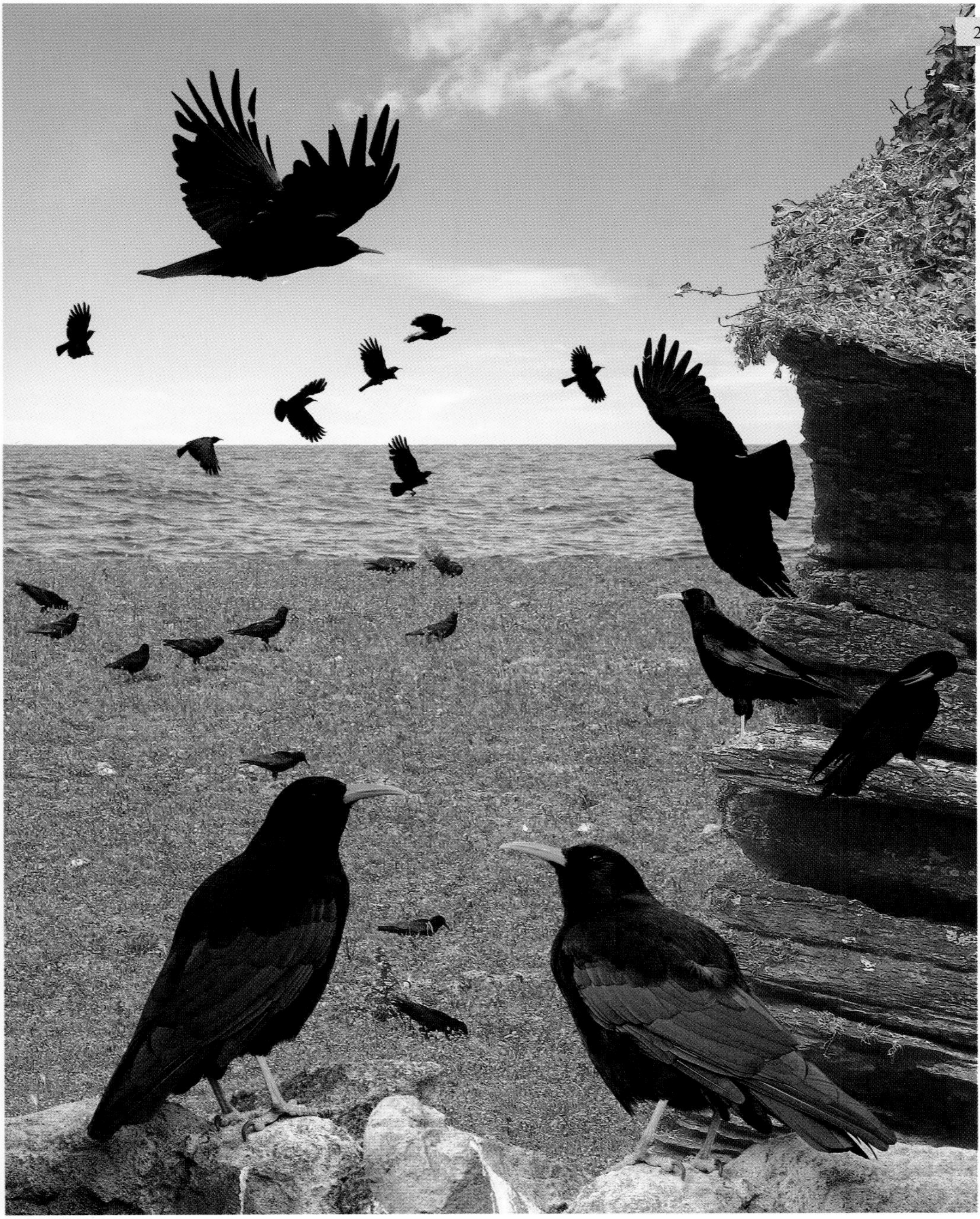

Chough *Pyrrhocorax pyrrhocorax* **CHOUG/CF** L 40cm

UK: s. 300 pairs

Rare playful crow of western coasts, where it occurs on maritime cliffs; also on a few mountaintops inland. Breeds in sea caves, disused mine shafts, rock crevices, and ruined buildings. Very different ecology from other crows: feeds mainly on invertebrates in the soil, probing, digging, and turning items over. Comes alive in flight, where it rides clifftop turbulence with exuberant ease in small groups, frequently making daring closed-wing plummets and twisting and turning in the air. Distinctive call a cheerful cheeough, a bit like a ricocheting bullet. **ID:** Unmistakable, with long, downcurved scarlet bill and red legs. Sexes alike but juv has brownish yellow bill. In flight, underwing two-toned, outer wings broadly 'fingered'.

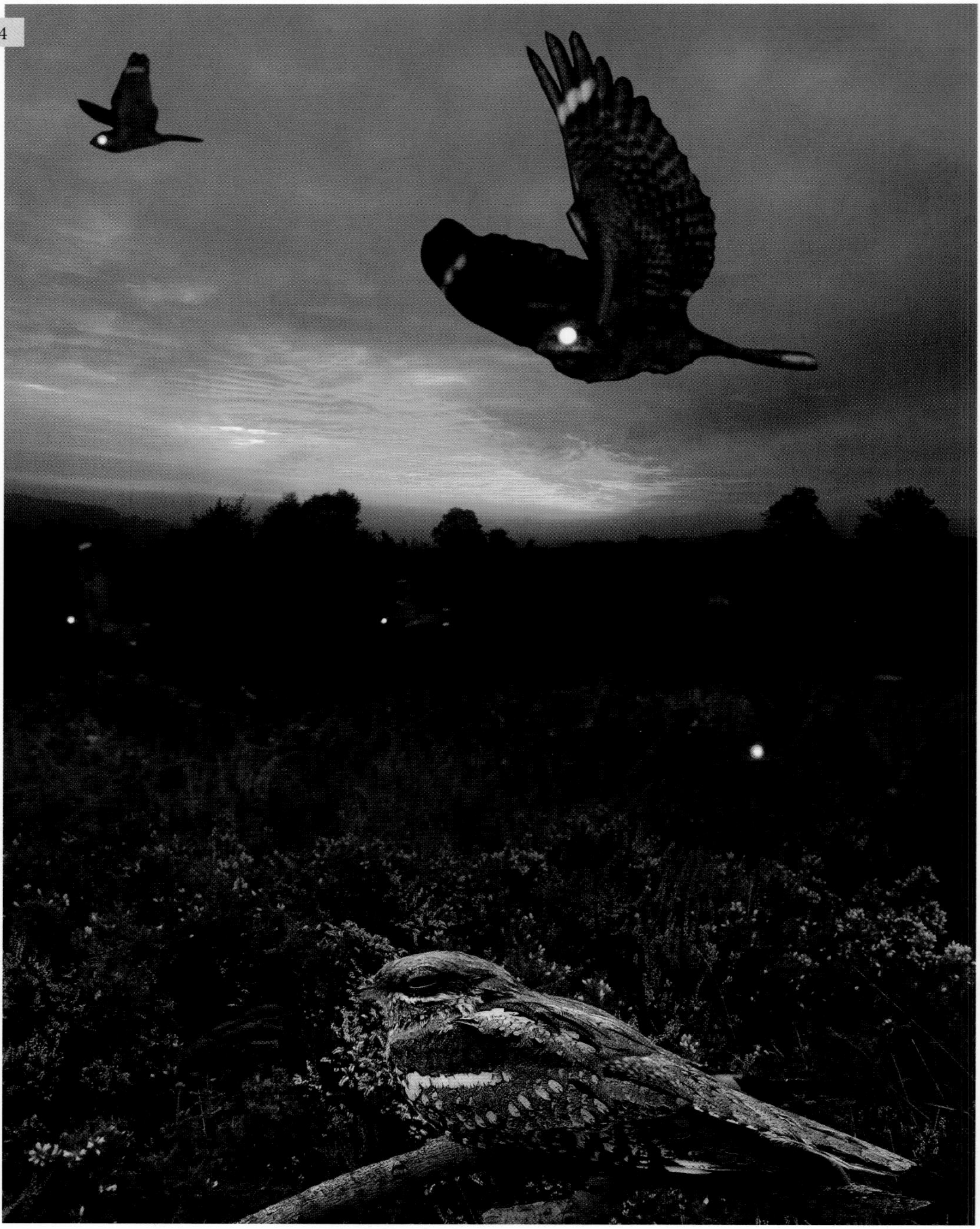

Nightjar *Caprimulgus europaeus* **NIJAR/NJ** L 27cm

UK: s. 4,600 pairs

Uncommon nocturnal species of southern heathland, woodland edge, moorland, and open conifer plantations. Summer migrant May–Aug, rarely seen on migration. Specialises in foraging for flying insects in summer night skies, catches moths and beetles one at a time, either in flying bout or quick sally from perch; often most active at dawn and dusk. Nest on the ground in bare scrape. Male makes very weird, long-lasting hollow trilling on 2 pitches, a song known as 'churring'. Also has distinctive froglike *cru-ick* flight call, and wing-claps in display. Can sometimes be attracted by waving white handkerchief. Eyes reflect torch light. **ID:** Unmistakable on ground, with enormous head, minute bill but large gape, and impeccable cryptic camouflage. Perches longways on bare branches, wires; also atop posts. Ad ♂: white sides to tail and white patches near wingtip, missing on ad ♀ and juv/1st-w. Has long, pointed wings and long tail (sim to KESTR in shape), flies with deep wingbeats, moving along in jinking course with quick changes of direction, brief hovers, and glides. Flight completely silent. Most easily found at night by reflective torch 'eye-shine'.

Cuckoo *Cuculus canorus* **CUCKO/CK** L 33cm

UK: s. 16,000 pairs

Fast-declining icon of woodland, farmland, marshes, and moors, where its wondrous, sonorous *cuck-oo* song is a stirring part of spring and summer atmosphere. Remarkable behaviour involves subcontracting care of eggs and young to small songbirds, mainly REEWA, DUNNO, MEAPI, and ROBIN; nestling Cuckoo evicts nestlings of host. Female may lay 20 eggs, in nests of host who brought her up. Arrives in Apr, adults may leave by Jul, young by Sep. Song varies and may be elaborated into coughing series; additionally, ad ♀ makes loud, theatrical ringing call. Eats hairy caterpillars. Often perches on wires and treetops, wings may be held characteristically drooped, tail raised. Typically flies low and fast and is hard to spot; in flight, wings barely raised above horizontal. **ID:** Slim, hawklike shape, with sharply pointed wingtips. Mainly ash-grey but white underneath with dark cross-barring. Undertail dark with white bars. Feet, bill base, and eye-ring yellow. Ad ♀ may show variable rusty wash to upper breast, extra barring on throat. Some ♀s quite different, a rich rusty brown on upperparts—the rare 'rufous' form. Chick barred in front, huge orange gape. Juv: dark brown above with pale scaling, white patch on nape.

Swift *Apus apus* **SWIFT/SI** L 16cm

UK: s. 85,000 pairs

Very common summer visitor, here only for the cricket season, late Apr–Aug. Breeds in small colonies on ledges in tall buildings, such as churches, but ability for efficient flight means that it can be seen anywhere, even over urban centres. Seemingly always airborne, in fine weather usually above rooftop height; at dusk, parties may circle high out of sight and roost aloft. In poor weather feeds over waterbodies, where insects are emerging, and low down. Typically flies with long glides interspersed with fast but relaxed flaps; capable of effortless, quick accelerations and changes of height. Catches very small invertebrates one by one. Never perches on such as wires; can only cling. Utters distinctive 'screaming' call with slightly strained air. Colony members often club together and zoom around roofs, screaming. **ID:** Distinctive sickle shape with very long, sharply pointed wings, made up largely of 'hand', with reduced 'arm'; head barely protrudes and bill tiny (gape larger). Quite long, forked tail. Mainly dark brown with white throat. Juv: has larger white throat patch and, at close quarters, slightly scaly plumage pattern.

Alpine Swift *Apus melba* **ALPSW/AI** L 21cm

Rare visitor from southern Europe, may turn up anywhere between Mar and Nov, but records most common Apr–May and Aug–Oct in southern counties. Any out-of-season swift is worth checking. Has habit of flying very high. **ID:** Larger than SWIFT, with distinctly slower wingbeats and even longer glides, which may recall HOBBY. Has slightly broader wings, but otherwise shape sim. Given a good view, neatly demarcated white belly and throat, and also narrow dark collar unmistakable; also slightly paler brown than SWIFT.

Red-rumped Swallow *Cecropis daurica* **RERSW/VR** L 16cm

Annual visitor to Britain, esp in Apr–May and again (fewer) Oct–Nov, esp south and east England. Tricky species to pin down, often doesn't stick around when visits coasts, reservoirs, marshes, and the like. Distinctive flight, with much more gliding than SWALL, often higher up. **ID:** With pale rump and gliding flight, almost a cross between SWALL and HOUMA, but long tail streamers immediately obvious. Head reddish brown and underparts buff with light streaking, without chest band of SWALL. Undertail distinctively black. Adult: reddish rump. Juv: white rump, shorter tail streamers.

Swallow *Hirundo rustica* **SWALL/SL** L 19cm

Abundant summer visitor (Apr–Oct) to rural areas, esp farmland, villages, and the vicinity of fresh water; also abundant anywhere as a passage migrant. A lively, aerial bird that tends to fly lower than the others (martins, swifts), often taking food a couple of metres above ground. Flies less fitfully than martins, tending to move forward with upward and sideways twists rather than tight arcs, and looks fast and purposeful. Has distinctive 'rowing' action to wingbeats when flying. Often perches on wires, esp flocks on autumn migration, and males also will sing their fast-paced, lively, somewhat grating twitter. Also flies around livestock, fielding insects disturbed as animals walk. Builds open-topped mud/hay nest indoors in a barn, loose colonies. **ID:** Long tail streamers best distinction from martins. Royal blue upperparts without white rump; tail with white spots. Adult: underparts buff except for deep red throat (which extends onto forehead) and dark blue breast band. Ad ♂: longer tail streamers than ad ♀. Juv: much paler, and washed-out reddish colour on throat and forehead, whiter on underparts, shorter tail even than ad ♀.

Sand Martin *Riparia riparia* **SANMA/SM** L 12cm

JK: s. 54,000–174,000 pairs

Fairly common, early arriving (Mar) and early departing (Aug) summer migrant, usually found near fresh water. It depends on sandy riverbanks, gravel workings, and similar sites for breeding, making a tunnel about 1m long for its nest. Breeds in colonies of various sizes. Can be seen far from colony, for example over reservoirs, fields, almost anywhere rich in small, low-flying invertebrates. Has a distinctive weak flight, with rather rapid flaps and short glides, and rarely flies high. In flight, often seems to hold wings close to body. Perfectly able to perch for example on wires and joins SWALL and HOUMA on migration. Roosts in reed beds. Call is a gentle buzzing rasp, not as hard as HOUMA's call. **ID:** Small, weak-looking martin with predominantly pale brown upperparts and whitish underparts; no white rump, in contrast to HOUMA. Has short tail with only a shallow fork. Always look for distinctive brown band across the chest. Darker underwings contrast with white belly. Juv: throat and neck side tinged brown, not pure white, and wings and mantle look slightly scaly.

House Martin *Delichon urbica* **HOUMA/HM** L 12cm

UK: s. 510,000 pairs

Common, declining summer visitor much attached to buildings in towns and villages. Builds a very distinctive cup-shaped mud-nest where horizontal and vertical meet, with small side-door entrance, usually in a small colony. Arrives mid-Apr and departs Oct to wintering grounds in Africa still largely unknown. Roosting habits also poorly known. Forages on flying insects quite high up, among SWIFTs rather than SWALLs, and scours skies with short movements, with many turns, glides, and arcs, rather than sweeping fast like a SWIFT. Requires nearby water (or at least mud source) for breeding, and often found by waterbodies such as reservoirs. Often lands near puddles to collect mud and shows off its white feathered legs. Call is hard *prrit*, of which it makes many variations, including long 'conversations' in the nest. **ID:** Compact, with broad wings and shortish tail with decent fork. Very conspicuous and diagnostic white rump. Ad br: clean white underneath without any breast band, and underwings also pale. Dark glossy blue. Juv: has less glossy upperparts and soiled dirty-white underparts

SONGBIRDS

Shrikes are solidly built birds with relatively long and often rounded tails they sometimes fan and swish to the side. They sit tall on the tops of trees, bushes, hedges, fences, or walls—anywhere with a good view. They swoop or drop down, sometimes hovering, to catch insects, mammals, reptiles, birds, and other small critters which they rip apart with hooked bills. If they have a surplus, they will impale it on spikes to create 'larders', hence the name 'butcher bird'. They often fly significant distances between perches with undulating flight. At times they sit quietly out of view for long periods. All show facial masks and mostly pale underparts. Most show faint barring on the underparts, stronger in winter and in juveniles. All species are uncommon, and others, not covered in this book, occur as vagrants.

Thrushes are a familiar group of birds that can often be seen in the back garden. They are as happy feeding on the ground as in fruit-bearing bushes. Often in flocks, they can be quite approachable, particularly when they are busy feeding. All have distinct plumages.

Tits are a charismatic group of birds that are woodland dwellers but familiar to gardens and feeders. They're always on the move, and their nice colours, small size, and habit of hanging upside down make them very popular. They are mostly year-round residents.

Warblers are a large group of small insect-eating birds. They have relatively distinctive songs and calls. All are migrant. Warblers are notoriously hard, sometimes impossible, to identify. Why? Because they are small, hard to see, and constantly on the move, plus their colour patterns are rarely distinctive. Most are subtle shades of green, grey, and brown. Judging these and accounting for variation within each species adds to the difficulty. When assessing colour, it is very important to understand the effect of light and how it reflects off vegetation. The problems are even greater when looking at photographs.

Most of these warblers are grouped into five genera. Knowing the differences between these groups is important for narrowing down your search image.

Sylvia often skulk around in dense, scrubby vegetation and are more often heard than seen, though some do make song flights. Songs are a fast array of notes, usually with more musical quality than acrocephalus warblers. Calls are an array of similar *chack*. Sylvia are large and robust with powerful bills and strong legs. Upperparts are unstreaked, often with white outer tail feathers. The throat often contrasts strongly with the rest of the head, and the underparts are pale and unstreaked.

Acrocephalus (often shortened to acros) are usually found clambering around reed beds or damp areas with bushes, typically staying well hidden. On migration, birds can show up anywhere and can be doubly confusing outside their normal environs. Brown-toned to blend in, their upperparts can be either streaked or unstreaked. These birds are slim, with pointed head and bill and a broad-based tail rounded at the tip. None have white outer tail feathers. Sexes are alike. They often sit still for periods of time and sing for periods of time out of sight. Song is often a repetitious series of sharp agitated notes that include mimicry. They have a wide array of calls, some similar to sylvia warblers.

Locustella are dark with upperparts and underparts that can be streaked or not. Undertail coverts are often dark. They are skulkers, quite happy to scamper away on the ground. They have cricket-like, reeling songs.

Hippolais are somewhat intermediate in appearance between Acrocephalus and Phylloscopus.

Phylloscopus (often shortened to phylloscs) are small, cute woodland birds, often staying in the higher branches to glean and flit after insects. Small and slight, they are small billed and have short, square-ended or even slightly forked tails. They have green, yellow, and white tones with unstreaked upperparts. Some of these gems have one or two wing bars.

Warblers rarely have strong plumage patterns. Identification involves using a combination of other characters. Size and shape are always fundamental. For the beginner, these differences may at best seem subtle, but with practice they will become more noticeable. Bill and tail are good places to focus on size, shape, and colour when looking for additional clues. Wing length and how far the primaries project beyond the longest tertial (primary projection) can also be vital tips. Leg colour is often useful, but can be variable and difficult to judge. Colour tones are important but need to be used in conjunction with other characters. Habitat and behaviour are great clues, particularly on the breeding grounds, but not as reliable when the bird is on migration.

Pipits are another group of similar-looking birds. Typically heavily streaked above and below, they spend a lot of time strutting along on the ground, often in loose flocks. Often inadvertently flushed, they usually call repeatedly on take-off. Learning their call and their song (usually delivered in flight) is a great help when identifying them. Habitat, bill size, underpart streaking, size, and colour are the most important features for identification.

Wagtails, like pipits, spend a lot of the time walking purposefully on the ground. They also have white outer tail feathers but much bolder colour patterns that lack streaking.

Finches eat seeds and have pointed conical bills for this purpose. They often fly in tight flocks that can be seen overhead in their characteristic deeply undulating flight that shows their forked tails. Some stay in the north in winter so are known as 'winter finches'. They feed mostly on seeds and fruit but can eat insects. Dependent on food supplies, they tend to be nomadic and occur a long way south of their usual range in some years. Knowing the success of northern food supplies, such as cone crops, can lead to fairly good predictions of future bird movements of a number of species.

Buntings also have powerful conical bills like finches. They tend to spend lots of time on the ground feeding on seeds. Most are strongly patterned, particularly around the head and have white outer tail feathers.

In many cases, it is better to leave birds unidentified. It can sometimes be shocking to go back to look at a bird later and find it looks and behaves differently. Knowing how to evaluate the certainty of an observation is a skill that comes with practice and expertise.

Many birders enjoy trying to age and sex, as well as identify, all the birds they see. In most cases it is not possible to do either. In others there is much overlap in plumage between ages and sexes. In this book, the age and sex of many of the captioned birds are certain; others are not so clear. Some captions are used to give a general idea of appearance.

In most species, adult males are brightest, with the most contrast in colour patterns. Features such as wing bars and supercilium tend to be the boldest. Immature females are at the opposite end of the spectrum. In the fall, adult females and immature males are intermediate and tend to be very similar in general colour patterns and tones.

By spring, males (1st-summer) show a number of adult-male-type characters while retaining some old immature feathers—these are contrastingly worn and usually faded brown. For example, 1st-summer Pied Flycatcher is adult-like but has retained juvenile flight feathers and a variable number of wing coverts. This is a typical pattern of a number of species and makes many of these birds quite easy to age and sex, which tends to impress beginners, even though it is not difficult to work out. They also sing. These general patterns are shown in many other families.

Juvenile and adult feathers have many different characteristics. These features are used by banders for ageing and sexing birds in the hand; however, with careful field observation (or photographs), we can often also see them. Juvenile tail and flight feathers are typically narrower and more pointed than those of adults. They also tend to be brown rather than black. Juvenile greater primary coverts and alula (small feathers at the bend of the wing) are usually more pointed and paler.

Britain and Ireland are famous for vagrants, the first, or last, places where birds over the Atlantic Ocean make landfall. With suitable weather conditions, birds regularly show up from as far away as Asia, the Middle East, and North America. Once birds set out the wrong way, they can easily end up thousands of miles out of range, so anything is possible just about anywhere. Most vagrants are blown off course while migrating, and juveniles are particularly prone to show up in late fall. At this time of year, never rely on assumptions!

Ornithology is still in its infancy, and one of its most exciting aspects is that there is so much left to learn. So look and study closely. What you might be learning for yourself may also be valuable to others. As this book goes to press, the definition of a species is no longer as clear-cut as it once was. Analysis of DNA has had a big effect on taxonomy and on status of species. Many subspecies or races are now being elevated to full species status by some birding bodies, and the taxonomic order continues to change significantly. More 'splits' are sure to come.

Golden Oriole *Oriolus oriolus* **GOLOR/OL** L 24cm ***s. 2–5 pairs***

Beautiful but rare breeder, usually in East Anglian poplar trees near water. Rare migrant, mostly late spring (85/year). Despite its gaudy colours it stays well hidden near the tops of trees—glimpsed flight calls are the norm. Fluid flight style is a cross between a JAY and a BLABI. Gorgeous, exotic flute-like song as stunning as plumage, like a liquid wolf-whistle. Has a variety of grating, cat-like calls. **ID:** Ad ♂: unmistakable yellow and black, with yellow at corners of the tail and base of wing. Ad ♀/1st-yr: a subdued version with finely streaked underparts. If in doubt, always look at size, shape, and variably reddish bill.

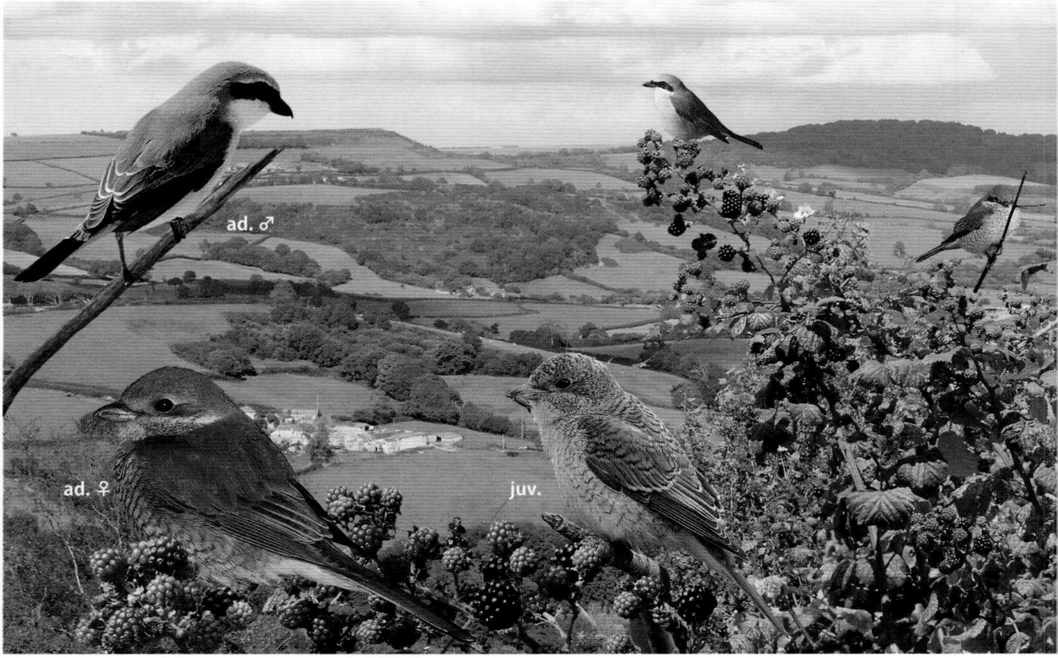

Red-backed Shrike *Lanius collurio* **REBSH/ED** L 17cm ***1–3 pairs***

Once a breeder on southern heathland, now reduced to the occasional pair. Migrants are most regular in the east and south (250/year). Exciting predatory species, catches just about any live prey smaller than itself, including birds. Old nickname 'butcher bird' derived from habit of impaling cached prey on thorns to create 'larders'. Like other shrikes, often sits upright on side branch of tree, or even on fence, with a good vista. Sometimes swishes or fans tail. **ID:** Compact shrike. Ad ♂ distinctive, with bold black face mask, chestnut upperparts, pink breast. Ad ♀: more subdued pattern with reddish brown tail, variably greyish brown head, and heavily barred underparts. Juv/1st-w: similar to ♀ with mostly pale-edged feathers above, brown tail.

Woodchat Shrike *Lanius senator* **WOOSH/OO** L 18cm

Rare passage migrant, particularly in the south. **ID:** A striking bird in adult plumage with black mask and pale underparts as other shrikes but the chestnut cap and nape are always distinctive. Ad ♀ average duller with browner back, paler forehead, duller mask, and paler fringes to wing coverts. Juv trickier with scaly plumage similar to REBSH. Look for pale median coverts and scapulars. Other differences include paler and greyer tones with often contrasting rufous nape. Western subsp. *badius* has less white in scapulars and base of primaries.

Great Grey Shrike *Lanius excubitor* **GRGSH/SR** L 24cm ***w. 63***

Rare winter visitor to heaths, moors, and bogs, often traditional sites. Highly predatory; perches high, scanning for rodents, insects, small birds, and other prey. It swoops down, sometimes hovering, before pouncing. Usually unapproachable. Often disappears for stretches of time, probably sheltering in bushes. Goes considerable distances with bouncy flight between perches. **ID:** The largest shrike, it is bulky but long tailed and elegant. Ad: shades of grey with black mask and wings. 1st-w: sim to ad with some juv flight feathers and wing coverts. Others much browner and more heavily barred, often with pale base to bill.

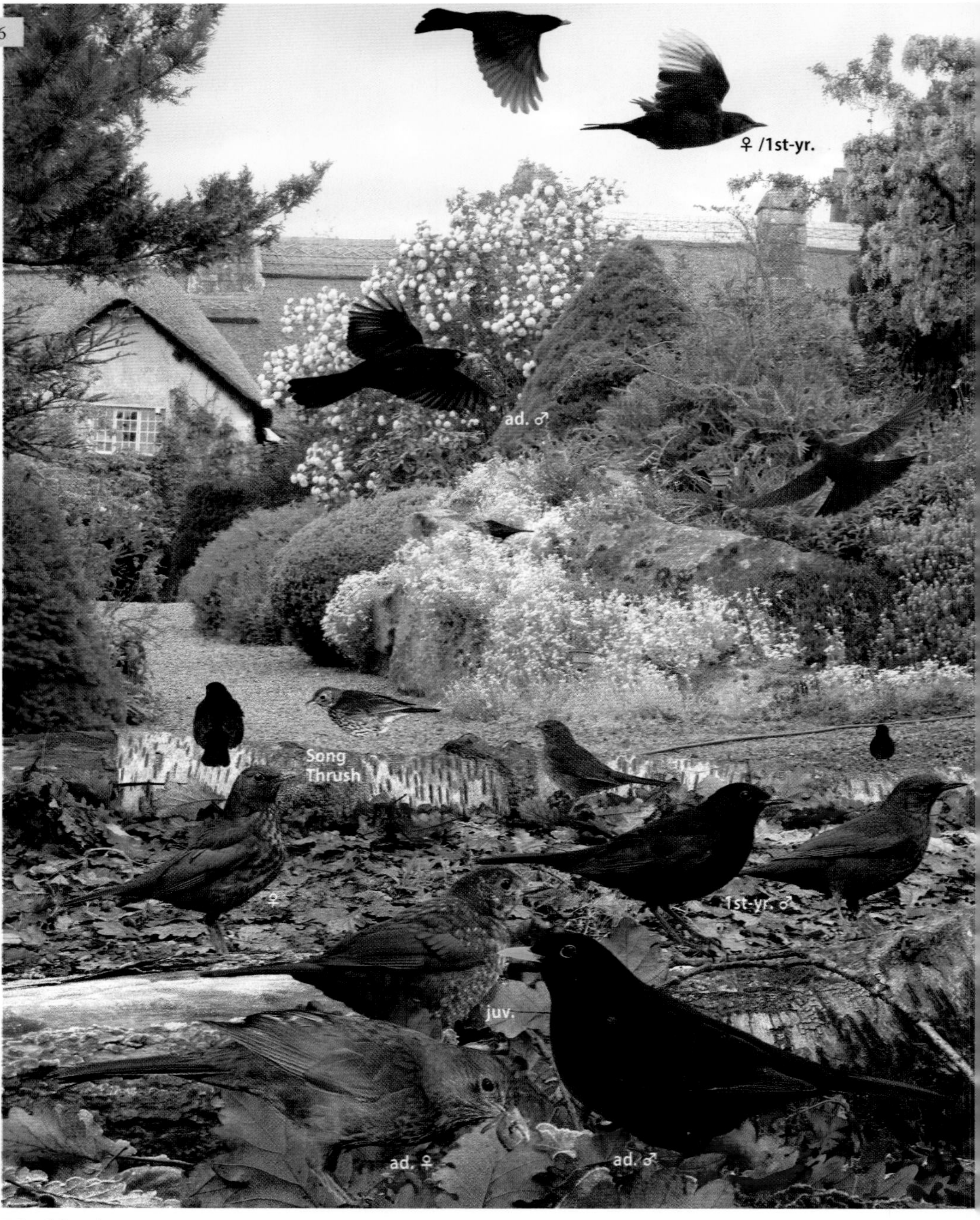

Blackbird *Turdus merula* **BLABI/B.** L 25cm

UK: s. 5,100,000 pairs

Abundant woodland bird, also found in gardens, hedgerows, farmland, heaths and moors. Very familiar to everyone. Forages on lawns or fields for worms, standing still for a few moments, then making scampering runs forward to grab prey, or stand watchful again; may also make 2-footed hops forward. Scratches among leaf litter for invertebrates, takes berries from shrubs, feeds below bird tables. Utters over-panicky alarm rattle. Also makes angry *chink chink* calls at communal roosts, or during day to mob cats or bird predators. From Feb to May, sings gorgeous tuneful song with reassuring air; phrases well spaced, not repeated, often end in squeak or chuckle. Often sings from roofs. **ID:** Well proportioned, with quite long, square-ended tail. Ad ♂: jet black all over, orange-yellow bill and eye-ring. Indivs sometimes have white patches on plumage. 1st-w ♂ sim but plumage slightly brown tinged, and bill variably dark. Ad ♀: essentially dark brown (some rustier), but paler on throat and breast, with light streaking; bill dull yellow. Juv: slightly paler brown than ad ♀ and with copious pale spots and speckles over much of plumage. Dark bill. Ground colour much darker than SONTH.

Ring Ouzel *Turdus torquatus* **RINOU/RZ** L 24cm

UK: s. 6,200–7,500 pairs

Uncommon summer visitor (Mar–Oct) to upland moors above 250m, in mixed sites with grassy swards, scrub, streams, and the like. More widespread on migration, when visits coastal fields, downland, lowland scrub, and so forth, in company with other thrushes. Much shyer than BLABI at all times, and often flushes far when disturbed. Flight call is soft *tack*, quick unlike BLABI. Song clear repetition of mournful piping notes with some interspersed twitters. **ID:** Similar to BLABI, but has scalier plumage and pale edges to wing feathers; also slightly longer, more pointed wings. Ad ♂ is black with bold white band across breast, like tucked-in napkin. Bold black accentuates pale wing panels. Bill yellow,with dark dirty tip, eye-ring not yellow. Ad ♀: dark brown version of same, with dirty-white gorget and obvious scaling on underparts. Juv/1st-w: dark sooty-brown (much darker than juv BLABI) with very obvious pale scaling below and black streaks on throat. At best a slightly paler band across breast, often missing in 1st-w ♀.

Mistle Thrush *Turdus viscivorus* MISTH/M. L 27cm

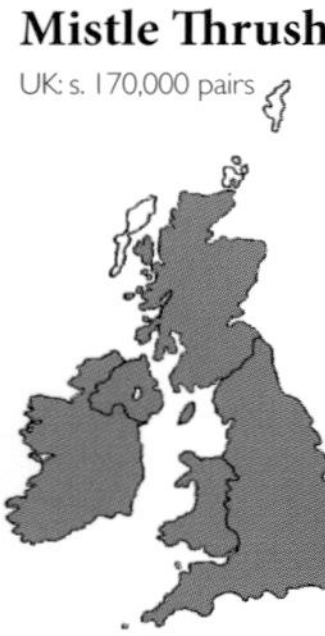

Fairly common, easily overlooked thrush of open fields, large gardens, and woodland with tall trees. Often the thrush seen right out in the middle of fields, further from cover than SONTH, and also seen on tops of tall trees; rarely on small garden lawns. When flushed, has distinctive unhurried undulating flight. Not sociable, usually in pairs, family parties at most. Pairs or singles aggressively defend clump of berry-bearing shrubs/trees, including mistletoe, sometimes throughout winter. Has distinctive harsh, loud, rattling call. Song similar to BLABI, but faster with shorter phrases, and has distinctive far-off, melancholy air; often sings in afternoon and in poor weather. **ID:** Large thrush, moves with heavy, confident hops and runs. Longer tail than SONTH and has proportionally small head and big body with 'beer gut'. Whiter underparts than SONTH, with rounder spots that often coalesce into patch on breast side. Paler brown upperparts with obvious pale rump and pale wing panels; white corners to tail, white underwings. Sexes alike. Juv: as ads but with large tear-drop-shaped pale spots on mantle. Looks odd.

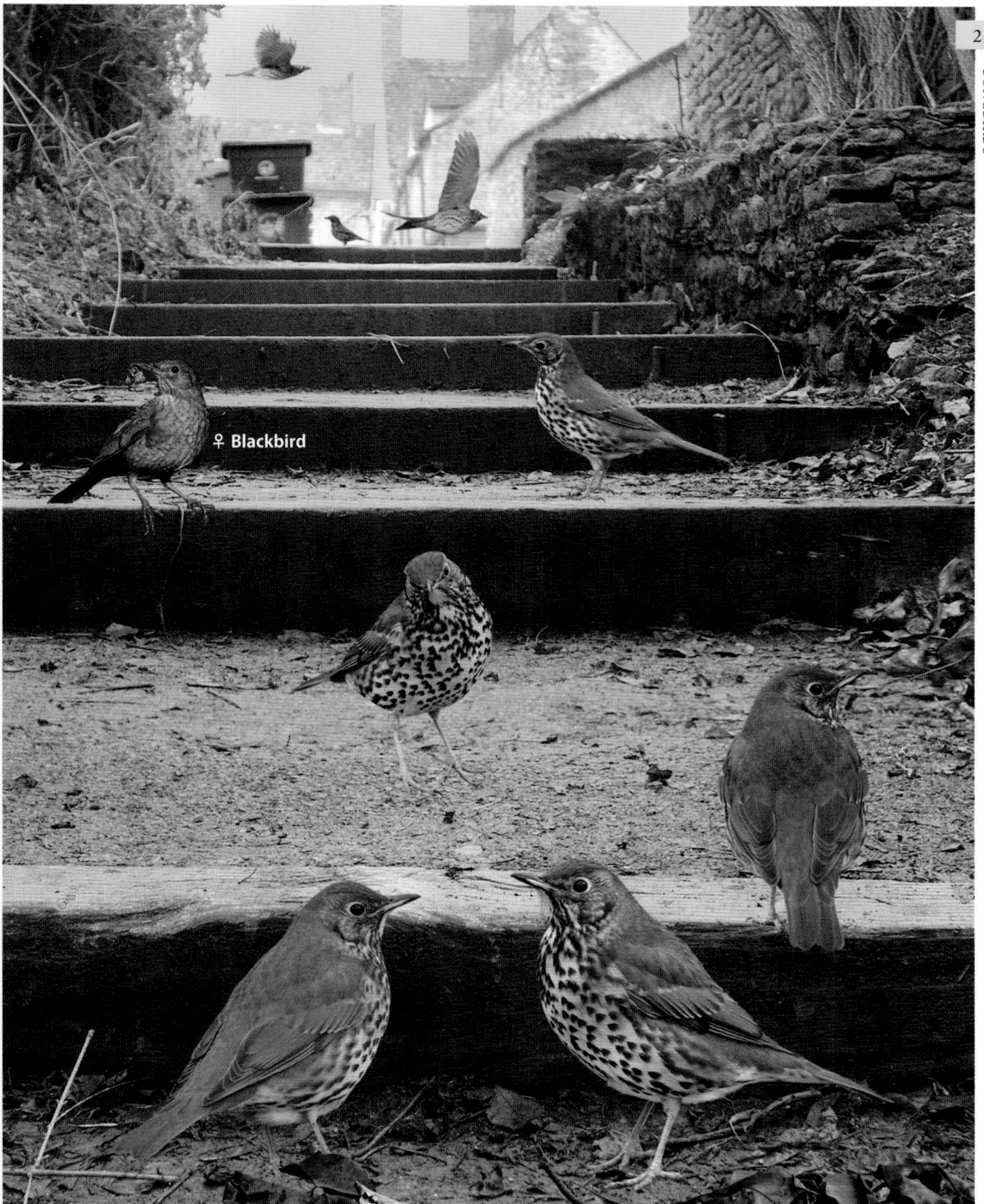

Song Thrush *Turdus philmelos* **SONTH/ST** L 23cm

UK: s. 1,200,000 pairs

Familiar, much-loved thrush of gardens, scrub, and woodland edge. Famous for its loud, clear, varied song, with well-spaced, short, high-pitched phrases repeated several times each before the next. Also famous for its unique habit of striking snail shells against hard surface (e.g., stones, paving) to break them. Runs across lawns BLABI-style, takes berries, feeds in leaf litter. Feeds close to cover and not as much in open as MISTH. Call a short *tsip*. **ID:** Smaller than MISTH and BLABI and more compact. Doesn't stand up as tall as MISTH. Neat spots on breast pointed on upper tip (arrowhead) and often arranged in neater lines down breast and flanks than MISTH. Spots set against warm buff colour on upper breast and flanks, quite different from MISTH. Also darker olive-brown upperparts, no pale panels on wings, rump not obviously paler than back. Flies fast and low, straight into cover, quick wingbeats; underwings pale sandy-brown. Sexes alike. Juv: as ads except for subtle pale streaks on crown and down mantle, soon lost; breast spots smaller and not as neat.

Redwing *Turdus iliacus* REDWI/RE L 21cm

UK: s. 4–16 pairs
w. 690,000

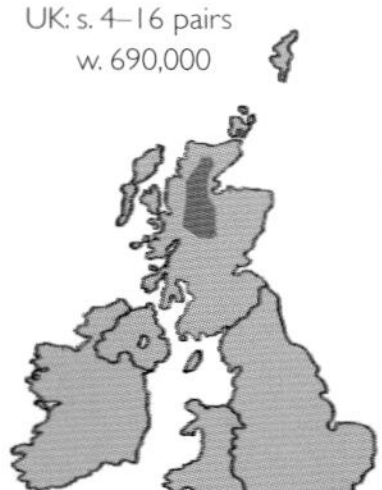

Common winter visitor (Oct–Mar) to hedgerows, fields, and woodland edges, usually in flocks. Mixes freely with other thrushes, esp FIELD. Most often seen raiding berries from trees and shrubs, but also feeds on invertebrates in soil and, unlike FIELD, forages in leaf litter in woodland. Visits suburbs and gardens in later winter, esp in snowy weather. Rare breeding bird in Scottish waterside scrub. Call a sharp *tseep*, like a sharp intake of breath, a common winter sound and also heard from migrants passing overhead on starlit autumn nights. In early spring, flocks make excited babbling. **ID:** Obviously a thrush, but smaller than SONTH and differs in bold 'made-up' face pattern, with strong white supercilium and white submoustachial stripe. Named for conspicuous bold rusty red patch leaking down from underwings onto flanks; also has whiter breast and belly than SONTH with bold stripes rather than discrete spots. Sexes alike. 1st-w: can sometimes be aged by pale tips to tertials and buffer supercilium.

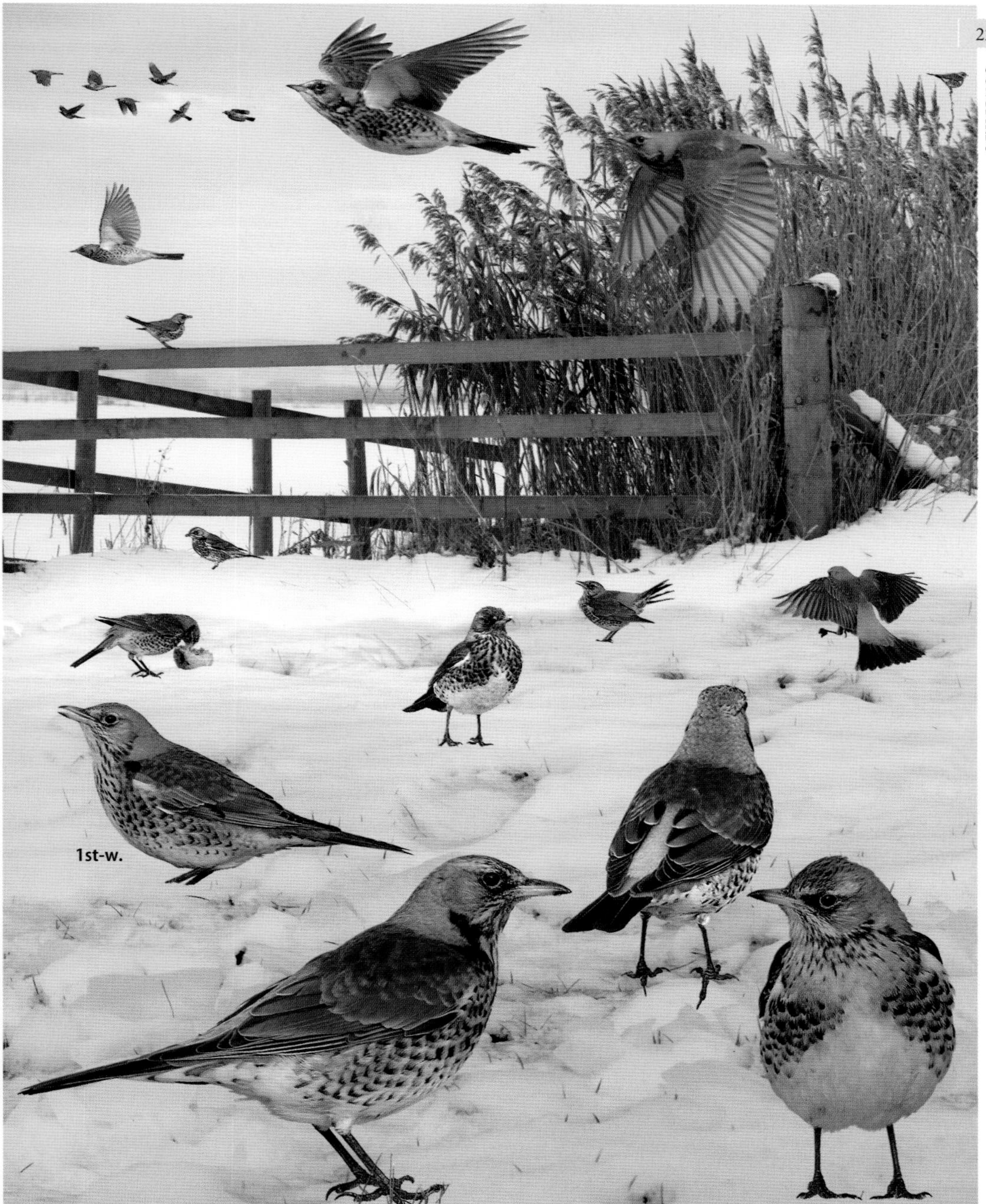

Fieldfare *Turdus pilaris* FIELD/FF L 26cm

UK: s. 1–2 pairs
w. 720,000

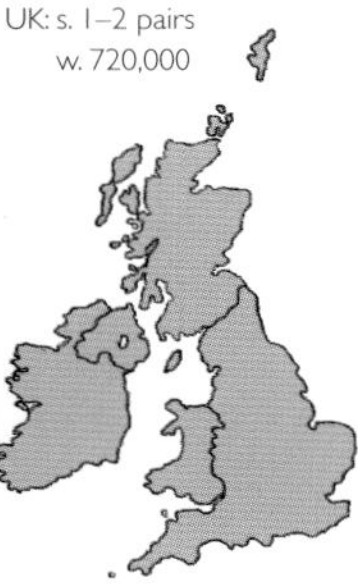

Comes here in flocks in autumn and winter (Oct–Mar) to feed on berries and soil-living invertebrates, living a nomadic existence on fields, hedgerows, and scrub, often in company with REDWI. Flocks move like army troops over wide open fields, each bird moving along in typical thrush stop-start foraging fashion until field covered. Only visits gardens when berries running short, and often moves in large numbers in response to spells of bad weather, turning up in places overnight. Makes quite pleasing *shack-shack* call. Flocks fly in loose, undisciplined fashion like wind-blown autumn leaves. Flight less undulating than MISTH. **ID:** Large, distinctive thrush with ash-grey head and rump/upper-back panel; pleasing velvet mantle and scapulars; black tail. Has ochre band across breast, and lines down breast turn to chevrons on flanks; belly and underwings whitish. Has surprisingly obvious nick of white at bend of wing, also whitish supercilium. 1st-w: can be aged by white edges to retained juv greater wing coverts.

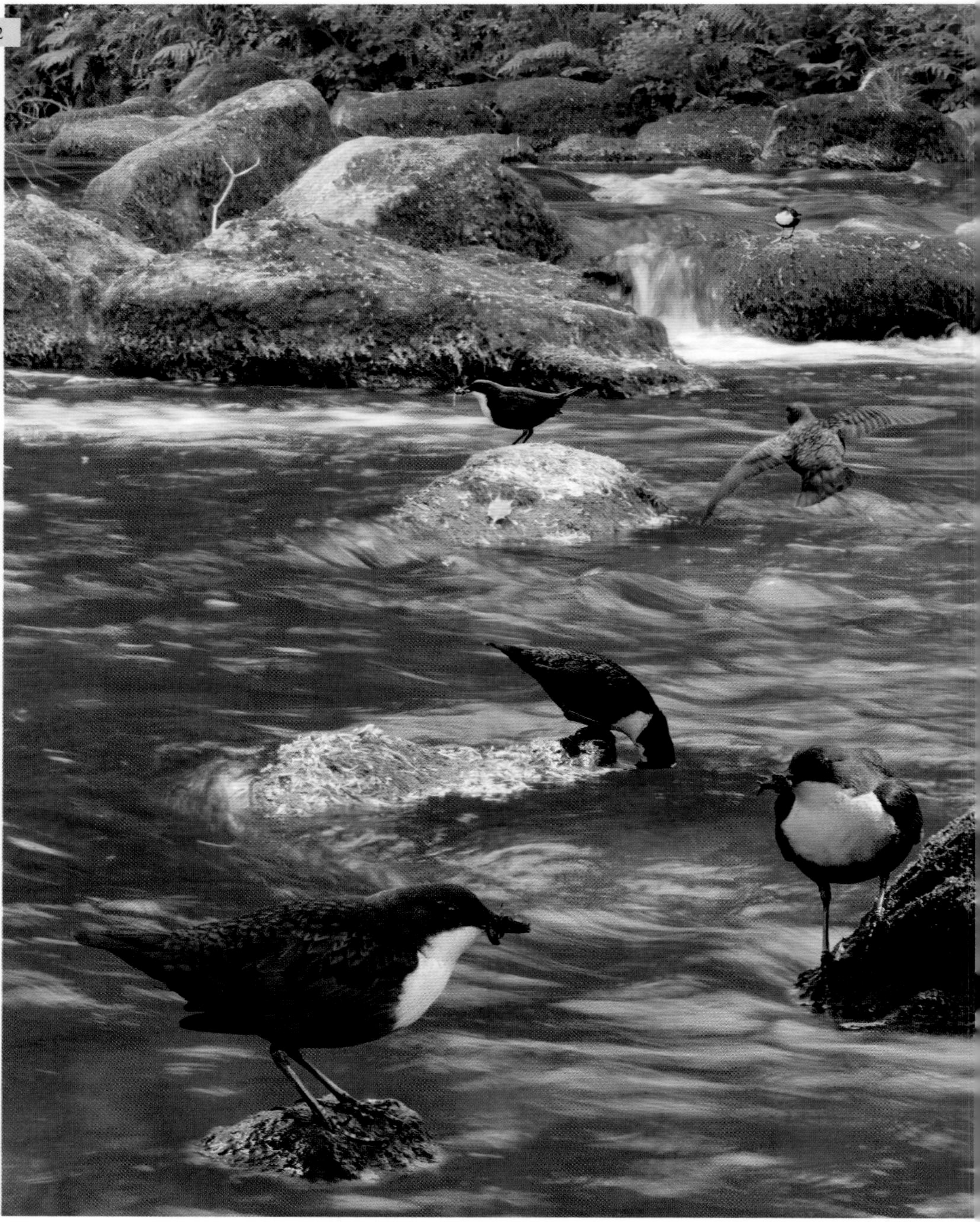

Dipper *Cinclus cinclus* **DIPPE/DI** L 18cm

UK: s. 12,000 pairs

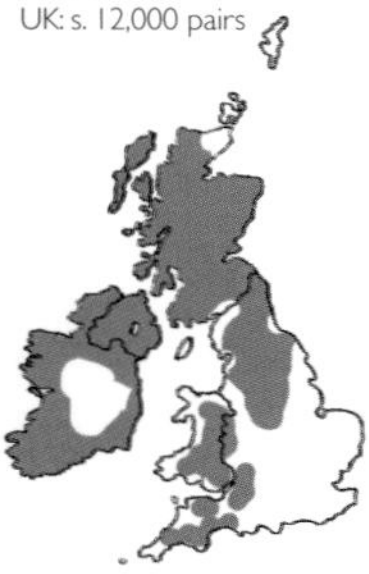

Unique aquatic songbird of fast-flowing streams with rocks and rapids, and also where rivers flow into freshwater lakes. Often found by waterfalls, weirs, and bridges. Fairly common in west and north; very habitat-specific. Usually seen flying fast and low over water with whirring wings, veering to follow direction of watercourse. When foraging, perches on rocks, then simply walks into the water, belly-deep and then totally immersed; bobs up and out without fuss or shaking plumage. Also swims easily, with wings open. When perched, habitually curtseys, bobbing quickly up and down, and cocks tail. Loud call is metallic *zit*; also has loud, slow, strained song often heard in midwinter. **ID:** Unmistakable starling-sized plump bird with short tail. Mainly dark brown, with brilliantly contrasting white throat and breast, and rustier red-brown belly and crown. Long, straight, dark bill. Often 'blinks' white eyelid. Juv: strange-looking grey bird with scalloped pattern and white throat, but shape and behaviour as ads.

Waxwing *Bombycilla garrulus* **WAXWI/WX** L 18in

UK: w. 11,000

Birders' favourite, a rare winter visitor, with numbers varying from year to year. Good numbers, 'irruptions', occur when rowan berry stocks collapse in northern taiga, esp after good breeding season. Whole lifestyle revolves around berries, and one bird can eat 600–1000 a day. In Britain, moves around nomadically in flocks, often turning up in suburbia and, bizarrely, car parks planted with berry-bearing shrubs. Also takes midges in fly-catching sallies. Call a distinctive, trilled *sree*, sibilant like a pea-whistle. Often tame and immune to human activity.

ID: Plump STARL-sized bird with unmistakable crest. Headgear, sleek pink-brown 'fur coat' plumage, and smart black throat and eye-stripe make it look dolled up for a night out. Undertail coverts russet. Flight STARL-like, in close formation, slightly more undulating. Adult: wingtips with V marks, secondaries with waxy red tips, broad yellow tail tip. Vs, yellow inside and white outside, are most clearly defined in ♂, which also has broadest yellow tail band and most obvious waxy tips. 1st-w has single yellow line along wingtip, without outer webs making V; lacks waxy tips.

Bearded Tit *Panurus biarmicus* **BEATI/BR** L 11cm

UK: s. 640 pairs

Exciting scarce and localised resident of large reed beds; will wander to smaller stands in autumn and winter. Difficult to see, esp in windy conditions, but frequently makes short flights over reeds, its long tail and whirring wings instantly identifying it. Very sociable and almost invariably seen in small parties. Often comes to base of reed stems in summer to pluck insects from water surface. Feeds on seeds in winter, mainly from feathery tops. In autumn, may make short 'high-flying' excursions, zooming high upwards calling loudly, then dropping down again. Call is distinctive, pinging *zching*—beware, this is sometimes imitated by REEWA. **ID:** Almost unmistakable, with small size, long tail, and rich tawny colouration; nothing is really similar. Has short, orange, tit-like bill. Clings to reed stems in tit-like fashion, hence name; much-used alternative is Bearded Reedling. Ad ♂: smart with blue-grey head and black drooping moustache (not beard!), black undertail coverts. ♀ head unmarked pink-brown, undertail pale. Juv: as ♀ but black back and tail sides.

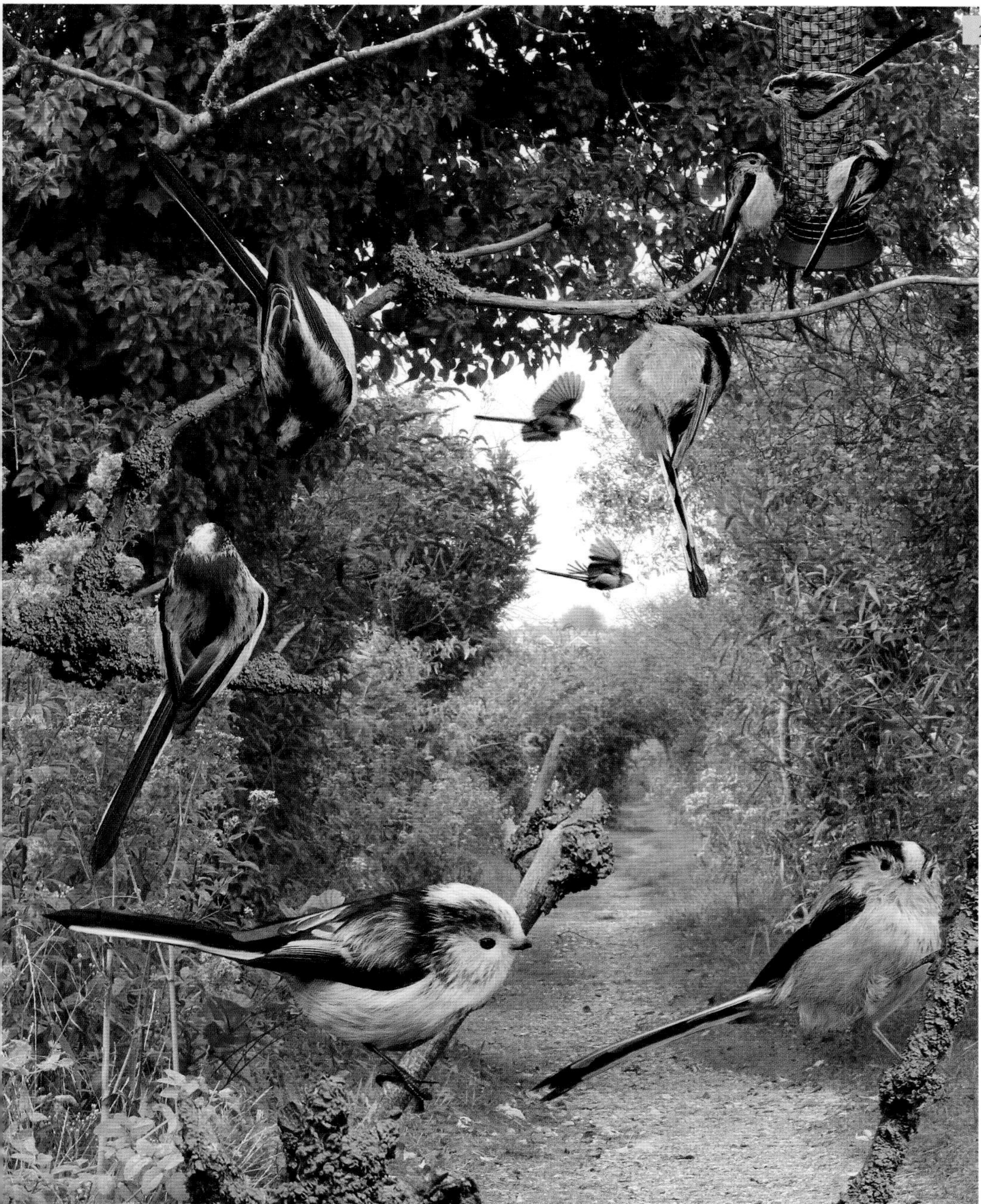

Long-tailed Tit *Aegithalos caudatus* LOTTI/LT L 14cm

UK: s. 340,000 pairs

Very common mite of woodland and scrub, now increasingly visiting gardens, where it feeds from hanging feeders. Bands of 5–10 relatives spend autumn and winter patrolling large territory, where individuals feed in branches for just a few moments before moving on to the next tree, one after the other, always restlessly passing through. Forages acrobatically at any height, using tail as counterbalance, often holding on upside down. Flocks break down in early spring, pairs build remarkable domed nest of moss, cobwebs, lichen, and feathers, usually in low (thorny) bush. Groups make persistent, fast *see-see-see-see* calls to keep together, with gentle *tupp* noises at close quarters and louder splutters if birds separate. Flocks roost at night cuddling together, as do fledglings. **ID:** Unmistakable: tiny size, very long trailing tail, and weak flight with rapid undulations rule out anything else. Adult: pink-flushed body plumage, head white with black stripe curling round eye and widening onto mantle; crown white. Juv: head with sooty face mask covering eye, no pink on body, shorter tail.

Great Tit *Parus major* **GRETI/GT** L 14cm

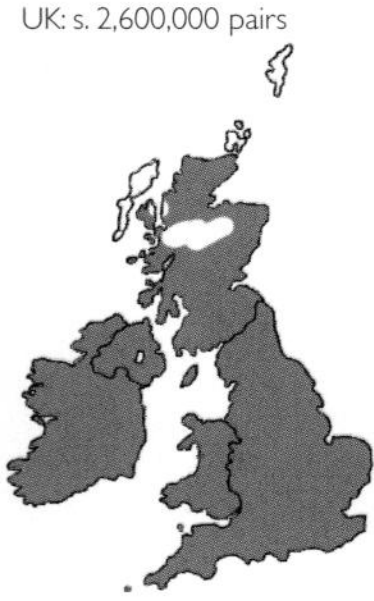

Superabundant bird of woods, gardens, shrubbery, hedgerows, and so on. Occurs in all types of trees, including pure coniferous stands. Has a tendency to feed by trunks and larger branches, and forages on the ground frequently; however, also acrobatic like other tits, and feeds in canopy foliage, hanging upside down. Unable to resist hanging feeders and bird tables, and is usually one of the first visitors. May be found in roaming flocks of birds in autumn, winter, and esp late summer, when juveniles form same-age gatherings. Cheerful chiming song, a much varying repetition of 2 notes *TEEcher, TEEcher*, can be heard everywhere from late Dec until May. Makes *pink-pink* and huge variety of other calls. **ID:** Largest tit, size of CHAFF, and only one with white outer tail feathers. Longer tail than e.g. BLUTI. Distinctive plumage with yellow breast split by black stripe; head with black cap, bold white cheek. Ad ♂ has broader breast stripe, esp obvious between legs; ♀: paler yellow breast. Juv: yellow cheeks, sooty-black head, and reduced stripe.

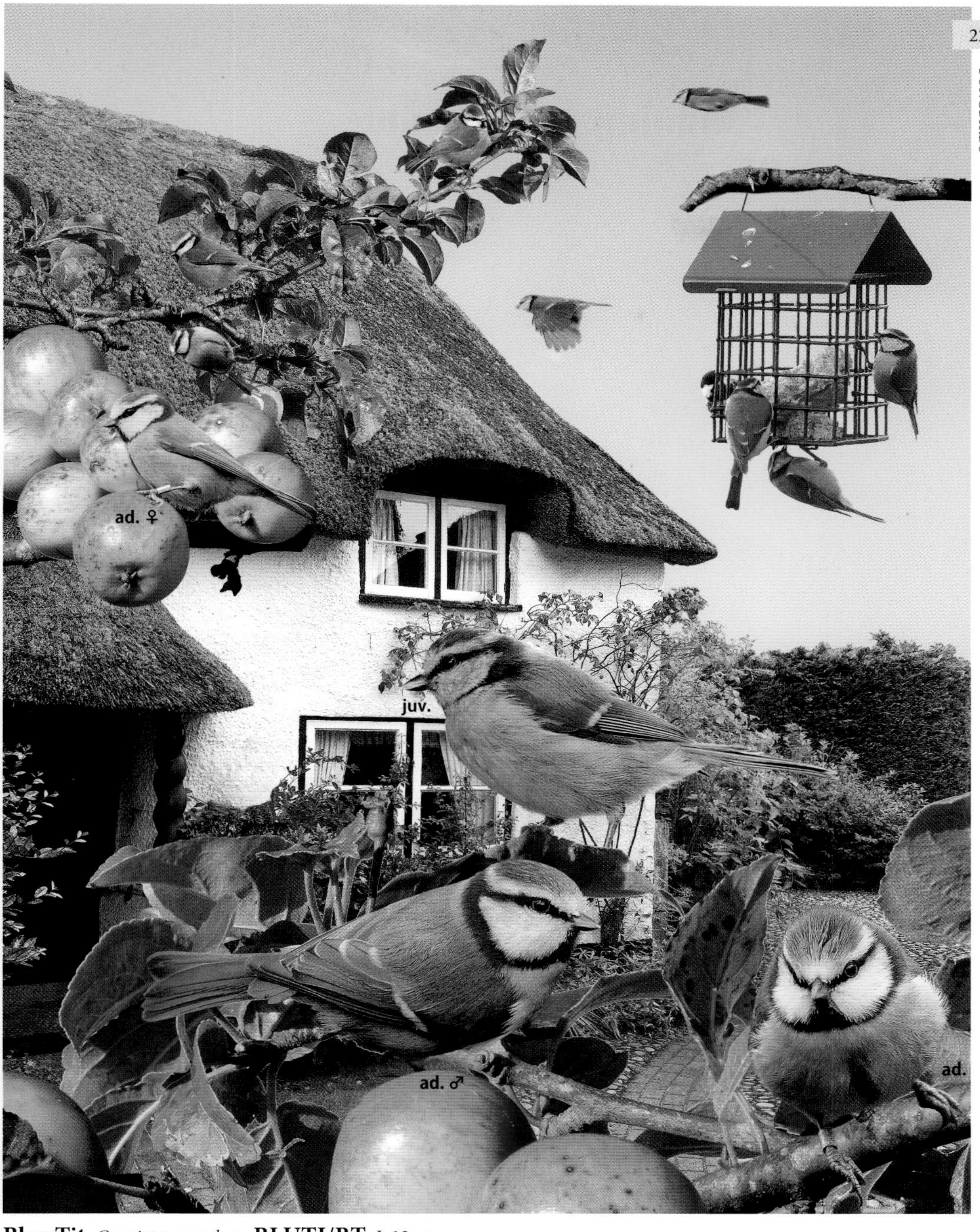

Blue Tit *Cyanistes caeruleus* **BLUTI/BT** L 12cm

UK: 3,600,000 pairs

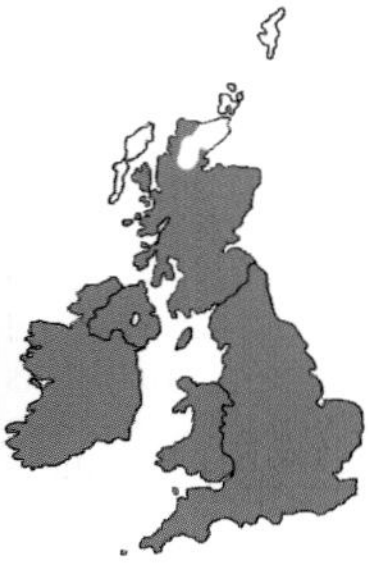

One of Britain's commonest birds, found in woodland, gardens, shrubbery, and many other places, but usually absent from conifer plantations. Very perky, inquisitive, fearless, and downright aggressive species; holds its own at garden feeders, even against much larger GRETI. Strong legs confer acrobatic ability, so feeds high up in canopy, even among thinnest twigs; will come to ground too. Uses garden feeders and competes with GRETI for nest boxes. Parents feed large broods (average 10+) for 2 weeks, making 1000 visits a day carrying caterpillars. Sociable, often in parties, incl with other tits. Complex songs include silvery trills on one note; lots of calls, including drawn-out scold. **ID:** Brightly coloured small bird, with brilliant yellow breast with very narrow, not very neat, black stripe down belly. Stunning cobalt-blue cap above mainly white face, with narrow black eye-stripe and throat—quite distinct from GRETI. Short blue tail. Sexes alike, the brightest extremes are ♂. Juv has wash of yellow on head instead of white, and cap greyish green. Frothy calls of begging juvs is one of sounds of midsummer.

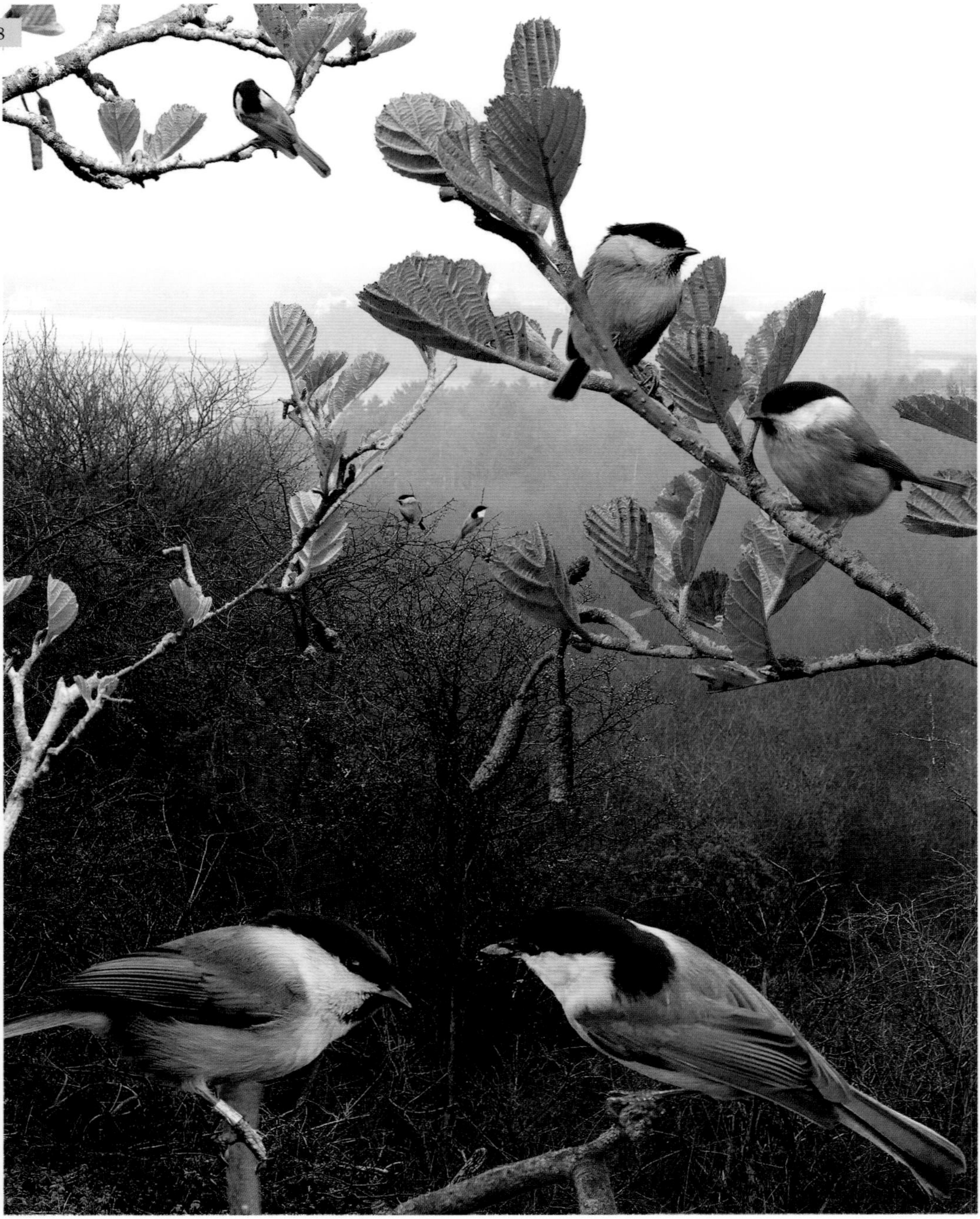

Willow Tit *Poecile montanus* **WILTI/WT** L 12cm

UK: s. 3,400 pairs

Uncommon tit of damp woodlands and scrub, esp of willow (of course), alder, elder, and birch; also occurs in hedgerows, scrub around lakes and gravel pits, and, quite unlike MARTI, in coniferous woodland, esp in Scotland. A quiet and undemonstrative species, calls much less often than MARTI and other tits, and is also a little shyer. Usually seen only in singles or pairs. Diagnostic call is drawn out, nasal *eez-eez-eez*, often combined with introductory notes to give *chick-a-bee-bee-bee*; rarely heard song is repeated, rather sweet *piu-piu-piu* (Feb–Apr). Unlike MARTI, excavates its own nest hole. **ID:** Neat tit with smart black cap and bib and brown plumage with no wing bars. Frighteningly similar to MARTI, but is a little larger headed, fluffier, and bull necked. Cap is less glossy and bib often larger than MART's with slightly diffuse lower border. White of cheek extends further back towards nape. Best distinction probably pale edges to secondaries, making subtle wing panel. Sexes and juv alike.

Marsh Tit *Poecile palustris* **MARTI/MT** L 12cm

UK: s. 41,000 pairs

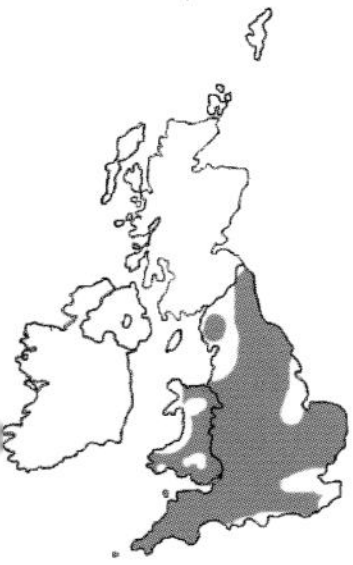

One of worst-named British birds, not found in marshes at all. Instead key habitat is mature deciduous damp woodland, usually with good understory (e.g., holly), where it is fairly common, but harder to find than other tits because it lives in pairs with large territories—you don't see flocks, at best small family parties in summer. However, pairs will join mixed tit parties when latter are in their territory. A perkier bird than WILTI, noisily drawing attention with distinctive *pit-CHOU!* call, which may become a scold. Song is repeated clipped note, sometimes just *chou, chouc, chou*. More often feeds on top of herbs than WILTI and much more likely to hammer seeds with bill. Doesn't excavate its own nest, but will forcibly take over WILTI construction. **ID:** Slightly smaller, slimmer, smaller headed, and better turned out than WILTI, but differences very subtle. Has glossier cap, smaller bib, and plain wing without pale panel. Cheeks are often duller brownish white towards nape. Very close up has white spot on base of upper mandible, above cutting edge. Sexes alike, juv with duller cap.

Coal Tit *Periparus ater* **COATI/CT** L 11cm

UK: s. 760,000 pairs

A small tit that breeds mainly in coniferous woodlands, but ranges more widely in winter, including commonly to gardens. Frequently seen feeding high in upper branches of conifers, easily manoeuvring out to tips of branches, acrobatically moving among needles, and often hovering to reach extremities. Takes invertebrates throughout year, but eats nuts in autumn and winter and will run gauntlet of BLUTI and GRETI to grab nut from feeder and quickly spirit it away. Has very similar song to GRETI but not as harsh and slightly squeakier, *soo-CHEE, soo-CHEE, soo-CHEE*. Most frequent call a questioning *twee?* **ID:** Looks big headed and pin tailed. Pattern like colourless version of GRETI, with same large white cheek patch and black crown, but has long white nape patch starting on top of crown. Easily distinguished from MARTI/WILTI by 2 white wing bars, often appearing to be made up from spots; also much colder olive-grey on mantle and buff on underparts. Lower border of black throat diffuse, giving messy look. Sexes alike. Juv: yellow wash to cheeks and nape.

Crested Tit *Lophophanes cristatus* CRETI/CI L 12cm

UK: s. 1,500 pairs

Uncommon resident in Scotland, mostly in stands of native Caledonian pine forest, but also ranges to other types of conifers. For breeding prefers plenty of old and rotten wood, esp tree stumps, and a rich herb layer. A quiet, retiring species; pairs found year-round in large territories. Usually detected by its distinctive if understated call/song, a trill that has an unmistakable bubbling quality interspersed with sharp, high-pitched *seep* notes. Often feeds on trunks and large branches; often joins flocks of woodland birds that pass through the territory. Excavates its own nest hole. Often visits feeding stations, in gardens or in woodland reserves. **ID:** Unmistakable if pointed crest seen; crest blackish with white scaling. Otherwise small brown tit without wing bars; has black throat and neck band, black eye-stripe. Sexes alike. Juv: just slightly shorter crest, difference doesn't last long.

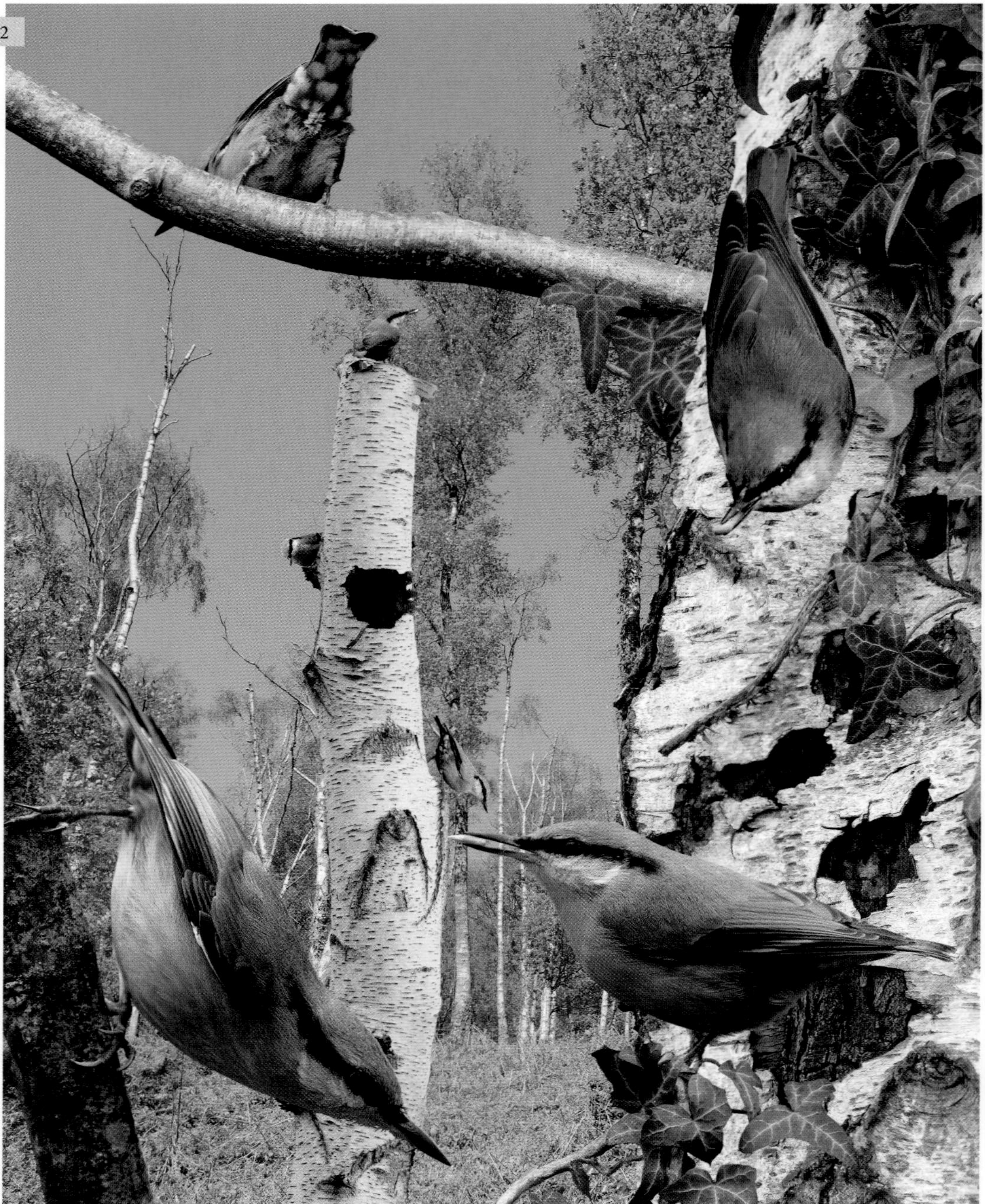

Nuthatch *Sitta europaea* **NUTHA/NH** L 14cm

UK: s. 220,000 pairs

Distinctive deciduous and mixed woodland bird that frequently visits gardens, slugging it out with tits on bird feeders. Lives most of its life, though, up in the tree canopy, where it clings vertically to tree trunks, both upright and, uniquely, upside down. Progresses along branches with sidling action, but rests on vertical trunks with one foot holding on above the other, head away from surface. Unusual shape, with very large head, little neck and long, sharp, chisel-shaped bill; also a short tail that isn't used for pivot, unlike woodpeckers and TREEC. Typically found in pairs. Makes variety of cheerful boyish whistles, also loud, plaintive *peeu* series. In autumn, collects large quantity of nuts from, for example, oaks and beeches to cache. Forages from ground at times. Nests in hole in tree or nest boxes, plasters mud around entrance for bespoke size. **ID:** 'Like KINGF without the glittering plumage', blue-grey above and light apricot and chestnut below, with long black eye-stripe; white corners to tail, white spots on vent. ♂ has warmer chestnut on flanks, contrast to belly; juv sim to ad.

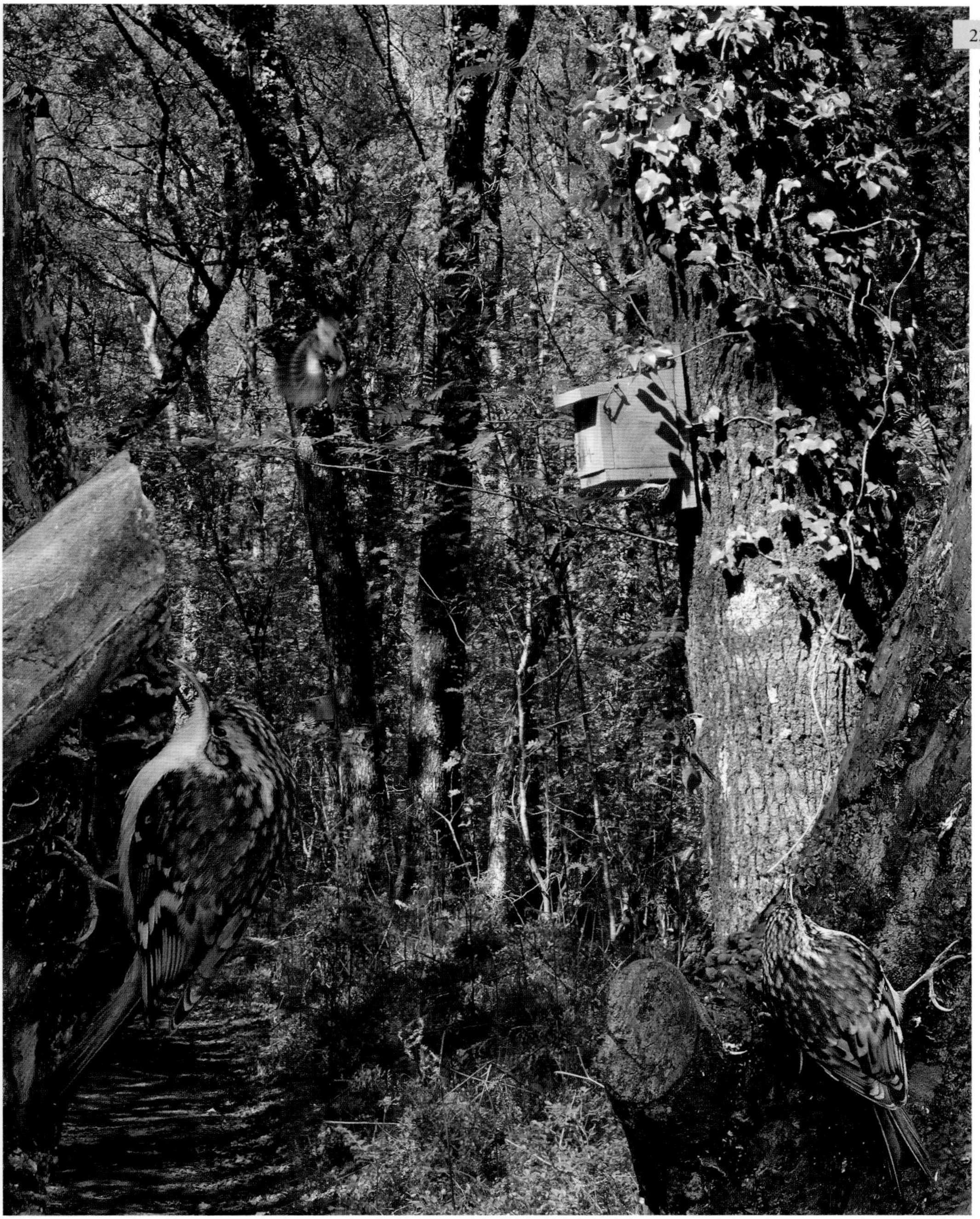

Treecreeper *Certhia familiaris* **TREEC/TC** L 12cm

UK: s. 200,000 pairs

Mouse-like bird that hugs tree trunks as it climbs, found in all kinds of woodland, including pure coniferous plantations. Also found in hedgerows and rural gardens, commons, heaths, and the like. Spends much of the day creeping up trunks and branches with 2-footed hops; typically starts near bottom of trunk, works upwards to near top of tree, then flies down to begin at neighbouring tree. Unlike NUTHA, cannot climb down headfirst because it uses long, stiffened tail as pivot, but can creep up overhangs. Feeds mainly on invertebrates, so doesn't usually visit feeding stations. Quiet species, uttering sibilant *sree* calls, in distinctively regular series. Song is gentle CHAFF-like phrase, falls down then rises in pitch at end. Usually nests behind flaking bark or amongst creeper, rarely uses boxes. **ID:** Behaviour usually identifies, but richly patterned brown above, pure white below, with long, slightly downcurved bill. Barring of wings visible in flight. Sexes alike, juv colder brown.

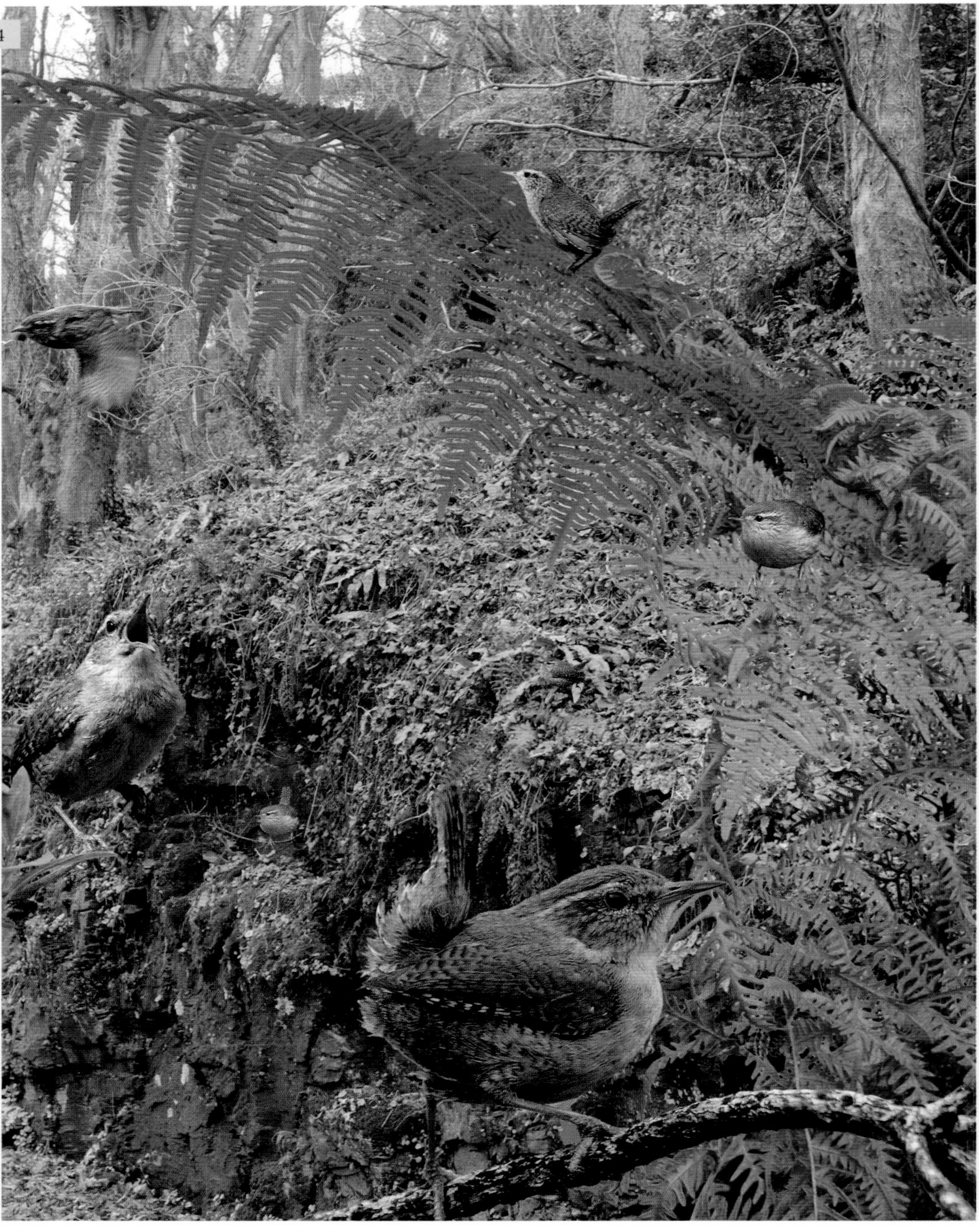

Wren *Troglodytes troglodytes* **WREN/WR** L 10cm

UK: s. 8,600,000 pairs

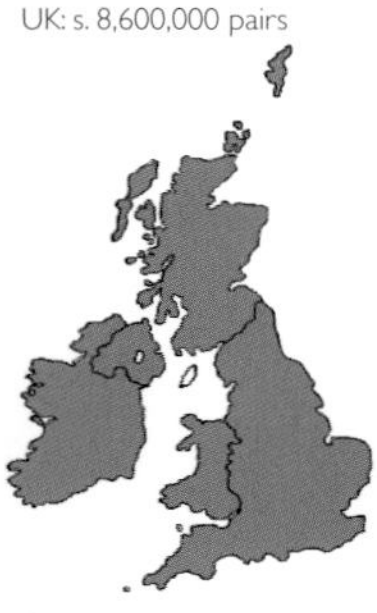

Extraordinarily abundant—probably Britain's most numerous bird—yet difficult to see well; keeps hidden in cover, creeping about on ground and just above. Most people think it's our smallest bird, but GOLDC and FIREC are tinier. Found in almost any kind of low vegetation, from deep woodland undergrowth to windswept offshore islands (Hebrides, Fair Isle, Shetland have distinct subspecies). Rarely seen or heard much above 5m, almost never high in trees. Compensates for size by noisy and overwrought personality. Unexpectedly loud song explodes from near ground level, a hurried jumble of sweet, liquid notes, including a jarring trill mid-phrase, overall like excitable commentator enthusing over finish of race. Call testy, spitting *teck, teck*. Restless, curtseys when perched, cocks tail; often inquisitive, scolds. Builds ball-shaped nest, main construction by male, furnished by female. **ID:** Minute brown fine-barred bird with pale supercilium and long, sharp-tipped, slowly downcurved bill; wings and tail short. Has low, whirring flight. Sexes and ages sim.

Dunnock *Prunella modularis* **DUNNO/D.** L 14cm

UK: s. 2,500,000 pairs

A woodland edge species that is now a familiar sight in gardens, as well as hedgerows, heaths, moors, and all kinds of dense shrubbery. Quite sparrow-like, but instead has thin bill and habit of creeping or shuffling along the ground, legs flexed, rather than hopping. Much less sociable, not in flocks. Also constantly flicks wings and tail, looks nervous and twitchy. A good songster; both sexes deliver a cheerful but limited cyclical warble that can sound like the squeaky wheels of a trolley; heard almost all year. Often sings half a dozen times before moving perch. Main call a loud, also squeaky *seep*. Has a red-hot sex life in which both males and females may hold multiple mates, with fractious consequences. Males often wave wings at each other in obvious display. **ID:** Well proportioned with very thin bill and pink legs. Head and breast suffused with grey, while much of plumage richly striped, including on underparts, unlike HOUSP. Tail plain brown. Sexes alike. Juv: same colour scheme as ad but more boldly striped all over, including on head.

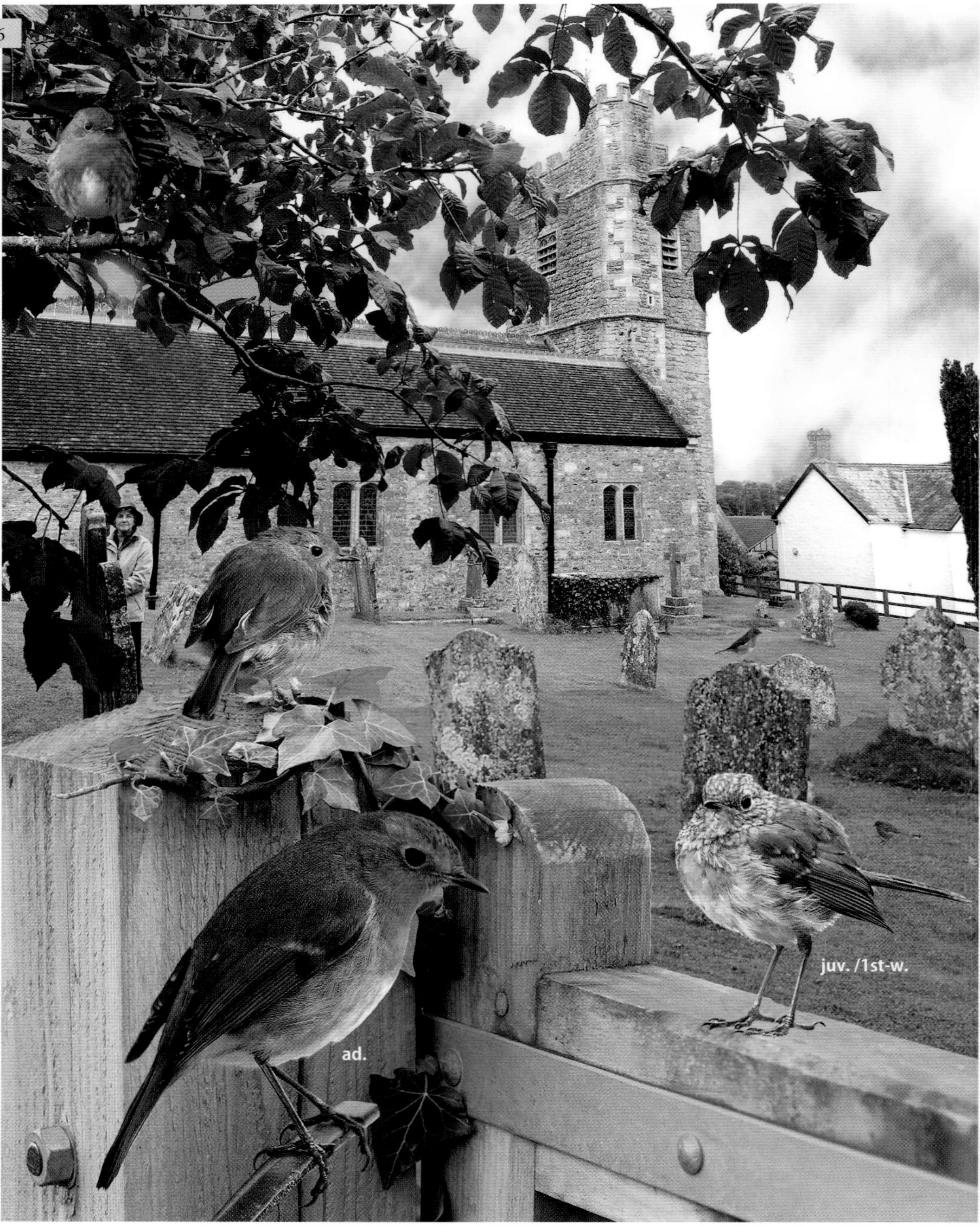

Robin *Erithacus rubecula* **ROBIN/R.** L 14cm

UK: s. 6,700,000 pairs

Great garden favourite, originally a woodland bird but now ensconced in suburbia and in people's affections. Also occurs in scrub, hedgerows, and wherever dense cover is adjacent to open ground for feeding. Famed habit of perching on spade handles derives from technique of watching for food from low perch, and then dropping down onto any invertebrates spotted. Astonishingly aggressive; spats routine, killing regular. Often extremely tame, benefits from gardener turning over soil and also from free handouts, esp of mealworms. Often bobs up and down, hops across lawns; has rapid, fluid flight, usually down low. Often sings in complete darkness, even in winter. ROBIN's is perhaps most frequently heard bird song in Britain. Pattern: bird sings phrase, leaves gap, sings different phrase, and so on; phrases characteristically include slow and fast cascading sections, overall a bit squeaky and wistful. Call clean *tick*. **ID:** Nothing else has sim plumage. Garden visitors in winter are often continental birds. Sexes alike, briefly held juv plumage v different, brown with mottling on breast and pale spots on upperparts.

Bluethroat *Luscinia svecica* **BLUTH/BU** L 14cm

Extremely skulking rare passage migrant and occasional breeder, with average of 113 records/year Mar–May and Aug–Oct. Usually found in coastal scrub, often marshy. Shape and mannerisms on ground similar to ROBIN, has longer legs. Call *chack*. **ID:** Consistent features include conspicuous russet base to tail, very strong pale supercilium and some form of breast adornment. Ad ♂ br: throat/breast scintillating blue, with white (c/s Europe) or red (n Europe) central spot, then black/white/reddish bands across chest. Ad ♀/1st-w ♂: usually some but less blue, variable bands, black submoustachial stripe; other ad ♀ and 1st-w ♀ just creamy throat with black 'pearl necklace'.

Red-breasted Flycatcher *Ficedula parva* **REBFL/FY** L 12cm

Rare passage migrant Aug–Nov (avg 86/year), mainly to northern Scottish isles and along the East Coast. Very rare in spring. Small and active, often stays in canopy of trees, warbler-like, does fly-catch. **ID:** Would be a dull bird if not for long tail, which is black with white sides and incessantly cocked high over back; also has large, dark staring eye with pale eye-ring. Ad ♂ with grey head and orange throat; ♀/1st-w plain brown head, ♀ with white throat, 1st-w with buff throat.

Spotted Flycatcher *Muscicapa striata* **SPOFL/SF** L 14cm

UK: s. 36,000 pairs

Widespread summer visitor (May–Sep) to forest and woodland edge, parks, and gardens; more widespread on migration, often in scrub. Lives primarily in the tree canopy, feeding by making brief aerial sallies from elevated perches (e.g., dead branches and twigs) in which flying insects are snapped up. Habit of returning to perch after acrobatic, fluent flight is what gets it noticed. Will perch on fences lower down, and even feeds on ground in rainy weather; regularly sallies over rivers and streams from nearby trees. Often takes large insects such as butterflies and bees. Terrible song of disjointed squeaks, from canopy, easily missed. Alarm call *wiss-chuck*. **ID:** Surprisingly distinctive: upright posture when perched, with slim body, large head, very long pointed wings, and small feet. Upperparts mainly mousy grey-brown, underparts white except for consistently, neatly etched streaks down throat and chest. Sexes alike, and only juv is actually 'spotted', with pale spots on upperparts, a little mottled below. 1st-w sim to ad but with broader and buffer fringes to wing feathers creating very thin bars.

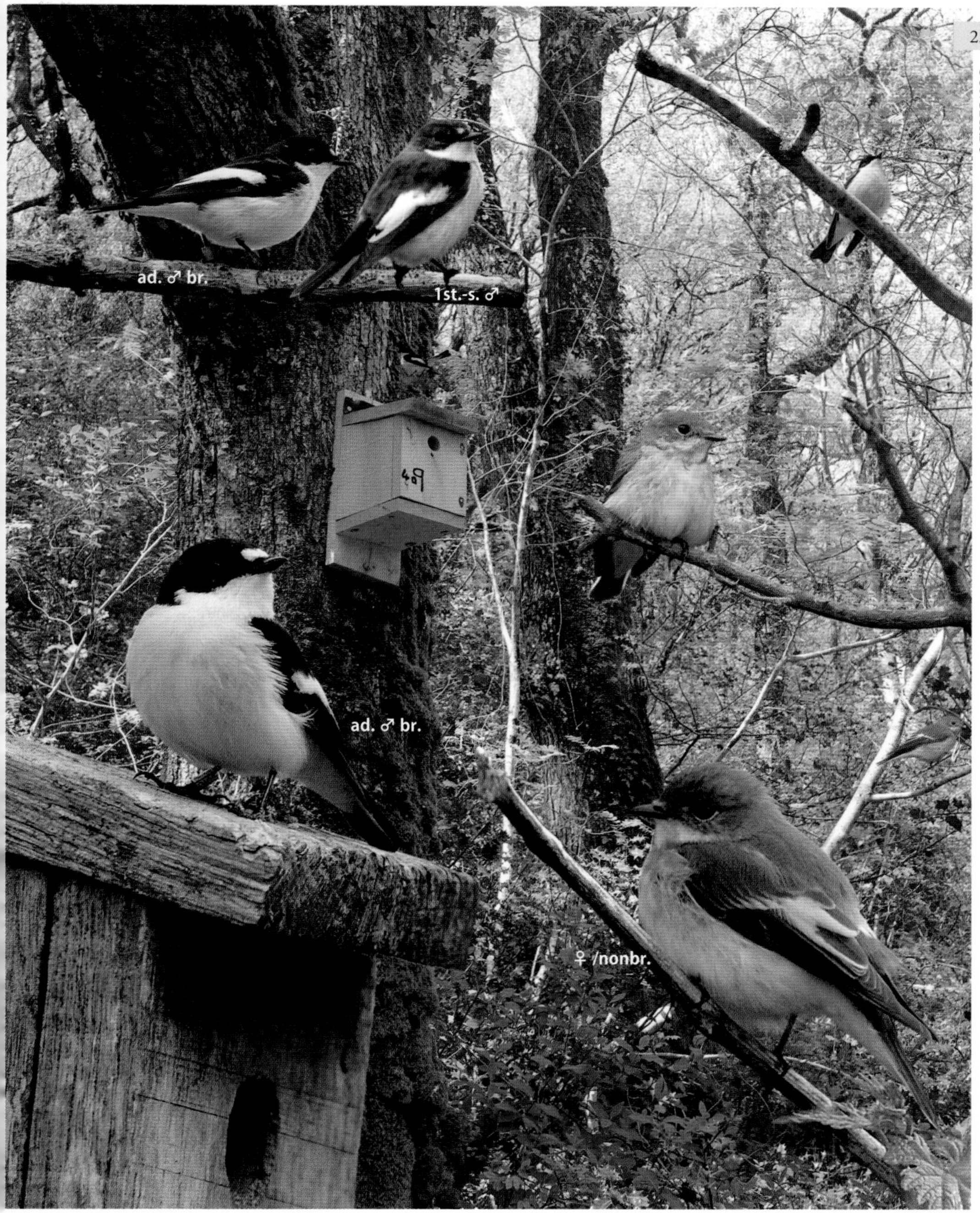

Pied Flycatcher *Ficedula hypoleuca* **PIEFL/PF** L 13cm

UK: s. 18,500 pairs

Summer visitor (Apr–Aug) to deciduous woodland and glades, particularly in the west and north. In many places associated with sessile oak woods, but also birches and other woodland; more widespread on migration. Similar in behaviour to SPOFL, aerial sallies to catch flying insects, but less often returns to the same perch it has just left; also, tends to remain inside canopy when feeding, less attracted to sunlit perches. Small, restless bird repeatedly flicks wings (sometimes just one wing) and cocks tail. Nests in holes in trees, finds nest boxes irresistible. Male often sings at entrance hole, a fast ditty with repeated up-down pitch changes and slightly strained air; call *pik*, a little like GOLDF. **ID:** Small neat, plump bird with short, white-sided tail. Always has broad white/buff-tinged wing bars. Ad ♂ br: smart black above and clean white below, with small white forehead patch and half-collar; some are browner (esp 1st-s). In ♀, dark brown replaces black, except on wings, although white patch smaller. Juv: spotty version of ♀. 1st-w/nonbr: sim to ad ♀ but may have blacker rump.

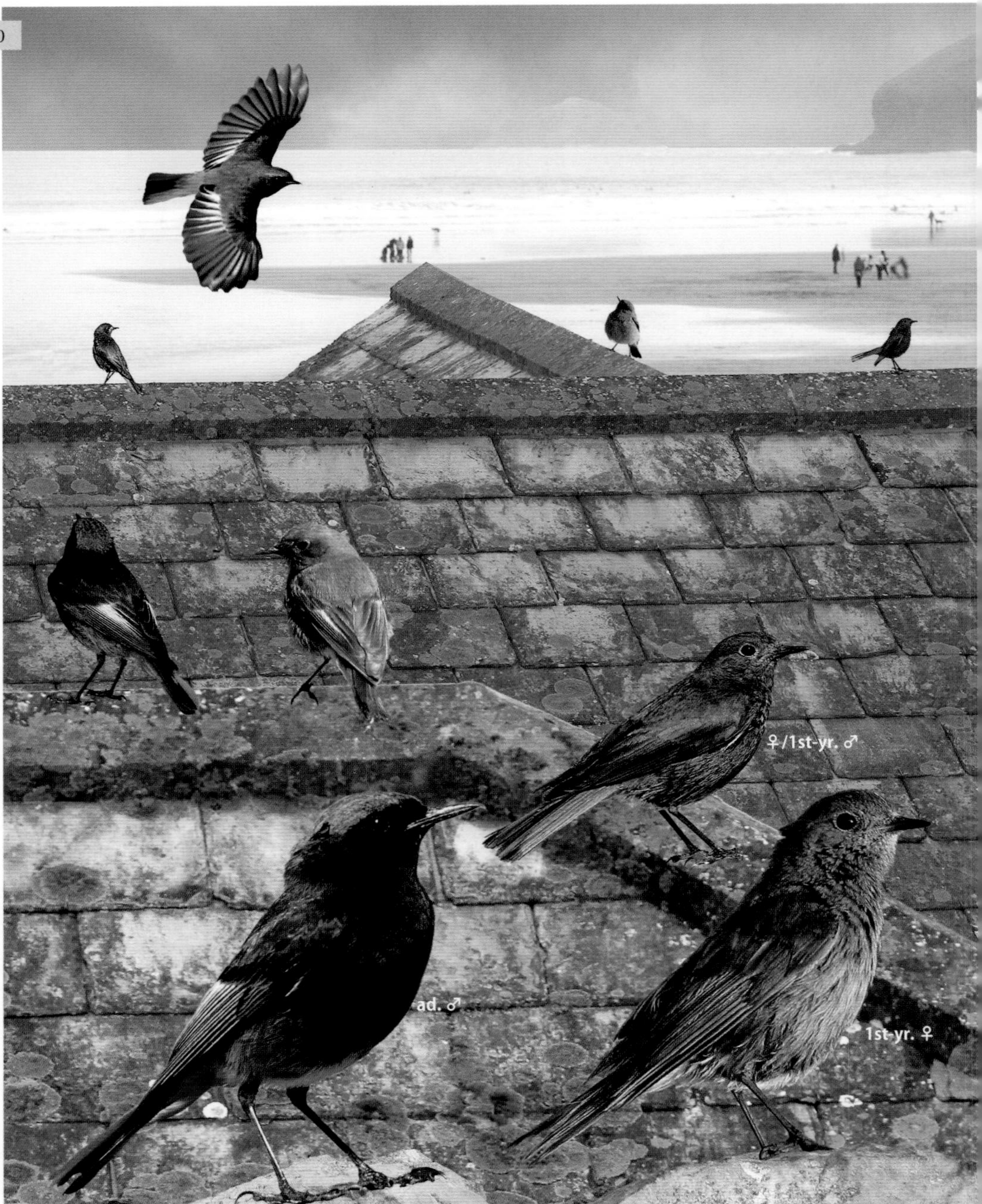

Black Redstart *Phoenicurus ochruros* **BLARE/BX** L 14cm

UK: s. 19–44 pairs
w. 400

Rare breeding and wintering bird, but commoner and more widespread as passage migrant Mar–Apr and Sep–Nov. The very few breeders are in urban/industrial areas (e.g., London, Birmingham) or on cliffs. Migrants often found on cliffs, shores, rocky places, farms, roofs, and so on. Quivers orange tail in style of Redstarts, but compared to REDST more often on buildings and never likely seen perched in tree. Feeds more often on ground and runs more and longer. Sings from high (e.g., top of building, crane, aerial), often in twilight, song includes short introductory phrase followed by unique sound like ball bearings rubbing together. Call *tucc, tucc.* **ID:** Small ROBIN-like bird with orange tail. Like REDST but darker in all plumages. Ad ♂ br: slate-grey, darkens to black around face and breast; white wing panel on secondaries. 1st-s ♂: lacks panel. ♀/1st-w: mainly plain sooty-brown, including on underparts, which don't contrast much with upperparts.

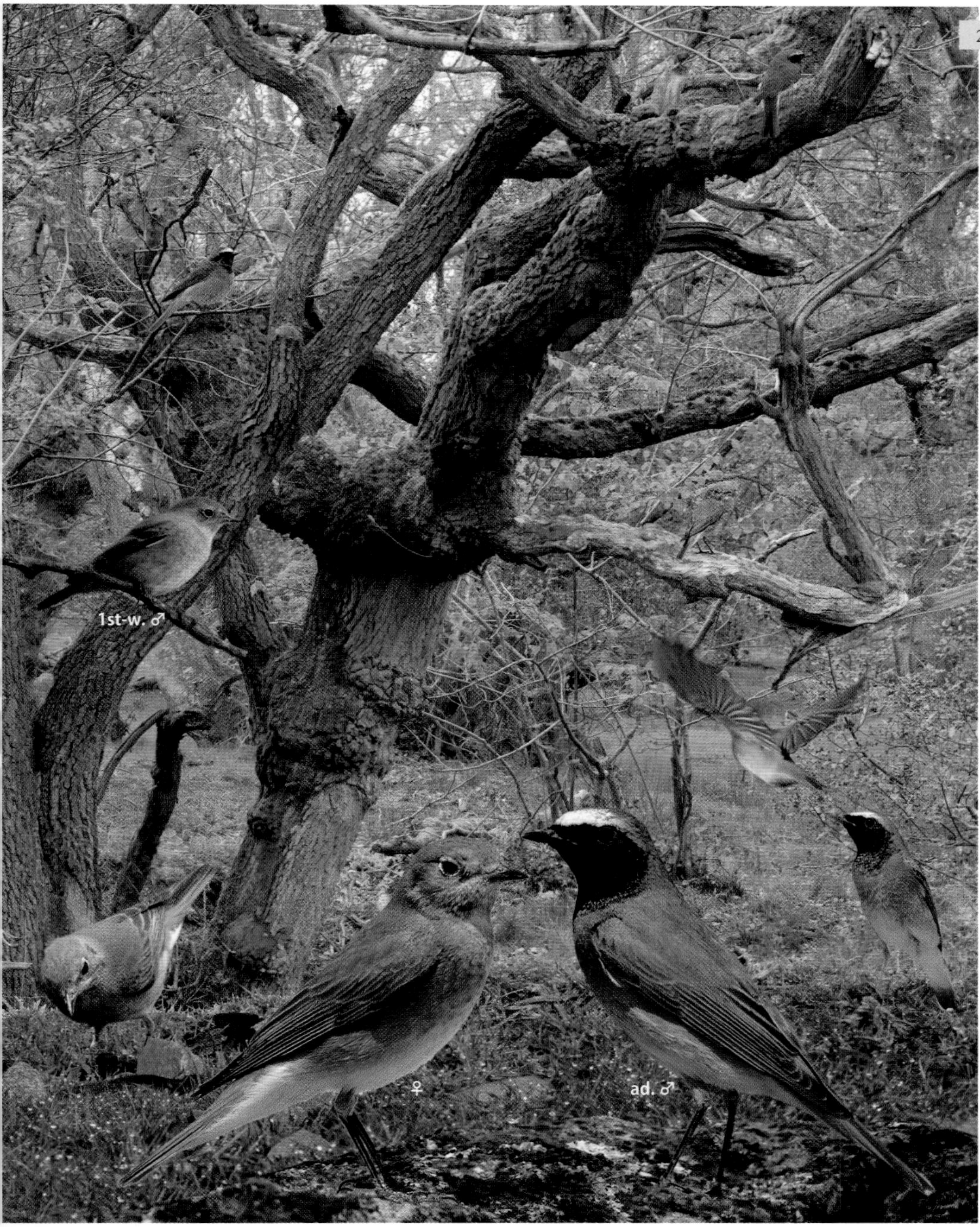

Redstart *Phoenicurus phoenicurus* **REDST/RT** L 14cm

UK: s. 100,000 pairs

Widespread summer visitor (Apr–Sep) to deciduous (esp sessile oaks) and mixed woodland, uplands, open country with scattered trees; common passage migrant in scrub. Restless ROBIN-like songbird that has odd habit of quivering orange tail relentlessly (unique to both redstarts). Arboreal, feeds in branches of trees, also on the ground, where makes brief hops. Very active, flitting about a lot. Often retiring, incl on migration. Song of 2 parts: a slightly sorrowful *hey diddle, diddle* followed by second part that varies phrase to phrase and is often imitative. Call is distinctive *hweet*, often *hwee-tk-tk*. **ID:** Warmer brown than BLARE, without pale wing panel. Ad ♂ br: handsome, with black throat and white forehead; in nonbr these sullied by brown fringes. ♀ brown with orange tail; throat pale, often whitish, in contrast to BLARE, and underparts usually obviously paler than upperparts. 1st-w: brown fringes to flight feathers; ♂ may show hint of black on face.

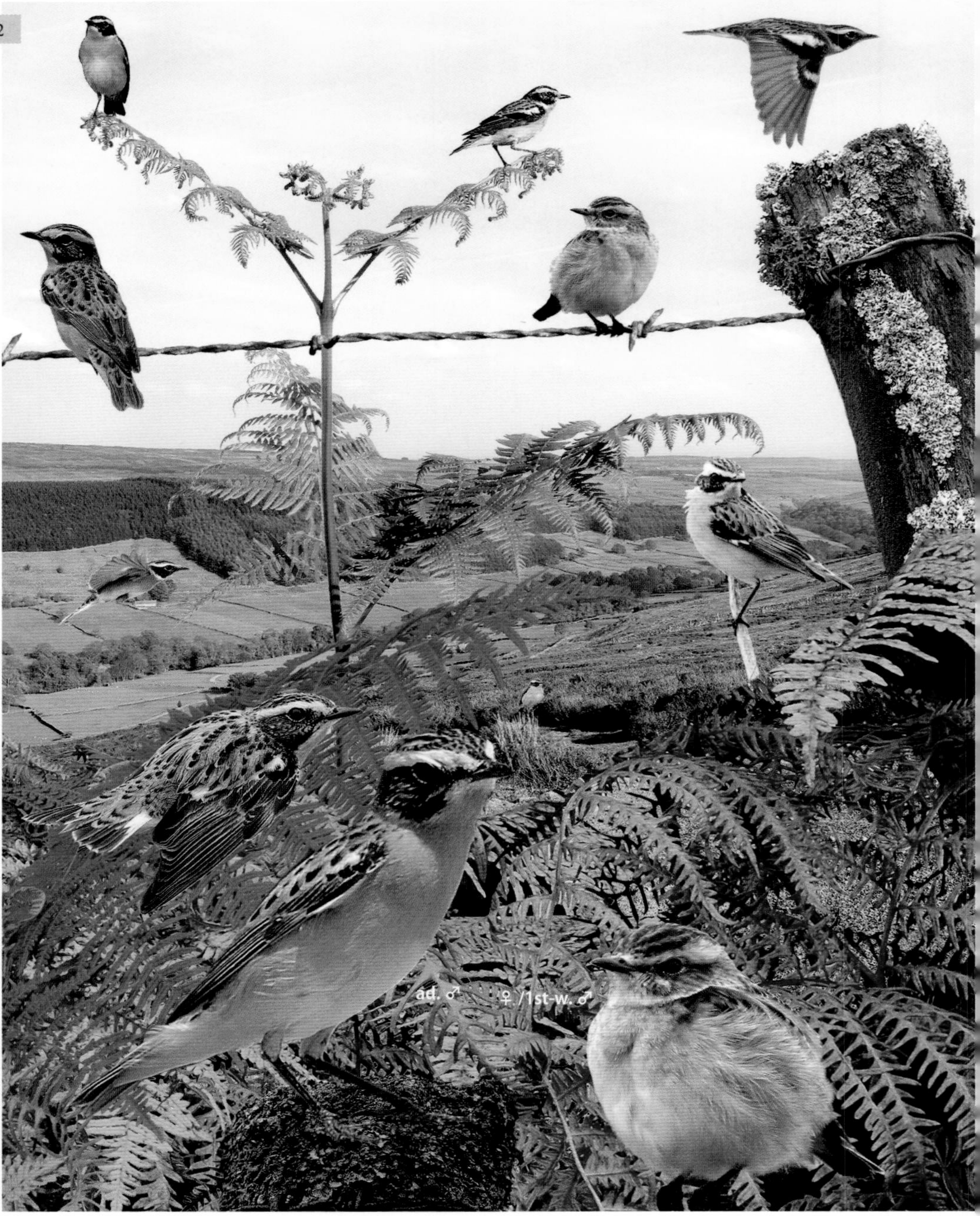

Whinchat *Saxicola rubetra* WHINC/WC L 12cm

UK: s. 47,000 pairs

Fairly common summer visitor Apr–Sep and widespread passage migrant. Breeds in rough terrain, often in uplands, typically dominated by bracken; on passage, any sort of overgrown grassy habitat. Typically hunts by perching sentinel-like on raised perch (e.g., tall weed) and, once prey spotted, dropping to ground and pouncing on it. Restless, often flicking wings and tail. On perch, may adopt slightly leaning forward posture. Song slightly fitful, with short phrases, often rather strained in tone and containing excellent mimicry; typical call *u-tic*. **ID:** Small, upright perching songbird like STOCH, but has noticeably longer wings and more fluent, less whirring flight. Crown flatter, accentuated by prominent broad white or buff supercilium, the best field mark. Tail with prominent white sides to base. Ad ♂: apricot breast and black cheeks surrounded by white malar stripe and supercilium; large white wing patches. Ad ♀: buff supercilium, little white on wing. Juv/1st-w: beautiful creamy-buff fringes to upperparts, some with small white spots; often some black spots on breast.

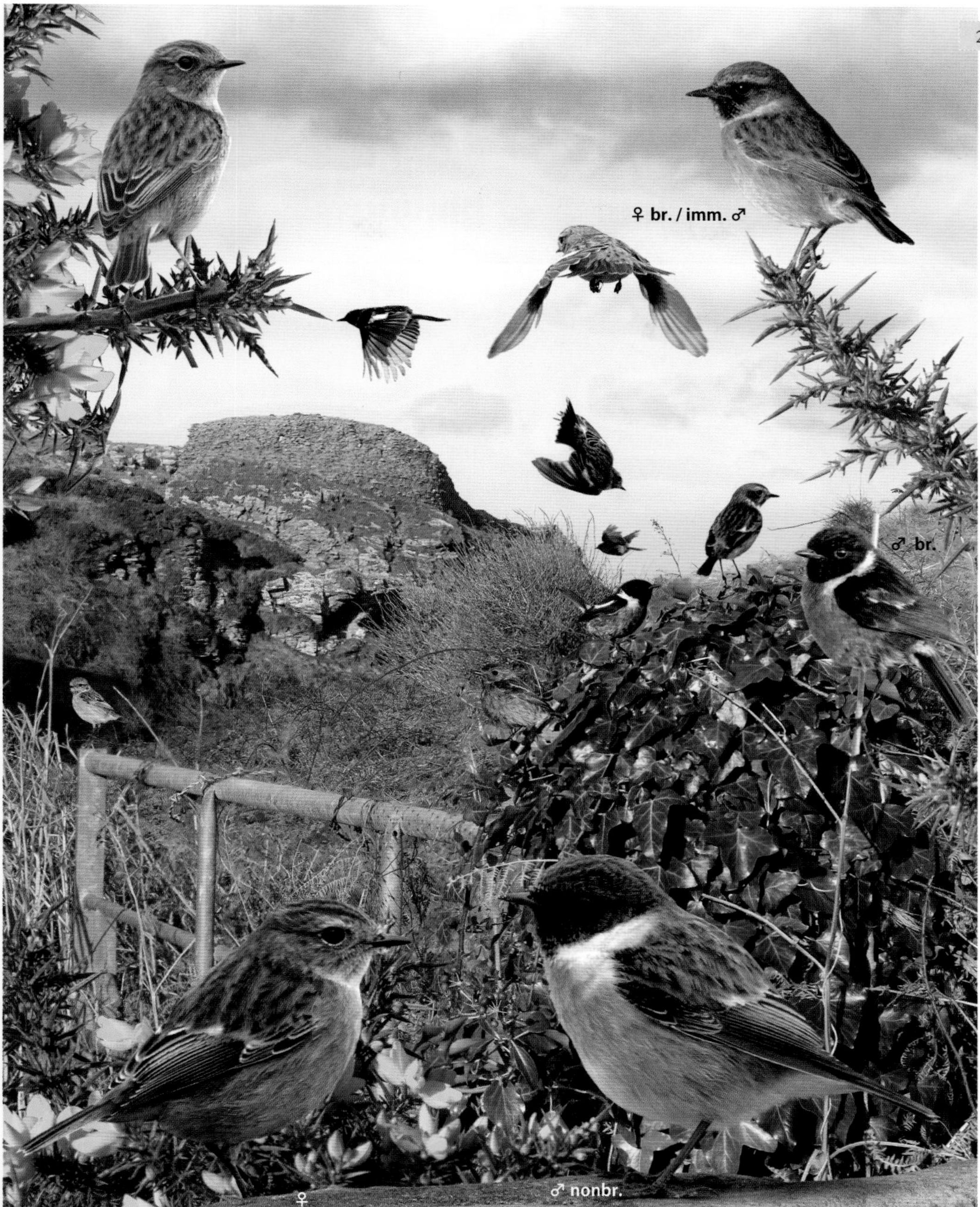

Stonechat *Saxicola torquata* **STOCH/SC** L 12cm

UK: s. 59,000 pairs

Highly strung resident of bushy places, heaths and moors, clifftops, coastal scrub, and the like. Often associated with gorse, and spends much time sitting on top of bushes, from where it scans for insects on the ground before flying down and snapping them up. Habit of sitting upright on raised perches and returning high after a sally makes it a birder's favourite. Fidgety, frequently flicking wings and tail, and also noisy. Calls a lot, and when young are about, incessantly: scolding tone to *sweet-sack!* notes. Song is a squeaky phrase similar to DUNNO but more metallic; sometimes delivered in brief song-flight. **ID:** Small, compact songbird with short wings and tail, upright posture when perched. Flight whirring. Rounder crown than WHINC, and lacks white on tail. Ad ♂ br: bold plumage with black head and white half-collar, dark wings with white patch, orange breast. Ad ♂ nonbr: colours dulled by brownish feather tips. Ad ♀: dark brown head, less obvious collar, smaller white wing patch. 1st-w: pale throat and head, browner. Juv: more spotted.

Wheatear *Oenanthe oenanthe* **WHEAT/W.** L 15cm

UK: s. 240,000 pairs

Breeds in rocky places, from shingle below sea level to the tops of the highest mountains. Often selects nest holes in dry stone walls. One of earliest summer visitors to arrive, even in late Feb, and one of last to disappear (by Nov); a common migrant almost everywhere. Perky, upstanding, long-legged ground-hugging chat, spends much time running over short turf, picking up invertebrates that it spots while standing still briefly on eminence such as a rock. Quite shy, flies off showing unmistakable white rump and black inverted T on tail. Call a hard *chack*; song is series of short, rushed phrases of often harsh notes; sometimes delivered in song-flight. **ID:** Brilliant tail pattern unique, unmistakable. Ad ♂ br: jet-black face mask, raincloud-grey back, solid dark wings, apricot breast. Ad ♀ br: sim to ♂ br but no mask, back brownish. Ad nonbr/1st-w: Smartly coloured shades of peachy orange with boldly marked wings. Ad ♂ has bolder black mask bordered by whiter supercilium. Migrant Greenland race *leucorhoa* averages bigger, with more intense colouration on underparts.

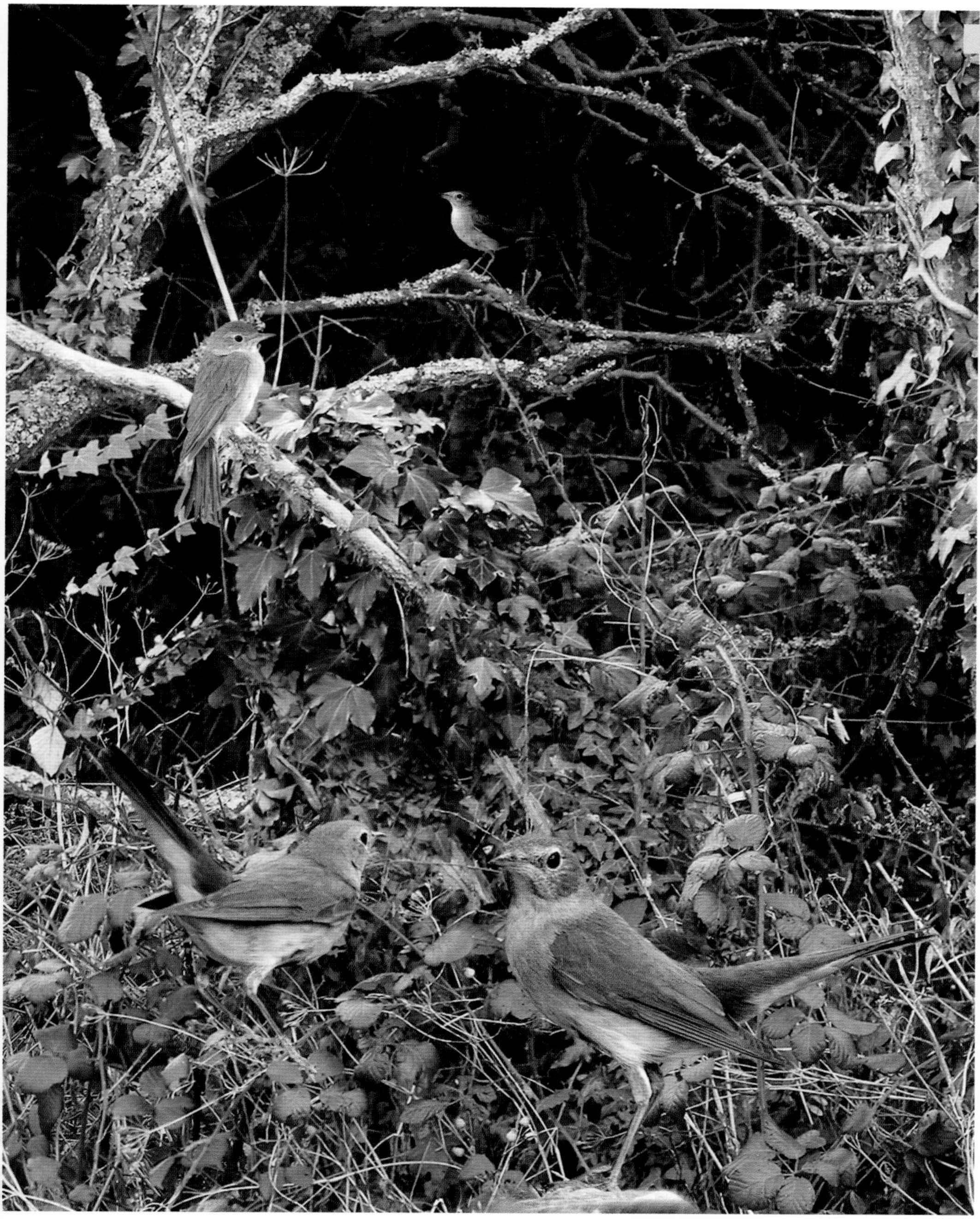

Nightingale *Luscinia megarhynchos* **NIGAL/N.** L 16cm

UK: s. 6,700 pairs

Celebrated songster that lurks in southern thickets, coppices, and scrub between Apr and Aug. Famously sings at night, but also by day. Usually a well-concealed, disembodied voice, hard to see. Song rich, varied, virtuoso but not esp sweet; phrases last 2–4 s, with gap in between, sometimes with soft introductory *tew, tew* whistles, and often with long trills. Perhaps most remarkable for volume variation, from whispers to shouts. Easy to recognise once heard; night singers in gardens are usually ROBINs. Song Apr–May. Almost as distinctive is unusual call, a soft croak, like a quiet frog/toad. Feeds mainly in shade underneath bushes, but will sometimes hop out, ROBIN-like, wings often droop to side, tail raised. Very rarely seen on autumn migration; departs very early. **ID:** Plain warm brown songbird with broad, chestnut tail (might recall a REDST), underparts paler. Beady dark eye. Juv as ad but with mottled breast and pale spots on upperparts.

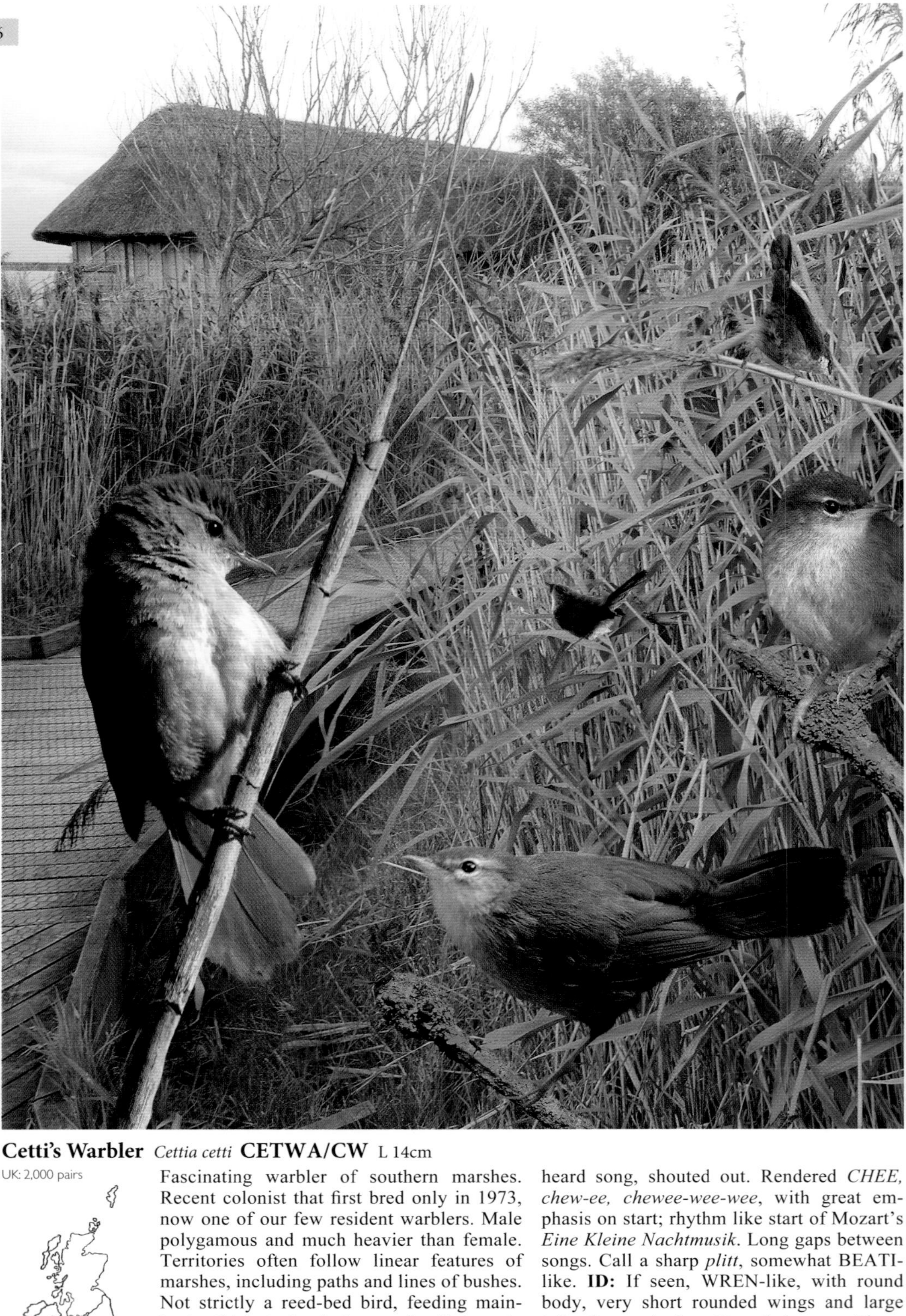

Cetti's Warbler *Cettia cetti* **CETWA/CW** L 14cm

UK: 2,000 pairs

Fascinating warbler of southern marshes. Recent colonist that first bred only in 1973, now one of our few resident warblers. Male polygamous and much heavier than female. Territories often follow linear features of marshes, including paths and lines of bushes. Not strictly a reed-bed bird, feeding mainly in thickets bordering reeds. Extremely skulking, keeping low in waterside vegetation and hiding so well that some birders haven't seen it over years of trying. Frustration made worse by its explosive and easily heard song, shouted out. Rendered *CHEE, chew-ee, chewee-wee-wee*, with great emphasis on start; rhythm like start of Mozart's *Eine Kleine Nachtmusik*. Long gaps between songs. Call a sharp *plitt*, somewhat BEATI-like. **ID:** If seen, WREN-like, with round body, very short rounded wings and large tail, often cocked up. Rounded crown. Plumage warm plain brown above, paler below, with definite grey on sides of head, noticeable pale supercilium. All plumages sim.

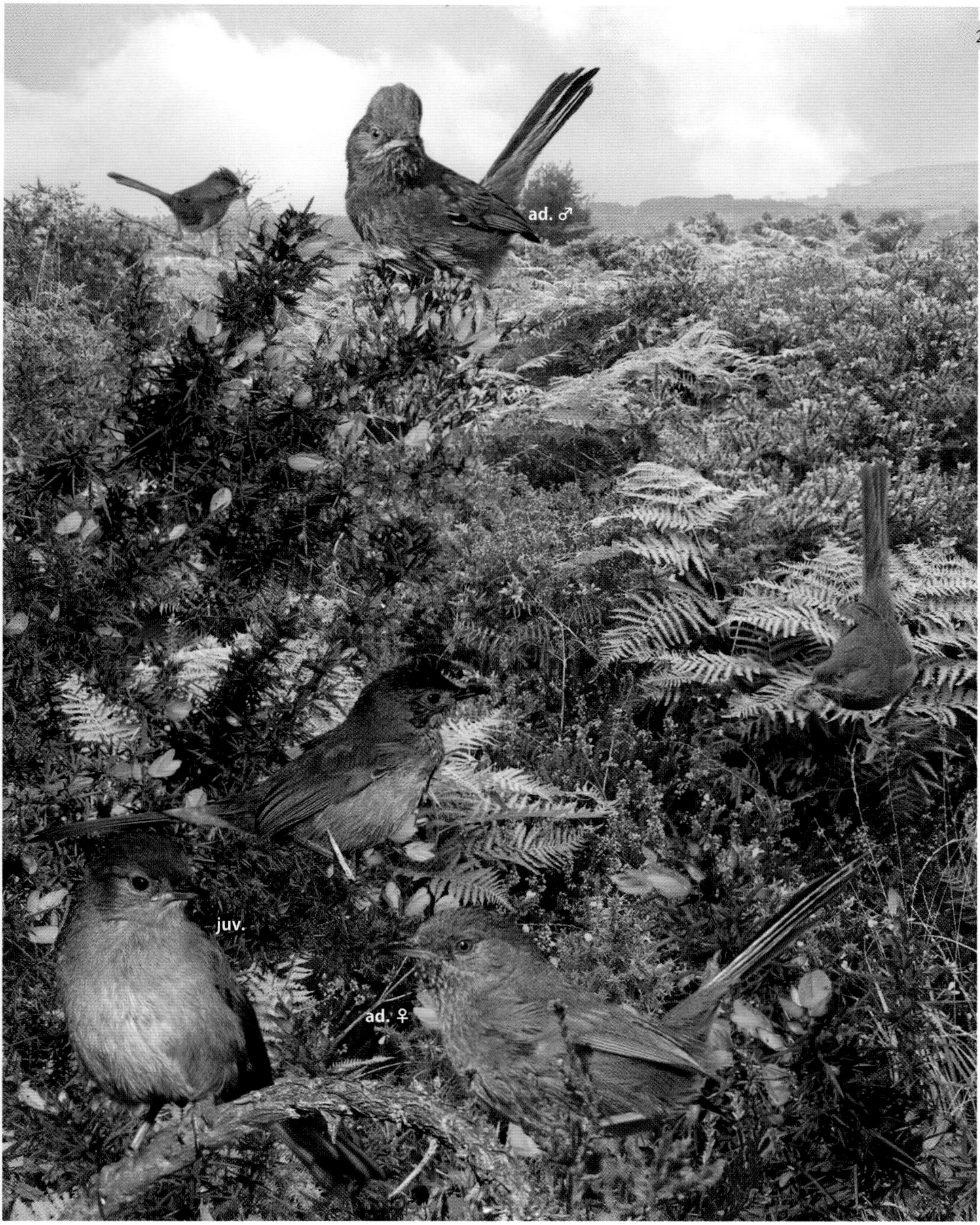

Dartford Warbler *Sylvia undata* DARWA/DW L 12cm

UK: s. 3,200 pairs

Rare mite of southern heathland, skulking and difficult to see. Unusual for being resident, but some move out of heathland in winter and can be seen in other low scrub such as bracken. Population is hit hard in severe winters. Feeds low down, often out of sight in gorse and heather. Also flies low, usually less than 1m above ground, with fast, whirring flight, tail seemingly out of control behind. Easiest to see on still and sunny days, when more likely to perch briefly on top of gorse, or even on low branches of trees such as birch. Often spotted close to feeding STOCH, using latter's vigilance. Has odd, harsh-voiced *chai-eer* alarm call; song chattering but overfast, like jabbered verse, sounds cyclical. Sings in short bouts. **ID:** Very distinctive, like very dark WREN with super-long tail, often cocked up. Ads with scarlet eye-rings. Orange legs. Ad ♂: grey above, rich rhubarb-red below (except for whitish belly), with small white speckles on throat. Ad ♀ duller, esp underparts. Juv/1st-w: browner still on back, and with greyish underparts; lacks red eye-ring.

Garden Warbler *Sylva borin* **GARWA/GW** L 14cm

UK: s. 170,000 pairs

Widespread summer migrant, late Apr–Sep. Breeds in verdant habitats, including woodland edge, overgrown hedgerows, and tall scrub, where it sings well but keeps low profile inside foliage. Not normally in gardens. Widespread early autumn migrant (Jul, Aug) often drawn to berry-bearing shrubs. Compared with relatives, occurs when breeding in more airy, less dense woodland than BLACA, but in much taller bushes than WHITE; often sings from tree on edge of scrub. Song consists of fast, bubbling phrase on even tempo, without change either end of phrase (unlike BLACA); to some it has the feel of SKYLA about it. Doesn't sing in flight. Call a decidedly gruff *chek*. **ID:** A heavyset warbler. Lack of features is characteristic. Very plain and unremarkable, except for surprisingly short, thick bill. Just brown above, a little paler below, with definite tinge of grey on sides of neck. Dark beady eye, negligible supercilium. Legs are dark grey. Sexes alike and juv sim.

Blackcap *Sylvia atricapilla* BLACA/BC L 14cm

UK: s. 1,100,000 pairs

Very common woodland warbler that skulks in undergrowth but often sings from higher up, even in canopy. Mainly an early arriving summer visitor, from first week of Apr, and departs late Sep, but in recent years, central European population has taken to wintering here, Oct–Mar, usually in scrub and gardens. Often unexpectedly aggressive at bird table. Typical fidgety warbler, constantly moving around in vegetation; on migration feeds on berries from elder and the like. Makes loud *tack* call, often incessantly. Song is upbeat, like somebody cheerily whistling as they walk through the wood. Tune starts hesitantly, then suddenly develops into tuneful ditty by the end. Later in season, leaves off opening; may sing right through summer. **ID:** For a warbler, quite well built and decidedly greyish; bill fairly short and thick (less so than GARWA). Legs strong, grey. Essentially plain greyish brown (♀ a shade browner) except for boldly coloured cap, jet black in ♂ and caramel-brown in ♀. Juv as ♀, but 1st-w ♂ may have brown or black cap or admixture of both.

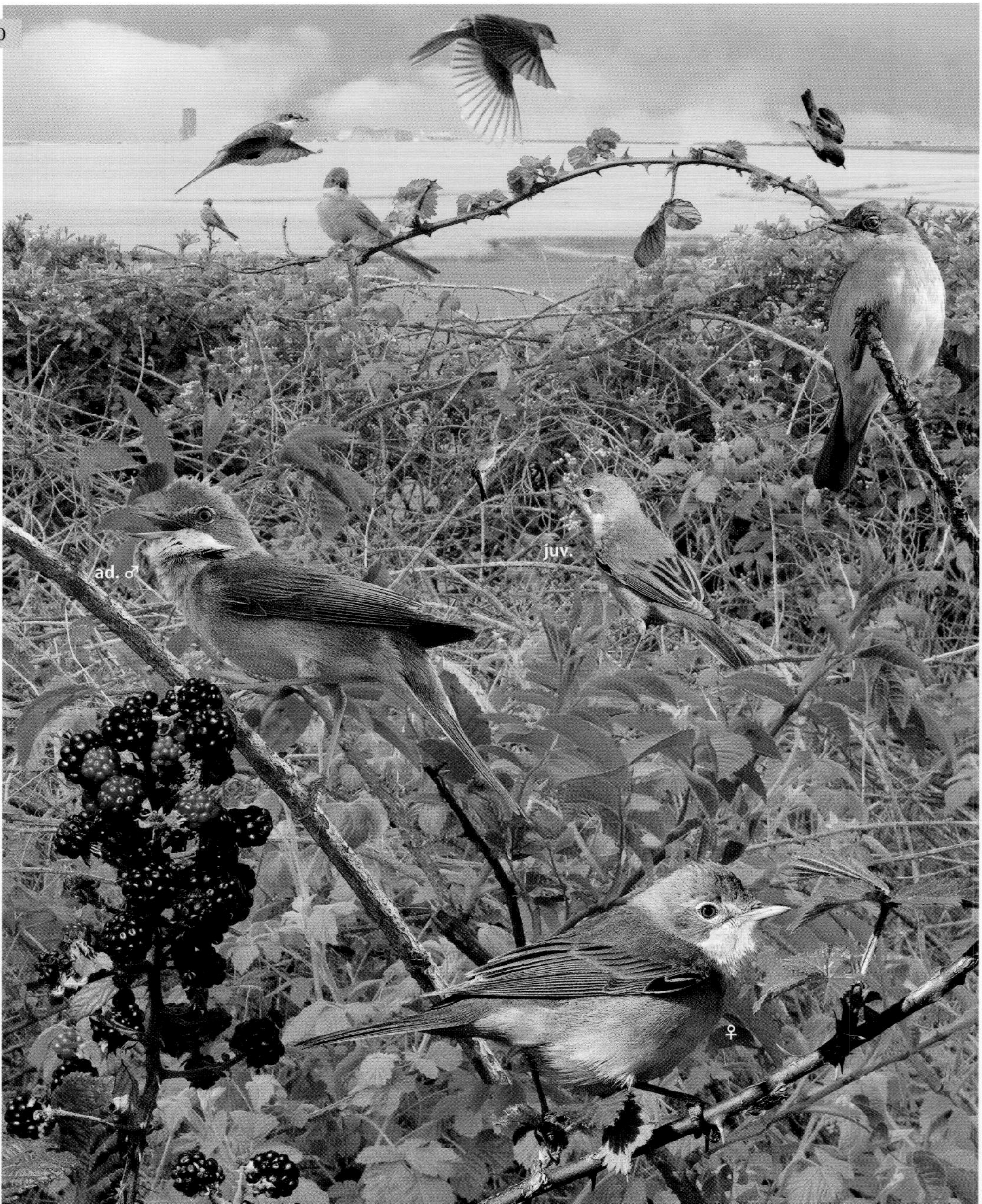

Whitethroat *Sylvia communis* **WHITE/WH** L 14cm

UK: s. 1,100,000 pairs

Sun-loving, effervescent summer visitor, Apr–Sep. Occurs anywhere with low, thick scrub, including brambles, nettles, hawthorn, for example hedgerows, heaths, commons, and overgrown gardens. Although skulking like most warblers, is show-off when singing, frequently perching on bush-tops, lower overhead wires and sprays. Often launches into song-flight, in which rises up a few metres, hovers fitfully (dangling like toy spider on string), and sings long version of song before dropping down quickly. Song usually fast and scratchy, with slight attack at start; most perched phrases very short. Call: nasal *churr*; also a scold faintly like BLUTI. **ID:** Medium, slender warbler with long tail; latter looks unruly, 'glued on'. Often raises crown feathers. Distinguished from relatives (esp LESWH) by rich, toffee-coloured panel on inner wing; pink legs. Ad ♂: grey head, brilliant white throat (fluffed out when singing, like shaving foam), white eye-ring, pinkish breast; ad ♀ subdued version of same, e.g., grey-brown head. 1st-w sim to ♀ but softer, more evenly buff.

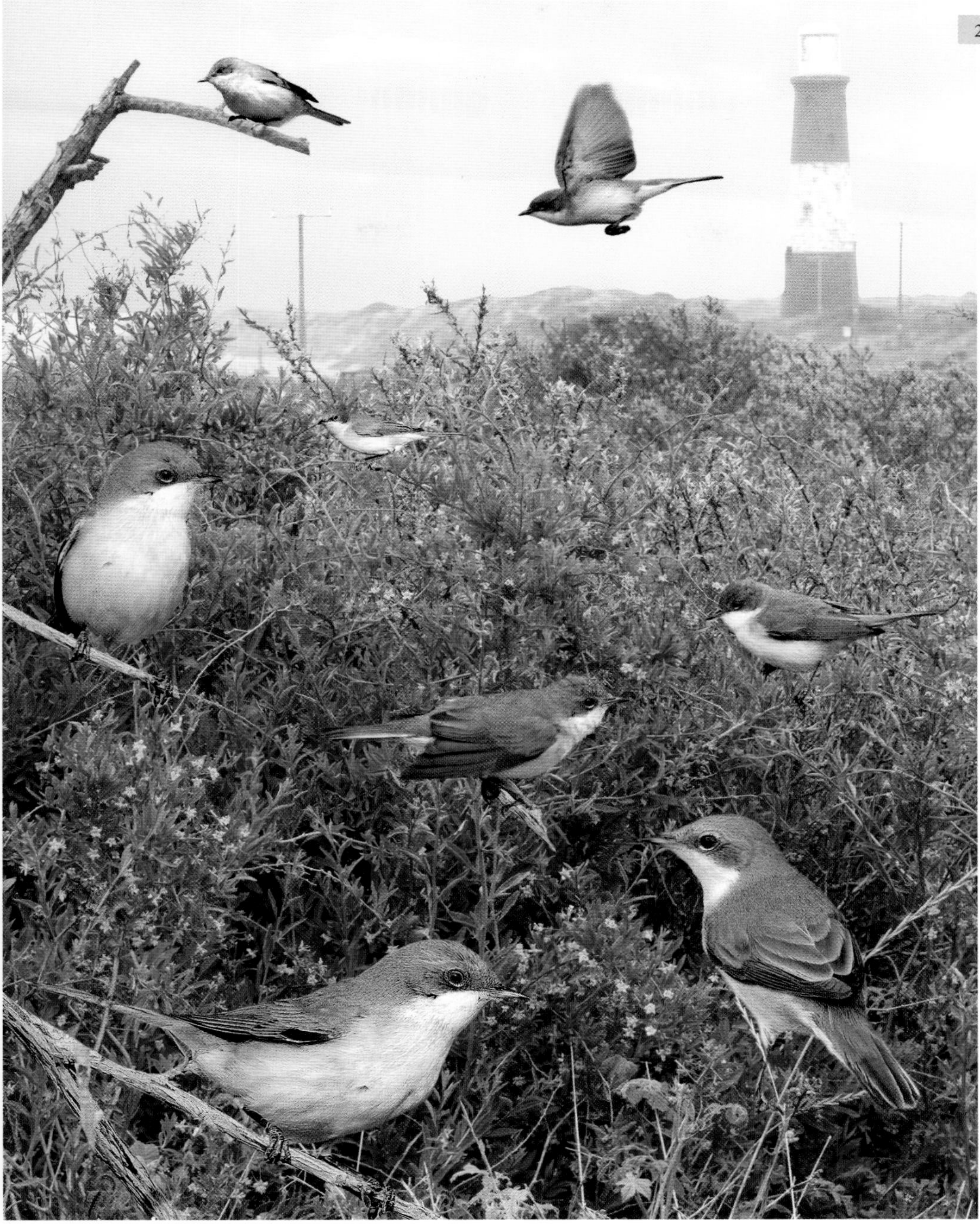

Lesser Whitethroat *Sylvia curruca* **LESWH/LW** L 13cm

UK: s. 74,000 pairs

Summer visitor as WHITE, but winters on opposite side of Africa, the east. Not as widespread or common as WHITE, and nowhere near as conspicuous. Breeds in taller vegetation and makes habit of staying concealed, not perching on tops of bushes or wires, and not singing in flight. All in all, highly skulking and, if anything, easier to see on migration, when it shares berry-bearing bushes with other warblers. Song quite different: briefly scratchy (and often inaudible) prologue leads in to a distinctive rattling trill, not dissimilar to start of YELHA. Call *tkk*, like knocking £1 coins together. **ID:** Smaller, neater, and more compact than WHITE. A bird of grey tones with dull dark brown upperparts and wings without warm colouration, and black legs. Ad: head darker grey than WHITE, and off-white underparts look cleaner and shinier; there is often a black face mask, more or less well defined. Juv/1st-w often whiter below, may have narrow pale supercilium.

Grasshopper Warbler *Locustella naevia* **GRAWA/GH** L 13cm

UK: s. 16,000 pairs

Uncommon and very secretive summer visitor (Apr–Sep) found in thick, tangled vegetation in a variety of habitats: low scrub, young conifer plantations, wetland edges, tussocks, rank grassland, and so on. Lives low down in these habitats, often actually feeding by creep-walking (not hopping) on the ground. Sometimes flushed when observer walks through tall grass, esp on the coast at migration watch-points, but usually very difficult to encounter. Does, however, have remarkable song that betrays presence. It is an insect-like, fast, reeling trill (actually 26 double notes per second) on constant pitch; also sounds like a cyclist freewheeling. Volume rises and falls as bird turns head while perched. Sometimes bird sings while visible on low perch (with bill open, sound not always audible), but often from cover. Call a fairly loud *tschik*. **ID:** Small warbler that recalls DUNNO. Basically all-over olive-brown, paler on underparts. Heavily dark spotted on upperparts, has streaks on flanks and sometimes a few spots on breast. Weak supercilium. Has quite heavy, rounded tail and long, streaked undertail coverts. Juv: yellower below.

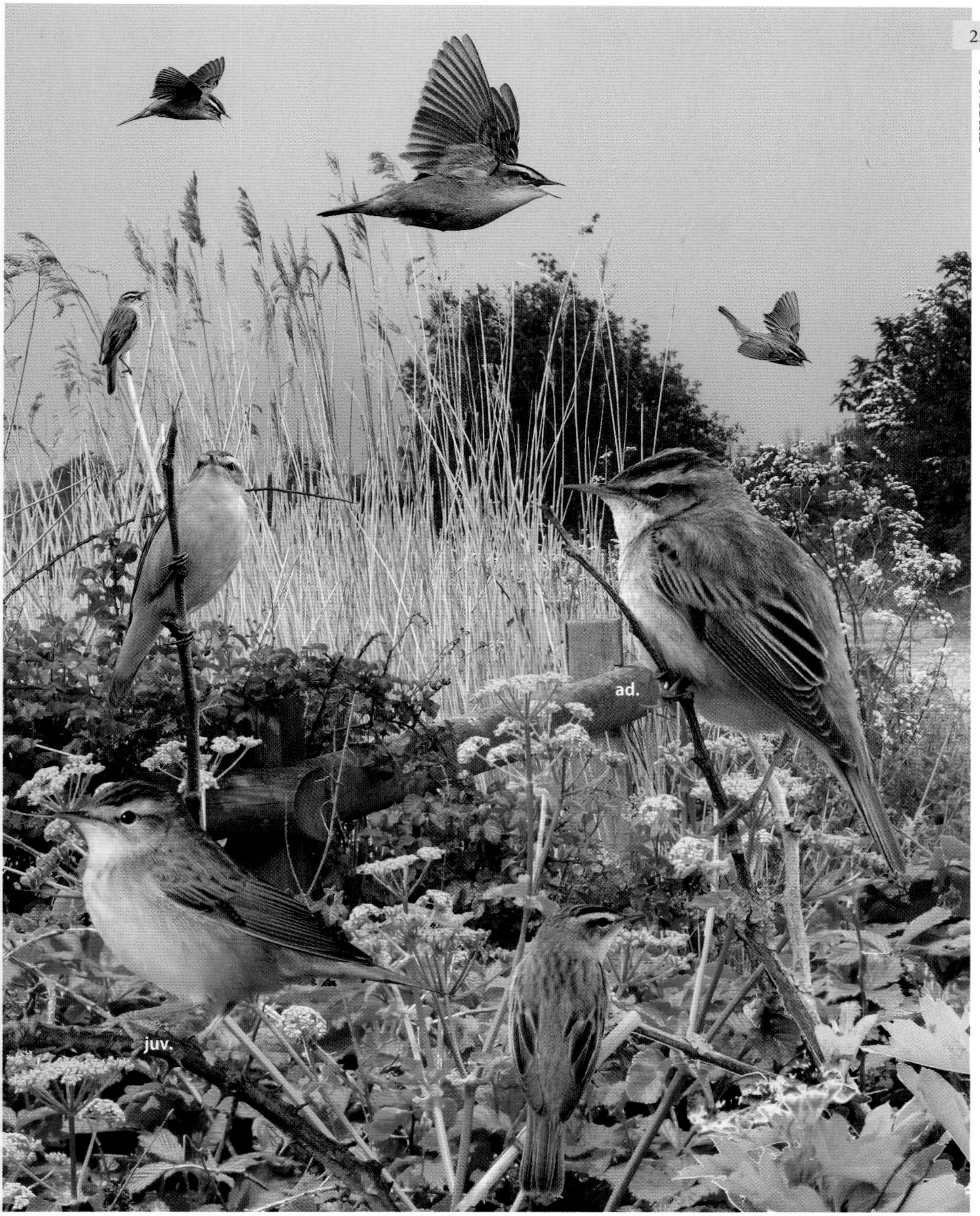

Sedge Warbler *Acrocephalus schoenobaenus* **SEDWA/SW** L 13cm

UK: s. 290,000 pairs

Common and irrepressible warbler of the margins of marshes and reed beds; sometimes found in drier, scrubby habitats. While breeding, REEWA is usually seen among reed stems, SEDWA is found on bushes on the edge or within reed beds, at least when singing. Unlike REEWA, builds nest over dry ground. A summer visitor, Apr–Sep. Vivacious, bursting with curiosity, and has spirited song, sometimes delivered (unlike REEWA) in a brief up-and-down song-flight. Song itself sung in long sequences, with super-fast, complicated delivery, including some mimicry. In contrast to REEWA song, lacks obvious rhythm and contains regular harsh, scratchy notes. Sings in full view on side of bush; often lands low and makes its way upwards while singing. Call: insignificant *errr* or *teck*. **ID:** Smallish warbler with short narrow tail and flattish crown that often looks peaked. Conspicuous long, broad, pale supercilium. Also has dark crown sides, streaked back and warm-brown rump. Juv/1st-w: may have more obvious pale central crown stripe than ad. Also some have light streaking on breast.

Aquatic Warbler *Acrocephalus paludicola* **AQUWA** L 13cm
Very skulking and secretive autumn migrant (Jul–Sep) to marshes, juvs turning up mainly in ringers mist nets on the South Coast, 20–40 records/year. Globally threatened. **ID:** Similar to SEDWA, but over-all paler and yellower, with broad creamy 'tramlines' and dark stripes down back, buff central crown stripe, spiky-tipped tail feathers, and pale lores. Ads are duller with narrow black streaks on flanks, juvs lack these.

Barred Warbler *Sylvia nisoria* **BARWA** L 16cm
Rare autumn migrant on East Coast, Aug–Oct, with about 150 records/year. Call: loud scolding rattle. **ID:** Large and slightly clumsy warbler with lethargic character, moves around slowly. Nearly all records are of 1st-winters, which look like large mean GARWA, but have distinctive pale double wing bars and pale fringes to tertials, plus usually some barring on the flanks and rump. Heavier bill and longer tail than GARWA. Ad completely barred below.

Marsh Warbler *Acrocephalus palustris* **MARWA/MW** L 13cm ***s. 2–8 pairs***
Rare migrant, with about 50 records/year, and irregular breeder. Remarkable for its late arrival on breeding grounds, in late May or even Jun. Sings amazing, demented, fast song consisting almost entirely of mimicked elements, expertly intertwined with repeated *tizay* and other phrases. Sings with mouth wide open, unlike REEWA, and is not a reed-bed bird, but actually of nearby waterside herbs and drier rank vegetation. **ID:** Almost identical to REEWA, but slightly colder, greyer upperparts, incl on rump, and yellower underparts. More pot-bellied and with shorter bill, but often barely separable.

Reed Warbler *Acrocephalus scirpaceus* **REEWA/RW** L 13cm

UK: s. 130,000 pairs

Lives up to its name and is rarely seen away from reed beds or shrubs adjoining reed beds, such as willows. Broader habitat on migration, even bushes in dry areas. A common summer migrant, mid-Apr to Sep, and in spring is a dominant force in marshes, where it lives in dense pockets. With strong legs and feet, adapted to hold tightly onto vertical stems. Quite irascible, often squabbling, and also curious. Song is a long, rhythmic series of grumpy chirping notes, ticking over like an uninterrupted monologue. Often delivered low down, in green parts of reeds, but sometimes higher. Bird often appears to have bill only half open when singing. Builds nest over water, bound to vertical stems. **ID:** Medium-sized brown warbler with specialist habitat and distinctive shape, with sloping crown and long bill giving 'arrow-shaped' head. Always has a white throat. Plain brown without streaks, and with modest pale supercilium. Rump richer brown than back. Juv/1st-w: warmer brown on top and buff on underparts. Duller birds, often of eastern origin, v sim to MARWA.

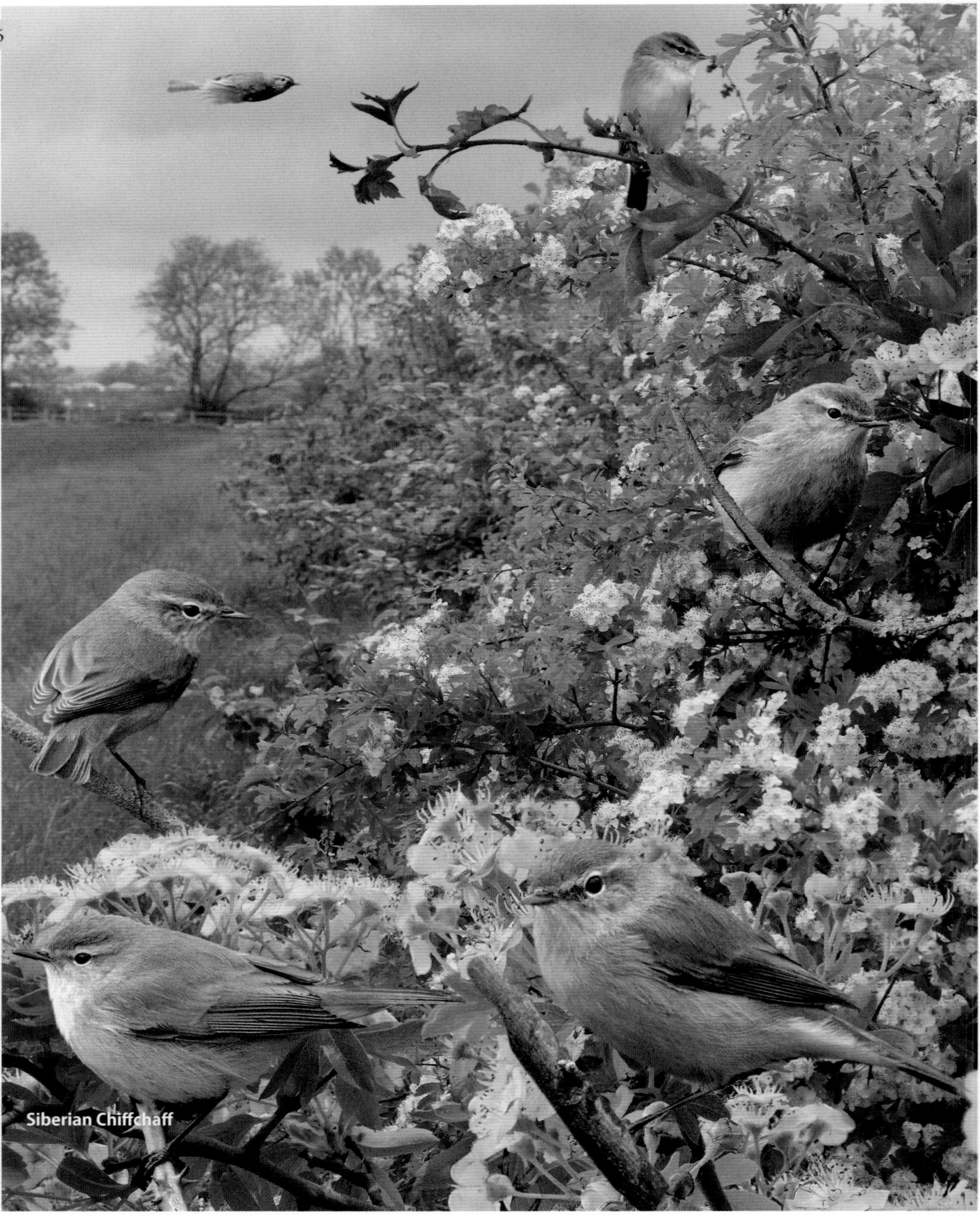

Common Chiffchaff *Phylloscopus collybita* **CHIFF/CC** L 11cm

UK: s. 1,200,000 pairs

Starts arriving early Mar, when can be seen in coastal bushes, clumps of willows, and thickets near water. Latter habitat used increasingly in winter; however, is at heart a bird of mature deciduous woodland, where sings from the treetops, often bare/dead branches. Feeds among leaves ('leaf warbler') very actively, darting about and often hovering briefly. Song is distinctive *chiff-chiff-chaff-chiff-chaff...* in long sequences at steady metronomic pace; sometimes adds short stammering sounds at end of sequence. Sings throughout season, even on autumn migration. Call cheerful *hweet!* ('hweet from the chaff'). **ID:** Really small BLUTI-sized, mainly dull olive-green. Has distinctive habit of constantly flicking tail. More rounded crown than WILWA, with fine, short bill, fat body, shorter wing points, and black legs. Dark ear coverts make white eye-ring obvious above and below eye, supercilium looks shorter. Ad spring: not as bright or clean looking as WILWA, darker above (brownish green) and below (buff-white). Ad autumn/1st-w: looks greener, esp above, but without much yellow. Siberian Chiffchaff (*tristis*) rare but regular, dowdy, greyish brown above, buff supercilium with green tones restricted to wing and tail fringes.

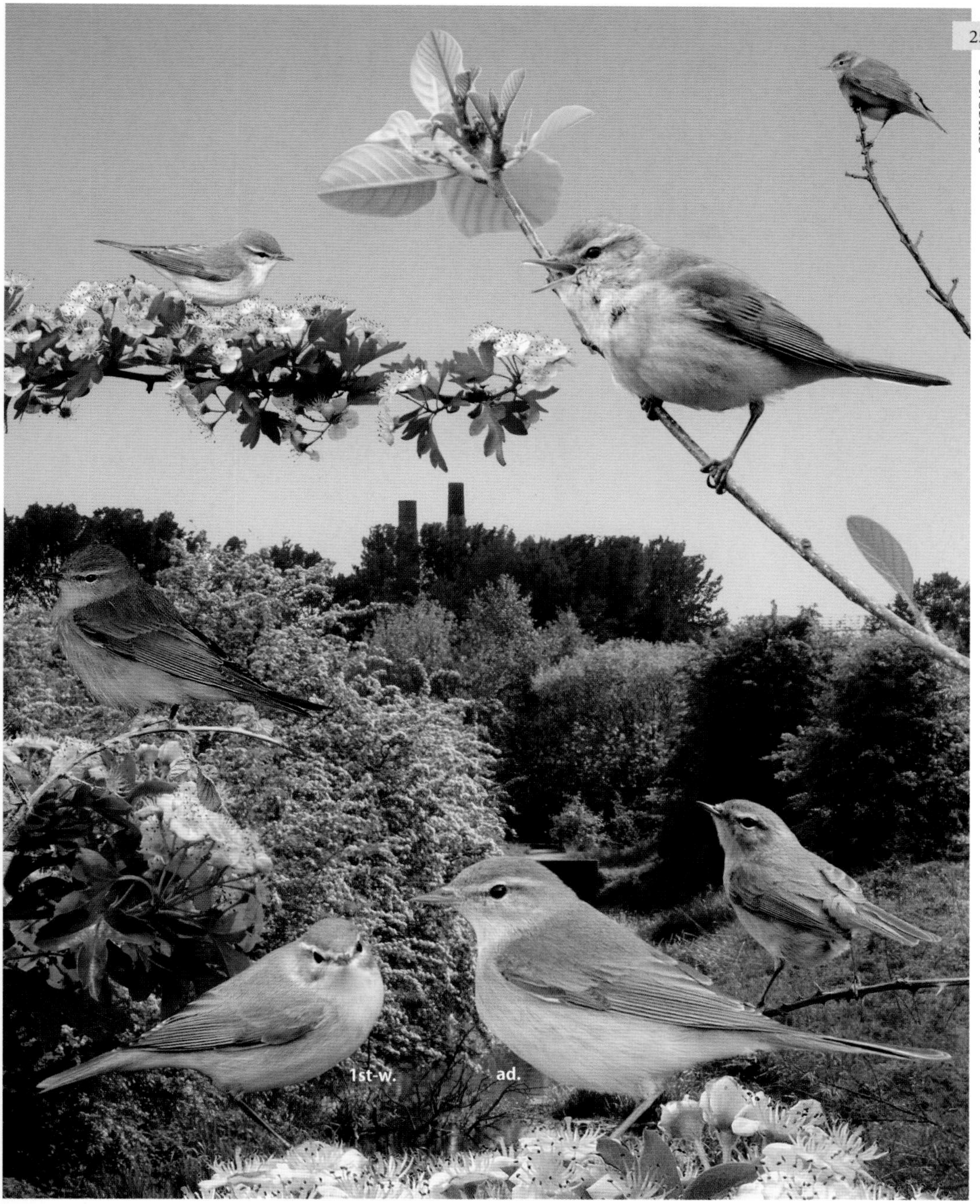

Willow Warbler *Phylloscopus trochilus* **WILWA/WW** L 12 cm

UK: s. 2,400,000 pairs

Common warbler of scrub and smaller trees, such as birches and willows, often on edge of woodland. Abundant in the north. Doesn't winter. Arrives late Mar and leaves mid-Sep; main departure well before CHIFF. Feeds actively in canopy of small trees, flitting about as CHIFF, sometimes hovering. Lacks CHIFF habit of constantly dipping tail down, but will do this intermittently. Sings delicious descending phrase, whispering and effortless, begins almost apologetically, the steadier as it drops down; call more mournful and 2-syllabled than CHIFF: *hoo-eet*. **ID:** Slightly larger, slimmer, a little yellower than CHIFF and more contrasting. Has longer wings (wingtips project well beyond tertials at rest) and usually pale legs. Has distinctly more 'open' face than CHIFF, with paler mottled ear coverts providing less contrast to eye-ring, with longer, yellower supercilium and rarely cleanly defined dark eye-stripe. Bill longer than CHIFF and pale, almost orange base. Ad spring: upperparts greener and underparts whiter and cleaner than CHIFF, with more contrast. Ad autumn/1st-w: underparts strikingly yellow, upperparts quite bright green, supercilium yellow.

Wood Warbler *Phylloscopus sibilatrix* **WOOWA/WO** L 12cm

UK: s. 6,500

Fairly common summer visitor to mature woodland, esp of sessile oaks, but also beech stands with minimal undergrowth. Much the least common of the three main 'leaf warblers', and hard to see on migration, esp in autumn when it seems just to disappear by Aug. First arrives Apr. Mainly a canopy-feeding bird, but nests on ground. Has far-carrying, trilling 'shivering' song, likened to a spinning coin coming to rest; also a repeated plaintive *pu-pu-pu...* interspersed with shivers. Call is *pu* uttered in isolation. Sometimes performs flight-song in canopy, a mainly horizontal perch-to-perch flight of 1–5m, landing during trill. **ID:** Slightly larger than WILWA. Has different shape, thick neck, with such long wings that the tail looks short. Usually distinguished by bright lemon-yellow face, supercilium, and breast, which contrasts sharply with clean white lower breast and belly. Also check for beech-leaf–green back and dark tertials with striking pale fringes. All plumages sim, though a little duller in autumn.

Yellow-browed Warbler *Phylloscopus inornatus* **YEBWA/YB** L 10cm ***w. 8***

Rare but remarkably regular autumn vagrant (320 records/year), which breeds in Siberia and seems to take wrong turns to get here (should winter in tropical Asia); Sep–Nov. Quick moving and elusive, but has distinctive call, a loud COATI-like *hoo-eet!* that attracts attention. Often in willows and sycamores in coastal scrub. **ID:** CHIFF-like but smaller, and with obvious broad yellow wing bars and long, broad, pale yellow supercilium; crown dark olive-green, sometimes with just a hint of a pale stripe. Tertials with broad white fringes. Dark rump, whitish underparts, yellowish legs.

Pallas's Warbler *Phylloscopus proregulus* **PALWA** L 9cm

Rare autumn vagrant, Oct–Nov, with avg 78 records/year, mostly to south or east. Moves around even faster than YEBWA and is inveterate hoverer. Call nasal *tseu*, not conspicuous. **ID:** Smaller than sim YEBWA, more GOLDC-like, with short tail. Main diff from YEBWA conspicuous yellow rump (seen when hovering), narrow golden crown stripe, bright yellow front of supercilium.

Greenish Warbler *Phylloscopus trochiloides* **GSHWA** L 10cm

About 10 records/year, mainly on East Coast and Northern Isles Aug–early Oct; occasionally in spring, when sings stuttering phrase, cross between WILWA and WREN. Call sparrow-like *tse-lee*. **ID:** CHIFF-like but notice whitish underparts contrast with dark olive-green upperparts, greyish on mantle; narrow whitish wing bar, pale fleshy-orange lower mandible.

Radde's Warbler *Phylloscopus schwarzi* **RADWA** L 12cm
Autumn vagrant, 5 records/year, Oct–Nov. Incredibly skulking in scrub near or on ground. Often heard first, slightly clicking *tleck*. **ID:** Dark like DUSWA, mustard vent area and buff-yellow underparts. Supercilium whiter behind eye, not as narrow in front; ear coverts mottled. Shorter, thicker bill than DUSWA, overall more strongly built, paler pinkish legs.

Dusky Warbler *Phylloscopus fuscatus* **DUSWA** L 11cm
Autumn vagrant from Siberia, 6 records/year, Oct–Nov. Skulks low down. **ID:** Like dull, dark brown CHIFF, clincher is tack call. Check for reddish brown (or brown) legs, long supercilium, narrow and whitish before eye, broader and often tinged buff behind. Short wings make it look quite portly and WREN-like; often flicks wings and raises tail as if constantly restless.

Icterine Warbler *Hippolais icterina* **ICTWA** L 14cm
Rare migrant, May and Aug–Sep, on East Coast; average 137 records/year. Has bred. Call trisyllable *dee-deroid*. **ID:** Like large WILWA, but plain face and long bill immediately obvious. Washed yellow below. Weak pale supercilium merges into pale lores. Legs obviously grey. Wings long and pointed (looks flycatcher-like in flight) and pale fringes to secondaries make panel (less obvious in autumn).

Melodious Warbler *Hippolais polyglotta* **MELWA** L 13cm
Rarer than very sim ICTWA, with just 30 records/year, most Aug–Sep. **ID:** Shares yellow colouration, long bill with pinkish lower mandible, and plain expression of ICTWA. Bill slightly shorter and wings much shorter (primary projection half length of tertials), without pale panels. Legs paler, sometimes brownish. In autumn, juv may show subtle wing panel, but unlike ICTWA, not on greater wing coverts.

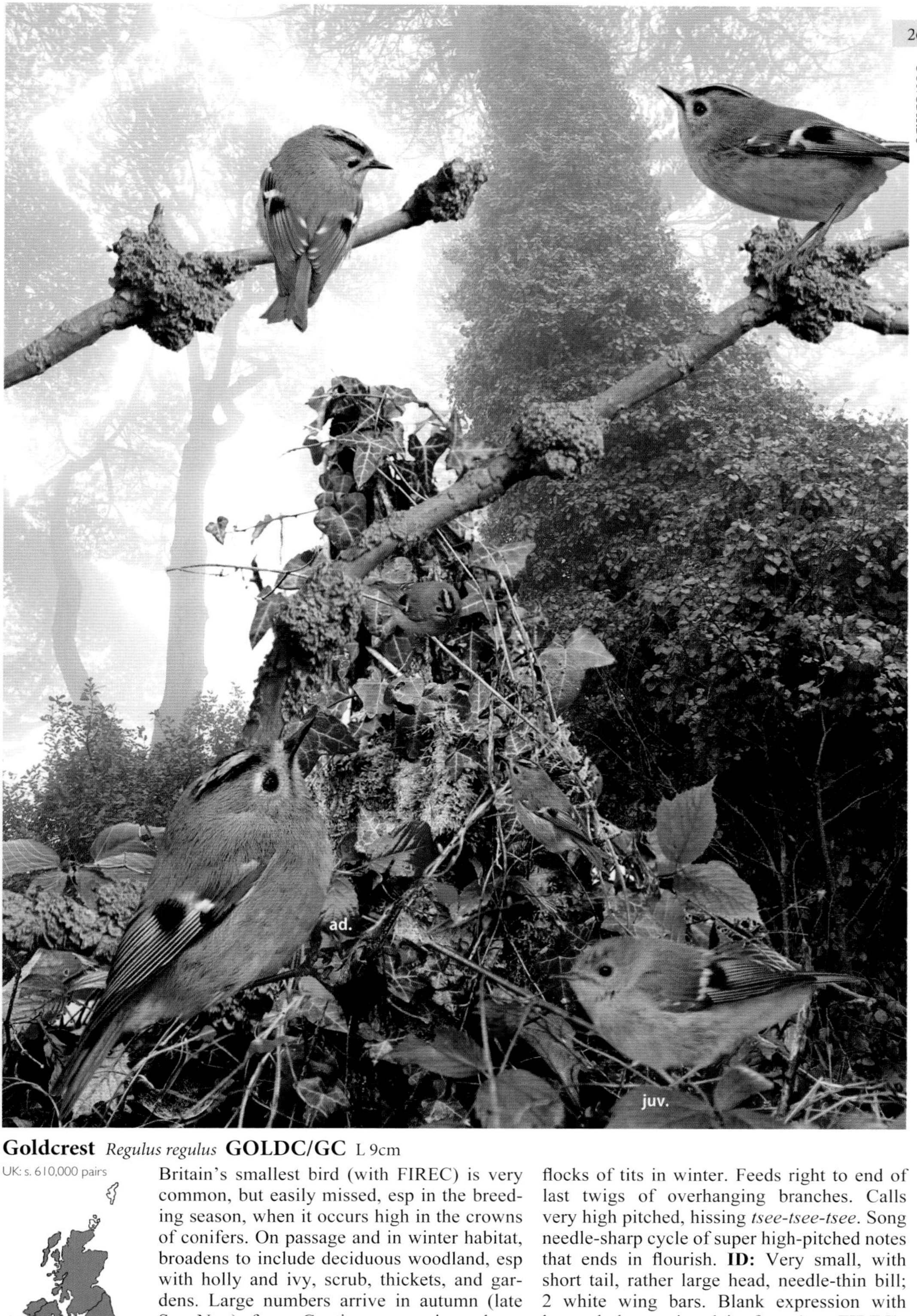

Goldcrest *Regulus regulus* GOLDC/GC L 9cm

UK: s. 610,000 pairs

Britain's smallest bird (with FIREC) is very common, but easily missed, esp in the breeding season, when it occurs high in the crowns of conifers. On passage and in winter habitat, broadens to include deciduous woodland, esp with holly and ivy, scrub, thickets, and gardens. Large numbers arrive in autumn (late Sep–Nov) from Continent to winter here. Tiny, fast-moving mite that restlessly flits from branch to branch, hovers, flicks wings, raises crown; essentially unafraid of people, so will allow close approach. Often joins flocks of tits in winter. Feeds right to end of last twigs of overhanging branches. Calls very high pitched, hissing *tsee-tsee-tsee*. Song needle-sharp cycle of super high-pitched notes that ends in flourish. **ID:** Very small, with short tail, rather large head, needle-thin bill; 2 white wing bars. Blank expression with large dark eye in plain face (see FIREC); sides of crown with thick black stripes. Ad ♂: crown yellow, with touch of orange towards nape; ad ♀: crown just yellow. Juv: no head markings or crown stripes, just plain face.

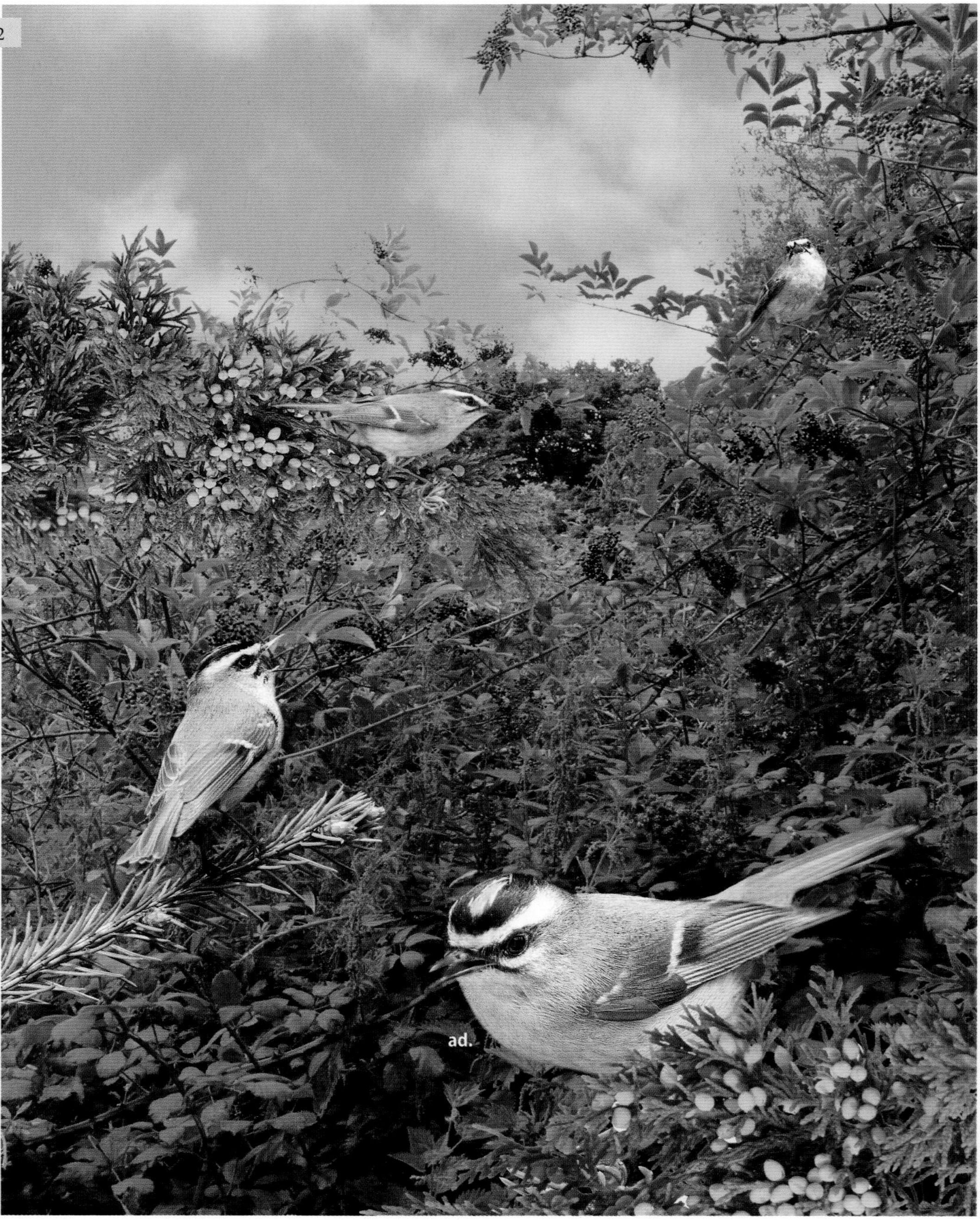

Firecrest *Regulus ignicapillus* **FIREC/FC** L 9cm

UK: s. 550 pairs

Much less common than GOLCR, small numbers breed in stands of spruce and, locally, in holly among oaks. Scarce passage migrant, esp in coastal scrub; check out holm oak trees and ivy. Small wintering population on the South Coast in similar habitats to migrants. Just as small as GOLDC and with similar behaviour, said to be even more restless, remaining in same trees for shorter time. When breeding, sticks to the treetops. Call is cleaner and less hissy than GOLDC, a tit-like *si-si*. Song lacks cyclical nature of GOLDC, just high-pitched notes accelerating to short flourish. **ID:** Really quite different from GOLDC, glimpsed often enough—brighter, more jewel-like. Face completely distinctive, with black stripe though eye and broad white supercilium—no staring face like GOLDC. Also underparts slightly paler and cleaner (contrast with upperparts), mantle deeper moss-green, bronzy neck patch. Black crown stripes meet on forehead. Ad ♂ crown orange, ad ♀ crown yellow. Juv lacks ornaments but has narrow dark eye-stripe and pale supercilium.

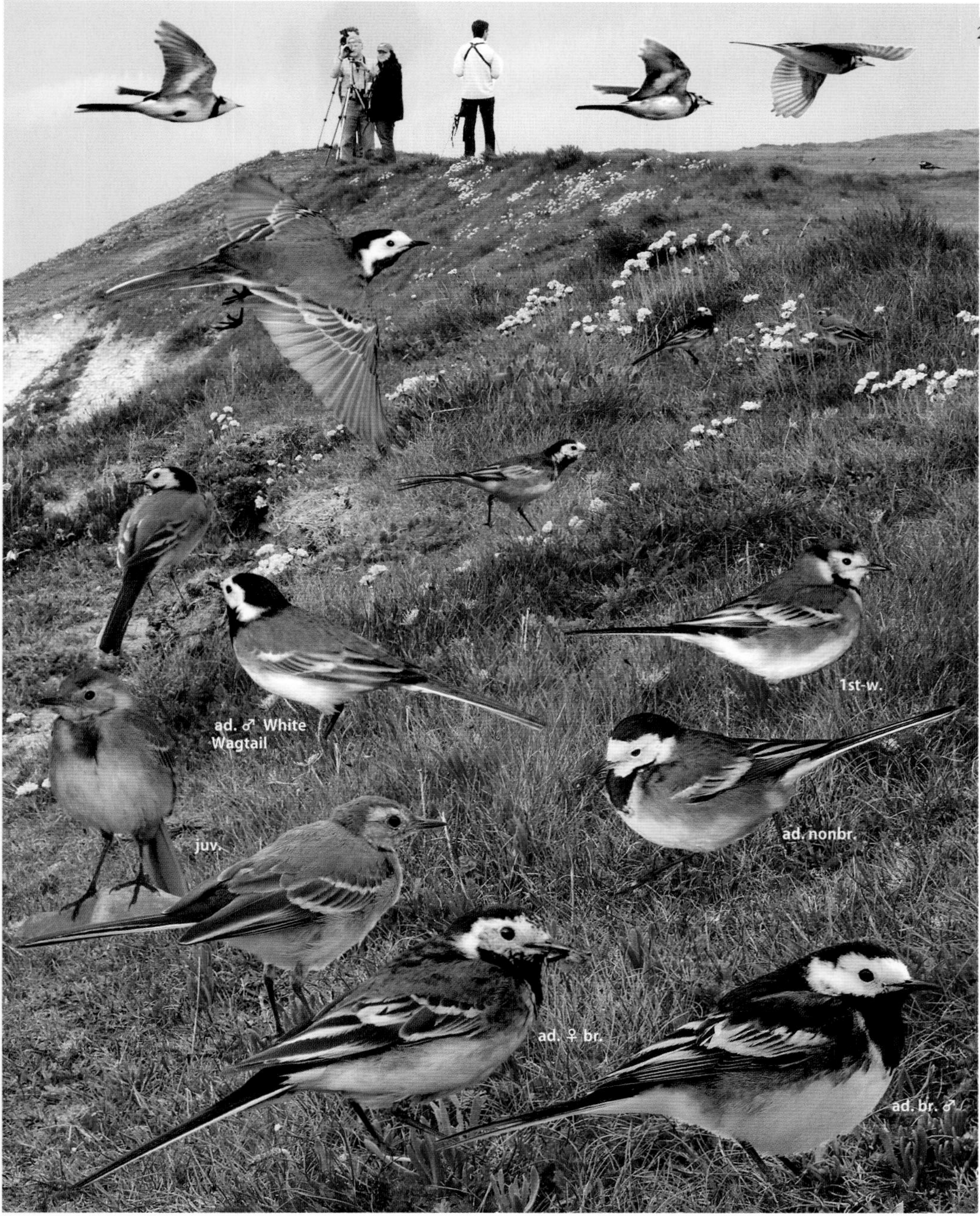

Pied Wagtail *Motacilla alba* PIEWA/PW L 18cm

UK: s. 470,000 pairs

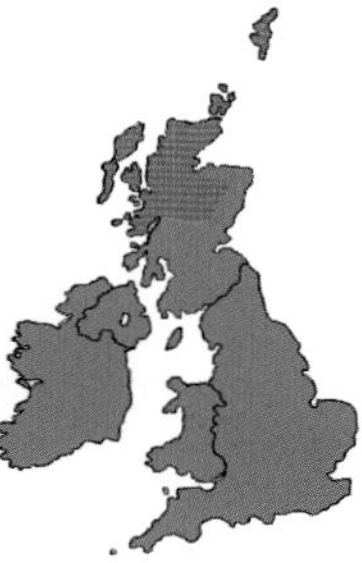

Very common resident in open habitats, including waterside, lawns, farmland, fields, urban areas, car parks, roads, and so forth. In winter often roosts communally on roofs (e.g., of supermarkets), sewage farms, trees in town squares, etc. Easily recognised by its long tail which is persistently wagged; also runs and walks along the ground, doesn't hop. Often in small flocks. Flight very undulating, makes cheerful call *chissick* in flight. Song rambling series of chatters and twitters. Nests in cavities of many kinds. **ID:** Distinctive slim and long black-and-white bird, with long black tail with white outer tail feathers; legs black. Wing feathers white fringed and tipped. Ad ♂ br: white face, black crown and back, black throat and upper breast, whitish underparts with dusky flanks; ad ♀ same but mantle dark grey, not black. Ad nonbr loses much black on throat and breast, leaving broad black band. 1st-w sim, head may be tinged yellow. Juv: greyish cap and back. White Wagtail: passage migrant from Continent, fairly common. On ad br, black nape contrasts strongly with pale grey back (neat border in ♂); flanks not dusky. Others very difficult to ID.

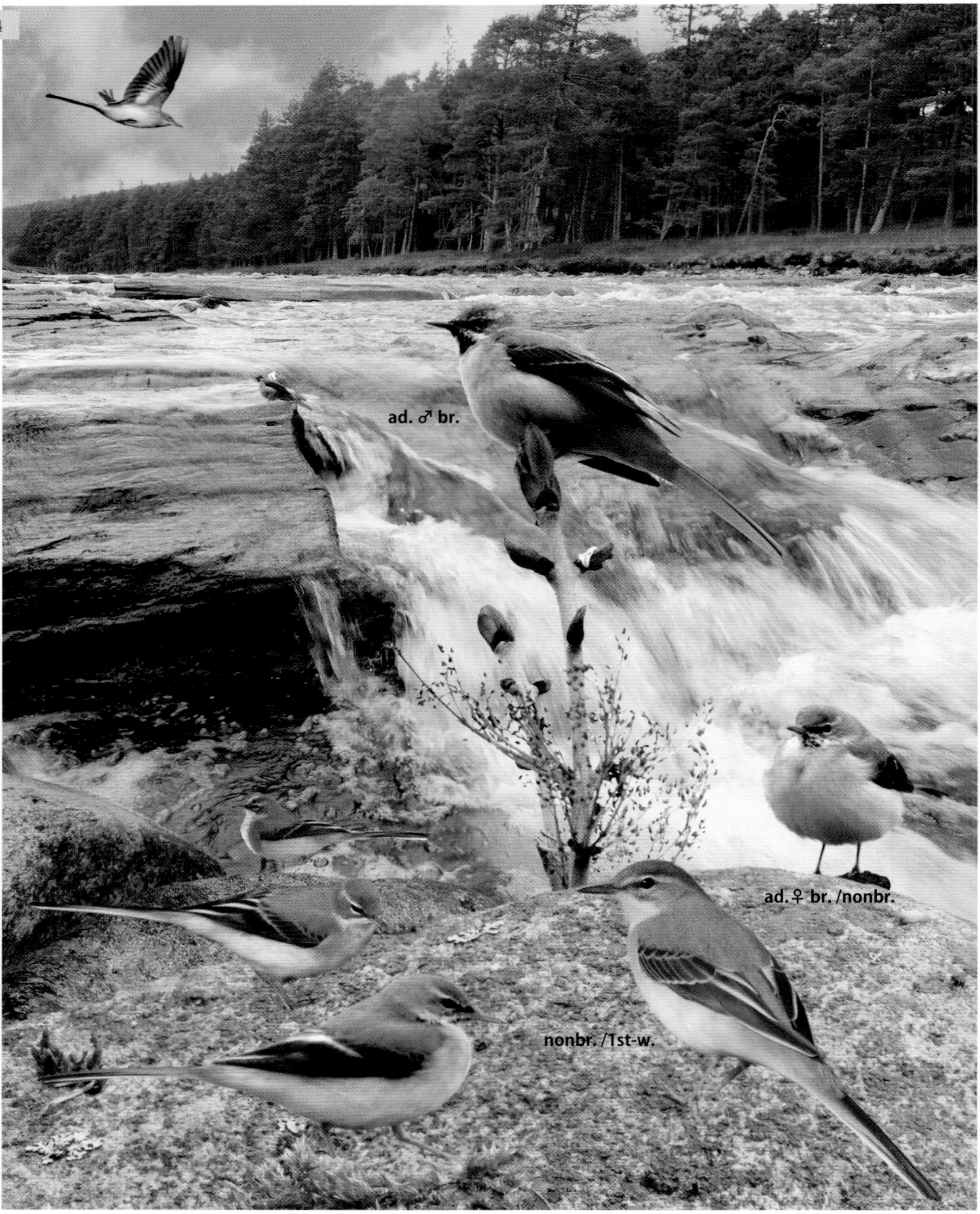

Grey Wagtail *Motacilla cinerea* GREWA/GL L 18cm

UK: s. 38,000 pairs

Breeds beside fast-flowing streams and weirs, esp in upland areas. In winter, leaves colder hills and is found in wider range of habitats, including the edges of lakes and slow-flowing rivers, sewage farms, canals, and even garden ponds. The 'ultra wagtail', with the longest tail and rear body and the heaviest undulations in flight. Wags tail incessantly, walks and runs over mud, hops from rock to rock in rivers, sometimes flies out over river to catch flying insects. Main call better enunciated than PIEWA, clean *zi-zit*. Song a series of insect-like *si-si-sit* phrases, often delivered when bird perches on branch of tree. Like PIEWA, often spends time on roofs, catching insects in sun. **ID:** Badly named, but does have grey upperparts. Much more distinctive are lemon-yellow underparts (always on undertail coverts), and also, in flight, single central white wing bar noticeable above and below; also pink legs and white tertial fringes. Ad ♂ br: most of underparts bright yellow, sharply contrasting with black throat; ad ♀ sim but throat whitish or mottled black (1st-s ♂ sim). Ad nonbr/1st-w: whitish throat, 1st-w may have buff on underparts.

Yellow Wagtail *Motacilla flava* **YELWA/YW** L 25cm

UK: s. 15,000 pairs

Fairly common summer visitor to wet meadows, pasture, marshy ground, and some arable fields. First arrivals mid-Mar, leave by Sep; quite widespread as a migrant, could turn up anywhere. Often feeds with livestock, including cattle and horses, feeding on invertebrates disturbed by their feet. Has distinctive, enthusiastic call *sweep!*, gives away its location in long grass and overhead. Truly terrible song, haphazard, jolting series of brief scratchy notes, like bad REEBU. **ID:** Clearly a wagtail, but shorter tail than the other two, with broader white outer tail feathers; black legs, unlike GREWA. Wing feathers pale fringed. Ad ♂ br: stunning bright buttery yellow on face and underparts, with yellow supercilium and green back; ad ♀ not as startling, paler but still yellow, and with browner back. Juv: dull brown, with conspicuous dark necklace and sub-moustachial stripe. Several races visit, commonest is Blue-headed Wagtail of near Continent: Ad ♂ br with different head pattern, bluish on crown, nape, and ear coverts, with bold white supercilium, yellow throat and underparts. ♀ similar, but paler yellow below, with whitish throat.

Meadow Pipit *Anthus pratensis* **MEAPI/MP** L 14cm

UK: s. 2,000,000 pairs

Abundant small bird of various open country habitats, sometimes occurring where there isn't much else, for example vast tracts of moorland or upland grassland. In winter, just about anywhere. Migrates within the country, and is very common in spring (Mar–Apr) and autumn (esp Sep–Oct) on visible migration watches. Feeds on ground simply by walking and picking, like a person idly window-shopping. Easily flushed and then overreacts, shooting upwards with panicking *sip-sip* calls, then flying this way and that, not sure what to do. Perches freely on bushes, wires, trees. Often sociable in nonbreeding season. Flight weak, with bursts of wingbeats seemingly just enough, jerky. Song is repeated *slip-slip-slip-slip* notes, gradually changing in pitch and accelerating to a *twee-twee-twee*... ending. Often in long songflight, rises from ground, sings and parachutes back down to ground, legs dangling and tail up. **ID:** Small streaked bird like miniature thrush, white outer tail feathers. Heavily streaked on mantle and underparts with 'HB pencil lines', reach down with same thickness to flanks. Ground colour variable, from brownish to greyish; in summer, worn birds whitish below, otherwise buff. Hind claw long, legs pink. All plumages sim.

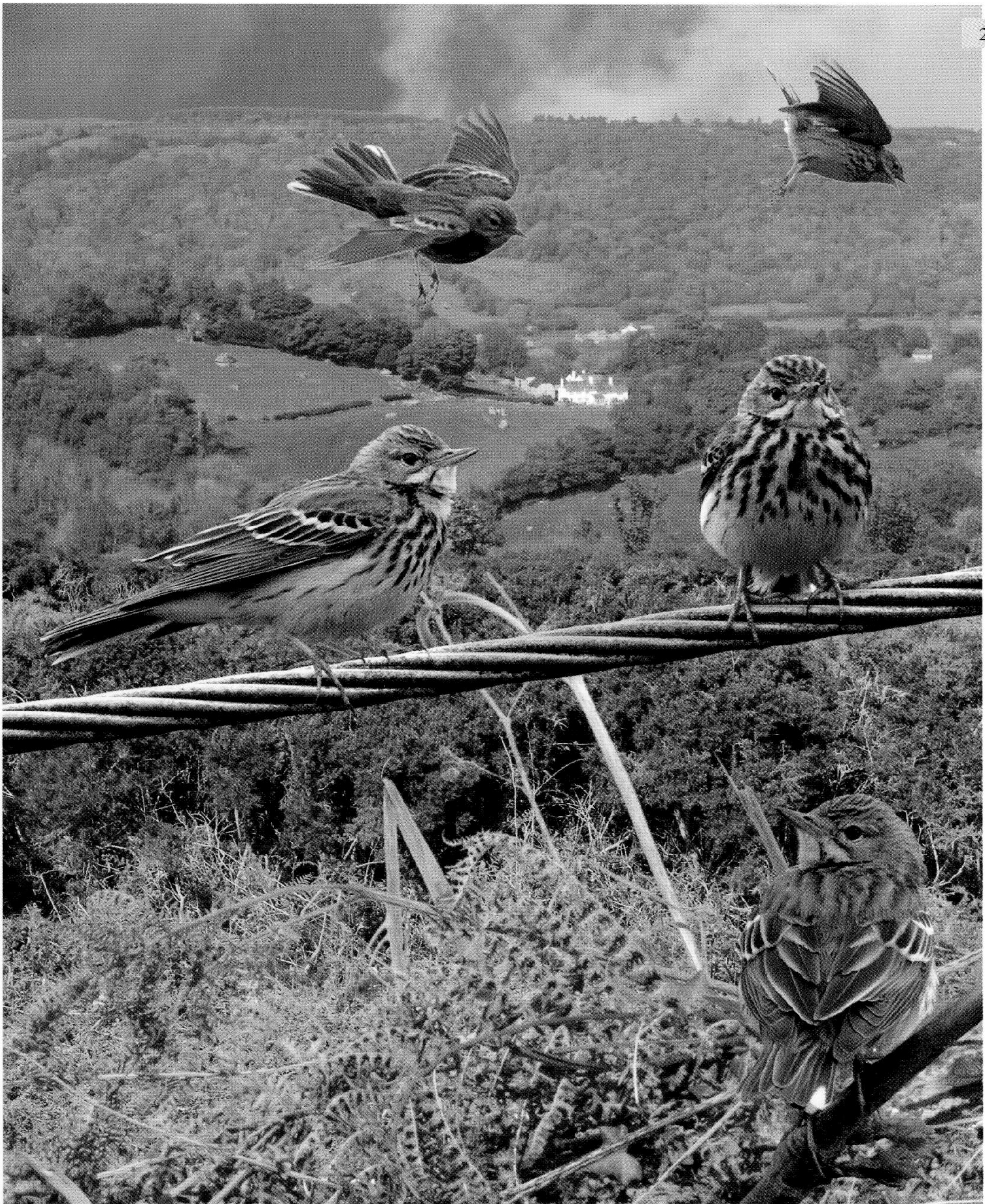

Tree Pipit *Anthus trivialis* **TREPI/TP** L 15cm

UK: s. 88,000 pairs

Summer migrant (Apr–Sep) to open woodland, heathland, and young conifer plantations; requires open areas that nonetheless have trees from which male can take off on song-flight. Rises steeply, reaches maximum height, then starts to glide down in parachute drop, with legs dangling and tail up, looks like a child's paper aeroplane. Song (on ascent) has distinctly fast CHAFF-like beginning, then a series of trills on different pitches as it descends. Also sings perched. Call *speez*, often heard from migrants. Flies off with more confidence than MEAPI, without dithering, often goes far. Has habit of incessantly pumping tail when perched. Not sociable like MEAPI, usually alone or pairs. **ID:** Slightly larger and heavier than MEAPI, with short, curved hind claw. Much thicker bill gives different expression, together with clearer pale supercilium. Good distinction is streaks on underparts: on breast they are thick and bold, but transition to v narrow and light on the flanks (on MEAPI bold all way down). Streaks on mantle less obvious than MEAPI; belly may be contrastingly white. All plumages sim.

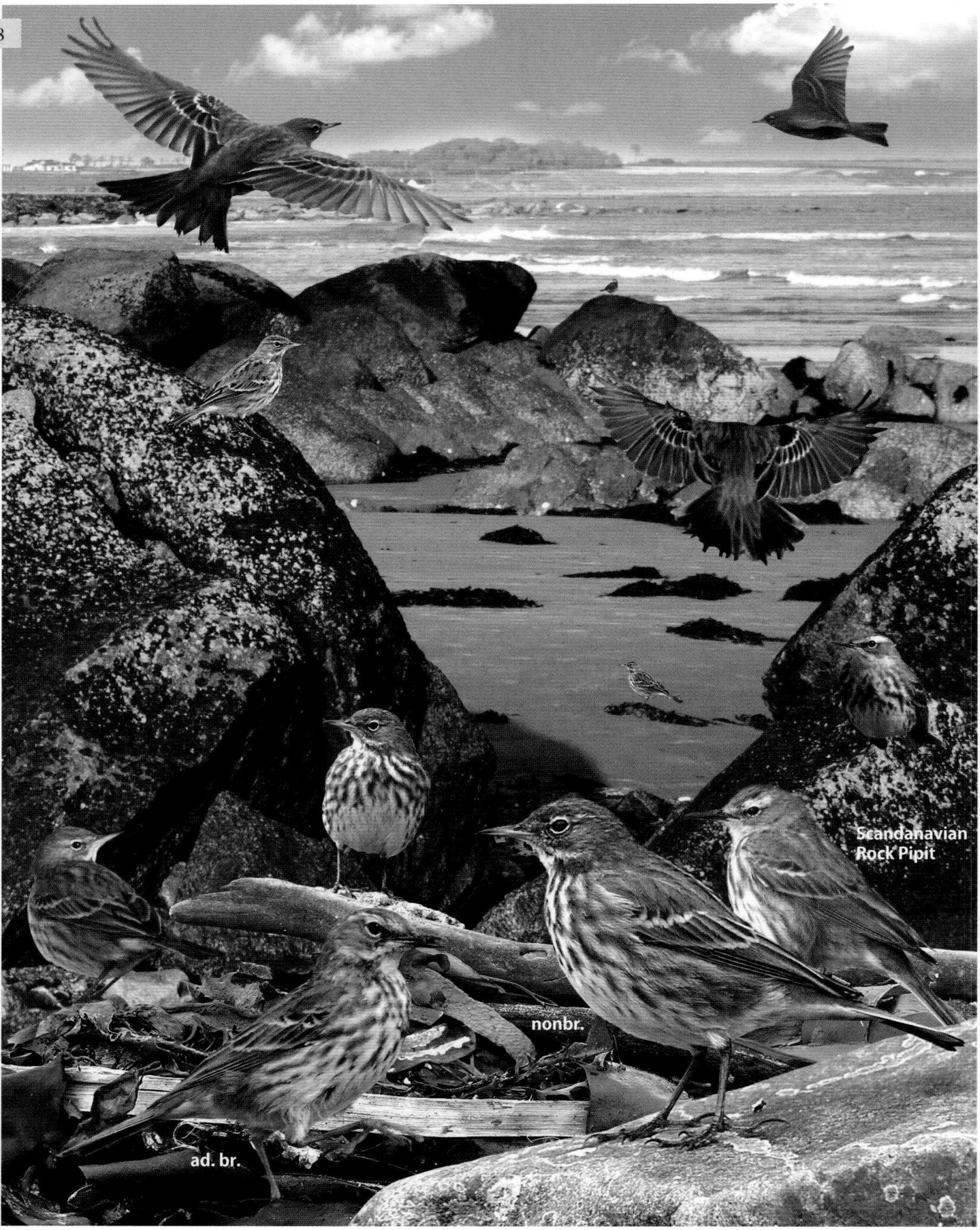

Rock Pipit *Anthus petrosus* **ROCPI/RC** L 16cm

UK: s. 36,000 pairs

The pipit of rocky shores, cliffs, islands, and coasts. It is seen walking among seaweed and pebbles on the beach or salt marsh getting its feet wet, or flying around seabird colonies. In winter also found sparsely inland. Has parachuting display-flight like other pipits, beginning and ending at ground level. Song very similar to MEAPI, but first repeated notes more obviously double, and song elements a little sharper; includes usual pipit accelerations and tone changes. Call like a 'MEAPI call with an S at the start', a sharper and more emphatic *feest!* **ID:** Larger than similarly plumaged MEAPI, which may overlap in habitat, and invariably darker hued all over: duskier ground colour of underparts provides backdrop for thicker ('B pencil-line') and more diffuse, smudged streaks, while dark upperparts make mantle streaks harder to see. Also, legs are dark red or black (not pink), outer tail feathers are smoky-grey, not white. If in doubt look for much larger bill. Ad br: black bill, lightens in winter. Scandinavian Rock Pipit: winter visitor, sometimes separable in spring when acquires pink throat and breast. Greyish head and back, and white supercilium also shown by some resident birds.

Water Pipit *Anthus spinoletta* **WATPI/WI** L 18cm ***w. 190***

Uncommon winter visitor that breeds high in central European mountains, then migrates north in autumn (unexpected direction), and oddly chooses lowland freshwater sites such as sewage farms, watercress beds, edges of marshes for wintering. Often seen feeding on the edge of puddles or lakes. More flighty than confiding ROCPI, flushing far and high. Call like cross between ROCPI and MEAPI, very difficult to be sure of. **ID:** Build as ROCPI, and has dark legs, but outer tail feathers diagnostic white. Ad nonbr: like ROCPI, but whiter underneath, with cleaner breast streaks; also more obvious pale supercilium and white wing bars. Ad br (Feb–Mar): prominent white supercilium, grey head, beautiful peachy wash to breast, which is almost unstreaked. Scandanavian Rock Pipit in spring has more streaking and duller tail edges.

Red-throated Pipit *Anthus cervinus* **RETPI** L 15cm

Rare visitor May–Jun and Sep–Oct, esp to East Coast and Scilly, average 8 records/year. Often beside lakes and puddles. Best detected by distinctive call, a soft but explosive *pseee*, like TREPI but sweeter, like a dog whistle. **ID:** MEAPI-sized, but thick bodied, decidedly short tailed, and heavily streaked. Rump streaked. Underparts whiter than other pipits. Adult: obvious from sandy-orange wash to head and chest, brightest in br ♂. 1st-w: no orange, but note heavy black streaking on dark brown back, with white tramlines.

Olive-backed Pipit *Anthus hodgsoni* **OLBPI** L 15cm

Rare autumn visitor Sep–Oct, esp to East Coast and Northern Isles, average 7 records/year. Call sim to TREPI. Usually on the ground staying well hidden but will perch in trees when flushed. **ID:** Typically striking olive-green back with diffuse streaks. Short broad supercilium broadest behind the eye, often with dark border above, and pale spot behind the ear coverts give a distinctive look with good views. The breast is usually boldly streaked, much finer on the flanks. If still in doubt check for brown tertial fringes.

Tawny Pipit *Anthus campestris* **TAWPI/TI** L 17cm
Rare early autumn migrant, usually to south and east. Prefers dry areas. Call *schlup*, like soft PIEWA. **ID:** Immediately strikes as wagtail-like, long bodied and does wag tail. Frequently does short sprints. Bigger and longer legged than MEAPI. Ad looks buff, with plain mantle and a few streaks on upper breast. Shows complete dark eye-stripe and narrow moustachial and submoustachial streaks; 1st-w dark streaked on mantle, median coverts different shaped.

Richard's Pipit *Anthus richardi* **RICPI/PR** L 18cm
Regular autumn rarity, 70 records/year, Sep–Nov, in fields with long grass. Often detected by very distinctive, loud, very sparrow-like *scheep!* Often hovers before landing; when walking, peers over grass inquisitively. **ID:** Big, leggy pipit, with long hind claws. Heavy bill lark-like. Streaked only sparingly on upper breast, and usually has dark patch on side of throat. Warm buff flanks and pale lores distinguish from sim TAWPI. 1st-w has white edges to coverts (buff in ad).

Shorelark *Eremophila alpestris* **SHOLA/SX** L 16cm ***w.* 74**
Rare winter visitor to shorelines of the North Sea, where it feeds in small flocks among dunes and salt marshes, and sometimes rough fields just inland. Often feeds with SKYLA, SNOBU, and other seed eaters. Scurries along on ground, running, not hopping, with crouching gait. Flies off in close formation, often sweeping round behind observer and out of sight. Call a somewhat pipit-like *see-tew*. **ID:** Unmistakable, owing to bold black-and-yellow head pattern. In flight, tail pattern distinctive, with outer black triangles; black legs. Generally ad br ♂ with brightest yellow, in spring with small black 'horns'; ♀ duller.

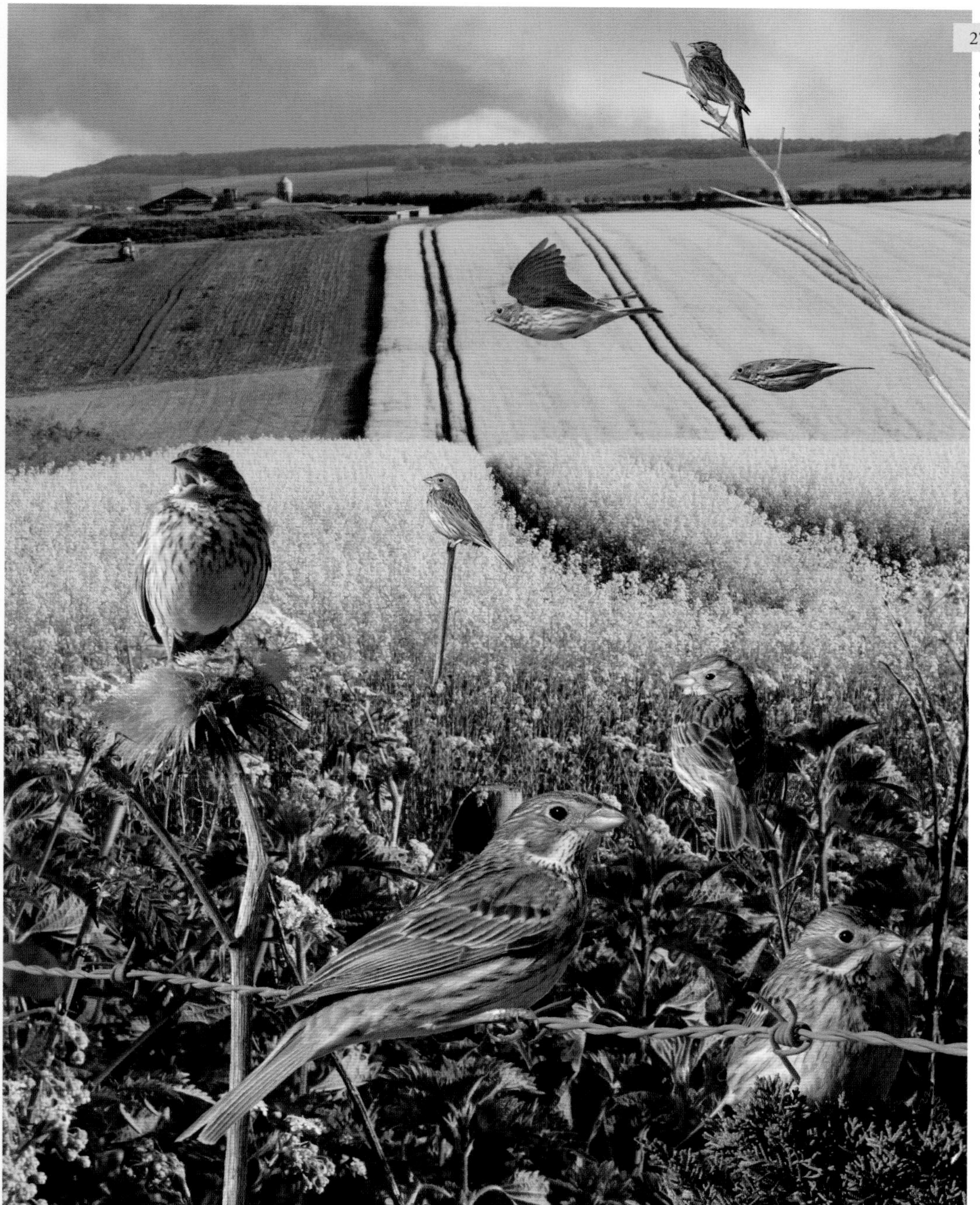

Corn Bunting *Emberiza calandra* CORBU/CB L 18cm

UK: s. 11,000 pairs

Fairly common but local in open fields, including arable crops and grassland. In winter, occurs in flocks in rough fields and stubble. Often seen perching on overhead wires, as well as fence posts and tall weeds. Has distinctive display, seen at most times of year, when flies up with legs dangling instead of being raised into undercarriage. Very distinctive song like the jangle of keys being shaken, starts slow and accelerates. Often sung incessantly all day, even in afternoon, and not just in breeding season. Call *dzik*. Flight swift and powerful, with shallow undulations. Male very polygamous, male in Sussex had 18 mates in a season! **ID:** Plump, streaky, rather featureless songbird with big head, short tail without white sides, and very thick pink bill with S-shaped cutting edge. Rounded crown separates from SKYLA, a bird of similar habitats. Breast streaks often coalesce into spot in middle of chest, upperparts heavily streaked. All plumages sim.

Skylark *Alauda arvensis* **SKYLA/S.** L 18cm

UK: s. 1,500,000 pairs

Celebrated open-country bird famous for its glorious song that cascades down from the sky, the singer itself often invisible high up. Bird rises slowly upwards in hovering style, singing all the while, remains aloft and high before slow descent and quick final plummet. Song ecstatic, shrill, continuous. Call a cheerful *chirrup*. Resident on farmland, moorland, grassland, and similar. Often associated with summer, but in winter gathers in flocks and feeds and roosts on ground, keeps low profile. Perches low, on tussock or fence posts. When flushed, often flies without panic, may hover before landing again. In level flight, slight undulations and fitful bursts of wingbeats; often seen on passage periods on visible migration watches. **ID:** Big for a songbird, approaches STARL in size; over streaky and straw coloured. Crest is good pointer, usually visible, if only as bump. In flight, shows white outer tail feathers and white trailing edge to wings. Heavily streaked on breast against buff background, shows something of breast band. Juv: looks oddly scaly above, no crest.

Woodlark *Lullula arborea* **WOODL/WL** L 15cm ***s. 3,100 pairs***

Uncommon in areas combining short vegetation, bare ground, and scattered trees: heaths, open woodland, and managed plantations in south and East Anglia. May winter on farmland stubble. Feeds on short-cropped turf, often out of sight for minutes on end. Flies with heavy undulations, often quite low. Makes circling flight-song high in the air. Song gorgeous, a trill that descends in semitones (like Doppler Effect), very pleasing. Call an almost apologetic *tit-loeet*. Often perches on trees and wires, unlike larger SKYLA. **ID:** Distinctive shape, with very short tail and, in flight, broad wings. On ground, look for spiky bill and bump for a crest, as well as v broad supercilium running to back, meets opposite number on nape; chestnut cheeks. Diagnostic is black-and-white patch on primary coverts. Lacks white outer tail feathers and trailing edge to wing. Tail tipped white. All plumages sim.

Short-toed Lark *Calandrella brachydactyla* **SHTLA/VL** L 15cm

Rare but annual visitor in spring (May) and autumn (Sep–Oct), particularly to the South Coast of England. Average 27 records/year, often on short grassland. Easily overlooked. Call *chirrup*, like HOUMA. **ID:** Pale finch-like passerine with stubby bill. Look for dark patch on side of neck (on most), virtually no streaks on underparts, v long tertials covering to wingtip. May be rusty capped. Median wing coverts dark centred.

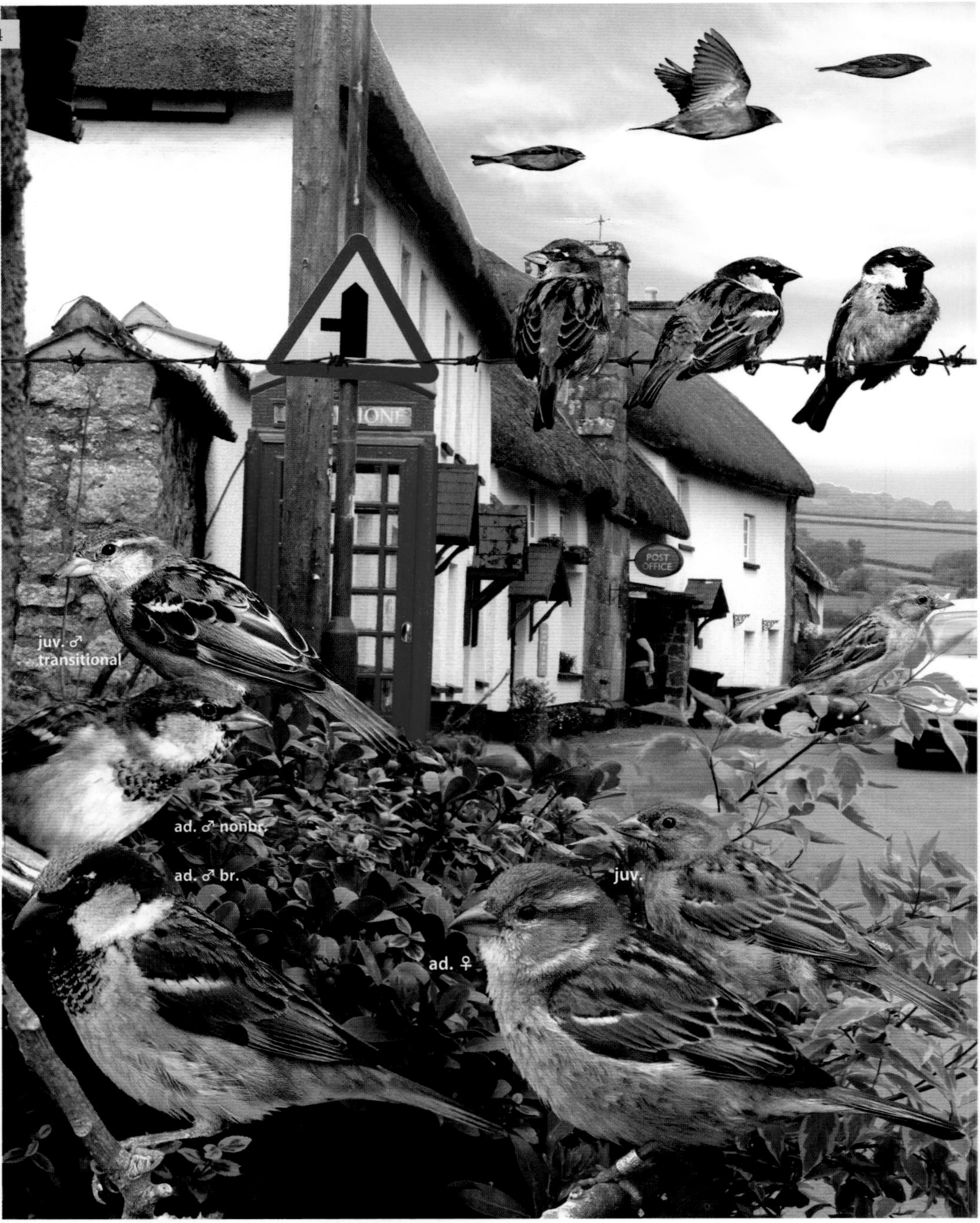

House Sparrow *Passer domesticus* **HOUSP/HS** L15cm

UK: s. 5,300,000 pairs

Very common city, town, and village bird, tough and adaptable, lives on the coat-tails of people. Often the first bird you encounter where you get your takeaway coffee, go into a farmyard, visit the shoppers' car park. Uses feeders in gardens, nests in the eaves of buildings (any cavity), gathers on roofs. Tame but not reckless, usually in small groups feeding on the ground or sunning on a hedge, or dust-bathing. Several chirping notes, sometimes repeated constantly. Flight powerful and straight with fast steady wingbeats. **ID:** Quite robust, scruffy LBJ (little brown job). Dull unstreaked underparts, boldly streaked upperparts, and short tail without white sides. Sexes different. Ad ♂ br: nicely marked with grey crown, black bill, mostly brown upperparts, grey cheeks, and black bib. Nonbr ♂: a much duller version of same pattern with paler bill. ♀: pale dingy brown, indistinct supercilium contrasts with darker cap and eye-stripe. Pale bill. Juv: as ♀ with buffier underparts and fringes to coverts, soft-textured feathers, and rounded tips to flight feathers. 1st-w: moults in adult plumage through autumn.

Tree Sparrow *Passer montanus* **TRESP/TS** L 14cm

UK: s. 200,000 pairs

Country bumpkin cousin of HOUSP, somewhat localised. Commonest on farmland with hedges and trees, but also on woodland edges and in parks with scattered mature stands. Nest is usually in a hole, either in a tree or in a nest box, and birds prefer to breed in small colonies. Call slightly higher pitched than HOUSP, sharper and more metallic; also utters *teck* in flight, a call missing from HOUSP. **ID:** Smaller and very much neater and classier than HOUSP. Also differs radically in that sexes are alike. Has neatly defined chestnut crown, clean white cheeks with a black spot in the middle, pale collar, v clean, pale brown underparts, and smart black bib. Bill dark with yellow base (more obvious in winter). Juv: dusky cheeks and collar, and overall not such clean markings on head.

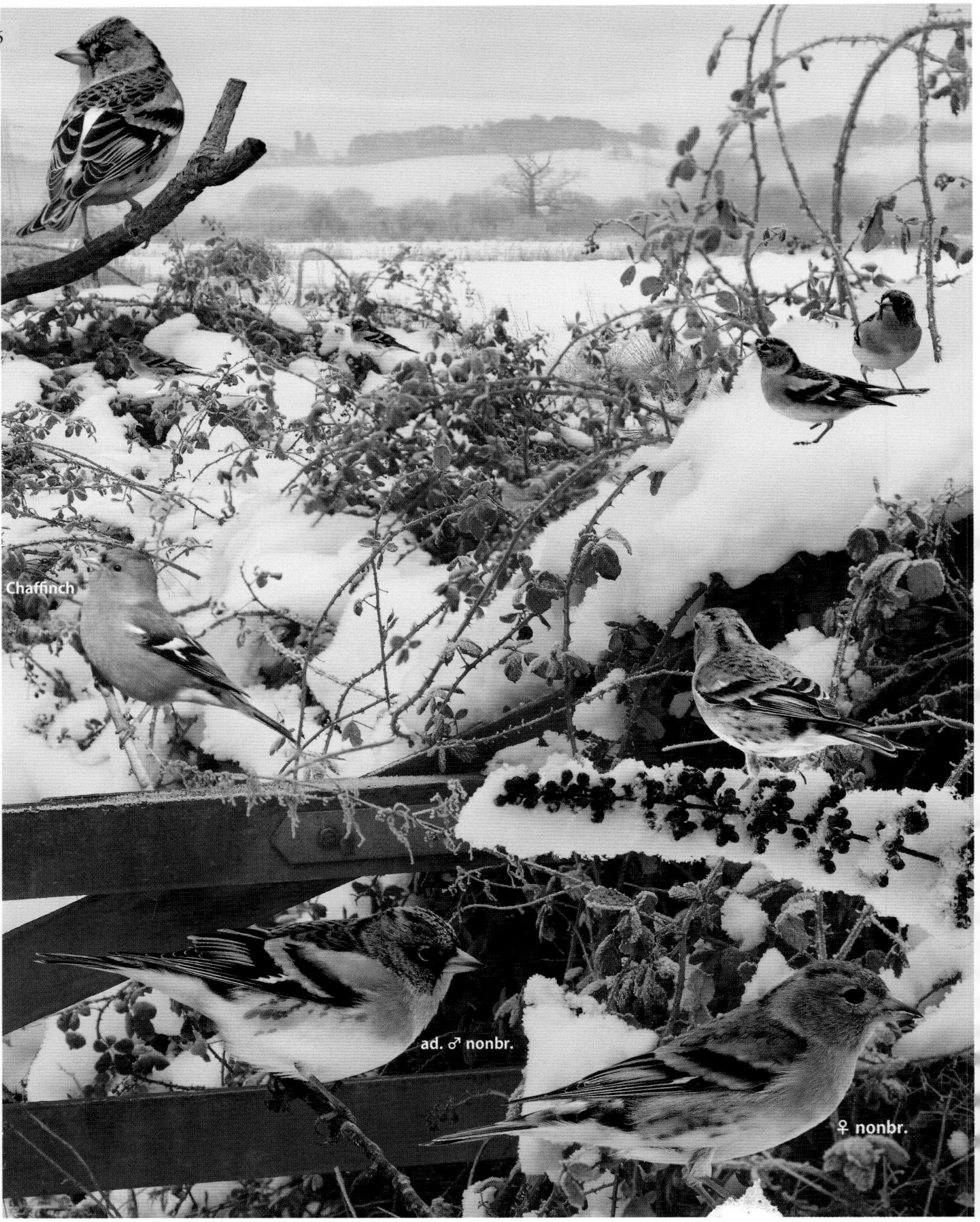

Brambling *Fringilla montifringilla* **BRAMB/BL** L 15cm

UK: w. 45,000–1,800,000

Winter visitor Oct–Apr, esp to beechwood, but later in winter also in fields and hedgerows, sometimes gardens and feeders. Varying numbers visit Britain, according to beech mast supplies elsewhere. Occasionally breeds in birch scrub. Usually gregarious, gathering in flocks with CHAFFs on woodland floor, grubbing among fallen leaves. Roosts communally, sometimes in large numbers. Perched call a loud, parrot-like *ye-ick!*, flight call a soft *jep*, and song is like GREFI wheeze on flat pitch. **ID:** Similar to CHAFF but invariably orange washed (colour of autumn beech), usually bright on upper breast and shoulders; rash of dark spots on flanks, belly white. Has shorter, more forked tail, which is black without white edges. White rump always obvious when bird flushed. Very slightly thicker bill is distinctively yellow with black tip in winter. Nonbr ♂ mainly buff-mottled black on head and mottled dark brown on mantle. 1st-w ♂ similar, but shoulders dark speckled. ♀ has greyish sides of head, with dark-streaked crown and nape. ♂ br by Mar, head and mantle jet black, bill black.

Chaffinch *Fringilla coelebs* **CHAFF/CH** L 15cm

UK: s. 6,200,000 pairs

Superabundant woodland finch, also occurring in gardens, hedgerows, and, in winter, farmland fields. Common visitor to garden feeders, usually prefers to feed on ground, where it both hops and shuffles. Sings cheerful, rattling, accelerating song with flourish at the end; among many calls are upbeat *pink, pink!* and soft *chup* flight call. In summer, lives in woodland canopy, gleans leaves for insects and also snatches them in brief aerial sallies. In autumn, diet switches to seeds, including beechmast. **ID:** Slim finch with long tail (outer edges white) and quite horizontal posture when perched. Easily recognised by multiple white wing patches, including white shoulders and Y-shaped mark on coverts, stained yellowish. Bill grey/pinkish. Rump green. Ad ♂ br: pink chested and has blue cap and nape around pink cheek; brown mantle. Nonbr ♂: pale feather tips subdue plumage, through winter get worn away to reveal bright colours beneath. ♀ dowdy, pink-brown on breast, with dull greyish head markings and narrower white wing markings. Juv: sim to ♀, but 1st-w ♂ has pink tinge to breast.

Linnet *Carduelis cannabina* LINNE/LI L 14cm

UK: s. 430,000 pairs

Resident of bushy areas such as hedgerows, commons, and rough ground, as well as fields and salt marshes in winter. Highly sociable finch, gathering in large flocks in winter and small 'neighbourhood groups' when breeding. Feeds on very small seeds, either on ground or by perching on herbs; doesn't feed in trees like LESRE. Song a lively, fast series of twitters with periodic zooming off at a tangent, like experimental musician; call hard but quiet *ch-chup*. Flies with great freedom, with big undulations and twists and turns; flocks adhere closely. **ID:** Very slim, with long forked tail and very small, conical bill, which is grey. White sides to tail and white wing bar made by primaries. Pale patches around face in all plumages, including around eyes and on cheeks, a 'badly powdered face'. Ad ♂ br stunning, with deep crimson breast and forehead, grey head, and warm brown back. Nonbr ♂ much duller, red largely hidden, buff below. ♀ mainly brown above and buff below, with neat streaks. Juv: plainer face, plumage more speckled.

Twite *Carduelis flavirostros* **TWITE/TW** L 14cm

UK: s. 10,000 pairs

Upland version of LINNE, breeding on moors and coastal heaths, islands, and near isolated farms and crofts. Reliant on small seeds, as LINNE. Populations in Scotland and Ireland don't move far, but Pennine breeding population moves to North Sea coasts for the winter. Highly sociable, often forming large flocks. Tends to feed on the ground, where it can be difficult to see; in winter, forages closer to tideline than other finches. Will perch on trees, but doesn't feed from them. Calls include *chut-ut,* like cross between LINNE and LESRE, also eponymous metallic *tveet*; song not like LINNE, a series of twitters with harsh buzzes and brief wheezes, altogether like electricity crackling. **ID:** Heavily streaked brown finch, with characteristic warm 'bran-coloured' wash to face in all plumages. Seen well, more LESRE-like than LINNE-like. Shares LINNE's silvery wing bar, tail is slightly longer. In nonbr easily told from LINNE by yellow bill. Ad ♂ br with grey bill and diagnostic pink rump; rather dark above; ♀ sim but lacks pink rump. Nonbr/1st-w: strongly buff below, with less streaking.

Common Redpoll *Carduelis flammea* **COMRE/FR** L 5.75in

UK: s. 220,000 pairs

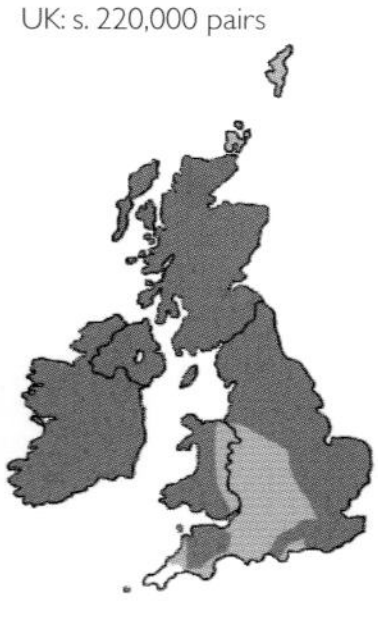

Fairly common woodland finch associated mainly with birch all year-round; in winter, also in alders. Found in scrub in the north. Nomadic. Feeds on seeds, often hanging upside down like a tit. Takes off in a tight, noisy, 'bouncing' pack giving buzzing *chid-chid-chid* calls, often mixed with *tswerr*. Although easily spooked, can be tame. **ID:** Highly variable in appearance (taxonomy is uncertain). Appears as a small ball of feathers with a narrow but strongly forked tail. Small head, stubby bill and raspberry red cap give it a cute look. Brown streaked upperparts, pale rump, and buff wing bars. Underparts are brown-washed, with blurry streaks, mostly on the flanks. Ad ♂: raspberry red on breast, extensive on some but highly variable. ♀/imm: lacks red and more heavily streaked. The slightly larger Common or Mealy Redpoll (*flammea*) is a winter visitor in highly variable numbers, differs on average from the resident Lesser (*cabaret*) in having white wing bars, colder greyish cast to plumage, and bolder face pattern. Scarcer winter visitors from Iceland (*islandica*) and large, dark, streaky Greenland birds (*rostrata*) cloud the picture further.

Arctic Redpoll *Carduelis hornemanni* **ARCRE/AL** L 14cm ***w. 13***

Remarkably hardy visitor from north, on average 16 records/year. ID with care! **ID:** Some told by a combination of paler mantle, fewer streaks on underparts, less contrasting and paler face, few or no streaks on undertail coverts, and all or mostly white rump. Sometimes has shorter 'nipped in' bill, and more feathering around legs. ♂: only lightly pink breasted and more lightly streaked. Two races: *exilipes* (Scandinavia) and rare *hornemanni* (Greenland and Canada), latter is noticeably larger, beige faced, and bigger headed, in comparison, also averages paler.

Serin *Serinus serinus* **SERIN/NS** L 12cm

Rare migrant, esp Mar–Apr, has occasionally nested; 60–70 records/year. A bird of gardens and parks, churchyards, and other well-wooded areas. Often sits on wires and on conifer treetops and has light, deeply undulating flight. Usually feeds unobtrusively on ground. Fast, jingling song, like shaking very small car keys or ball bearings rubbing together. Call liquid *tri-lil-it*. **ID:** Heavily streaked green finch with minute grey bill. Narrow wing bars, unmarked tail. Ad with bright yellow rump. ♂ brilliant lemon-yellow on head; ♀ duller. Juv browner with only slightly greenish rump.

Siskin *Carduelis spinus* **SISKI/SK** L 12cm

UK: s. 420,000 pairs

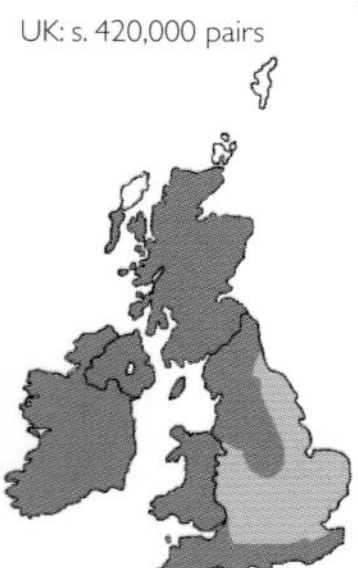

A woodland and forest finch that has developed the habit of visiting garden feeders, where it has habit of holding on upside down. Breeds widely in spruce and pine forest, and is common winter visitor to alder trees and birches. Very sociable, breeds in small groups and can be in large flocks in winter, feeding in the treetops. When such flocks flushed, they 'explode' from branches in all directions, but often wheel round and come back. Flight light and undulating. Feeds on ground when seeds fallen in late winter, otherwise acrobatically in branches. Main call a *sissy*, feeble, sighing *dwee* with metallic ring; also make sparrow-like calls and song is quiet babbling chatter interspersed with little flatulent buzzes. **ID:** Small green tree-feeding finch with 2 bright yellowish wing bars and neatly streaked flanks, white belly. Bill quite long and pointed. ♂ with coal-black cap and bib, bright yellow rump; ♀ unmarked face and duller rump. Juv heavily streaked all over, but still tinged green, with yellowish wing bars.

Greenfinch *Chloris chloris* GREFI/GR L 15cm

UK: s. 1,700,000 pairs

Abundant finch of verdant gardens, woodland edge, churchyards, parks, and all sorts of scrubby habitats. A well-known bully at garden feeders, monopolising the seed supplies. Feeds on ground, from herbs (including sunflowers) and also on trees such as yew and other berries. Sociable, often in small flocks, and pairs may nest in close proximity. Has exuberant spring songflight, in which describes circle or figure of eight at treetop height, may sway from side to side with full wingbeats, giving unexpected SWALL-like impression. Also sings from treetop (e.g., cypress), a series of canary-like trills on one note, often including a drawn-out, emphatic *dzweeee*. Call in flight *chp-chp* and variants. **ID:** Sparrow sized but usually unmistakably apple-green. Has a huge pale pink bill, frowning expression, rather short tail, and upright stance when perched. Yellow wing bar down edge of wing only (in SISKI goes across wing), tail yellow sided. ♂ bright apple-green (duller nonbr), with much yellow on wings and tail, greyish tinge to side of head and on wings; ♀ duller, with subtle streaks on mantle and breast. Juv heavily streaked, with whitish breast.

Goldfinch *Carduelis carduelis* **GOLDF/GO** L 12cm

UK: s. 1,200,000 pairs

Common brilliantly coloured bird of weedy, overgrown rough ground with thistles, its staple food. Also scrub, woodland edge, and, increasingly, gardens, where it comes to feeders providing small seeds (sunflower heats, nyjer). Usually seen adorning thistle-heads, where it can perch horizontal, hold onto the side or hang upside down, often fluttering its wings for balance. Also feeds on teasel (mostly males), and on the ground. Nest on end of branch, often over water. Once largely a summer visitor, now found as resident most areas, although still more numerous Apr–Sep. Lively and conversational, uttering liquid *ticklit* call or singing its twittering song, which tinkles like small brook. **ID:** Small, compact finch with unmistakable plumage, esp the brilliant golden yellow panels in the middle of the black wings. Also has white spots on wingtip and tail. Bill ivory coloured. Ad has tricoloured head with scarlet face, toffee-coloured mantle, flanks, and 'bra'. Juv completely lacks face markings, just beady dark eye in bland face; lightly streaked grey-brown.

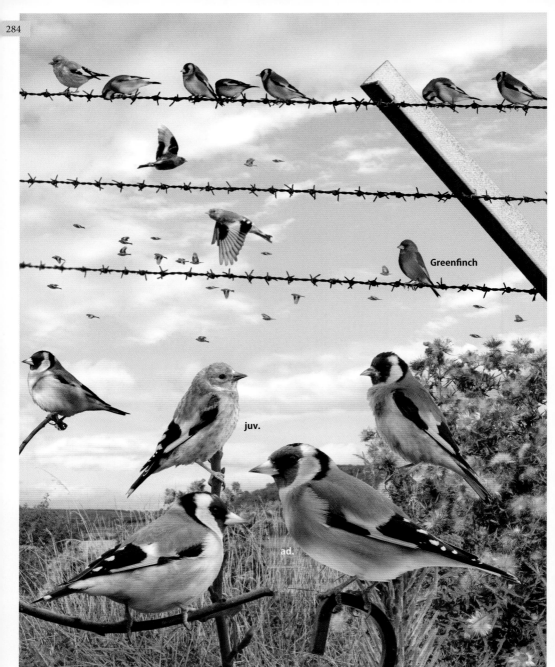

Bullfinch *Pyrrhula pyrrhula* **BULLF/BF** L 15cm

UK: s. 220,000 pairs

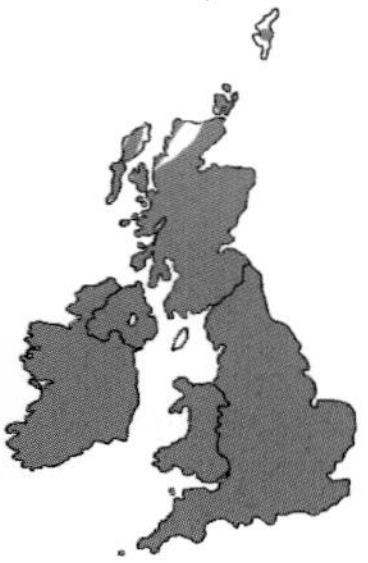

Low-profile finch of woodland, scrub, orchard, and hedgerow, also now a regular at garden feeders. Quieter than relatives, just uttering rather plaintive, irregular whistling *pu* calls, and is much less sociable, usually being seen only in modest family parties. Rarely heard song consists of broken sounds and calls, sounding like a rusty sign swinging in the wind. In breeding season, feeds on buds and soft fruits, turning to seeds in the autumn; once persecuted in orchards for eating fruit-tree buds. Resident, but a few northern birds winter here. **ID:** Well-built finch with smart plumage. Thick black bill, of which culmen seems in smooth line with rounded crown. Often looks plump, with long black tail, no white sides. White rump easily distinguishes it from superficially similar CHAFF, as does black cap in ad. Ad ♂: fulsome plum-red breast and side of head, grey back. Ad ♀ with pink-brown breast, brownish back. Juv: like ♀, but is duller, lacks black cap, and has staring dark eye. Northern birds brighter reddish pink, larger.

Crossbill *Loxia curvirostra* **CROSS/CR** L 16cm

UK: s. 40,000 pairs

Widespread but uncommon conifer specialist; has crossed bill for prying out seeds of spruce and pine. Nomadic, moving to other areas when food is scarce, so may go missing in 'normal' areas. Also feeds on larch in autumn. Able to breed throughout the year if food supplies good. Often feeds quietly in small flocks, hanging from any angle, parrot-like. Sound of falling cones may be clue to whereabouts. Uses bill to manoeuvre in trees. Most easily seen flying high overhead giving loud *jip-jip!* notes. Song is slow trilling series of calls. Often perches on treetops. **ID:** Crossed bill is diagnostic except for SCOCR and PARCR. Chunky with oversized head and short forked tail. All have dark wings and tail. Ear coverts subtly dark, often appearing as thick eyeline. Some show weak wing bars. Ad ♂: uniform dark red on underparts, head, and back. Undertail coverts white with dark centres. Ad ♀: mostly olive-green but variable and can show yellow, orange, or red. 1st-yr ♂: patchy green and red. Juv heavily streaked underparts.

Scottish Crossbill *Loxia scotica* **SCOCR/CY** L 16cm ***s. 6,800 pairs***

Found in Scots pine woods, esp the native Caledonian Forest of northern Scotland, but also in commercial plantations nearby. The only bird species confined entirely to Britain. Differences from CROSS are subtle. Voice similar to CROSS, but quiet *chup* calls deeper, others higher; only sonograms make differences clear. **ID:** Almost identical, but has heavier bill than CROSS. Head neckless, with bill larger, deeper, and blunter than CROSS (intermediate with PARCR). Tail and wings fractionally longer. Plumage as CROSS.

Parrot Crossbill *Loxia pytyopsittacus* **PARCR/PC** L 18cm ***s. 65 pairs***

Rare resident in Scottish Highlands, esp Caledonian pine forest; rare migrant elsewhere. Voice very similar to CROSS, but song is lower pitched and slower and calls generally louder, deeper, and more metallic. **ID:** Slightly larger than CROSS and with noticeable bull-neck and larger bill; top of lower mandible not visible above upper when bill shut. Lower mandible deep 'keeled' (bulges down), making bill almost square, while upper mandible seems to curve down more sharply. Differences subtle. Plumages and sequence as CROSS.

Hawfinch *Coccothraustes coccothraustes* **HAWFI/HF** L 18cm ***s. 500–1,00 pairs***

A famously shy and elusive treetop bird of mature deciduous woodland. Favourite trees wild cherry, hornbeam, elm, oak, beech. Able to crack very hard seeds and nuts (cherry stones). Secretively feeds on ground in leaf litter, easily flushed. Often perches to side of treetop, hard to pick up. In flight, overly fast wingbeats give slight out-of-control look. Often flies high, shows big white wing bar. Call *tsip*, like very loud ROBIN. **ID:** Large, top-heavy finch with massive head and bill, creamy-pink plumage, black chin and mask. Short tail. Ad ♂: dark grey bill when br, yellow in winter. Ad ♀: less colourful plumage, yellow bill, grey secondary patch. Juv: spotted below.

Common Rosefinch *Carpodacus erythrinus* **SCARO/SQ** L 14cm

Rare passage migrant that occasionally breeds in open country with scattered trees and thick bushes. About 100 are recorded each year, usually at eastern coastal sites. Call strained *zhwee*. Song is unmistakable, cheerful *pleased to meet you* or similar phrase. **ID:** Oddly bulbous dark bill, rounded crown and long wings and tail. Ad ♂: from 2 yr, rich strawberry crown, head, breast, and rump, so unmistakable. Ad ♀: plain dark brown; dark eye in plain face, neat narrow streaks on mantle and underparts. Juv browner, with 2 buff wing bars.

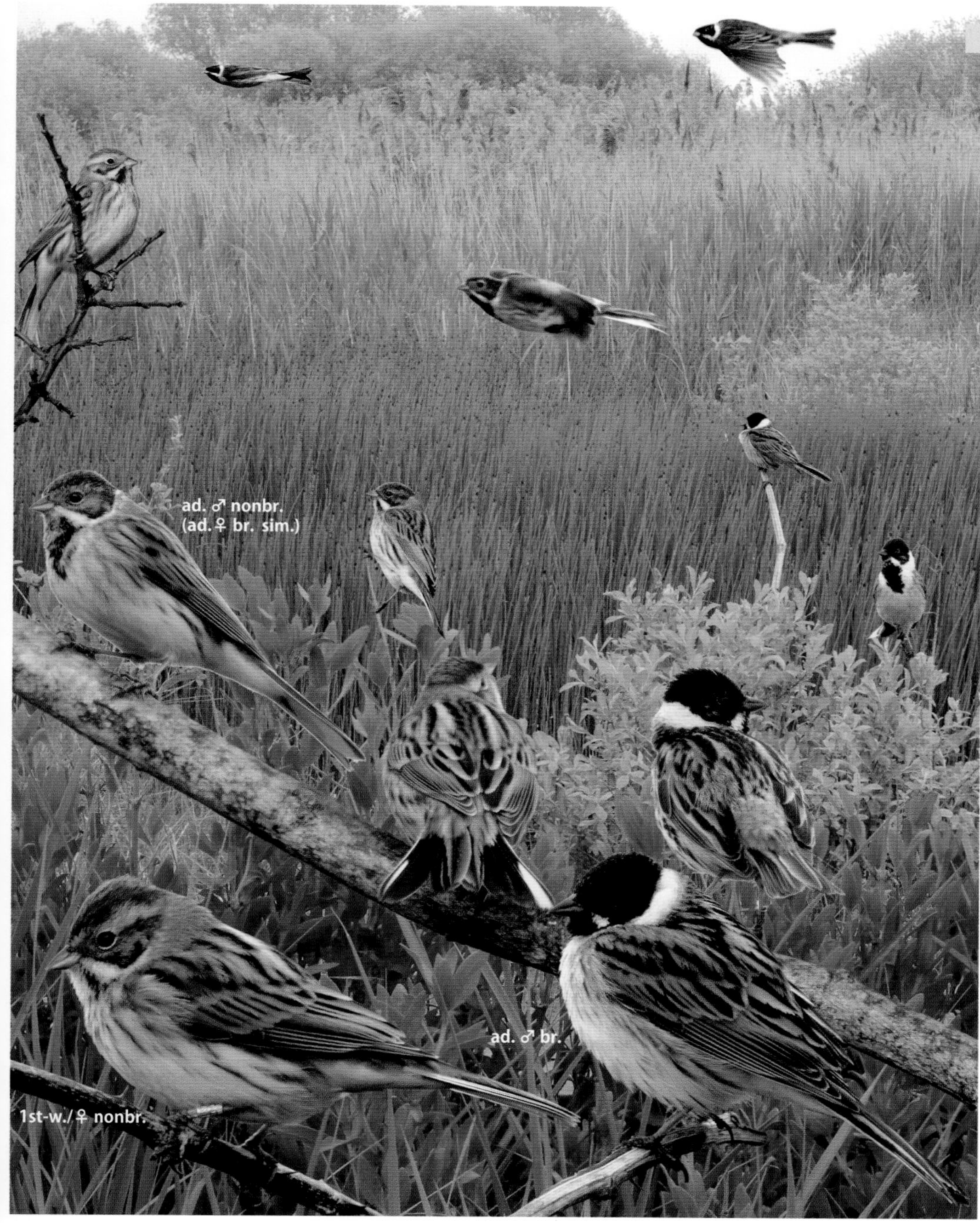

Reed Bunting *Emberiza schoeniclus* **REEBU/RB** L 25cm

UK: s. 250,000 pairs

Easily overlooked bird of freshwater marshes and other wetlands, and a few drier habitats such as heaths and farmland. Easily dismissed as a sparrow, but has curious habit of constantly flicking tail when perched. Flight is also distinctive, with fitful bursts of wingbeats. Main call is a falling *tseeu*, while song is series of staccato phrases *tsweek, tsweek tssizzit*—sounds like child hesitantly counting and forgetting what comes next. Sings from high perch on reed or willow, well in view, but often rather skulking. In winter, gathers in modest flocks and often joins other species for example on farmland. **ID:** Sparrow-like, but has long tail with narrow white edge. Bill smaller, dark grey, and in most plumages streaked in front. Ad ♂ br: jet black head and throat, white collar and moustachial stripe. Ad ♀ told by stripy face, with pale supercilium and v obvious white moustachial stripe, dark lateral throat stripe. ♂ nonbr: sim, but usually has some mottled black on bib. Juv/1st-w: clear buff supercilium and moustachial stripe, bold streak down from bill.

Snow Bunting *Plectrophenax nivalis* **SNOBU/SB** L 16cm

UK: s. 70 pairs
w. 12,000

Remarkably hardy, breeds further north than any other songbird. Small population on high Scottish mountain tundra all year-round, but mainly winter visitor to coastal dunes and large beaches. Occurs in tight flocks from a few birds up to 100. Crouches to feed but then walks fast on short legs and can be deceptively tough to see on snow, sand, or earth. Often take off in unison, a beautifully patterned mosaic of brown and white, and will move to another area only to return 10 minutes later. In flight, gives a soft ripple *tirirrip* (quite like CRETI). Also mellow *tew*. **ID:** Large bodied with small head. Ad ♂ br: solid black bill and upperparts. Ad ♀ br: like ♂ with dark markings on head and back. Ad nonbr/1st-yr: sim when sitting, with warm brown breast patches, cap, ear coverts, and back (with black streaks). Bill mostly yellow-orange. In flight, age and sex sometimes become clearer. Ad ♂ has extensive white in upperwing, imm ♀ the least. By late winter, wear starts to produce darker, more contrasting, breeding plumage.

Lapland Bunting *Calcarius lapponicus* **LAPBU/LA** L 16cm ***w. 710***

Scarce winter visitor (Sep–Mar) to coastal beaches, dunes, and rough fields, often with SNOBU. Usually in small parties. Call is distinctive *ticky-tick, tew*. **ID:** Long wings and broad body give lark-like appearance. All plumages have rufous nape, plus dark markings on breast and flanks contrasting with white belly. Short yellow bill a good distinction from REEBU, also SKYLA. Ad br ♂: unmistakable, ♀ is faded version. In other plumages, check 2 narrow white wing bars either side of rufous greater coverts, plus head pattern, emphasised by dark-bordered ear coverts with dark patches at rear corners. Nonbr ♂ usually with black marks on breast.

Little Bunting *Emberiza pusilla* **LITBU/IJ** L 14cm

Average 29 records/year, mainly passage periods, occasional overwintering. Sharp *zick* call attracts attention. **ID:** Small and neat, with sharp-tipped grey bill with straight culmen, chestnut face and lores, rather obvious pale eye-ring, black-edged ear coverts, and rusty central crown stripe with black either side. Neat black streaks on breast and flanks.

Rustic Bunting *Emberiza rustica* **RUSBU** L 15cm

Average 9 records/year in passage periods. Call *zick*. **ID:** Sim to REEBU in size and shape, but crown noticeably peaked and has straight culmen, giving sharp bill tip; bill also has distinctive pink lower mandible and greyish upper. Legs pinkish brown, paler than REEBU's. Look also for reddish brown nape and pale whitish spot on edge of ear coverts.

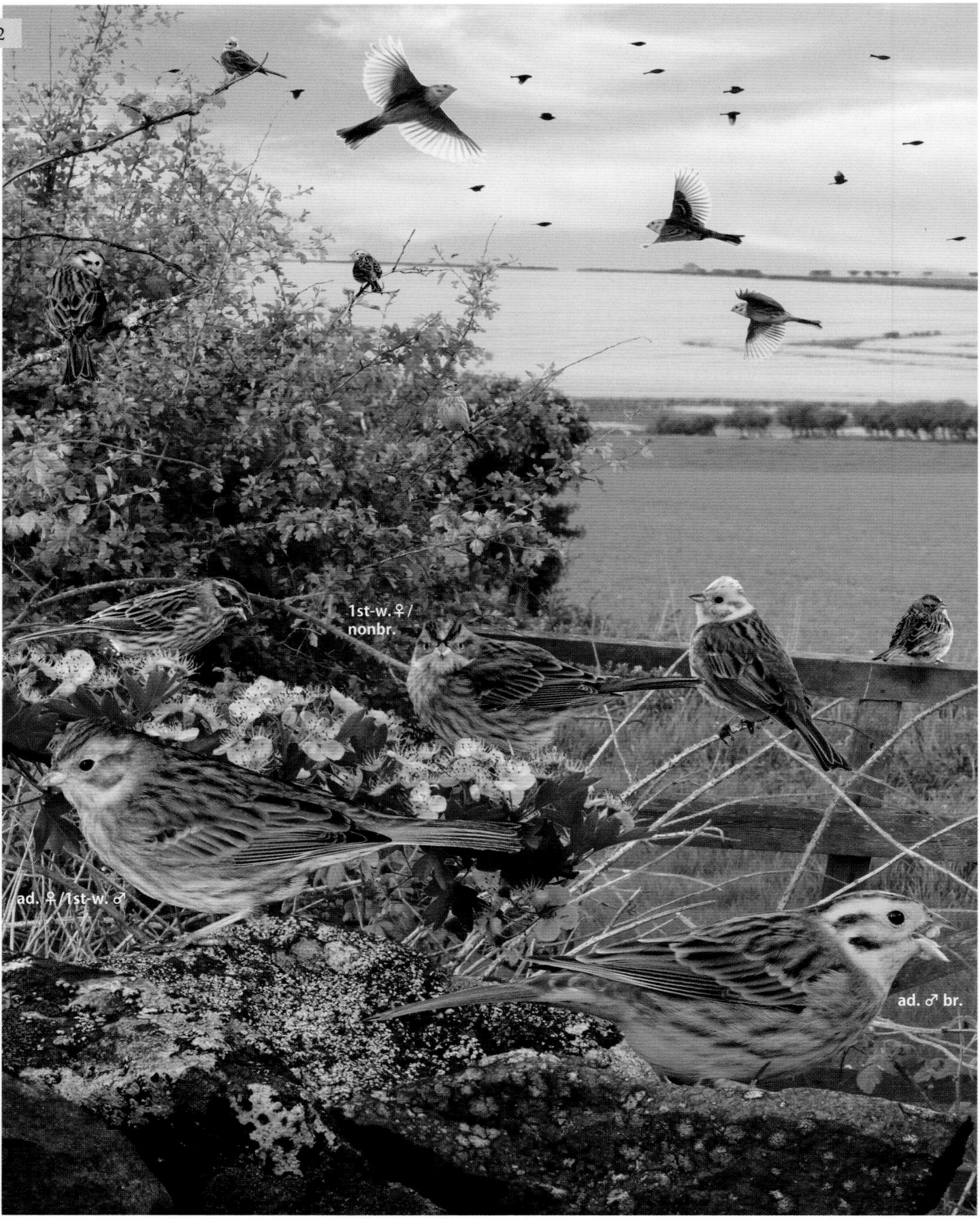

Yellowhammer *Emberiza citrinella* **YELHA/Y.** L 16cm

UK: s. 710,000 pairs

Familiar and widespread resident hedgerow and farmland bird, also seen on heaths and commons. Famous for its unusual yellow colour (very few birds like this) and its dry-sounding song, often rendered *a little bit of bread and no chee-ese*, sounding like the rattle makes the bird run out of breath, exhaling heavily at the end. The *cheese* is often left out, leaving just the rattle. Call *zit*. The song is often heard all season long, and even during the afternoon (3000 repeats a day). Males hold linear territories along hedgerows, and perch prominently. In winter, lower profile, feeds in flocks on farmland. **ID:** Sparrow sized but distinctively long tailed. Look also for variable yellow wash and chestnut rump. Ad ♂: easily recognised by bright marigold-yellow head, with variable dark markings, and yellow underparts with tinge of chestnut on breast. ♀/nonbr ♂: essentially sim but not as bright, head with olive-green ear coverts and crown sides. Juv: quite brown and tricky, check for tinge of yellow on underparts and chestnut rump.

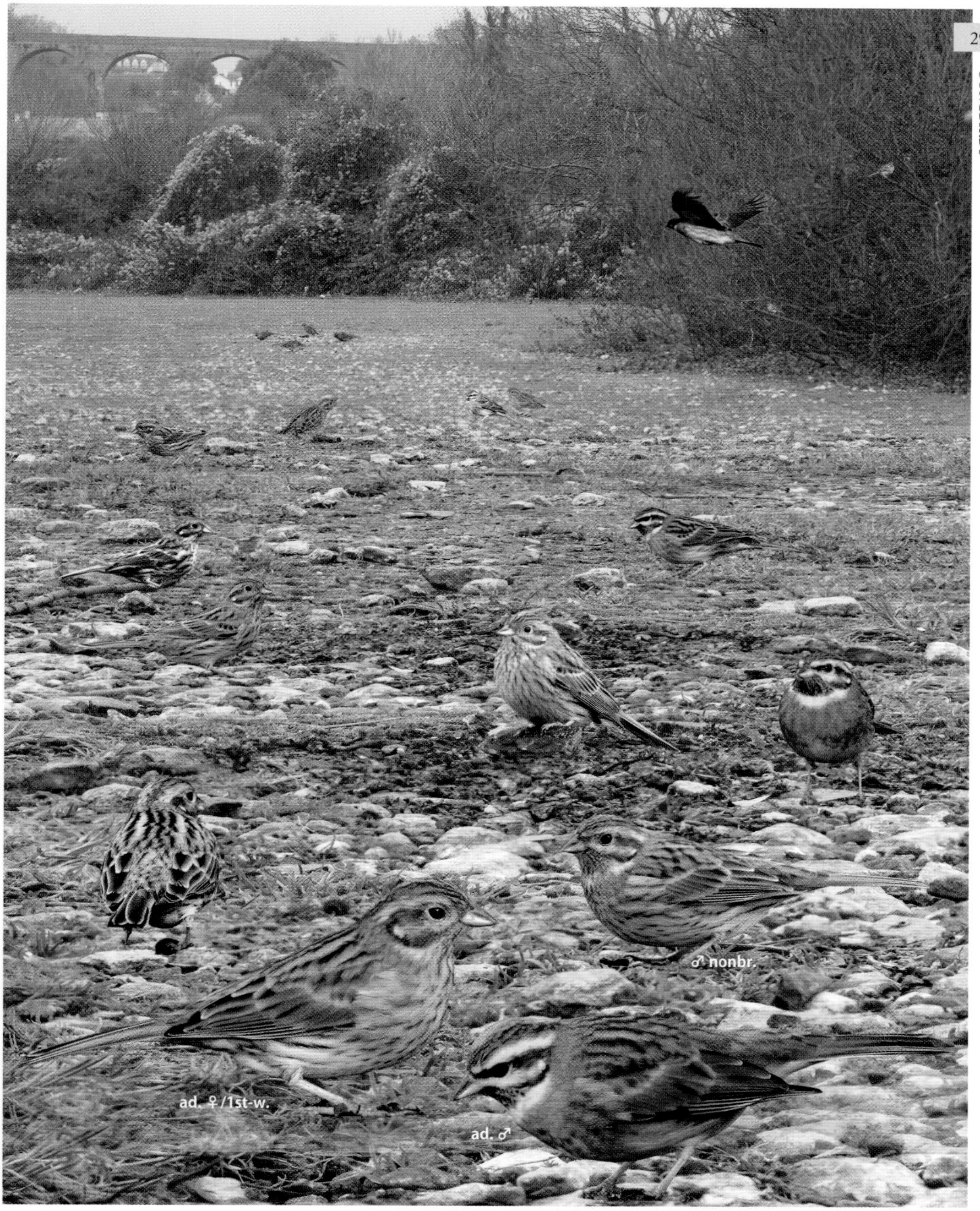

Cirl Bunting *Emberiza cirlus* **CIRBU/CL** L 16cm

UK: s. 860 pairs

Rare breeding bird in sw England, mainly Devon, where found in patchwork of small fields and hedges. Much harder to find and more skulking than YELHA, often feeding quietly on the ground close to cover. Will perch prominently to sing, for example on wires, tops of bushes. Song superficially like YELHA without *cheese*, but faster and more insect-like, with flatter tone (may recall LESWH). Call not as sharp, more like *sip*. In winter may gather in small flocks, often with YELHA. **ID:** Just slightly smaller than YELHA, and has olive-green, not chestnut rump, greenish crown, and more reddish brown back. Consistent difference is that streaks on throat and breast finer and not so smudged. In all plumages head stripier. Ad ♂ br: unmistakable bold black eye-stripe and throat, leaving yellow band on ear coverts and yellow supercilium. Black often subdued in nonbr ♂. Ad ♀/juv: grey-green stripes behind eye and below ear coverts, yellowish either side.

Ortolan Bunting *Emberiza hortulana* **ORTBU/OB** L 16cm

Rare but regular migrant Apr–May and Aug–Sep, with about 70 records/year. Quite shy and unobtrusive, spending much time on the ground. Calls *see-up* or *tlip*. Song short dry rattle with lower-pitched finishing note, like start to Beethoven's Fifth Symphony. **ID:** Unusual combination of pale, yellowish eye-ring and pink bill IDs it; also pink chest and yellow submoustachial stripe. Ad ♂ br: unmarked greyish green head and breast band, yellowish chin, ♀ with diffuse streaks on head and breast. 1st-w: head duller and underparts more heavily streaked.

Rose-coloured Starling *Sturnus roseus* **ROCST/OE** L 22cm

Rarity from west Asian steppe country, sometimes arrives in small numbers in late spring; otherwise autumn juveniles that sometimes overwinter. **ID:** Shape sim to STARL, but bill shorter and blunter. British birds usually mixed in with STARL flocks. Ad br: unmistakable pink and black. Ad nonbr: pink not as bright. Juv: similar to juv STARL but paler (milky coffee), with contrasting dark wings, pale rump. Bill pale yellow.

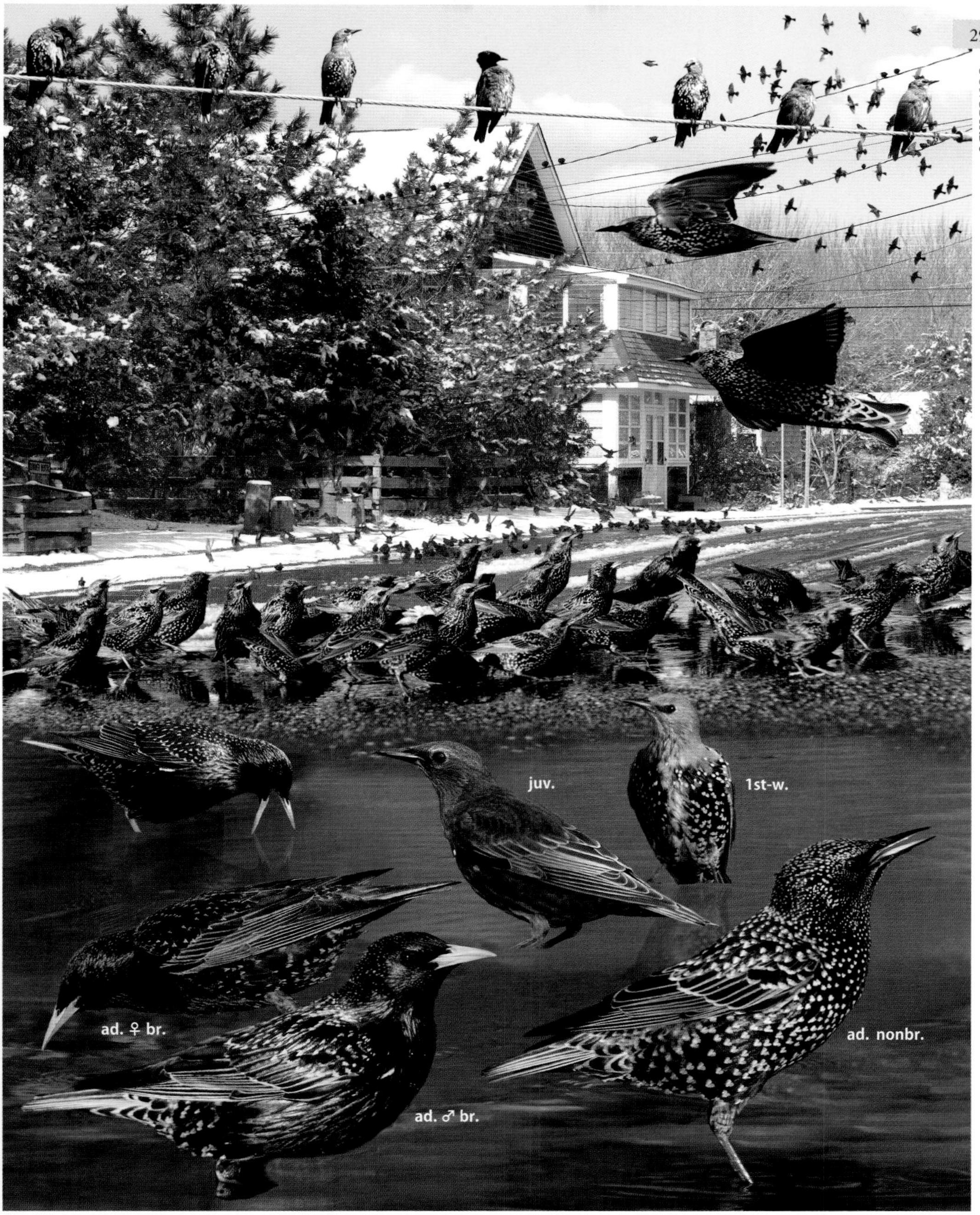

Starling *Sturnus vulgaris* **STARL/SG** L 22cm

UK: s. 1,900,000 pairs

Abundant and familiar in all kinds of habitats, including urban areas, gardens, farmland, and coast. In addition to breeding birds, millions come from the Continent to winter. May gather in enormous winter roosts that sometimes perform aerobatics at dusk. Normal flight path level, with rapid shallow wingbeats; wings look triangular. Nests in holes in trees and eaves, and regularly comes to bird tables for scraps. Familiar song includes rapid clicks, whistles, chatters, and some mimicry; many phrases quickly repeated. Has *wherr* flight call. Birds often sing while waving wings. Has jaunty walk; probes in soil; flies off low. **ID:** Plump, with short tail and sharp, spiky, jabbing bill. Plumage oily iridescent; legs pink. Ad dark with green and purple iridescence and yellow bill, ♂ with grey-blue base to bill and ♀ with paler base. Nonbr: copiously speckled with whitish spots on underside, buff on upperparts, with buff edges to flight feathers. Bill black. Juv: basically unmarked dirty brown-grey, paler on throat, with light streaking on breast, dark patch between bill and eye.

ACKNOWLEDGMENTS

Dominic Couzens for such professional, speedy work in writing much of the text. He brought his own style and meshed it with *The Crossley ID Guides*.

In life and with any major project, it's always a strong foundation that counts. For that, I thank my wife, Debra, and daughters, Sophie and Sam. Their endless patience during the months of travel, missed dinners and the countless hours of putting books together is appreciated. Likewise, Dominic would like to thank his wife, Carolyn, and children, Emmie and Sam.

My parents, Brian and Margaret Crossley, as always supported and encouraged me from the start. My father's artistic influence has been the cornerstone of my appreciation for colour and patterns. In many ways this book is for them. They are still looking for that bird book which helps them identify all the local birds they see—this one has their name on it. I hope it makes up for my not taking football and cricket all the way!

Robert Kirk, Ellen Foos, Lucinda Treadwell, John Hussey, Jessica Pellien and the staff at Princeton University Press for all their help.

Several great birders looked over drafts of the book. Their constructive comments and encouragement made a huge difference. These included Paul Baxter, Bruce Mactavish, Killian Mullarney and Andy Musgrove.

It is impossible to name all the people who have helped with this project—on so many levels. A book like this involves business, birding, photographic, design, and many other skills that have been acquired over a lifetime from so many people. A lot of these are close friends but others with strong input are people I met in passing who were generous enough to help with advice or information. The sum of it all is this book! I apologise for omitting any people, authors or organisations from the following list. Helpers have included: Jessie Barry, BTO/BirdTrack, Olivia Crowe, Paul Cook, Mike Crewe, John Crossley, Eric Dempsey, Nils Van Duivendijk, Dick Forsman, David Foster, RSPB, Simon Gillings, Baz Hughes, Derek Moore, Stephen Moss, Andy Musgrove, Paul Sterry, Roy Sutton, Jonathon Wasse, Chris Wood.

CREDITS FOR PHOTOS AND MUCH MORE

I always try to take all the images for Crossley Books myself. This book contains around 5,000 images, not only of birds, but also of scenic backgrounds and vegetation. Inevitably, I fall short. Filling the gaps at short notice is crucial and difficult. A number of the following people are good friends who have gone out of their way to dig through their files, and in some cases went out to take pictures, with the sole purpose of helping complete this book. Their contributions and knowledge on so many levels are priceless.

Peter Adriaens:	BLTDI, WOODC, STOCU, LESWO, CUCKO, BEATI, AQUWA, YEBWA, PALWA, RICPI
Jan Baert:	TEMST, JACSN, MONHA, REFFA
Paul Baxter:	GRESK, CORNC, QUAIL, REBSH, WOOSH, REBFL, BARWA, MARWA, GREWA, ICTWA, MELWA, OLBPI, ARCRE, CROSS, HAWFI, SCARO, LITBU, ORTBU
Johan Buckens:	BEAGO, GRCGR, BLTDI, GOSHA, LESWO, GOLOR, RINOU, BEATI, RADWA, DUSWA
Jon Buxton:	GARGA, WWBTE, BLATE, LITGU, TEMST, BITTE, PURHE, GRWEG, WATRA, WHTEA, MONHA, HENHA, HONBU, REFFA, KINGF, LESWO, REBSH, REBFL, PIEFL, CETWA, ICTWA, GOLDC
Martin Cade:	DOTTE, HENHA, LITOW, BLARE, GARWA, YEBWA, PALWA, GREWA, RICPI, ROCST
David Castor:	GOLPH
Richard Chandler:	SPORE, WOODC, STODO, GREWO, CUCKO, SNOBU
Andrej Chudi:	WOODL
Mike Crewe:	GRESK, ALPSW, REBFL, STOPE
Debra Crossley	Cover portrait (Richard)
Raymond De Smet:	GARGA, POCHA, SMEW, GOSHA, MONHA, RINPA, GOLOR, CORBU
Stuart Elsom:	LITAU, SPOON, CORCR, REFFA, FIREC, WOODL

Wouter Faveyts:	MONHA, BLATE, NIJAR, BEATI, AQUWA
Miel Ferdinande:	CUCKO
Charles Fleming:	DARWA
Hubert Gallagher:	COMCR, WILWA
Christopher Gibbins:	LITGU, CASGU, ICEGU, GLAGU, SPOON, ROCST
Paco Gomez:	GOLOR
Doug Gochfield:	REDPH
Steve Howell:	WHBDI
Lip Kee:	GOLOR
Carol Kent:	LITGU
Derek Moore:	HONBU
Killian Mullarney:	GARGA, BLAGU, PUFFI, MANSH, BALSH, STOPE, WWBTE, BLATE, ARCTE, ROSTE, GRESK, ARCSK, MEDGU, LIRPL, SPORE, SPOON, LITEG, COOT, REFFA, WOODP, BEEEA, BLABI, ROCPI, WATPI, BULLF
Artur Mikolajewski:	BARWA
Ferran Pestana:	GOLOR
Rab Rae:	PARCR, SCOCR
Cameron Rutte:	WHBDI, PTARM
Ellen Sandberg:	VELSC, MERLI, LOEOW, RINPA, CUCKO, SCARO
Norman D. van Swelm:	SPOCR
Jan Svetlik:	WOODL
MiMarnix Vandegehuchte:	FERDU, PTARM
Michael Unwin	Cover portrait (Dominic)

Index

Grey Plover *Pluvialis squatarola* **GREPL/GV** L 28cm*

UK: w. 43,000

Common winter visitor to estuaries and sandy beaches. May gather in large numbers at roost sites, but at low tide bad tempered, and individuals space themselves out, some maintaining territories. As with other plovers, has distinctive run-stop-pick feeding style, easy distinction from KNOT or REDSH. **ID:** Easily the largest and heaviest of the plover group, with muscular neck and large body. A big head and large bill give it a distinctive

UK: w. 43,000—estimated pop. (w:winter - numbers of individuals, s:summer—numbers of territorial pairs. Additional non-territorial birds also occur). Numbers from A. Musgrove et al. (2013) and RSPB website.

**Please note that the population count is listed after the bird's length on pages without a map.*

Scientific name

5 or 2 digit BTO shorthand codes used by ringers, note takers, texting etc. 2-word common names are usually given as the first 3 letters of the first name, and the first 2 of the second.

Length in cm. This is an average usually taken from the tip of the bill to the tip of the tail.

PLATE GLOSSARY

ad. nonbr. adult nonbreeding is the typically duller 'winter' plumage but occasionally birds like this are seen in summer. These are often 1-year-old birds.

ad. ♂ br. adult breeding is the typically brighter 'summer' plumage. Males (♂) and females (♀) are frequently different.

ad. term used when there is no difference in appearance between sexes or seasons.

juv. juvenile is the first set of feathers. They are the only feathers all grown at the same time and so have a uniform appearance.

1st-w. first-winter is a combination of juv. feathers and newer second-generation feathers worn in winter.

1st-s. first-summer is a combination of juv., 1st-w., and new bright adult-type breeding plumage feathers.

1st-yr. term used when there is no significant change in appearance through the first year.

♀/1st-yr. some birds are difficult to age and sex. The plumage shown is reprentative of the classes indicated.

Please note that all representative ages and classes are labelled in at least one place in each plate. Have fun working out the remainder! On rare occasions where labels are mid-distance between two birds, the label applies to both birds.

Regular breeding range—birds are typically faithful to breeding sites from year to year.

Regular year-round range—few individual birds stay year-round in one place; they often make local movements and are replaced seasonally by others of the same species.

Regular winter range—tends to change from year to year and day to day due to factors such as food supply and weather. Assume that species showing no winter range winter mostly to the south of our region, in Europe and Africa.